THE ELUSIVE IDEAL

*Equal Educational Opportunity
and the Federal Role in Boston's
Public Schools, 1950–1985*

ADAM R. NELSON

D0068234

The University of Chicago Press

CHICAGO AND LONDON

ADAM R. NELSON is assistant professor of educational
policy studies and history at the University of Wisconsin-Madison.

The University of Chicago Press, Chicago 60637
The University of Chicago Press, Ltd., London
© 2005 by The University of Chicago
All rights reserved. Published 2005
Printed in the United States of America

14 13 12 11 10 09 08 07 06 05   1 2 3 4 5

ISBN: 0-226-57189-0 (cloth)
ISBN: 0-226-57190-4 (paper)

Library of Congress Cataloging-in-Publication Data

Nelson, Adam R.
The elusive ideal : equal educational opportunity and the federal role in Boston's
public schools, 1950-1985.
p. cm. — (Historical studies of urban America)
Includes bibliographical references and index.
ISBN: 0-226-57189-0 (cloth : alk. paper)—ISBN: 0-226-57190-4 (pbk : alk. paper)
1. Educational equalization—Massachusetts—Boston—History—20th century.
2. Education and state—Massachusetts—Boston—History—20th century. 3. Federal
aid to education—Massachusetts—Boston—History—20th century. I. Title.
II. Historical studies of urban America.
LC213.23.B67N45 2005
379.2'6'09744'61—dc22
2004021956

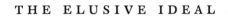

THE ELUSIVE IDEAL

HISTORICAL STUDIES OF URBAN AMERICA

Edited by Kathleen N. Conzen, Timothy J. Gilfoyle, and James R. Grossman

ALSO IN THE SERIES

Parish Boundaries: The Catholic Encounter with Race in the
Twentieth-Century Urban North *by John T. McGreevy*

Modern Housing for America: Policy Struggles in the
New Deal Era *by Gail Radford*

Smoldering City: Chicagoans and the Great Fire,
1871-1874 *by Karen Sawislak*

Making the Second Ghetto: Race and Housing in
Chicago, 1940-1960 *by Arnold R. Hirsch*

Faces along the Bar: Lore and Order in the Workingman's
Saloon, 1870-1920 *by Madelon Powers*

Streets, Railroads, and the Great Strike of 1877 *by David O. Stowell*

The Creative Destruction of Manhattan, 1900-1940 *by Max Page*

Brownsville, Brooklyn: Blacks, Jews, and the Changing Face of the
Ghetto *by Wendell Pritchett*

My Blue Heaven: Life and Politics in the Working-Class Suburbs
of Los Angeles, 1920-1965 *by Becky M. Nicolaides*

In the Shadow of Slavery: African Americans in New York City,
1626-1863 *by Leslie M. Harris*

Building the South Side: Urban Space and Civic Culture in
Chicago, 1890-1919 *by Robin F. Bachin*

Places of Their Own: African American Suburbanization
in the Twentieth Century *by Andrew Wiese*

Downtown America: A History of the Place and the People
Who Made It *by Alison Isenberg*

Block by Block: Neighborhoods and Public Policy on
Chicago's West Side *by Amanda I. Seligman*

When the educational enterprise is going smoothly, the public does not often exercise its right to evaluate. It is after the system begins to break down and the public finds itself inadequately served that the issue comes to the fore.

McGeorge Bundy, *Reconnection for Learning,* 1967

CONTENTS

Preface & Acknowledgments ix

INTRODUCTION xiii
The Evolution of School Reform in Boston

CHAPTER ONE I
Pursuing Federal Funds, 1950–1963

CHAPTER TWO 31
Defining Disadvantage as Disability, 1963–1966

CHAPTER THREE 61
Aggravating Racial Imbalance, 1966–1968

CHAPTER FOUR 91
Seeking Program Effectiveness, 1968–1971

CHAPTER FIVE 121
Making "Appropriate" Placements, 1971–1974

CHAPTER SIX 151
Reconfiguring School Finance, 1974–1977

CHAPTER SEVEN 181
Evading Local Accountability, 1977–1980

CHAPTER EIGHT 211
Compelling Better Results? 1980–1985

CONCLUSION 241
The Complex History of American School Reform

Notes 255 · *Index* 325

W hen I tell people I've written a book about the federal role in Boston's public schools, they often ask, "Is it another book about the busing crisis that rocked the city in the 1970s?" I answer, "No, not really." While court-ordered busing certainly figures into this narrative, the issue of racial desegregation is only part of a larger story told here. My goal has been to examine a wide range of interconnected policies, which, between 1950 and 1985, dramatically reshaped the city's—indeed, the entire nation's—public schools. Ultimately, this book is about the struggle to make the elusive ideal of equal educational opportunity a reality for all children.

To document this struggle, this book traces a sequence of complex and sometimes contradictory school-reform policies that emerged at the federal, state, and local levels in the 1950s, 1960s, 1970s, and early 1980s. It investigates policies related not only to racial desegregation but also to special education, compensatory education, bilingual education, school finance, and student testing. Each of these policy areas saw great change between 1950 and 1985, and each had a significant effect on the operation of schools. The specific implementation of various school-reform policies differed from city to city (in some ways, Boston was unique), but the basic aim—equal educational opportunity—was shared by every city in America. For this reason, a study of the federal role in Boston's schools can shed light on the federal role in American education in general.

As any student of "policy implementation" knows, the process involves diverse groups making contributions to a product that inevitably differs from its original conception in unexpected ways. In this regard, policy implementation is much like scholarship. Scholarly ideas, like policy ideas, circulate widely among many people before they "hit the ground." Certainly, the writing of this book fits such a description of scholarly production. Mutual collaboration and assistance have, I hope, resulted in a final publication that is better—more thoroughly researched, more cogently argued, and more clearly expressed—than the original idea. I therefore take this opportunity to thank some of the people who helped with the "implementation" of this project.

First and foremost, this study would not have been possible without the assistance of Carl Kaestle at Brown University. In the fall of 1997, when I was in my final year of doctoral study in the Department of History at Brown, Professor Kaestle hired me as a research assistant. The following year, he received a grant from the Spencer Foundation for a project on "The Federal Role in Elementary and Secondary Education, 1950–2000," and he involved me in his research. At the same time, he received support for his work from the Annenberg Institute for School Reform, based at Brown, and used some of these funds for assistants, including me. Both the Spencer Foundation and the Annenberg Institute supplied funds—through Professor Kaestle—to aid the initial stages of my own work on the federal role in Boston's public schools.

In the spring of 1998, Professor Kaestle assembled a team of skilled researchers to discuss his ongoing research, and, in subsequent years, my own work has benefited from the input of these colleagues. Special thanks go to Jack Dougherty of Trinity College in Hartford, Connecticut; David Gamson of the Pennsylvania State University; and Matthew Davis of Rowan University in Glassboro, New Jersey. Together with Carl Kaestle, these individuals helped me develop the general analytical framework that guides this study, including its chronological boundaries (1950–85), its focus on a series of key episodes in the evolution of federal aid to education, and its emphasis on the dilemmas of policy implementation at the local level. Jack Dougherty was especially helpful in outlining a model of two-way interaction between local and federal education agencies, with state agencies playing a stronger and stronger intermediary role over time.

Between 2002 and 2005, I was fortunate to participate in the Advanced Studies Fellowship Program at Brown, supported by extremely generous grants from the Spencer Foundation and the William and Flora Hewlett Foundation. Under the direction of Carl Kaestle, the Advanced Studies Fellowship Program provided financial support for a full year of research and writing. It also assembled a community of junior and senior scholars to engage in semiannual discussions of major issues in American school reform. I have benefited immensely from the insights generated by this community, which has included Howard Chudacoff, Marguerite Clarke, Liz DeBray, Kim Freeman, David Gamson, Nora Gordon, Chris Lubienski, Katie McDermott, John Modell, Marion Orr, James Patterson, Doug Reed, Beth Rose, Wendy Schiller, and Warren Simmons.

Every historical research project depends on the assistance of countless librarians, archivists, and other reference experts to put scholars in touch with the primary sources they need to construct their narratives. I owe a major debt of gratitude to librarians in the Government Documents Room at the Boston Public Library and the Massachusetts State House Library, the archives of the Boston Public Schools, and the reference departments of the Beebe Communications Library at Boston University, the Rockefeller Library at Brown, Widener Library at Harvard, Memorial Library at the University of Wisconsin–Madison, and the State Historical Society of Wisconsin. These professionals have been invaluable in helping me track down useful documents of every variety. I must also thank my Boston-based cousin, Nathan Schafer, for his excellent work as a research assistant.

My colleagues in the Department of Educational Policy Studies at the University of Wisconsin–Madison offered helpful suggestions on various drafts of this project. Bill Reese and Michael Fultz have been especially generous with their time and critical comments. I would also like to thank the students who offered advice on an early version of this book. Neema Avashia, Karen Benjamin, Sarah Glick, Daria Hall, John McKinley, Joanna Miller, Katie Shelton, Scott Spector, and Adriene Williams all provided feedback that made my analysis clearer than it otherwise might have been. Jennifer Sandler, in particular, helped immensely by photocopying countless reports and articles related to this project. I must also thank Carl Kaestle's able administrative assistants over the years, including Jen Meeropol and Tia Malkin as well as Mimi Coughlin and

Alyssa Lodewick, the Assistant Directors of the Advanced Studies Fellowship Program, who solved myriad technical and bureaucratic problems along the way.

My editors at the University of Chicago Press, particularly Robert Devens, have proven unfailingly helpful. I would also like to express my gratitude to the editors of the series "Historical Studies in Urban America," Kathleen N. Conzen, Timothy J. Gilfoyle, and James R. Grossman, and to the reviewers who read my initial manuscript, including Maris Vinovskis and another anonymous reader. The comments of Robert Schwartz and Charles Willie helped me reconsider some of my interpretations at a late stage in the project, and manuscript editor Mara Naselli scoured my prose for errors both grammatical and syntactical. Publicist Mark Heineke and designer Matt Avery helped make the book more appealing to readers, indexer Amanda Grell came to my aid in a pinch, and editorial associate Elizabeth Branch Dyson coordinated every aspect of the process with efficiency, patience, and good humor. While I hope all my mistakes have been corrected, I take full responsibility for any that remain.

Finally, I wish to thank my family: my parents and my brother, Matt. As with my first book, this project reflects their indefatigable love and support. In various ways, they acted as a corps of unpaid—and perhaps unwitting—research assistants by reading multiple newspapers and forwarding copies of all education-related articles and editorials they discovered to me. I doubt they realize how helpful they were as second, third, and fourth pairs of eyes, scanning the political and journalistic landscape for data to deepen the analysis presented in this study. My aunt and uncle, Kathy and Karl Nelson, offered very helpful comments on my manuscript during our annual vacation "at the lake" in the summer of 2003, and for their insights I am grateful. Although my brother spent much of the past several years in Islamabad, Kathmandu, Bangkok, Kuala Lampur, and Manila before joining the faculty at Bates College in Maine, he has continued to offer much-appreciated words of encouragement. This book could not have been completed without the help of my family.

The Evolution of School Reform in Boston

On June 21, 1974, federal district court judge Wendell Arthur Garrity Jr. ordered the immediate desegregation of the Boston public schools. It was a bold decision—one only a federal judge could make—and it promised to bring equal educational opportunity to all students in Boston. Yet, in a city with such a long and turbulent history of racial conflict, few Bostonians believed the court's ruling could be enforced without hostility or resistance. And they were right. When classes began in mid-September, the city exploded in violence. School buses carrying black students to the formerly all-white South Boston High School faced mobs of white protesters hurling bricks, bottles, eggs, and epithets. By mid-October, full-fledged race riots had erupted in the virtually all-black neighborhood of Roxbury, and, in early December, a black student at

Hyde Park High School assaulted a white student with a knife. Television networks broadcast nightly updates on "the Boston school crisis," and street fighting continued for the remainder of the year.[1]

When the turmoil finally subsided, three questions emerged from the controversy. First, was federal court action really the best way to equalize educational opportunities for all students in the Boston public schools? Second, was this particular form of federal intervention most effective in the long run? Third, what approaches, federal or otherwise, might have produced more lasting or thorough reform in the city's troubled schools? This analysis of the evolving federal role in Boston's schools seeks to address these questions by placing them in historical context.[2] In recent years, the federal role in education has become a subject of increasing debate. Few studies, however, show the interplay between local, state, and federal school policies over long stretches of time; even fewer attempt to show the overlapping development of local, state, and federal policies targeted at diverse groups of urban students—from the economically disadvantaged to the limited-English-proficient to the mentally, physically, or emotionally disabled—all at once.

This book does so. In the process, it begins to reveal the complex relationships that existed between local and federal officials as both tried to give meaning to the phrase *equal educational opportunity* in the public schools. Those familiar with Boston's fierce opposition to school desegregation and busing in the 1970s may be surprised to learn, for example, that Boston was often ahead of the curve in developing and implementing new policies that later became part of federal law. Indeed, throughout the postwar era, Boston launched new programs, served new constituencies, and devised new ways of controlling expenses *before* the federal government required such programs, services, or cost-control strategies. Contrary to the belief that federal agencies imposed unwelcome ideas on local schools "from outside" or "from above," this study shows that, in Boston, federal policies in the realm of education tended to expand programs already initiated at the local or state level.

In 1952, for example, Boston bolstered its programs in mathematics, sciences, and foreign languages—as well as its programs for "gifted" students; six years later, in 1958, Congress passed the National Defense Education Act (NDEA) to strengthen programs in precisely these areas. In 1963, Boston launched its first compensatory education program for socially and economically disadvantaged students in the inner city; two years later, in 1965, Congress passed the landmark Elementary and Secondary Education Act (ESEA) to meet the same need. As early as 1960, Boston offered English-language instruction for immigrant pupils; eight years later, in 1968, Congress added the Bilingual Education Act (Title

VII) to the ESEA. In 1972, under pressure from Boston activists, the Massachusetts legislature passed the nation's most comprehensive program of special education for the disabled; three years later, in 1975, Congress adopted the Education for All Handicapped Children Act (P.L. 94-142), which borrowed heavily from Massachusetts's model.

Scholars have examined each of Massachusetts's innovative programs in turn, but no scholar has yet examined all of these programs together in a single historical narrative. As this study demonstrates, the years prior to 1975 marked a period of expanding access to educational services in the public schools, while the years after 1975 marked a period of managing the high costs and refining the administration of these new services. In times of retrenchment, as in times of expansion, Boston routinely explored new ideas and tested new proposals *before* these ideas and proposals reached the federal level. For example, in 1980, when the nation's economy was mired in a deep recession, Massachusetts voters passed Proposition 2½, a referendum limiting property taxes and sharply curtailing state aid to schools. In 1981, just after Ronald Reagan's inauguration, Congress passed its own cost-control law, the Educational Consolidation and Improvement Act (ECIA), to reduce spending and replace various categorical programs with block grants to the states.

Each of these reforms at the state and the federal level won popular approval, but none seemed to bring dramatic improvement to Boston's inner-city schools. The question is, why not? Why did local, state, and federal policies fail to offer a clear path to equal educational opportunity for all students in the 1950s, 1960s, 1970s, and 1980s? To answer this question, this book explores a tension between two goals that have guided American educational policy ever since the Supreme Court's unanimous ruling in the case of *Brown v. Board of Education* in 1954.[3] The first goal is integration; the second is academic achievement. Both of these goals have been linked to the constitutionally significant concept of equal educational opportunity, and, over time, many have presumed that integration would lead almost automatically toward achievement. Yet, as this history of federal aid to Boston's public schools reveals, the link between integration and achievement has never been entirely secure.

It is at least possible that integration may not always foster achievement for all students. To many, such a statement itself seems heretical. Yet, in order to place the elusive and evolving ideal of equal educational opportunity in historical context—that is, to see how diverse individuals and groups understood this ideal over time—this book and its readers must step into the past and ask, as others, both black and white, rich and poor, Democrat and Republican, asked, with great sincerity and seriousness, in earlier periods: what if the best way to equalize educational opportunities was to place different students with different needs in different environments with different services, even if this strategy grouped students by ability, by language, or perhaps, directly or indirectly, by race? What if the goal of equal educational opportunity (especially in urban areas) involved trade-offs between maximum integration and maximum achievement, between the total inclusion of all students in the same classes and the optimal performance of each student individually?

Which of these two goals, integration or achievement, held greater social value? Which promoted the political, economic, or moral well-being of nation? Which promised to advance the overall development of children? Which should federal policies or federal resources support? These are the difficult—indeed, wrenching—questions that shaped the federal role in public schools between 1950 and 1985, and these are the questions that have guided this study. A blend of policy history, urban history, and intellectual history, it describes the frequent and often bitter conflicts that erupted between integration and achievement as competing federal goals. While this study does not take sides in these debates, it does show how well-intentioned policies at the local, state, and federal level could work at cross-purposes with one another and how the dilemmas of policy alignment became more and more convoluted over time. As a work of history, this book tells the story of a particular time and place, but, in the process, it also sheds light on later and larger events.

In general, the book saves its interpretive conclusions for the end, but a few points require clarification at the start. Unless otherwise specified, the book uses the term *integration* to refer to the inclusion of *all* types of pupils in the same learning environment. The use of this term is not necessarily restricted to racial integration (or desegregation) as commonly understood in the discourse on public education. Rather, as the narrative will make clear, its use is tied to the much broader movement for civil rights and educational opportunities in the postwar years. All too often, in the popular mind and in the scholarly literature, the struggles of racial minorities, handicapped students, "non-English-speaking" pupils, and low-income children appear separately, yet in most urban schools, these groups overlap. The plight of racial minorities is closely interwoven with the plight of linguistic minorities, the handicapped, and the poor. Thus, if integration is truly a goal for all students, the terms used to describe this goal cannot be dissociated.

Yet, the notion that the nation's public schools could—or should—integrate all students into the same "equal" learning environment is, and has been, controversial because the concept of *total* integration seems to preclude the possibility of identifying and effectively addressing students' "special" educational needs, which minority students (of every kind) are almost always presumed to have. This book does not evaluate the pedagogical or philosophical merits of integrated or nonintegrated schooling, nor does it seek to test the relative effectiveness of different classroom programs. It simply notes that, between 1950 and 1985, it became increasingly problematic for schools to offer programs, integrated or not, that yielded unequal student "outcomes." Indeed, at the heart of this book lies the observation that in Boston, the meaning of *equal educational opportunity* shifted perceptibly over time from an emphasis on integration to an emphasis on measurable academic achievement.

One final note. Since the history of federal aid to education is complex, this book uses a loose focus on a wide-ranging theme—"special-compensatory programs" for students considered disabled—to trace the changing circumstances under which Boston came to define the key phrase *equal educational opportunity*. The study begins with the rise of special programs for the handicapped in the 1950s, then follows this development into related concerns over poverty, desegregation, and bilingual education in the 1960s. It returns to the issue of special education in the 1970s, moves on to the various cost-control reforms of this decade, and ends with the emergence of standardized testing in the 1980s. The devil, they say, is in the details, and this book is filled with innumerable details. The basic narrative, however, is this: as new services proliferated and local expenditures rose, the question in Boston was whether or not to seek federal aid. Sensing a sort of Faustian bargain in this decision, school officials moved cautiously to accept federal grants while avoiding federal oversight. It did not take long to see, however, that, for better or worse, "federal aid without federal control" was an impossible combination.

CHAPTER ONE

Pursuing Federal Funds, 1950–1963

Boston has had a long history of involvement with the issue of special education for the disabled. As early as the 1840s, two reformers, Samuel Gridley Howe and his wife Julia Ward Howe, established a small school for twelve mentally and physically disabled children in nearby Malden. Chartered as the Massachusetts School for Idiotic and Feeble-minded Youth, this school later moved into a wing of the Perkins Institute for the Blind in Watertown, which had been founded in the late 1820s as the nation's first school for the visually impaired. Both of these early institutions received state funding for the first time in 1856, and, toward the end of the nineteenth century, the City of Boston began to allow mildly handicapped children into its public schools—so long as they did not disrupt the "regular" classroom environment. These programs were far ahead of their time, but they did not include all the city's hand-icapped children, most of whom remained at home with their parents. Even in the state's publicly and privately supported asylums, handi-capped students received only limited academic training—that is, if they received any at all. A proposal to include the city's most severely disabled children in its regular public schools did not emerge until 1940, when a group of mothers asked the Massachusetts department of mental health to recruit a teacher to work with their mentally retarded children in lo-cal neighborhood schools. This initial group of women, calling them-selves the Boston Child Betterment Association, subsequently pushed to enroll *all* disabled children in the public schools. At the end of World War II, the Boston Child Betterment Association changed its name to the Boston Association for Retarded Children and set up offices at the Bos-ton Street Health Unit. Over the course of the next half-decade—from 1945 to 1950—the association pressed for the integration of disabled children into the public schools and the provision of special services to facilitate their educational development.[1]

The gentle persistence of the Boston Association for Retarded Chil-dren surprised the five-member Boston school committee, which prided itself on a decades-old network of special programs for handicapped children. As school superintendent Dennis Haley commented in his an-nual report in 1950, "Boston has for many generations pioneered in helping children who, for some reason, are not able to keep pace with their classmates. Many of these children have a physical handicap; some are slow learners; and others have difficulty in adjusting themselves so-cially. All need special assistance, and the Boston public schools have been far in advance in providing it." Certainly, compared with other states, Massachusetts was far ahead of the curve in providing educational services for the disabled. Hearing-impaired students attended the inter-nationally renowned Horace Mann School for the Deaf, founded in 1869, while those with more serious physical or mental handicaps at-tended the Walter E. Fernald School for the Retarded (the successor to the Massachusetts School for Idiotic and Feebleminded Youth, of which Fernald was the first superintendent). Emotionally disturbed and delin-quent young men attended the Gertrude Godvin School for Boys, and in the late 1940s, Boston opened two new hospital centers for the handi-capped, one for polio victims at the Haynes Memorial Hospital for Infectious Diseases and another for convalescent children and "spastics" at the Joseph P. Kennedy Memorial Hospital. Even students confined to their homes with illnesses such as rheumatic fever, epilepsy, tuberculo-sis, broken bones, or mumps received individualized instruction from "a well-trained corps of teachers" who made weekly house calls. All in all,

Superintendent Haley noted, Boston's programs for disabled children were well above average for the 1950s. In his words, "By all these means, children who at one time might have known the discouragement of failure now have the hope of a normal education."[2]

The Boston Association for Retarded Children did not discount the value of these programs, but it believed that all disabled children should be permitted to attend the *same* public schools as nondisabled students—and, increasingly, others throughout the country agreed. In 1952, the Boston Association for Retarded Children joined twenty-three other groups to form a Massachusetts state chapter of the two-year-old National Association for Retarded Children, which had become a prominent advocate for the mainstreaming of disabled children in public schools.[3] Also in that year, the Boston public schools joined the Perkins Institute for the Blind in developing a regional plan for students with various physical disabilities. As Edward Waterhouse, the director of the Perkins Institute, commented, "it is now apparent that New England public schools must adopt programs for the education of the handicapped." The John Greenleaf Whittier Elementary School in Dorchester was the first to designate one of its classrooms specifically for the use of blind pupils. As the *Boston Post* reported just before the beginning of the fall semester, "The classroom will be equipped with special furniture, Braille materials, and all special supplies necessary for the education of the blind."[4] Calling this classroom an intriguing and novel experiment, Superintendent Haley remarked in his annual report for 1952–53 that "the most interesting classroom in the whole City of Boston is the Braille class at the John Greenleaf Whittier School, the only one of its kind in New England. Here, in its second year of operation, the pupils are not segregated, but move about, run errands, and deport themselves like their seeing friends. The pupils learn to read and write Braille with ease, Braille books paralleling the reading books used in regular grades. The class is filled to capacity and has attracted many visitors, particularly nurses, social workers, and others interested in this phase of public school work."[5]

When Haley commented that blind students were "not segregated" in the Whittier School, he meant that they were not isolated in a completely separate institution as they had been in the past; he did not mean that blind students sat side-by-side in classes with sighted peers. Like most of his contemporaries, Haley insisted that the best way to ensure equal educational opportunities for all students was to place disabled students in isolated classes suited to their needs. Moreover, he drew a distinction between physically disabled students, who were capable of average academic achievement within regular schools, and mentally disabled students, who were not.[6] This distinction made sense to Haley, but it did not make sense to the parents of mentally disabled students, who persuaded the state legislature in 1952 to create a "special commission to make an investigation and study relative to the training facilities available for retarded children."[7] This commission began work in 1953 with six members: Philip Bowker, a state senator; Meyer Pressman, a state representative; Philip Cashman, state supervisor of special schools, who represented the state Department of Education; Malcolm Farrell, director of the Walter E. Fernald School, who represented the state Department of Mental Health; Helen Freeman, president of the Massachusetts Special Class Teachers Association; and Mrs. David Hurwitz, president of the Massachusetts Association for the Retarded.[8] Over the next two decades, the special commission issued sixteen major reports, each of which stressed the idea of integrating retarded and nonretarded students into regular schools, if not into regular classrooms. It sponsored research on the educational needs of the retarded and gathered data from both teachers and administrators. As one observer noted, "Most legislation concerning special education from 1952 onward was first proposed by the commission," which saw itself as a veritable "state seminar on the rights of handicapped children."[9]

The commission's first report, written in the fall of 1953 and released in January 1954, outlined its primary objectives: "It is the hope of this commission to interpret to the legislature the rights of handicapped children, more particularly mentally handicapped children, to their rightful share of education in their local communit[ies]. It is the hope, further, to demonstrate to the legislature the *responsibility* . . . to implement this right so that cities and towns will provide these rights for mentally retarded children." For the special commission, including retarded children in the public schools was a fundamental right that no tax-supported education system could legally deny. In its words, every child in the public schools was "entitled . . . to every aid we can give him to function within his handicap as a child; that is, whatever special facilities the law can set up to develop him to [his] maximum capacity."[10] This argument was not lost on Massachusetts's legislators. In 1954, after receiving the commission's first report, the legislature amended Chapter 71 of the Massachusetts General Laws (one of three chapters dealing with public schools) to guarantee every mentally retarded child the right to a free education in a public school—provided that he or she could sit still in class and provided that his or her presence would not distract nondisabled pupils. This amendment accompanied another new law, Chapter 514, which established a separate division of special education within the state Department of Mental Health and allocated funds to reimburse up to 50 percent of local costs associated with special services for all "educable mentally retarded" students. Chapter 514 also required annual re-examinations for children placed in special classes to make sure their original diagnoses were valid—the presumption being that special classes hindered rather than helped students who were not "truly" disabled. In this way, the state legislature promised all retarded pupils access to the state's public schools.

Taken together, these new laws marked a substantial increase in Massachusetts's commitment to school aid for the disabled.[11] They did not, however, increase the level of interaction between disabled and nondisabled students in public school *classes*. In 1955, a year after the passage of these new laws, Superintendent Haley commented proudly that the Boston public schools were already "living up to the letter of the law that 'all public school children of school age found to be retarded in mental development shall be placed in special classes.' . . . Children who are not at home in the regular classroom or whose ability deters them from average achievement are given special consideration and instruction in subjects that eventually will lend them to become self-supporting and useful citizens. This work is now carried on in 105 special classes and 17 sub-special classes."[12] While services for the disabled were undoubtedly expanding and improving in Boston's schools, Superintendent Haley's emphasis fell squarely on the provision of isolated rather than integrated programs. He continued to insist that retarded students benefited from the "special consideration and instruction" they received in physically separate classes designed to meet their unique educational needs. Such classes were necessary, he contended, for students whose disabilities rendered them "incapable" of average academic achievement. Indeed, for him, incapacity for average achievement was the very definition of *disability* and the basic justification for "special" or supplemental services. And, yet, it was this view—the view that mentally disabled students were fundamentally incapable of average academic achievement—that generated the most trenchant controversy over time. If Haley was prepared to include physically disabled students in regular classrooms in the public schools, critics asked, then why not include mentally disabled students in regular classrooms, too?[13]

The idea of including all disabled students in regular classes was still new in the mid-1950s, and it was not universally welcomed. To many, the notion of placing disabled and nondisabled students in the same class seemed absurd—a disservice to *both* groups. Most educators continued to believe that the best way to raise academic achievement for all was to provide special services for the disabled in isolated classrooms tailored to their specific needs. Yet, the principle of integration was slowly gaining ground—not only in the schools but also in the federal courts. The recent case of *Brown v. Board of Education of Topeka, Kansas* in 1954 dealt not only with racial segregation, but also, less directly, with the issue of segregation among *any* group found to have "special educational needs." In fact, the defense attorneys in this case explicitly warned that court-ordered integration might eventually lead to a situation in which public schools would be required to include *all* students in the same schools—despite varying individual needs—in order to meet the vague standard of equal educational opportunity. In the attorneys' words, "if segregation of black children was unconstitutional, [then] surely it will be found that segregation of children defined as disabled is also unacceptable."[14] By advancing this line of argument, the defense hoped to convince the court that integration per se was ultimately irrelevant to pupils' academic achievement and, thus, to their educational opportunities. This point backfired, however, when the justices accepted the notion that black and white students had different educational needs but rejected the notion that different needs among different races necessitated different schools. Instead, they stated unequivocally that, where race was concerned, "separate schools are inherently unequal" and, in their remedy-phase decision in 1955, *Brown v. Board of Education II*, held that the only way for all students to enjoy equal opportunities was to integrate them into the same schools— and even the same classrooms—"with all deliberate speed."[15]

The full complexity of this decision was not obvious in 1955. Few predicted the extent to which "the segregation of children defined as disabled" would be tolerated (or even applauded) in the future, and few predicted the extent to which integrated classes themselves could be considered "discriminatory" if they treated all students in exactly the same way and overlooked individual differences. Instead, most observers saw the court's rulings in *Brown v. Board of Education* as a victory for those who advocated integration for all students—regardless of differences—in the same learning environment. Certainly, Massachusetts's special commission for the retarded saw the court's rulings this way. In its second report, in 1955, the commission asked that special programs for the retarded be incorporated into regular classrooms. "Programs for helping retarded children are based on the belief that [these children] need extra help so that they can have equal opportunity with normal children," the commission wrote. If a principle of integration could apply to black students despite their special needs, then, according to the special commission, the same principle could apply to disabled students despite *their* special needs. The special commission argued that "the objective is not to transform those of limited mental capacity into geniuses. . . . The goal . . . is to allow them to function as well as possible at their own level of intelligence."[16] Responding to Superintendent Haley's view that full integration was appropriate only for students who were capable of average academic achievement, the commission held that students' academic potential could not be ascertained until *after* their placement in integrated classes. (The commission failed to realize, however, that Haley could use the same reasoning to argue that disabled students' academic potential could not be discerned until after their placement in *isolated* classes.)

$$\diamondsuit$$

In the mid-1950s, it was not clear whether integration or isolation was more likely to foster the educational progress of disabled students in public schools. What *was* clear was that virtually every state faced growing demands for special services. In its report in 1955, Massachusetts's special commission for the retarded reproduced a letter from President Dwight Eisenhower declaring National Retarded Children's Week and urging support for the National Association for Retarded Children. Using this letter as leverage, the commission lobbied for more research on education for mentally disabled pupils. In its third report, in 1956, the special commission drew attention to several federal grants that had become available for special educational services on a matching basis. These grants (P.L. 84-825, P.L. 84-880, and P.L. 84-922) were designed to support teacher-training programs, diagnostic equipment (for hearing, vision, and IQ tests), and vocational rehabilitation facilities. Massachusetts's special commission urged the state to seek federal aid under these programs and also mentioned the Cooperative Educational Research Act (P.L. 83-565), which had been authorized in 1954 and was scheduled for its first distributions in 1957. Much of the aid appropriated under this law was earmarked for research into the educational needs of the mentally retarded, and Massachusetts's special commission strongly encouraged the state departments of education and mental health to apply. Never suspecting that federal aid for "special services" might result in programs set apart from regular classes, the special commission worried instead that Massachusetts was not seeking enough financial help from the federal government. According to the commission's third report in 1956, the state was "not availing itself of the opportunity to obtain these federal funds"—and this failure to seek federal aid was, in turn, having a negative effect on the educational opportunities of disabled students.[17]

Indeed, Massachusetts *did* miss its first opportunity to apply for federal matching funds for special education, and the reason, according to the special commission, was not that the state feared overbearing federal control but that state officials assumed federal money, once appropriated, would always be available.[18] According to the special commission, officials in both the state Departments of Education and the state Department of Mental Health failed to understand how tenuous these first grants really were and how much more assistance was actually needed. The commission observed, for example, that the recently passed Cooperative Educational Research Act required congressional reauthorization on a yearly basis, so its grants might conceivably end within months. Determined not to let external funds go to waste, the special commission began in 1956 to push for additional programs at the state level that would qualify for federal matching grants. It called for the establishment of clinical nursery schools for mentally retarded students as well as state programs to accommodate physically handicapped, emotionally disturbed, and aphasic (i.e., nonverbal or noncommunicative) students.[19] The legislature responded to the commission's appeals with two new laws, Chapter 570 and Chapter 635, to put Massachusetts in a better position to capture federal aid. In the meantime, Congress expanded its own involvement in special education with two more laws: P.L. 85-308 for books for the blind and P.L. 85-926 for special-education training courses in colleges and universities.[20] Each of these initiatives at the state and federal level added services for the disabled, but none required the integration of handicapped and nonhandicapped students in the same classes. Rather, lawmakers tended to assume that disabled students benefited from physically isolated programs.[21]

At a time when local school districts received extremely limited external support, administrators did not immediately grasp the usefulness of federal funds. For instance, in 1956, Boston received only about 0.2 percent of its total school budget from the federal government, chiefly for vocational education programs created under the Smith-Hughes Act of 1917 and the Vocational Rehabilitation Act of 1920. Yet, once federal aid arrived in school-department coffers, officials quickly sought more. In Massachusetts, the election of Governor J. Foster Furcolo in 1956 further bolstered the state's receptivity to federal aid. Furcolo, a Democrat, had served two terms in Congress from 1948 to 1952 as a representative from Massachusetts's second district (in the middle of the state). After Eisenhower's election in 1952, he had returned to Boston to serve as state treasurer and, in that capacity, had become more and more convinced of the desirability of pursuing federal aid, including aid to schools. Upon his election to governor, he appointed a new state commissioner of education, Owen Kiernan, to coordinate the schools' pursuit of new grants. Kiernan, a graduate of Bridgewater State Teachers College with a master's degree from Boston University as well as a doctorate from the Harvard Graduate School of Education, had served as a teacher, principal, and superintendent in the affluent Wayland-Sudbury school district in suburban Boston before assuming the commissionership. He was fully aware of recent increases in both state and federal aid to public schools and, as commissioner, seized every opportunity to obtain additional grants. Indeed, over the course of his eleven years as commissioner, Kiernan oversaw an unprecedented rise in the amount of aid flowing into Massachusetts's public schools, particularly into the state's urban areas. For both Governor Furcolo and Commissioner Kiernan, the pursuit of aid for public schools was a top priority.

From their point of view, the most urgent need facing Massachusetts's schools in the mid-1950s was a need for more classrooms and more teachers to accommodate rapidly expanding enrollments. Between 1945 and 1955, the baby boom had added more than four million children a year to the nation's elementary schools. Massachusetts had watched new births rise from 76,455 in 1945 to 98,933 in 1948 to 99,619 in 1951. In 1954, the state had 107,086 new infant arrivals, and in 1955, that number jumped to 109,610. The birth rate peaked in 1957 with 115,065 babies — a 66 percent increase over just twelve years.[22] Massachusetts tried desperately to keep pace with its ever-increasing school enrollments, but its efforts fell short. Class sizes ballooned, and teacher shortages were chronic. Part of the problem was that most districts had not built a single new school in more than two decades. Birth rates had declined throughout the Great Depression, and scarce resources had gone to meet other needs during World War II; thus, little new construction had taken place in these years, and urban areas such as Boston found themselves with aging and undersized buildings in the 1950s.[23] In the winter of 1955, in response to this predicament, Superintendent Haley launched a major construction campaign to try to alleviate Boston's need for new buildings. "High on the list of accomplishments recorded in this annual report is the inception of the first major building program in many years," Haley asserted in his annual report that year.[24] His construction program called for ten new schools and three new additions at a cost of more than $10 million. These new schools helped, but, as both Haley and Kiernan emphasized, more buildings were still needed, and more buildings required more money.

At a time when the total annual budget for all of Boston's public schools was $30 million, voters had authorized two separate $5 million bonds (the first in 1953, the second in 1954) to supply the funds needed to erect Haley's first ten new schools in high-growth areas throughout the city. Then, in 1956, the superintendent announced a *third* $5 million bond to build seven more elementary schools and a new vocational high school closer to the inner city. His proposals focused on low-income neighborhoods such as the South End, Dorchester, Hyde Park, Roslindale, Columbia Point, Mattapan, Orient Heights, and Roxbury. In his annual report for 1957, Haley described the work in progress: "Four new elementary schools, one eight-room addition to an elementary school, and a junior high school gymnasium completed and in use. Construction work begun on the Boston Trade High School addition and three elementary schools. Preparation of plans and securing of land authorized and in process for six more building projects: a new technical high school, addition of a gymnasium for a district high school, three new elementary schools, and an eight-room addition to an elementary school. Four new play areas constructed adjacent to existing school buildings. Fifty-eight major maintenance projects completed as part of modernization program."[25] All told, Haley's plan called for "the ultimate expenditure of $41,000,000 by 1961 to replace existing school buildings which have become obsolete and to supply adequate modern plant facilities."[26] It was an ambitious plan, but funding remained tight. Citizens soon tired of school-construction bonds, and property taxpayers demanded relief— either from the state legislature or, if not from the state, then perhaps from the federal government.

Starting in 1957, both Superintendent Haley and Commissioner Kiernan began to pursue federal assistance for school construction projects already underway in the Boston public schools. In particular, they began to investigate the possibility of receiving aid for schools in federal "impact" areas. Two laws, P.L. 81-815 and P.L. 81-874, had passed in 1950 to provide supplementary grants to schools located in places where federal military installations or other federal activities had reduced local property tax revenues. A number of state leaders believed that Boston might be eligible for this type of aid—which, by the mid-1950s, was the largest source of federal support for public schools. Since this money was intended to substitute for lost property tax revenues, administrators were permitted to blend it into regular operating budgets and use it for virtually any purpose.[27] Such loosely regulated aid was understandably desirable from an administrative point of view, not only to Commissioner Kiernan at the state level, but also to Superintendent Haley at the local level. The only catch was that both laws stipulated that districts receiving impact aid had to have either 6 percent of their students residing on federally owned land or 6 percent of students' parents working in federal jobs. Thus, in order to receive any impact aid, the Boston public schools had to identify approximately 5,500 children who fit at least one of these criteria.[28] Representative Robert Crawley of the state legislature's subcommittee on education later remarked that "if only 5,500 Boston school children reside with a parent employed at a federal installation, the city [could] receive this type of assistance. . . . At the rate of approximately $200 per pupil, this amount could well be in the range of $1 million."[29] Unfortunately, Boston was not able to find enough children to meet the 6 percent cut-off, so the city was not eligible for impact aid. Federal support for school construction would have to wait, at least for a while.

◈

Despite this failure to secure impact aid, the Boston public schools continued to be successful in applying for small-scale federal grants to support special services for the disabled. Indeed, Massachusetts's special commission for the retarded acknowledged in 1957 that a basic level of educational opportunity had been established for all children in the state—a worthy accomplishment, even if the larger goal of integrating the disabled and nondisabled into the same classes was still on the special commission's agenda. The year 1957, however, was no ordinary year in the history of American education. It was the year of *Sputnik,* and many observers began to claim that supplemental services for the disabled had slighted another group of "exceptional" children: the gifted. After the Soviet Union launched the world's first orbiting satellite in October 1957, the rhetoric surrounding the public schools shifted rapidly from the needs of below-average students to the needs of above-average students. Viewing *Sputnik* as a "sobering symbol of Soviet genius and power potential," schools focused on the needs of the best and brightest, and, in the midst of all this flurry, the needs of the handicapped faded into the background.[30] When the Soviet Union launched a second satellite just a month after the first, the needs of academically talented students became a central preoccupation in the nation's schools. A week after the launching of *Sputnik II,* a federal policy paper, "Education in Russia," stressed the Soviets' cultivation of academic talent and called on American educators to do the same, but better. In order to "beat the Russians" and win "the race for space," the report urged public schools to produce a new generation of leaders capable of competing with the best minds from abroad.[31]

In the late summer of 1958, in an attempt to hasten reform in the nation's schools, Congress hurriedly approved the "emergency" National Defense Education Act (NDEA), which sent an unprecedented infusion of federal funds into the public schools. According to President Eisenhower, the United States needed to outdo the Soviet Union "on the Communists' own terms—outmatching them in military power, general technological advance, and specialized education and research." The NDEA, therefore, targeted exactly these areas, shoring up the nation's educational and research facilities, fostering technical development, and improving academic achievement among the nation's most outstanding students. In particular, federal resources under the NDEA supported new instructional programs in science, mathematics, engineering, and foreign languages. While few, if any, of the nation's schools had been seeking aid in these areas (most sought federal aid for school construction and teacher salaries), they nevertheless jumped at the chance to purchase additional materials with external funds. Indeed, administrators found plenty of ways to use NDEA grants at the local level. They bought millions of new microscopes, telescopes, Bunsen burners, and other devices for their science labs, as well as new radios, televisions, reel-to-reel players, and other audiovisual equipment. (In Boston, the schools assembled an unparalleled collection of educational filmstrips on virtually every subject imaginable.) The schools justified each purchase as a contribution to "national defense"—or, more accurately, to the academic achievement of students who would be responsible for the nation's military strength and its resistance to domestic subversion. One columnist, noting the scramble for new algebra textbooks in the fall of 1958, commented in an essay for the *Saturday Review*, "Without mathematics, democracy cannot hope to survive."[32]

The chief architect of the NDEA was Boston native Elliot Richardson, who served as President Eisenhower's assistant secretary of health, education, and welfare in charge of legislative affairs. Over the course of a lengthy career in both state and federal government, Richardson became a celebrated public servant. His first success, however, came in 1957 and 1958 as a result of his involvement with the NDEA. A graduate of both Harvard College (class of 1941) and Harvard Law School (class of 1947), Richardson had participated in the D-Day landing at Normandy in 1944 and had earned a Bronze Star for valor. After law school, he had clerked for Judge Learned Hand of the Second Circuit Court of Appeals and, subsequently, for Justice Felix Frankfurter of the U.S. Supreme Court. In the summer of 1953, at age thirty-three, he had joined the congressional staff of Massachusetts senator Leverett Saltonstall, a Republican (and "Boston Brahmin") who had served as governor from 1939 to 1945 (at which point he left to succeed Massachusetts senator Henry Cabot Lodge Jr.). By the time Richardson joined Saltonstall's staff in Washington, the senator had attained the rank of majority whip, and he gave his young protégé a thorough introduction to all aspects of the federal legislative process. Indeed, as the senator's aide, Richardson was able to work closely on legislative issues with both President Eisenhower and Vice President Richard Nixon. For example, in 1953, when Saltonstall became chairman of the Senate Armed Services Committee, he included Richardson in the committee's deliberations over the armistice that brought an end to the Korean War. Also in 1953, he included Richardson in the planning for a new Department of Health, Education, and Welfare (HEW), which Eisenhower created shortly after his inauguration. Four years later, after Eisenhower's re-election to a second term, it was this department that Richardson joined as assistant secretary for legislative affairs.[33]

Assuming his duties as assistant secretary in the spring of 1957, Richardson could not have predicted that the Soviet Union would launch its first *Sputnik* satellite just a few months later. However, this momentous event on October 4, 1957, set the terms of Richardson's legislative agenda for the next full year. Almost immediately, he and HEW secretary Marion Folsom began to coordinate a response to the *Sputnik* crisis, focusing especially on the nation's schools. Upon his arrival in the second Eisenhower administration, Richardson had been appointed to a presidential task force on federal aid to colleges and universities, and this experience had significantly broadened his view of the federal role in the nation's education system. With *Sputnik*, he saw a chance to extend federal aid not only to the nation's colleges and universities (aid his home state of Massachusetts was particularly likely to receive, given its wide array of postsecondary institutions), but also to the nation's elementary and secondary schools. Historian Barbara Clowse described his role in building support for federal aid to education after *Sputnik*. "From February [1958] into the summer, Richardson moved back and forth on a triangular course from the Hill to the department [of health, education, and welfare] to the White House," she explained. "Those who were most deeply involved with passage of the NDEA agreed ... that Richardson 'did more of a job of direct discussion with [the bill's principal congressional sponsors, Representative Carl] Elliott [D-Ala.] and [Senator Lister] Hill [D-Ala.], than any one person did.' ... Since he had access to the chief executive, Richardson was able to explain to those on the Hill 'what the reasons for the [Eisenhower] administration's approach were and what things ... the President would not accept.'"[34] With remarkable speed and skill, Richardson built a case for the NDEA as a package of large-scale federal aid to the nation's public schools.

Previously, such aid had foundered on a combination of three issues: racial segregation, fears of "federal control," and concerns that federal grants might go to parochial schools and, thus, violate the separation of church and state. Richardson allayed the second and third issues by emphasizing the strictly "voluntary" nature of the proposed NDEA grants and the fact that religiously affiliated schools would be barred from applying for direct aid, but the first issue—racial segregation—was harder to resolve. Two members of the Senate Labor and Public Welfare Committee, Barry Goldwater (R-Ariz.) and Strom Thurmond (D-S.C.), maintained that federal aid would give the federal government a powerful tool to "force" racial desegregation in southern schools. Such an argument was probably exaggerated in 1958, because the Eisenhower administration—still reeling from its desegregation crisis in Little Rock, Arkansas, the year before—had no intention of using NDEA grants as a lever to integrate the nation's public schools. Nonetheless, any prospect of federal intervention in schools raised concerns. Richardson therefore went out of his way to reassure members of Congress that it was "the federal judiciary and not the executive branch of the federal government which is to determine how compliance with the Supreme Court mandate [in *Brown v. Board of Education II*] is to be brought about and what constitutes compliance in good faith."[35] Asserting that the aim of the National Defense Education Act was simply to meet "the urgent, overall educational needs of our country" and not to integrate public schools, Richardson promised southerners in Congress that section 305(c) of the NDEA "conclusively . . . rules out the possibility of discrimination" on the basis of race.[36] In other words, he argued, the NDEA would distribute aid equitably among the races, but it would not require schools receiving federal aid to be racially integrated.

Eisenhower signed the National Defense Education Act (P.L. 85-864) into law on September 2, 1958, but insisted that it should *not* be considered permanent federal assistance for the nation's public schools. It was, he maintained, only "an emergency undertaking to be terminated after four years."[37] Elliot Richardson, however, saw the law differently. In his view, the NDEA showed "that the federal government does indeed have an inescapable concern with the state of public education in this country," and by "inescapable," he meant ongoing.[38] Admitting that *Sputnik* had merely been an excuse to overcome past objections to federal aid, Richardson fully expected the federal role in public schools to grow over time.[39] "We certainly never intended to propose legislation that was merely related to mathematics or science," he noted. And, indeed, the federal office of education expanded rapidly beyond the areas of science and mathematics over the next four years.[40] Arthur Flemming, who replaced Marion Folsom as secretary of HEW in 1958, added more than seven hundred new staff positions to his department between 1959 and 1961, and the Office of Education, housed in HEW, established two new branches to handle additional responsibilities. Richardson welcomed this bureaucratic expansion (like many of his generation, he trusted bureaucracies to run large programs effectively), but he did not stay in Washington long enough to oversee the expansion himself. In the fall of 1958, he returned to Boston to take a new position as the U.S. attorney for the state of Massachusetts, a position he held for the next three years. It was, therefore, from the perspective of a federal official at the state level that he watched the NDEA take effect in the Boston public schools.

In many ways, the objectives of the NDEA were nothing new in Boston. The law passed shortly before the start of the 1958–59 school year, and when it was announced, Superintendent Haley reminded his fellow Bostonians that their local public schools were already doing what the federal government had only recently begun to support with large infusions of federal aid.[41] "The concern of the Boston public schools for the position of science and mathematics in the curriculum antedates by many years the successful launching of the first earth satellite by Russian scientists in October, 1957," he asserted.[42] Yet, once federal grants became available, new initiatives in science, mathematics, and foreign languages increased rapidly. Starting in 1959, a federally funded Science Institute for Able Learners provided "further enrichment for selected high school students of the Boston public schools [who are considered] capable of benefiting from the study of advanced material not ordinarily presented in the [regular] classroom." According to Haley, the goal of the program was "to group talented students together, start their science and mathematics studies earlier, and offer them an extra year of work in these subjects."[43] Although the Boston public schools had not requested federal aid for scientific programs, they readily accepted resources to bolster these areas. As Haley asserted, "Maintaining scientific and technical leadership is of vital importance to the progress and security of our nation. A new approach to the teaching of mathematics and science is considered urgent in order to stimulate interest and bring about proficiency in these fields in our educational programs."[44] Indeed, virtually every public school in the city accepted federal aid under the NDEA, and once the initial grants arrived, school officials enthusiastically asked for more. Within a year, the NDEA had injected previously inconceivable sums of federal aid into Boston's public schools.[45]

Boston's only condition in accepting this aid was that the federal government not intrude on local curricular decisions. Boston would accept federal funds, but it would not accept federal control. This distinction was important, because it indicated the extent to which federal aid and federal control were still considered separable in the late 1950s. Even with federal assistance flowing into the Boston public schools at an unprecedented rate, administrators wanted to be sure that centralized financial support would not lead to centralized educational decision making, which they considered potentially communistic in its implications. Such concerns were, however, frequently overstated. Throughout the 1950s, local and federal officials agreed on the democratic political aims of public schooling in the United States. For example, in the spring of 1952—well before *Sputnik*—Haley had noted that Boston's public schools would "be expected during the next decade to assume a steadily increasing responsibility in combating the insidious ideologies that are attempting to undermine the American way of life, at home in our own communities as well as far afield." In 1955, Haley assured parents that textbooks in "history, civics, economics, literature, and science come in for special scrutiny, so that objectionable, offensive, or un-American tendencies . . . may be detected and eliminated." Such rhetoric was not uncommon in Boston's schools. With the cold war as a menacing backdrop, lessons of patriotism and anticommunism were ever-present in the curriculum. Indeed, the curriculum in Boston reflected the nation's ideological mainstream—part of which was a staunch aversion to "federal control" in schools.[46] Particularly in 1959, when the first grants under the NDEA coincided with Fidel Castro's communist revolution in Cuba, the federal Office of Education carefully avoided any appearance of undue federal influence in local schools.

By the end of the 1959-60 school year, Boston was receiving significant federal aid. Small grants for the disabled and much larger grants for the gifted (under the NDEA) supplemented the school department's annual operating budget, and Haley looked forward to transferring local funds into other areas to meet continuing needs. Like most administrators throughout the country, he saw federal aid as a generous supplement to existing resources—an opportunity to direct other resources to other purposes. He was particularly eager to redistribute resources to meet the needs of mentally, physically, and emotionally disabled students whose numbers had been growing in the schools ever since state and federal aid had become available for the handicapped. At a time when the public schools enrolled approximately 90,000 students, Haley stated, "the number of pupils enrolled in special and sub-special classes on May 1, 1960, was 2,026," or 2.2 percent of the total. Even after the creation of additional classes for the disabled in several locations, the superintendent asserted, "there is need for more classes in certain elementary and junior high schools."[47] Indeed, no matter how much state and federal aid Boston received for its disabled students, Haley always found a need for more: the demands of the school budget were insatiable. And yet, Haley did not remain in office long enough to meet all these demands himself. In July 1960—after twelve years in office—he retired and turned his duties over to Frederick Gillis, a long-time assistant superintendent who had been responsible for, among other initiatives, the experimental class for blind pupils at the John Greenleaf Whittier School in 1952. Like his predecessor, Gillis made no secret of his desire for supplemental aid to the city's schools—especially for the disabled. In fact, Gillis's tenure marked a new era in the schools' pursuit of federal aid. Whereas such aid had been a relative novelty for Haley, it was a basic *expectation* for Gillis.[48]

◇

Gillis's arrival in the superintendency coincided with the presidential campaign of Massachusetts senator John F. Kennedy, whose election platform called for a significant increase in federal support for the nation's schools. Throughout 1960, all eyes were fixed on the race between Senator Kennedy and Vice President Nixon. Certainly, among Boston voters, Kennedy was the favorite. A contemporary of Elliot Richardson's at Harvard, he had graduated with the Class of 1940 (one year before Richardson) and had launched his political career in 1946 with his election to the U.S. House of Representatives. He served three terms as a congressman from Boston's heavily Irish-Catholic eighth district and was elected to the U.S. Senate in 1952 (at which point he passed his seat in the House on to another Irish-Catholic Bostonian, Thomas P. "Tip" O'Neill). As both a representative and a senator, Kennedy had consistently supported federal aid to schools. When he ran for the first time in 1946, he threw his support behind a new federally subsidized school lunch program; a dozen years later, in 1958, he voted enthusiastically for the NDEA. Over the course of his fourteen years in Congress, he had created a modest niche for himself as a leader in the realm of education: he had proposed legislation to provide grants for school construction and instructional materials as well as a wide array of auxiliary services, such as medical supplies for school infirmaries and items for the disabled. When he ran for the presidency in 1960, he was far more outspoken than his opponent in calling for general aid to schools, and he won considerable support from teachers who hoped to benefit from his election. (Although he distanced himself from the idea of aid to parochial schools, he still captured 80 percent of the Roman Catholic vote nationwide.) In Boston, teachers in both public and parochial schools cast their ballots for Kennedy and were delighted when he prevailed at the polls.

Kennedy's margin of victory was among the slimmest of the century, but, once in office, he did not forget his promises to schools. In February 1961, he proposed a major package of "general aid" to support both school construction and teacher salaries. While this proposal sailed through the Senate, it faced vehement opposition in the House, where southern Democrats on the powerful Rules Committee once again suspected that federal aid to education might be used to force racial integration in southern schools. To the disappointment of educators in Boston, neither Tip O'Neill, a member of the Rules Committee, nor John McCormack, the House majority leader and a congressman since 1925, could overcome the tactics of segregationists in their own party. Thus, "general aid" to public schools had to wait.[49] Kennedy did manage, however, to sign a number of smaller programs into law.[50] In particular, he succeeded in passing programs for disabled students, a group of particular interest to him, because his sister, Rosemary, suffered from mental retardation, and a second sister, Eunice Kennedy-Shriver, had recently initiated a national campaign to raise awareness about this condition.[51] In October 1961, Kennedy assembled a distinguished panel of experts to devise a "National Plan to Combat Mental Retardation," and he included on this panel a number of delegates from Massachusetts. The large number of delegates from Massachusetts was unsurprising, not only because Kennedy chose to invite people with whom he was personally familiar, but also because, a year earlier, Massachusetts had significantly expanded its state aid for disabled students in the public schools. A new state law—Chapter 750 of the Acts of 1960—encouraged schools to integrate emotionally disturbed students into classrooms with nondisturbed peers, and Kennedy's panel cited this law as a model of legislation to create "integrated" services for the disabled.[52]

In Boston, superintendent Gillis welcomed the prospect of additional state and federal aid for the disabled, but he did not welcome the prospect of integrating disabled and nondisabled students into the same classes. Following his predecessor, he insisted that disabled students benefited from placements in *isolated* classes and urged teachers to use state resources under Chapter 750 to place emotionally disturbed students in programs that were designed specifically to serve their "special educational needs." In 1961—the year Chapter 750 and its integrationist recommendations went into effect—he commented that the Boston public schools had created isolated programs "for about sixty disturbed children" and argued that "many more are needed." He explained (with regret) that "many districts have special-class cases who are still retained in regular-class groups because, first of all, there is no vacant classroom which can be provided for the class, and, in the second place, [there are] no special-class teachers . . . available. This poses a serious question, for the education of the special-class child is not what it should be, and, [when placed into a regular classroom,] that child deprives more able children of the attention they should receive from the teacher."[53] Despite the explicit integrationist intent of Chapter 750, Gillis continued to believe that the best way to provide equal educational opportunities to all students was to place those who were disabled in isolated programs. And, as long as supplemental aid was available for these programs, he saw no reason to change his mind. In 1961, he applauded two new federal laws—P.L. 87-276 for teachers for the deaf and P.L. 87-294 for books for the blind—neither of which required the integration of handicapped and nonhandicapped students in the same classrooms.[54]

By 1962, Gillis was accepting federal aid from a wide range of sources. He welcomed aid not only for the disabled, but also for the delinquent—under Kennedy's new Juvenile Delinquency and Youth Offenses Control Act—and for vocational education programs—under the new Manpower Development Act.[55] Of course, Gillis also purchased as much equipment as he could under the NDEA. "Probably the greatest single factor affecting the [school budget] during the past school year was the involvement of the NDEA," Gillis's audiovisual director commented in 1961. "Of the $186,000 in matching funds provided [by the NDEA], approximately $150,000 was spent on audiovisual equipment and materials that would not normally be either purchasable or replaceable through regular budgetary procedures." Subsequent years saw further use of the NDEA. As Gillis's audiovisual director observed in 1962, "full utilization of NDEA funds was made so that audiovisual equipment and materials constituted $175,000, or 75 percent of the $232,000 total spent." Along with new slide, film, and overhead projectors, Gillis also encouraged teachers to buy new cassette recorders, child-sized headphone sets, collapsible film screens, and of course, filmstrips. According to his audiovisual director, "the purchase of $75,000 of films on science, mathematics, and language, together with special-purchase commitments in other subject areas, enabled the film library to be almost self-sufficient. . . . Other benefits derived from NDEA participation are the availability of standby or loan equipment for immediate replacement of damaged equipment, and acquisition of special use or test equipment which will aid teachers in developing and utilizing new materials and practices."[56] Few schools in the early 1960s opted to forgo federal assistance. Indeed, the Boston public schools eagerly acquired as much new technology as the NDEA would allow.[57]

Even as Gillis acknowledged the usefulness of grants for technology, however, he observed that assistance was needed in other areas as well. What Boston really needed, he claimed, was not more flash cards, slide rules, or dissection kits but more classrooms and more teachers—needs that were not covered under the NDEA. While schools filled store rooms with new laboratory equipment, Gillis asserted, they were also filling classrooms with more and more students. Overcrowding was becoming a serious problem. When the first cohort of baby boomers began to celebrate their fifteenth, sixteenth, and seventeenth birthdays in 1960, 1961, and 1962, the enrollment crisis began to creep from junior high schools into high schools. At this point, Gillis began to publicize the city's desperate need for classroom facilities. His predecessor's $41 million school-construction campaign had ended in 1961, and Gillis began almost immediately to develop a construction agenda of his own. He knew the city's taxpayers were not eager to accept another bond issue—they had already accepted $15 million in school-construction bonds between 1953 and 1956—so he began to search for other sources of funding. In particular, he looked to the federal government. "With our population growing more rapidly than at any time in the history of our country, within a span of ten years there simply will not be enough high school and college teachers to meet the demand," he wrote. "Probably then, and only then, will the nation be sufficiently aroused to have the federal government take action—perhaps in some form of subsidizing." Over time, Gillis grew increasingly convinced that additional federal aid, on top of the NDEA and other smaller grants, was the only way to face the enrollment crisis threatening the Boston public schools. "If the cry of alarm sounded today continues to go unheeded," he cautioned, "before too long, it will be too late."[58]

Gillis's sense of urgency derived not only from the rising enrollments associated with the baby boom, but also from other demographic forces that were affecting the city's schools. Between 1950 and 1960, several thousand new residents had arrived in Boston—many of them black migrants from the rural South.[59] Eager to escape the sharecropping system, the daily humiliations of Jim Crow, and the terror of lynchings in both rural and urban areas, black families left the South after World War II in search of better-paying jobs and more respectful race relations in the North. This mass migration—the second of two great black migrations in the United States in the twentieth century (the other took place in the period before World War I)—brought unprecedented numbers of black residents to Boston as well as New York, Pittsburgh, Detroit, Chicago, and other northern industrial centers. The vast majority of these newcomers found housing in inner cities, and, gradually, the image of "black ghettos" grew up around them.[60] By 1962, 64,000 blacks constituted about 10 percent of Boston's total population, and 16,000 black children attended the city's public schools.[61] At the same time, growing numbers of foreign immigrants also arrived and took up residence in the same or adjacent neighborhoods. Foreign immigration had increased steadily in Massachusetts throughout the 1950s. In 1953, the U.S. Immigration and

Naturalization Service recorded 6,578 legal immigrants entering the state. Two years later, that number rose to 8,817, and in 1957, it jumped to 11,260—a 71 percent increase in four years. In 1960, more than 7,800 legal immigrants entered the Port of Boston—far more than the 4,293 immigrants who entered the Port of San Francisco or the 4,848 immigrants who entered the Port of Chicago that year. Of course, when combined with illegal or undocumented immigrants, these figures (still low in comparison with later years) would have been much higher.

The children of these new arrivals contributed to the enrollment pressures facing Boston's public schools. Starting in 1959, for example, refugees from revolutionary Cuba as well as citizens from Puerto Rico began filtering into the inner city, and Gillis wondered how their children would fit (both literally and culturally) into the city's overcrowded schools.[62] In the fall of 1960, in an attempt to hasten their assimilation, he authorized the implementation of a new English as a Second Language (ESL) program to give non-English-speaking elementary students extra help with language and to facilitate their transition into regular English-speaking classes. As the superintendent noted in his annual report for 1961-62, "classes for Puerto Rican in-migrants have been continued in the John Williams and George Bancroft Schools, and classes have opened in the Charles Bulfinch, Joseph Hurley, and Martin Milmore Schools."[63] Gillis emphasized that the city's ESL programs aimed to foster students' rapid integration into English-speaking settings. In his words, "these classes have teachers with non-Spanish backgrounds. It is our experience that, with a knowledge of Spanish, the teacher helps these pupils too much in their own language and so keeps the pupils from speaking English." In this way, the students who had English-language deficiencies spent most of their school day in regular English-speaking classes and were "pulled out" of these classes for two or three hours of intensive ESL instruction each afternoon. As Gillis noted, "the pupils remain in classes with their chronological peers and come to the 'English' room on schedule each day. There is a great deal of material available for these pupils to handle, for it is easy to talk about things one can see, touch, and play with. Shy children soon become part of the classroom group, and teachers say many who spoke no English on arrival soon become loquacious in English."[64]

Gillis was proud of Boston's programs for immigrant students, but he was unsure how the city would be able to add programs fast enough to meet the needs of its growing student population. "Education today is big business," he observed. "From the evidence available it becomes increasingly clear that education for tomorrow is going to require Herculean efforts in fiscal matters, as well as other areas of endeavor, if we are to remain firm in our commitment to educate every child who comes to our schools to the optimum of his potential." Observing that his budget had risen from $30 million to $38 million—a 27 percent increase—in just two years, Gillis insisted that Boston's local resources could no longer meet the schools' fiscal needs. "Local real estate taxes, even a state tax, will be inadequate to support the monolithic structure of mass education in the proportions which it will have reached in the next twenty years." According to Gillis, the schools' only hope for fiscal solvency was a dramatic increase in federal assistance. "Clearly," he asserted, "if we are to meet the needs of the present, and adequately prepare for the increasing numbers of young Americans who will come to our schools in the late 1960s and early 1970s, Boston must have full federal assistance—not [just] the type offered under President Kennedy's 'Juvenile Delinquency Act,' or by his 'Manpower Development Act of 1962,' both of which are restrictive, and sharply limited in terms of [duration] and application; but rather these federal funds must be made available on a permanent basis with only such federal controls . . . as are necessary for proper fiscal disbursement."[65] Gillis did not want to sound ungrateful for the federal aid that Boston was already receiving. He appreciated the help of the NDEA as well as the varied smaller matching grants for special education, which, together, added more than $500,000 a year to Boston's school budget. At the same time, however, he stressed the city's growing need for more.[66]

◇

Since federal aid for inner-city schools was scarce in the early 1960s, Gillis had to be creative in his quest for support. He could not depend on the passage of a general aid bill in Congress; instead, he had to make strategic use of existing federal programs. It was in this vein that he began in 1962 to seek federal aid for "urban renewal." Back in 1956, the Eisenhower administration had begun to shift the emphasis of federal housing policy (launched with the Public Housing Act of 1937 and then significantly expanded with the Federal Housing Act of 1949) from a national effort to provide basic shelter to a national effort to promote urban renewal. Rather than using federal resources to construct low-rent housing (as had been done when the first federal initiatives began during the depression), Congress in the 1950s began to allow cities to use federal resources to revive downtown areas. The hope was that central-city revitalization would act as a rising economic tide to lift all boats, including the poor. Thus, Congress granted aid to local projects designed to attract middle-class consumers to downtown areas. Civic centers, office towers, shopping malls, and luxury condominiums all benefited from federal urban-renewal support in the 1950s. The effect of this development was not, however, what Congress had anticipated. Urban-renewal projects added amenities for upper-income citizens—many of whom lived in the suburbs and commuted to work—and displaced lower-income residents into ghetto areas, which, in turn, became targets for further "gentrifying" projects because of their cheap land and politically marginal populations. By the late 1950s, the poorest urbanites found themselves squeezed into smaller and smaller neighborhoods isolated from the rest of the city by strategically placed highways. Adding insult to injury, these highways—the same elevated thoroughfares commuters took to work without ever seeing the ghettos around them—were constructed with federal aid from the Highway Act of 1956.[67]

As conditions in the inner city deteriorated, Superintendent Gillis began to wonder whether federal aid for urban renewal might be directed toward more helpful purposes.[68] Starting in 1962, he began to seek urban-renewal funding for school construction in Boston's most impoverished neighborhoods. In the fall of 1962, he asked Cyril Sargent of the Harvard Graduate School of Education to develop a comprehensive report detailing all of Boston's school-construction needs.[69] The report, when it was finished, called for $132 million worth of school construction to be completed over the course of eleven years (from 1963 to 1974). It listed eighty-six new projects, including a 3,000-student vocational high school and a sprawling 5,500-student campus-style high school to be located in the very heart of the city.[70] Most importantly, it explicitly outlined school projects in districts that were eligible for federal urban-renewal funds. As the *Boston Globe* explained: "Here's the way federal funds for urban renewal would help Boston build new schools as proposed by the $132,000,000 program outlined in the . . . Sargent Report. Suppose the city wanted to build a $1,200,000 elementary school on a two-acre site. If the school were constructed on a site ineligible for urban renewal assistance, it would cost the city $900,000. State school building aid would amount to 30 percent of the actual construction cost, about $300,000 in this instance. If, however, the school were constructed within an urban renewal area, it would cost the city only $210,000—$200,000 for construction and about $10,000 of the $200,000 cost of the site. That's what urban renewal means to school-construction costs."[71] The Sargent Report provided a clear and explicit plan to obtain federal aid for inner-city school construction, and it was exactly what Gillis wanted. It was not, however, the only proposal to suggest federal aid for school construction in 1962.[72]

In a separate report, the Boston Redevelopment Authority (BRA) recommended school-construction projects totaling $127 million. The BRA had been created by Boston's city council in 1957 to supplement the work of the depression-era Boston Housing Authority. Just as the housing authority had obtained funds from the Federal Housing Act of 1949, the BRA had been created to take advantage of federal urban-renewal funds authorized by Congress in 1956. In 1960, the BRA assumed the responsibilities of the Boston City Planning Board, including its responsibility to oversee all federally funded urban-renewal construction projects.[73] Thereafter, the BRA played a key role in obtaining federal aid for schools. For example, the BRA's report on school construction in 1962 took for granted the availability of at least $27 million in federal funds to cover building costs in Boston's inner city. Indeed, what was most notable about both the Sargent report *and* the BRA report was the fact that they simply *presumed* a federal willingness to help Boston build inner-city schools. School construction, in other words, was thought to overlap with the objectives of urban renewal.[74] This linkage of urban renewal and inner-city school construction constituted a savvy political maneuver on the part of Superintendent Gillis. Recognizing that urban renewal was popular among the middle classes, Gillis skillfully tied the needs of Boston's inner-city students to President Kennedy's concerns for urban revitalization—as well as the president's related concerns for juvenile delinquency, truancy, and crime. In this way, he cast inner-city school construction as a form of urban restoration and succeeded in winning political support at both the local and the national level. He also succeeded in obtaining critical financial aid to meet a need, which, if left to the vicissitudes of the Kennedy administration's ill-fated effort to win "general aid," might have gone unmet.

Gillis recognized that appeals for urban-renewal funding carried a risk of possible unwanted federal control, but he concluded that Boston could not avoid this risk. "We must take that chance," he admitted in 1962. "In point of fact, we have no alternative."[75] This decision to forfeit some local control in order to receive federal aid was momentous; indeed, it was a decision that ultimately transformed the structure of school governance in Boston. But it was also a decision that increasing numbers of large urban school systems were making in the early 1960s. The demographic changes weighing on Boston's public schools—rising enrollments; increasing racial, ethnic, and linguistic diversity; spreading poverty—were weighing on virtually every city in the country, and urban officials were beginning to coordinate their strategies for reform. Shortly before Gillis issued his annual report for 1962–63, he joined thirteen other superintendents to establish the Great Cities Program for School Improvement (later called the Council of Great City Schools, or CGCS).

Initiated in 1956 and incorporated in 1961, the Council of Great City Schools had two main objectives. First, it aimed to steer federal aid directly to city governments and away from state agencies that allowed funds to flow disproportionately to suburban areas. Second, it aimed to rewrite urban-renewal policies that tended to exacerbate rather than alleviate inner-city problems. Both of these aims appealed to Superintendent Gillis, who was tired of seeing federal resources serve wealthy suburbs more than the inner-city. In his annual report for 1961–62, Gillis insisted that the phrase *great cities* did not refer to "metropolitan areas where middle- and upper-class suburbanites live in commuter dormitories surrounding the core city"; rather, he asserted, the phrase *great cities* referred to "the inner city itself."[76] By joining the Great Cities Program for School Improvement, Gillis hoped to gain access to a larger portion of federal aid for Boston's schools.

The idea that large cities faced huge educational burdens was not new in the early 1960s, but this idea took on greater dimension and greater urgency in this period. Many observers began to argue that the most pressing challenges facing inner-city schools were not only financial, but also *cultural*. Superintendent Gillis—along with many of the most prominent sociologists of his day—began to suggest that students in ghetto schools were not just poor but "culturally disadvantaged" and "culturally deprived." As he put it in his annual report for 1961–62, "the subcultural patterns of the people living in these depressed [urban] areas serve only to encourage a rot of moral fiber. The common birthright of their children is squalor, disease, and crime. These boys and girls are the potential nonreaders, juvenile delinquents, unwed teen-age mothers, and dropouts. . . . The slum *per se* stamps the individual who lives in it as a second-class citizen—an inadequate person with zero for his aspirational goal." According to Gillis, children trapped in this "culture of poverty" rarely escaped, because anyone who attained middle-class status quickly moved out. "When this happens," he wrote, the inner city filled up with "culturally deprived immigrants, handicapped by a second-class education, or, worse still, by illiteracy. The rural backgrounds of these people, and their handlabor qualifications, make them unsuited for the skilled labor market which urban industrialization and automation demand. These people contribute to the pool of unemployables, and [then] go on welfare."[77] In Gillis's view, this debilitating cycle of poverty threatened the entire city, and the public schools had a responsibility to end it. "When the boy or girl comes to the public school from this kind of home, where the culture is several cuts below average," Gillis maintained, "the school, more than ever, must adjust to the needs of this child."[78]

According to Gillis, the great challenge facing public schools in the future was to find more effective ways of educating the city's neediest children—and he was not alone in this view. In an influential book, *The Other America,* published in early 1962, sociologist Michael Harrington also suggested that poor residents of the inner city shared a culture of poverty that severely restricted their social, economic, and educational opportunities. Harrington's theory of cultural deprivation struck a chord with middle-class Americans who often tended to attribute the causes of poverty to laziness, stupidity, damaged family structures, or other personalized weaknesses. Harrington, however, also drew attention to the structural and institutional causes of urban poverty in the 1960s. He explained that the lives of the poor were affected by the physical and built environments of inner cities—environments in which arterial and beltline highways as well as other obstacles such as empty lots and neglected border sites segregated poor and middle-class areas.[79] Lower-income residents were thus isolated from the services—such as schools, hospitals, supermarkets, banks, professional offices, parks, restaurants, specialty shops, libraries, and playgrounds—that made suburban neighborhoods so much more attractive, convenient, prosperous, and stable. According to Harrington, poverty in the United States was attributable to flawed city planning at least as much as individual moral failings. He therefore agreed with Gillis that one way to help "the other America" was to improve inner-city services—starting with the schools. Moreover, he asserted that the best way to improve inner-city schools was to supplement declining urban property tax revenues with funds from other sources, such as the federal government. In an argument that soon captured the attention of the Kennedy administration, Harrington drew a direct connection between public education and urban renewal.[80]

Gillis's own writings echoed Harrington's analysis as well as his conclusions. As he asserted in 1963, "fiscal help will have to come from the federal government, and the day has already passed when the issue of federal funds for education is an academic question. In our own city, it is an urgent, practical need." He noted further that "the requirement for federal aid is already approaching the critical point, because it costs so much more per student to educate an underprivileged pupil than it does to educate a boy or girl form a middle-class home." Each culturally disadvantaged student, Gillis declared, "needs 'field trips' to the museums, to the library, to places of business, to any and every place that will contribute to giving him a sense of belonging [in a big city] and to raising his aspirational goals. If the school fails this boy, he will become a dropout and, more often than not, a juvenile delinquent with a strong likelihood that his delinquency will be aggravated in adult life." Given the high cost of compensatory educational services—not to mention the potential cost to society if the city failed to offer them—Gillis insisted that the only way to improve urban schools was to obtain more aid from the federal government. He recognized that this goal was a lofty one—after all, President Kennedy had failed to push a general aid bill through Congress in 1961, and in 1963, the only federally funded education program aimed specifically at low-income students was the subsidized school lunch program, created in 1948. Yet, given the combined effect of a rapidly increasing student population and a rapidly decreasing urban tax base (an issue tied to suburbanization, which predated the rise of minority ghettos), Gillis believed that general aid from the federal government was Boston's only hope. "It is regrettable," the superintendent noted, "that we have to wait for an already sensitive fiscal situation to become a point of crisis."[81]

The financial plight of the Boston public schools was serious, but it was not solely attributable to an increase in urban poverty: it also derived from a lack of adequate state aid to schools. In 1963, Massachusetts used a so-called foundation formula for allocating state aid. Adopted in 1948, the formula established a minimum of $130 per year for the education of each student in the state and expected each city and town to devote 0.6 percent of its total property valuations to the support of local schools. If this local contribution fell short of the $130 minimum, then the state would make up the difference. If local contributions exceeded the minimum, then the state would spend nothing on that town's schools. In theory, this formula, which was common throughout the country in the 1940s and 1950s, equalized school spending throughout the state.[82] However, as school costs rose, the state did not raise the foundation amount. Moreover, most towns did not reassess their local property on an annual basis. As a result, the state found that a foundation formula based on an expected local contribution of 0.6 percent of assessed valuations did not yield enough money in most towns to cover the minimum of $130 per student. Since the state itself had only a fixed amount to spend on schools, and since localities refused to reassess their property or raise their own contributions, the state could not meet its growing obligations for school aid. In order to bring state aid into line with existing revenues, the state finally decided to cut the foundation amount in half, from $130 to $65—a sum that was grossly inadequate to meet school expenses in 1963.[83] As one study commented, "A foundation program of $65 per child obviously could not even begin to meet the requirements of financing a satisfactory education, even in 194[8], when the Massachusetts average expenditure per pupil in net average attendance was $175."[84]

The state legislature recognized this financial dilemma and tried to respond in two ways.[85] First, it appointed a commission to conduct an analysis of schools throughout the state. Codirected by superintendent of the

Chicago public schools Benjamin C. Willis and president of the Massachusetts state senate Kevin B. Harrington, the Willis-Harrington Commission was given two years and $300,000 to produce its report. Second, the legislature passed a new law, Chapter 660 of the Acts of 1963, which called for cities and towns to update their property valuations and promised more aid to schools. This law was an important step in the right direction; yet, property tax revenues still fell short of meeting the schools' needs, because, despite the passage of Chapter 660, only 25 percent of taxable properties throughout the state of Massachusetts were actually reassessed (the remaining 75 percent still used valuations from 1945). Furthermore, Chapter 660 kept the foundation amount static at $65 per pupil—a laughable figure in 1963, when average per pupil expenditures in Massachusetts were closer to $500 per year. Also, according to the Massachusetts Advisory Council on Education (created as a research organization by the Willis-Harrington Commission), "the $65 was applied only to children between the ages of seven and sixteen, ignoring the large number of children who began school at the age of six (or five) and those who remained in high school for one or two years beyond the age of sixteen. Therefore, from the very start, the Massachusetts foundation program was grossly inadequate."[86] Superintendent Gillis openly criticized Chapter 660, saying it was obvious the state needed to do more for its public schools—especially in large cities such as Boston. But his complaints fell on deaf ears. Having appointed a new commission and passed a new law, the legislature refused to listen, and Gillis was forced to retreat (albeit reluctantly) from his requests for additional state aid.

At the age of seventy, the superintendent was perhaps not as ambitious as he once had been. When Gillis took the helm of Boston's public schools in 1960, he had predicted that federal aid would become an integral component of the city's education budget, and this prediction had come true. Over time, Boston had pursued federal funds from a greater and greater range of sources, and the Boston public schools had used these funds to meet a wider and wider variety of needs—from special programs for the disabled to instructional equipment to major school-construction projects. The growth of federal aid to the Boston public schools had been extraordinary throughout the late 1950s and early 1960s (rising from 0.2 to 1.2 percent of a growing budget between 1956 and 1963), and Gillis, like his predecessor, had seized every opportunity to obtain more support. Now he was ready to turn his duties over to a new superintendent. In the summer of 1963, confident that he had guided Boston successfully through its most difficult years, he retired and left the schools in the hands of his deputy superintendent, William Ohrenberger.[87] It was a smooth transition, in part because Ohrenberger—who remained superintendent for the next decade—inherited a school system more comfortable with the idea of federal aid. Ohrenberger, even more than Haley or Gillis, simply *assumed* that federal aid would increase in the future, and he did all he could to maximize Boston's eligibility. Yet, the focus of this pursuit subtly changed. Stressing the plight of disadvantaged students in the inner city, Ohrenberger confronted a new version of the conflict between integrated and isolated programs for students with "special educational needs." Could isolated programs designed—and funded—to meet special needs nonetheless be considered "discriminatory"? Faced with this question, Ohrenberger soon realized that his predecessors' work had been simple by comparison.

CHAPTER TWO

Defining Disadvantage as Disability, 1963-1966

In 1963, Ohrenberger took up his predecessors' appeals for federal aid, and, like Haley and Gillis, he quickly found that it paid to be creative. For reasons both subtle and strategic, he began to focus his appeals on the issue of special educational services for the disabled. More specifically, he focused on obtaining federal aid for children diagnosed as mentally retarded or emotionally disturbed. This focus was politically astute, because in 1963, significant federal aid was not directly available to students who were socially or economically disadvantaged, but federal aid *was* available to students who were disabled. In February of that year, President Kennedy had announced the findings of his "National Plan to Combat Mental Retardation," and Congress had responded eight months later by passing two new laws: the Maternal and Child Health and Mental Retardation Planning Act, which authorized $265 million over five years for program development at both the state and local level, and the Mental Retardation Facilities and Community Mental Health Construction Act, which authorized nearly $330 million over five years for new buildings to serve disabled citizens.[1] When Superintendent Ohrenberger heard about the prospect of nearly $600 million in federal aid for the handicapped, he began to envision a windfall of federal funds for Boston—and he recognized that the way to maximize the city's eligibility for these funds was to identify as many disabled students as possible. Demonstrating his political acumen, he therefore began, in the fall of 1963, to frame the needs of impoverished students in the inner city not only in terms of social, economic, and cultural disadvantage but also in terms of mental and emotional *disability*. In short, he began to forge a direct link between cultural disadvantage and cognitive disability, and he encouraged teachers to place as many inner-city students as possible into classes that were likely to receive federal aid.[2]

Just as Superintendent Gillis had adjusted his school-construction agenda to fit the Kennedy administration's interest in urban renewal, so, too, Superintendent Ohrenberger adjusted his own priorities to fit Kennedy's interest in mental retardation. He knew that the President and Congress were starting to devote significant financial resources to special education programs, and he sensed that, if he could show a connection between cultural disadvantage and cognitive disability, he could increase his chances of receiving federal aid. Moreover, he realized that, if he could link the issue of mental retardation to other Kennedy concerns such as juvenile delinquency, urban decay, and poverty, then his chances of obtaining federal funds would improve even further. Fortunately, Boston had already begun in the fall of 1963 to launch several new programs designed specifically to meet the needs of "culturally disadvantaged" students—and a number of these programs were already benefiting from federal aid. For example, Ohrenberger received aid from the Manpower Development and Training Act to provide vocational and technical instruction to at-risk high school students whose academic achievement fell consistently below average; he secured resources from the Juvenile Delinquency and Youth Offenses Control Act for Operation Second Chance, a program to reduce the dropout rate among male middle-school pupils; and he obtained funding from the NDEA to offer counseling psychologists an in-service course, "Education in Disadvantaged Areas," which outlined various prekindergarten programs, supplemental reading techniques, and life-adjustment guidance services for elementary pupils.[3] As Ohrenberger pointed out, each of these new programs compensated for the deprivations of ghetto life, and each won federal aid. Now, the Mental Retardation Planning Act of 1963 promised similar fiscal rewards for linking compensatory education for the disadvantaged to special education for the disabled.[4]

Ohrenberger's conflation of disadvantage and disability did not seem odd to his contemporaries in the early 1960s—a time when the concept of a debilitating "culture of poverty" profoundly shaped the way educators viewed inner-city students. In their minds, cultural deprivation and cognitive disability almost always went hand in hand.[5] This point cannot be overstated. Just as a disability was defined as a life-long ailment or handicap (such as deafness or blindness), so, too, poverty was thought to be an inherited condition that resisted easy rehabilitation and, even if it responded to treatment or therapy, still left enduring scars. Like the effects of disability, the effects of impoverishment were thought to persist indefinitely; if poverty was present at infancy, childhood, or adolescence, then it was likely to cause problems in adulthood. Poverty thus resembled a disability, which, while perhaps treatable, was not really possible to "cure."[6] This element of "incurability" rendered the idea of compensatory education for the disadvantaged analogous to the idea of special education for the disabled. In the view of most educators, the culturally deprived were cognitively deficient, and their treatment frequently took on medical characteristics (indeed, in the 1960s, the terminology used to describe poverty was often medical in nature).[7] Moreover, when it came to teaching—or, rather, treating—disadvantaged students in special-compensatory programs, inner-city schools took on the qualities of hospitals. In an attempt to overcome the noxious effects of poverty, educators assumed that poor students, much like acutely ill patients, required "intensive care" in a facility that was both removed from the contagious environment of the slum and isolated from the healthy population. This special facility, a sort of hygienic ward in the cultural treatment center of the school, was the isolated remedial classroom.

The isolated remedial classroom constituted the critical care unit of the inner-city school. It healed the wounds and monitored the daily progress of the sickest—that is, the poorest and most culturally disadvantaged—children in the school. The isolated remedial class was located far enough away from the ghetto to prevent reinfection, but it was also quarantined from regular classrooms in order to avoid contamination. In some cases, the remedial class was quite literally a sanitized space for pupils who lacked access to clean homes or basic health care, a place where teachers could repair the damage that growing up in a slum could do. These comparisons between poverty and pathology, between schools and hospitals, between teachers and nurses clarify the idea that disadvantaged children suffered more or less permanent disabilities as a result of their encounter with poverty. In fact, only when *disadvantage* is defined as *disability* do the words of Ohrenberger and his contemporaries make sense. Ohrenberger truly believed that isolated remedial classes would improve the educational opportunities (and, in turn, the academic achievement) of poor minority students in inner-city schools. Inasmuch as these students were more likely to be mentally retarded—and up-to-date scientific studies concluded that they were—he held that special-compensatory classes were the best way to meet their needs. In fact, in his view, special-compensatory services for disadvantaged students in the inner city warranted federal aid in the same way that special services for disabled students in the suburbs warranted aid. Because the Kennedy administration had chosen to direct aid toward disabled rather than disadvantaged children, Ohrenberger insisted that Boston had an *obligation* to place as many low-achieving inner-city students as possible into this funding-eligible category—not only to maximize schools' receipt of federal aid, but also to maximize these students' educational opportunities.

Topping Ohrenberger's list of candidates for federal aid to the disadvantaged was a program called Operation Counterpoise, which had been launched in the fall of 1963 to serve poor minority children—or, more specifically, black children whose extremely low levels of academic achievement seemed to necessitate special-compensatory educational services. First introduced at the Henry L. Higginson Elementary School in the nearly all-black neighborhood of Roxbury, Operation Counterpoise had expanded rapidly in 1963–64 to include twelve schools at a cost of more than $350,000.[8] The program sought to reduce truancy rates, trim class sizes, expand libraries, and improve parental involvement in the schools. In a larger sense, it intended to rescue minority children from dysfunctional home environments in order to prepare them for academic achievement in the upper grade levels. As Ohrenberger's predecessor observed, "Operation Counterpoise is a preventive program designed to catch undesirable situations in their incipiency, to improve children's attitudes toward school, [and] to inspire standards of excellence which should be carried over into secondary education for all and beyond for many. It is our hope through this program to raise the achievement of these pupils closer to their potentials, which have for too long been submerged by parental lack of values."[9] In order to boost self-esteem and provide "cultural enrichment" for inner-city minority students, Operation Counterpoise built a remedial curriculum around "examples of what outstanding Negro leaders have done, thereby helping to make [black pupils] proud of their own cultural background and tradition."[10] In Ohrenberger's view, Operation Counterpoise was an ideal candidate for federal aid—if not under the rubric of federal aid for the disadvantaged (a rubric that did not yet exist), then certainly under the rubric of federal aid for the disabled.[11]

Programs for disadvantaged students spread rapidly in Boston in 1963–64, and each was cast as a contribution to "equal opportunity" in the inner city. As Ohrenberger's predecessor explained, "these programs should prove to all citizens with open minds that no child in the Boston schools is denied opportunity for maximum learning—irrespective of race, creed, or color."[12] An article in the *Christian Science Monitor* agreed, noting that Operation Counterpoise was "the sort of program Negro leaders have been urging, particularly for the areas of the city in which their people predominate. Cooperation between Negro parents and school officials in this program has been 'excellent,' say both sides." Indeed, many parents in inner-city neighborhoods welcomed Operation Counterpoise. As one mother commented, "this program should not be considered something novel. Our children now are beginning to get the kind of education they should have had all along." She added that, a year earlier, under the threat of program cuts in 1962–63, "we were told that there was simply no time in the school day to take our children on cultural field trips. This year, we have seen [these] become a reality, and we are most encouraged."[13] Superintendent Ohrenberger appreciated such approbation and applauded Operation Counterpoise as a major success.[14] And, yet, even as Operation Counterpoise expanded from one school to twelve in 1964, some inner-city parents began to insist that their children were *not* mentally deficient and were *not* eager to have their regular classes retooled for remedial instruction. Others charged that special-compensatory programs had been implemented in certain slum areas to mask the much deeper inequalities that existed between schools with predominantly black enrollments and schools with predominantly white enrollments. Between 1963 and 1964, these complaints escalated into accusations of widespread discrimination—and de facto segregation—in the Boston public schools.[15]

The Boston-based *Christian Science Monitor* noted that Operation Counterpoise had been "launched in some haste when charges of 'de facto segregation' were rife" in the city. The paper asserted that many black parents expressed suspicion about the program's tendency to place poor minority children in remedial classes—placements that promised access to special-compensatory services and potentially to allocations of federal aid.[16] Despite Ohrenberger's promise that special-compensatory services would improve opportunities for poor students (at a time when funds for predominantly black schools ran as much as 16 percent below funds for predominantly white schools), many black parents maintained that the best way to overcome racial inequalities in public schools, including disparities in academic achievement, was not to diagnose minority students as disabled and place them in special classes but, rather, to *integrate* them into schools (and classes) with average- or above-average-achieving white students.[17] Borrowing an argument from Massachusetts's special commission for the retarded (an ironic source), opponents of Operation Counterpoise claimed that the best way to equalize opportunities was to place all students together in the *same* classes.[18] Just as the special commission had advocated the placement of even the most severely disabled students in regular classes (with special services), so opponents of Operation Counterpoise advocated the integration of even the most gravely disadvantaged minority students in classes with (presumably less disadvantaged) white students. They contended that integration was inherently desirable and that "equal opportunities" were more likely to result from racially integrated regular classes than from racially segregated remedial classes. In sum, they argued, poor minority pupils in the inner city were educationally disadvantaged *not* because they were mentally disabled or culturally deficient but, rather, because they were de facto segregated.

So, which was likelier to foster equal educational opportunities: special services or racial integration? In 1963, this either/or question was hard to answer—even for black parents, who, in June of that year, staged a citywide boycott to protest racial inequalities in the public schools. On the last day of the spring term, black parents took their children out of class and organized a demonstration in front of school department headquarters.[19] Superintendent Gillis, confronting this rally a month before his retirement, had not been pleased.[20] In his final annual report, he noted that "an attempt was made June 18th to have Negro students effect a 'Stay Away From School Day.'" He concluded that "the operation was contrary to state law, and a dismal failure. Sit-ins and picketing of school headquarters proved equally futile."[21] Yet, by the time Ohrenberger arrived in July 1963, he could not ignore the fact that the parents' boycott reflected a growing movement for civil rights and racial equality on a nationwide scale. Under the charismatic leadership of Martin Luther King Jr., nonviolent action for civil rights and racial equality had spread from the South to the North. In 1960, students in North Carolina had organized a sit-in to protest segregated lunch counters; in 1961, the Freedom Rides had drawn attention to the problem of racism throughout the South; in 1962, federal marshals had guarded James Meredith as he enrolled at the University of Mississippi; and in May 1963, just a month before the school boycott in Boston, the televised brutality of police in Birmingham, Alabama, had revealed the urgency of the civil rights movement to millions of northern middle-class whites. By the time Ohrenberger

assumed the superintendency in 1963, he could not overlook the movement's strength within his own city. Indeed, after President Kennedy's
assassination in November—and the shift to Lyndon Johnson's administration immediately thereafter—the civil rights movement had become
impossible to disregard.

◇

At the heart of the civil rights movement in 1963-64 was the ideal of racial
integration, and, inasmuch as Operation Counterpoise appeared to thwart
this ideal, it—together with other special-compensatory services in de
facto segregated schools—became an object of bitter controversy. Some
argued that Operation Counterpoise served the unique educational needs
of poor minority students; others said it simply perpetuated their educational isolation. "It is good that there is [Operation Counterpoise] in Boston," wrote Robert Levey in an editorial for the *Boston Globe*, "but don't
let it be mistaken for a genuinely progressive or radical approach to a
problem. It is a conservative program and many of its features should
have always been a natural part of the school set-up. The school administration should not be proud that the enormous class loads in Roxbury
are just now being reduced. It should have made this item a high-priority
affair years ago."[22] The conservative nature of Operation Counterpoise
became all the more apparent when the newly elected chairwoman of
Boston's powerful school committee, a forty-year-old segregationist
from South Boston named Louise Day Hicks, gave the program her
strong support. A graduate (at fifteen) of the Wheelock Teachers' College
who held a bachelor's degree from Boston University's School of Education as well as a J.D. from the Boston University Law School, Hicks had
joined the Massachusetts bar in 1959 and had served as counsel for the
Boston Juvenile Court in 1960 before becoming treasurer of the Boston
school committee in 1962 and chair in 1963.[23] In Hicks's view, Operation
Counterpoise was designed to teach black children at what was considered "their own level" or on "their own terms"—and *apart* from white
students. It did not exist to foster integration among black and white students; rather, it existed to meet poor minority students' needs in their
own neighborhood schools and, in so doing, to compensate for their
cultural and cognitive deficiencies.[24]

Criticism of Operation Counterpoise increased steadily under Hicks—
even while superintendent Ohrenberger chose to devote his first annual
report to the subject "Education for the Culturally Disadvantaged."
Drawing a direct link between cultural disadvantage and cognitive disability, Ohrenberger praised the "successful" early implementation of

Operation Counterpoise as well as the work of Action for Boston Community Development (ABCD), a federally funded advocacy group that had collaborated with the schools to launch preschool programs and remedial reading programs for "culturally deprived children and youth."[25] He argued that each of these initiatives offered a necessary service to poor minority students and hinted that such initiatives might soon be eligible for federal funds. To parents concerned about schools' tendency to find high rates of mental disability among disadvantaged children, he replied that a *failure* to identify legitimate cognitive handicaps among pupils in slum areas might jeopardize the city's pursuit of federal aid (not to mention the educational opportunities of disadvantaged students themselves). As he asserted, poor minority students *needed* special programs, and the timing of this assertion was significant. Less than a month after it was made, the first appropriations under the federal Mental Retardation Planning Act of 1963 arrived in Massachusetts, and state officers began to identify areas of "need" for special services. The Massachusetts Mental Retardation Planning Project—which was duplicated in every state—commenced work in July 1964, under the direction of state commissioner of mental health Harry Solomon and included delegates from various other departments, including education, rehabilitation, public health, and public welfare. Solomon grouped these state delegates into nine subcommittees and charged each with the task of devising new programs to attract federal aid for the disabled—as well as the disadvantaged.

With federal aid to the disabled practically guaranteed, the Massachusetts Mental Retardation Planning Project established itself as a "permanent inter-departmental office for program development," the chief goal of which was to maximize the state's receipt of external grants. As Solomon noted, "history shows that the state failed to . . . meet local needs and demands for adequate services [for the mentally retarded]. Undoubtedly, this [failure] led to the necessity for federal direction in planning, and partial federal funding of new construction and staffing of local facilities."[26] In fact, it was not long before Solomon discovered that Massachusetts was eligible for previously unimaginable sums of federal aid for special-compensatory services for disabled (and disadvantaged) pupils. In Boston, Superintendent Ohrenberger was particularly intrigued by Solomon's finding that minority students in urban areas were more likely than white students in suburban areas to be diagnosed with mental retardation. This finding seemed to justify Ohrenberger's conflation of disadvantage and disability as well as his view that poor minority students required extra services to meet their special needs. If disabled white students in suburban schools were eligible for federal aid, then surely, he argued, disabled minority students in urban schools must also be eligible; indeed, the needs of poorer urban students warranted *prior* attention. As Ohrenberger pointed out, inner-city schools were far more crowded, their teachers less experienced, their materials less current, and their extracurricular offerings less plentiful than in the suburbs. Problems of unstable homes (or homelessness), absent parents, and drug abuse deepened the rut that placed inner-city minority students at risk of academic failure. At a time when below-average achievement was the key sign of mental retardation, it was no surprise that large numbers of inner-city minority students were being diagnosed as disabled.

Given his conflation of disadvantage and disability, Ohrenberger had no problem with the fact that programs such as Operation Counterpoise served poor minority students in their neighborhood schools. If anything, he saw this concentration of resources as an *advantage,* and he was not distressed when, in July 1964, the Massachusetts Department of Education, in an investigation of de facto segregation in Boston, found that the city had forty-five schools with over 50 percent nonwhite students, including twenty-seven with over 80 percent nonwhite students and sixteen with over 96 percent nonwhite students. He was entirely unconcerned that the (rather ironically named) William Lloyd Garrison Elementary School was 96.8 percent nonwhite, the Hyde Park High School was 99.1 percent nonwhite, and the George A. Lewis Middle School Annex was 100 percent nonwhite. One observer noted that "if this was not de facto segregation in education, then it was difficult to see what possible meaning that phrase could ever have"; but Ohrenberger saw nothing wrong with this situation, and he could not discern what useful lesson state officials intended to draw from these statistics.[27] Without any direct or explicit evidence linking racial balance to academic achievement, he pointed to ways in which these inner-city schools were trying to *improve* educational opportunities for their students. He noted that Operation Counterpoise and Operation Second Chance—which focused, almost by definition, on poor minority students in ghetto schools—were *solutions* to the problem of educational inequity, not problems in themselves. Moreover, he noted that this view was backed by the Massachusetts Mental Retardation Planning Project and the state legislature, which passed a new law, Chapter 650, in April 1964, to increase state aid to special-compensatory services in low-income areas. Chapter 650 did not require services to be housed in racially integrated schools; if anything, it required just the opposite.[28]

While the total authorization for Chapter 650 was small—only $50,000 for all of Massachusetts when Operation Counterpoise in Boston cost seven times that amount—it nonetheless set an important precedent for state-funded special-compensatory education in an era when only two other states, New York and California, had similar laws designed specifically to support programs for disadvantaged students.[29] Also, the timing of Chapter 650 was significant, because, in the fall of 1964, *federal* officials were also beginning to consider an increase in support for special-compensatory programs in low-income areas. Details of the federal proposal were still being worked out by a secret presidential task force, but it was clear that the Johnson administration was looking for ways to help local schools meet the needs of socially and economically disadvantaged students.[30] Whereas Kennedy had placed his educational emphasis on mental retardation, Johnson placed his emphasis on civil rights and poverty. Among his first legislative successes had been the passage of the landmark Civil Rights Act of 1964, which barred discrimination on the basis of race, color, or national origin in all programs receiving federal aid, and (a month or so later) the passage of the Economic Opportunity Act of 1964, which extended antidiscrimination provisions to the workplace.[31] By the fall of 1964, Johnson had laid a foundation for his War on Poverty, the centerpiece of his Great Society agenda, and the next major item on his agenda was federal aid to education. Johnson was, of course, familiar with his predecessor's failure to pass a general aid-to-education bill, but he also knew that existing federal aid—under the NDEA, the impact-aid program, and the urban-renewal program, as well as more recent programs for the disabled—had not sufficed to meet the needs of students who lived in low-income areas. It was time, he believed, for a massive increase in federal aid to disadvantaged students.

Coordinating this push was Francis "Frank" Keppel, a former dean of the Harvard Graduate School of Education whom Kennedy had appointed as federal commissioner of education in 1962. A contemporary of Kennedy's and Elliot Richardson's at Harvard, Keppel had graduated in 1937 (when Kennedy was a sophomore and Richardson a freshman).[32] He had served as secretary of the Joint Army-Navy Committee on Welfare and Recreation during World War II and had returned to Harvard as assistant dean of the college in 1945. In 1948, at the age of thirty-two, he was selected by Harvard's president James B. Conant to head the Graduate School of Education, and he remained in that post until his appointment as federal commissioner in 1962. Having witnessed firsthand the expansion of Boston's public schools between 1948 and 1962, Keppel was acutely aware of the difficulties facing the nation's urban districts. He knew that inner-city poverty combined with decreasing tax revenues, ever-growing racial, ethnic, and language diversity, and constantly mounting demands for special-compensatory services had placed the schools in a serious financial bind. Just as other Boston educators had looked to the federal government for help in the early 1960s, so, too, Keppel began to explore the possibility of boosting federal aid. In 1963, during his first year as federal commissioner, he proposed a bill for general aid "to improve educational opportunity and achievements of students attending schools in [those] areas—*both urban slums and rural depressed*—marked by high rates of unemployment and low per capita income and educational achievements." Over the next two years, this bill set the terms for a dramatic redefinition of the federal commitment to "educational opportunity and achievement" among disadvantaged students. Indeed, by the fall of 1964, it set an entirely new standard for federal aid to education in the United States.[33]

In 1964—after the passage of the Civil Rights Act and the Economic Opportunity Act—Keppel began to craft a politically palatable proposal for large-scale federal aid to education. Among the officials assisting him in this endeavor were Wilbur Cohen, who occupied the position once occupied by Elliot Richardson (assistant secretary of health, education, and welfare for legislative affairs), and Senator Wayne L. Morse (D-Ore.), who chaired the Senate Subcommittee on Education. It was Morse who suggested a strategy to carry the school-aid package through Congress. Determined not to repeat the mistakes of the Kennedy administration, Morse suggested attaching the bill to the largest and most popular federal aid-to-education programs: urban renewal and impact aid.[34] As Keppel later recalled, "the central point that he (Morse) made was [that], if we wanted this bill to pass, it would be wise to hitch it up to a piece of legislation that has plenty of congressional support (namely, the impacted-areas bill) and to the problems of the poor."[35] The virtue of the impact-aid laws was not only that they granted schools loosely regulated federal funds, but also that they granted funds based on total student enrollments in each state rather than just public-school enrollments. In this way, they avoided the dilemmas surrounding federal aid to parochial schools. As historian Julie Roy Jeffrey explained in *Education for Children of the Poor*, "an emphasis on giving money to the needy child rather than the school offered a good chance of avoiding the whole religious question, which focused on whether federal aid should go to parochial schools. Avoiding religious controversy was politically fundamental in Keppel's [view] as it was in Cohen's and the president's. Moreover, the poverty theme was politically popular."[36] Also, by continuing the NDEA's tradition of voluntary grants to local schools, Keppel, Cohen, and Morse were able to mitigate potential concerns about "federal control."[37]

In October 1964, Johnson asked Keppel to start building support for this proposal among key lobby groups such as the National Catholic Welfare Conference (NCWC) and the National Education Association

(NEA). Keppel was pleased to find both groups amenable to the bill. By the time of the presidential election in November, Keppel and his staff had devised a formula that distributed aid to local schools based on each state's total number of school-aged children with annual family incomes under $2,000 (for four people). Unlike earlier proposals for federal aid, which had foundered in the Rules Committee, Keppel's plan avoided previous problems in three ways. First, the problems facing urban education had become so overwhelming by the mid-1960s that many critics of federal aid were willing to set aside their long-standing fears of federal control. Second, the strategy of allocating aid on the basis of total enrollments rather than public school enrollments—that is, giving aid to the child rather than the school—skirted past controversies over federal support for parochial schools. Third, the recent passage of the Civil Rights Act of 1964 meant that Keppel could avoid any explicit references to desegregation in his bill, because racial discrimination was now officially illegal in *all* programs receiving federal aid. Once he had allayed these fears, Keppel was able to guide his bill smoothly through Congress. In the end, the tally was 263 to 153 in the House and 73 to 18 in the Senate. As Keppel recalled, "it [was] not easy [for Congress] to oppose a combination of the existing impacted areas program and an added program for the poor."[38]

On April 11, 1965, in a ceremony in front of his own former one-room schoolhouse in Stonewall, Texas, Johnson signed P.L. 89-10, the Elementary and Secondary Education Act (ESEA), into law. It was a landmark piece of legislation. Its first paragraphs affirmed the notion that disadvantaged children—like disabled children—had "special educational needs" requiring supplemental educational services, and its first title focused on the needs of the poorest students. As Julie Roy Jeffrey noted, "Title I was the heart of the bill where most of the money was concentrated. Focused on the children of poverty, Title I recognized their 'special educational needs . . . and the impact that concentrations of low-income families [can] have on the ability of local education agencies to support adequate educational programs.'" Henceforth, under the ESEA, it would be a policy of the federal government to help local education agencies "expand and improve their educational programs by various means . . . which contribute particularly to meeting the special educational needs of educationally deprived children." Along with aid for special-compensatory instructional programs, the ESEA also provided funds for "the acquisition of equipment and, where necessary, the construction of school facilities" in poor areas. Its only requirement was that federally funded programs, materials, and facilities had to help schools overcome the effects of poverty on student learning. Keppel admitted during the legislative hearings on the ESEA that there was no necessary link between poverty and academic performance—between economic and educational deprivation—but he insisted repeatedly that the two were related.[39] Indeed, his whole approach to the ESEA rested on the premise that disadvantage was a form of disability and that low income led inexorably to low performance in school. He therefore promised that federal aid would improve both the educational opportunities *and* the educational outcomes of disadvantaged students.[40]

◈

In Congress, the most outspoken supporters of the ESEA had been representatives of large northern cities, and Boston's representatives were no exception. Speaker of the House John W. McCormack supported the law on behalf of the ninth district (inner-city Boston), while Tip O'Neill supported it on behalf of the eighth district (the surrounding communities of Cambridge, Somerville, and Allston). The ESEA also won support from both of Massachusetts's U.S. senators: Leverett Saltonstall and Edward M. Kennedy, who had been elected in 1962 to fill the seat once occupied by his brother. All of Massachusetts's fourteen congressmen voted in favor of the ESEA, and, after the new law had passed, the whole state, especially Boston, did everything in its power to maximize its eligibility for federal aid. The *Christian Science Monitor* noted as early as May 1965 that "Boston's school department is working hard to get its maximum share of funds under the $1.3 billion federal aid-to-education law. School officials say the city is sure of getting about $3 million. They hope to snare as much as $5 million. It all depends on the proposals now being mapped by Action for Boston Community Development's (ABCD) special committee on educational planning and the school department's new Office of Program Development."[41] As state and local administrators scrambled to secure as much federal assistance as possible, the education bureaucracy in Massachusetts grew. The Office of Program Development was, in fact, an updated version of the old Permanent Interdepartmental Office for Program Development, which had been established two years earlier under the auspices of the Massachusetts Mental Retardation Planning Project. The new office, like the old one, had a single over-arching purpose: to coordinate applications for federal grants to special-compensatory services for disadvantaged/disabled students.

In June 1965—only two months after the passage of the ESEA—Superintendent Ohrenberger announced Boston's first application for a federal grant under the new law, and he was already confident that his application would be successful. "A federal grant of $172,000 under Title

II, Elementary and Secondary Act of 1965, will make school library materials available in every public school in Boston," he wrote in his annual report for 1965–66. "This money, to be used during the 1966–1967 school year, is the first-year grant for a five-year program designed to develop and improve school library services for students and teachers. Under the terms of the law this financial aid will be a supplement and not a substitute [for funds authorized locally]. With these federal funds, Boston hopes to institute a library or library services in every school in the system this fall."[42] Since, prior to 1965, *none* of Boston's elementary schools had its own library, this application marked a great leap forward in the provision of basic reading materials for all the city's public schools. Building on the theme of reading resources, Boston's director of program development, Evans Clinchy, announced that he would also seek an additional $500,000 under Title II for books as well as audiovisual equipment to help students read. He also promised to pursue $500,000 under Title III for special-compensatory services for low-performing students throughout the city.[43] Clinchy told a reporter from the *Boston Globe* that these initial requests were only a beginning. Within a year, he expected to obtain at least $1.1 million in federal resources to purchase new desks, chairs, and other classroom furniture for Boston's inner-city schools. "We're not just picking up spare federal change—we're in this game for a long time," he said.[44] Expecting federal aid to increase steadily in the years to come, he added that "our plans for Boston are based on spending a great deal more in the future."[45]

The biggest prize, of course, was Title I aid for children whose parents earned less than $2,000 a year. With more than 20,000 students fitting this description, Boston hoped to obtain nearly $2.4 million in Title I aid—a seemingly astronomical sum in 1965. Yet, there was a catch. The ESEA had been predicated on the terms of the Civil Rights Act of 1964, which banned the distribution of federal resources to any school that discriminated against students on the basis of race, color, or national origin. In 1965, the Boston public schools did not easily pass this test. Ohrenberger, for example, hoped to direct $2 million in federal funds toward Operation Counterpoise, but, schools in which this program operated had recently been criticized as de facto segregated. The question was whether de facto segregation constituted discrimination under the Civil Rights Act. According to Ohrenberger, it did not. If it did, he argued, then any program in any school that was discovered to be racially imbalanced could be accused of discrimination. Such a policy would be absurd, he maintained, because it would undermine the very purpose of the ESEA, which was to subsidize programs that were specifically designed to meet the special educational needs of disadvantaged pupils—pupils who, at least in the inner city, belonged overwhelmingly to minority groups and who attended schools in predominantly minority neighborhoods. As far as the superintendent was concerned, racial imbalance in Operation Counterpoise schools could not reasonably be considered evidence of racial discrimination or used to withhold federal funds. If it were, he asserted, then no school could ever serve any group of minority pupils in disproportionate numbers without being accused of discrimination and losing aid. In Ohrenberger's view, the ESEA specifically targeted grants for special-compensatory programs at poor students in inner-city schools, *most* of which were racially imbalanced.

Yet, as early as February 1965—two months before the passage of the ESEA—Alan Gartner, the head of the Congress of Racial Equality (CORE) in Boston, charged the city's schools with de facto segregation and urged commissioner Keppel not to release aid to Boston under any federal grants until its schools complied with the Civil Rights Act. Keppel pledged his support for this line of action and, two days after the ESEA was signed, sent a letter to HEW secretary Anthony J. Celebrezze suggesting that the ESEA enabled "a new approach in handling civil rights problems in education."[46] Then, in late April 1965, Martin Luther King Jr. visited Boston to lead a march in protest against de facto segregation in the city's schools. A month later, Walter Mode, regional director of HEW in Boston, held a press conference announcing he had "enough evidence of de facto segregation in Boston schools to warrant an investigation and to defer all further federal school aid grants."[47] By early June 1965, Massachusetts's state commissioner of education Owen Kiernan had agreed to withhold $1.2 million in federal aid—of a total of $3.3 million allocated to Boston's schools—pending investigation of racial imbalance.[48] This investigation marked the first time a northern school system had been charged with de facto segregation in violation of Title VI of the Civil Rights Act, and, by September 1965, it seemed that Boston, in order to secure its share of federal aid under the ESEA, would have to launch a rapid integration effort.[49] However, the Boston school committee refused to consider any such idea.[50] As Louise Day Hicks commented, "the policy of the Boston school committee has never been one of discrimination against the Negro child. I have no doubts that federal money will be coming to Boston when we submit our plan for use of the money. . . . If we are going to be judged on the true facts, the federal government has no right to withhold funds."[51]

Did racial imbalance constitute racial discrimination under the Civil Rights Act of 1964? Perhaps not. As the *Boston Globe* noted in June 1965, "the Civil Rights Act does not mention racial imbalance. Whether such imbalance, when due to neighborhood housing patterns and not to a gerrymandering of school-district boundaries, [constitutes] 'discrimination' under Title VI of the [Civil Rights Act] is the question the investigating committee will have to consider. The existence of racial imbalance in some Boston schools has been admitted by the school committee, but charges of de facto segregation have been consistently denied. . . . A report by Ohrenberger last week said [that] racial imbalance in some schools was 'a reflection of racially imbalanced neighborhoods.'"[52] In another article, Ohrenberger stated that "if federal funds are being held, . . . I will urge the Department of Health, Education, and Welfare to conduct its investigation immediately so as not to cause an unjustifiable delay in our [school] program. I am confident that any investigation of the facts will reveal that segregation in any form has never been and is not now practiced in Boston public schools."[53] Yet, the HEW investigating team—which included assistant secretary James Quigley, regional director Walter Mode, civil rights lawyer Arthur Menard, and policy analyst Ruby Martin—had other ideas. As the *Globe* reported, the team visited schools with large numbers of minority students and compared them with all-white schools, noting disparities in student-teacher ratios and building quality. Mode asserted, "We are charting a whole new area [of federal policy to ascertain] . . . what constitutes discrimination in the North. . . . We are also making a study in depth of the social and economic factors which affect education."[54] Was "discrimination" attributable exclusively to racial imbalance, or was it tied to other factors, such as unequal facilities, unequal resources, unequal teachers, or perhaps even unequal neighborhoods?

Put another way, was racial balance *required* in order for schools to avoid charges of discrimination and, in turn, to receive federal aid for special-compensatory services? In dealing with this question, Ohrenberger had to strategize, and, once again, he developed a subtle plan. Instead of seeking funds for programs such as Operation Counterpoise through the federal Office of Education (which administered the ESEA), he opted in 1965 to apply for a grant through the Office of Economic Opportunity (OEO), created by the Economic Opportunity Act of 1964.[55] He hoped that the OEO would agree with him that special programs in racially imbalanced schools did not discriminate against minority students but, rather, met their special needs. The OEO, however, did not agree; instead, it promptly rejected his application. Boston's assistant superintendent Marguerite Sullivan brushed the OEO ruling aside, saying that the "OEO decided to get out of the education business now that Title I money was being used for the same purpose," but, in fact, the OEO ruling had resulted from its finding that Operation Counterpoise lacked an effective "compensatory" program. The issue was not racial balance; it was program *effectiveness*. As the *Boston Herald* noted, "a key feature of compensatory education programs funded by the Office of Economic Opportunity is a comprehensive remedial reading program. In Atlanta, Ga., for example, the OEO has financed 'communications skills laboratories' to improve [the] reading and verbal skills of underprivileged children, most of them Negro, through extensive use of reading machines, remedial reading teachers, and small classes. . . . In Boston, no school has a full-time remedial reading teacher, and many Counterpoise schools do not have the services of even a part-time remedial reading teacher." One OEO bureaucrat observed that the Boston public schools "could have revised the program [to include a full-time remedial reading teacher] . . . , but, 'for some reason they didn't.'"[56]

Boston's school committee continued to insist that federal aid could flow to racially imbalanced schools and found a precedent for this position in Chicago, where Mayor Richard J. Daley persuaded the Johnson administration not to deny aid to that city's schools lest violence erupt on a huge scale. According to the *Boston Herald*, "Hicks made it plain she would be no less vocal than Chicago's Mayor Daley if the 'freeze' were put on Boston aid."[57] Noting that federal officials had quickly retreated from their attempts to integrate schools in Chicago, Hicks expected the same outcome in Boston—and she found support for her position even among some *federal* administrators. Assistant federal commissioner of education David Seeley admitted that the federal government lacked not only the resources to pursue all claims of de facto segregation but also a legal strategy to prosecute such claims under the Civil Rights Act. According to Seeley, "the problem [in Chicago] was caused by an HEW policy . . . which called for all new federal funds to be withheld from any school district against which a complaint of discrimination had been lodged, until the complaint was investigated and settled. In my view (with which Keppel concurred), this [policy of withholding funds while investigating allegations] was not legally permissible under Title VI [of the Civil Rights Act] and would be completely unworkable if enforced, since at that time we had no appropriation for enforcement staff to investigate complaints."[58] The problem of legal action against de facto segregation was twofold. First, the federal government was ill-equipped to collect information needed to prove the existence of de facto segregation in Chicago or Boston or other northern school districts. Second, proving the existence of de facto segregation did not necessarily mean proving *discrimination* as prohibited by the Civil Rights Act. As a result, Seeley argued, HEW had no authority to withhold federal aid before it could prove that a "crime" of discrimination had been committed.

As Seeley saw, the legal strategies involved in prosecuting de facto segregation in a northern school district were very different from the legal strategies involved in proving de jure segregation in a southern district. Unlike de jure segregation, which violated the equal protection clause of the Fourteenth Amendment and was, thus, unconstitutional, de facto segregation—that is, a phenomenon of different groups occupying different spaces without the intervention of any clear governmental policy to cause or perpetuate a pattern of group divisions—did not necessarily involve a constitutional violation. For example, a decade earlier, in the racial segregation case of *Briggs v. Elliot,* a federal district court in South Carolina ruled that the Constitution "does not require [racial] integration. It merely forbids [racial] discrimination." In other words, as long as the *laws* were race-neutral, the mere fact of racial division, delineation, or demarcation was not necessarily probative of a constitutional wrong.[59] Yet, with the passage of the Civil Right Act of 1964, the legal status of de facto segregation had changed dramatically. Title VI of the Civil Rights Act suggested that the mere existence of racial imbalance could provide at least a prima facie case of disparate or unequal treatment—and, thus, a prima facie case of discrimination. In other words, Title VI implied a strong link between evidence of racial imbalance, which was not necessarily illegal, and racial discrimination, which was. The only way to decide whether racial imbalance had, in fact, resulted from illegal discrimination was to discern whether different groups had received *intentionally* disparate or unequal treatment from some official governmental body. If racial imbalance resulted from deliberately unequal policies on the part of, say, a school committee, then such treatment could be considered proof of racial discrimination. Clear evidence of intentionality was, however, extremely hard to get.[60]

The problem was that, even if the office of education or the newly created office of civil rights within HEW pursued allegations of racial imbalance and discrimination in northern schools, cities like Boston would never admit that the separation of the races had resulted from "intentional" school policy. As Hicks had already stated, "the policy of the Boston school committee has never been one of discrimination against the Negro child."[61] In her view, racial imbalance in the Boston public schools was neither codified in law (in which case it would be prohibited by the Fourteenth Amendment) nor caused by intentional racial discrimination (in which case it would be barred by the Civil Rights Act). Instead, she maintained, racial imbalance in the Boston public schools was a natural consequence of citizens' independent housing choices and administrators' attempts to serve students' needs in their own neighborhoods. In her view, no student had ever been excluded from participation in or denied the benefits of any program or educational activity offered in the schools; indeed, if anything, Hicks implied, the separation of races in the schools was not discriminatory but *salutary*, because, in recent years, various state and federal agencies had targeted aid specifically at schools where special-compensatory programs could best meet the needs of poor minority students (i.e., racially imbalanced neighborhood schools). Using the same rationale that had blocked integrated programs for the disabled, she argued that integration might actually *jeopardize* students' access to programs intentionally designed to overcome educational inequities.[62] According to Hicks, the only way to "prove" the existence of discrimination in Boston was to prove somehow that schools intended to harm minority students, and, in her view, it seemed obvious that the schools intended to help.

◇

Confronted with a federal investigation of de facto segregation and discrimination in Boston, Hicks dug in her heels and prepared to sacrifice millions of dollars in federal aid to demonstrate that Boston did not intentionally discriminate against minority students. The Boston school department was not in complete agreement, however, on the idea of forfeiting large sums of federal aid. As the *Globe* reported, "The debate in [the] school committee over use of federal funds . . . usually pits committeewoman Louise Hicks against Evans Clinchy, director of program development, and others who feel that Boston should take all it can get. Mrs. Hicks has often maintained that government munificence in every field, including education, comes out of each of our pockets in the form of taxes and should be returned for our mutual benefit whenever possible. Clinchy . . . never looks the government gift horse in the mouth. Last week, he threw the debate squarely into the lap of the state Department of Education by pushing through . . . five supplemental programs to be funded under Title I of the Elementary and Secondary Education Act (ESEA). . . . 'I felt I would be remiss in my duty if we didn't try for it all,' he said." Whereas Hicks believed that federal grants should be available without any external regulations or oversight, Clinchy thought the city should maneuver around federal rules in order to maximize its eligibility for aid, which, he frequently reminded his colleagues, the city desperately needed. According to the *Boston Globe*, "Clinchy says he and his staff are willing to fight for the money, and they may win out. . . . But whatever happens, it is apparent they are chasing federal funds for Boston with a fervor unique in the state."[63] With Clinchy actively seeking federal aid and Hicks actively opposing racial balance, local officials split on the federal role in public schools. The key question was, did racial imbalance constitute racial discrimination?

The all-white school committee repeatedly answered this question in the negative and, in so doing, reflected the opinion of the city's white majority. Its five members were elected at-large for overlapping two-year terms, which meant that, each biennium, all five members ran against each other for reelection, and the candidate with the most votes usually occupied the chair. As one observer noted, "four wards of the city are ordinarily decisive in the vote—East Boston, South Boston, Hyde Park, and West Roxbury. All four have conservative constituencies in which the number of voters who are parents is small."[64] Most voters supported candidates not only on the basis of racial considerations, but also on the basis of *financial* considerations. Inasmuch as the school committee had the power to set the school budget (by far the largest component of the city budget), it also had the power, in effect, to set the property tax rate. Indeed, the school committee exercised tremendous financial influence and often justified its actions on economic as well as educational grounds. Louise Day Hicks, for example, insisted that it was more cost-effective to concentrate federally funded special-compensatory programs in areas with large numbers of poor minority students—a position endorsed by the Massachusetts Mental Retardation Planning Project. She also reminded critics that the state legislature's Willis-Harrington Commission had confirmed earlier studies showing that disadvantaged minority students in urban schools were disproportionately likely to suffer from cognitive deficiencies. Thus, she insisted, it was more important to pursue federal aid for special-compensatory programs than it was to pursue racial balance—particularly if academic achievement was the goal.

This position evidently prevailed in August 1965, when Operation Counterpoise received a last-minute grant for $2 million under Title I, *despite* the persistence of racial imbalance (but apparently not discrimination) in the schools. Massachusetts state legislators were not, however, willing to let Hicks win. A few days later—shortly after state commissioner Owen Kiernan announced his decision to withhold $1.2 million in federal aid to Boston—the legislature passed a so-called racial imbalance law, which declared that any public school with more than 50 percent minority students would forfeit state funds.[65] This law, which held unequivocally that racial imbalance constituted racial discrimination, was the first of its kind in the country, and it outraged Louise Day Hicks. In her view, the emerging theory of using state aid as a blunt instrument to change the racial composition of schools represented an unconscionable violation of local control.[66] According to Hicks, the racial imbalance law undermined local control in two ways.[67] First, it implied that the key purpose of state aid was not to meet the financial needs of local schools but, rather, to shift the locus of governance from local officials to the state. Second, and perhaps more importantly, it shifted the emphasis of school policy from *prohibiting racial discrimination* to *promoting racial balance*. For Hicks, these two concepts were not the same, because the second—promoting (or even mandating) racial balance—made it harder for schools to target special-compensatory programs specifically at low-achieving minority students in neighborhood schools. Moreover, Hicks argued, the idea underlying the racial imbalance law, the idea that equal educational opportunities for minority students *required* racially balanced schools, implied that minority students were somehow fundamentally incapable of average academic achievement unless their schools had white majorities.[68]

Clearly, the debate over racial imbalance was unlikely to disappear anytime soon. Although the legal status of racial imbalance was ambiguous at best, the federal view in 1965 was that racial imbalance was closely tied to racial discrimination and that schools should try to avoid both in order to make themselves eligible for federal grants. Indeed, Massachusetts's racial imbalance law was partly a way to bring schools into compliance with the Civil Rights Act, and, in turn, to help schools obtain federal aid under the ESEA (and other programs). The racial imbalance law thus had the support of Massachusetts's commissioner of education, Owen Kiernan, as well as Massachusetts's governor, John A. Volpe (who succeeded Foster Furcolo in 1960 and, after a defeat by Endicott Peabody in 1962, was reelected in 1964). The racial imbalance law also had the support of Volpe's lieutenant governor, Elliot Richardson, who, after leaving his post as assistant secretary for legislative affairs in HEW. in 1960 and serving as the U.S. attorney in Massachusetts from 1961 to 1964 (and briefly as assistant to U.S. attorney general Robert Kennedy), had decided to enter the realm of elective politics. Richardson's experience in both federal and state government had taught him the importance of meeting federal expectations in order to secure federal aid.[69] Despite his rather lukewarm attitude toward racial integration in the late 1950s when he was working on the passage of the NDEA, he knew that the legal climate had changed significantly in the wake of the Civil Rights Act, and he predicted that Boston would have to desegregate its schools if it wanted to qualify for federal aid. Even if schools had to find other ways of meeting the special needs of poor minority students in the inner city, Richardson advised urban officials to pursue, or at least *appear* to pursue, racial balance in the public schools.

Not so Massachusetts senator Edward Kennedy, who remained surprisingly quiet on the racial balance question. According to the *Boston Globe,* "Kennedy's silence on the present bill to withhold state funds from recalcitrant school systems . . . is confusing."[70] Perhaps Kennedy doubted the wisdom of criticizing racial imbalance when he knew that many of the special-compensatory programs his brother had created for disabled students served poor minority students in disproportionate numbers; perhaps he thought that racial imbalance was not inherently detrimental to student learning as long as it did not involve deliberate or intentional discrimination; or perhaps he believed racial imbalance was not unhelpful at a classroom level in cases where minority pupils shared certain educational difficulties that responded to "culturally relevant" programs or pedagogies. According to the news report in the *Boston Globe,* the junior senator hesitated to endorse the law because it relied on racial quotas and seemed to lead in the direction of cross-neighborhood busing to attain racial balance. (He apparently did not realize that the law's only sanction against racially imbalanced schools was the withholding of state aid; busing was not mentioned.)[71] And, yet, by remaining silent on the racial imbalance issue, Kennedy seemed to endorse a situation that perpetuated unequal education for poor minority pupils. While it was conceivable that racially imbalanced schools could serve minority pupils' "special educational needs" (certainly Hicks maintained this position), most observers in 1965 saw that Boston's public schools produced racially disparate educational outcomes and concluded that school leaders therefore discriminated, whether intentionally or not, against minority pupils. Indeed, racially disparate outcomes plagued even Operation Counterpoise, the federally funded program that school officials praised the most.[72]

In 1965–66, Operation Counterpoise faced a growing barrage of criticism, much of it coming from a recent Harvard graduate and Rhodes scholar named Jonathan Kozol, who had been hired as a teacher in the Operation Counterpoise program during the 1964–65 school year.[73] A seasoned civil-rights activist, Kozol did not accept the assumption that poor minority students were incurably underachieving, nor did he accept the notion that poverty was a form of pathology or the notion that poor minority students were more likely to be mentally retarded (and thus better served in remedial classes set apart from nonminority peers). By rejecting these views in his own Operation Counterpoise class, Kozol had enjoyed brilliant success with his inner-city fourth-graders. As one colleague observed, "in a matter of [a] few weeks, Kozol, taking over after eight other teachers had preceded him, raised the math average of his class from the mid-30s to the mid-80s."[74] After his first year as a teacher, Kozol wrote a detailed review of Operation Counterpoise and sent his ideas to assistant superintendent Marguerite Sullivan. Instead of praising the program as an effective way to improve the educational results of disadvantaged students, he accused it of papering over much deeper racial inequities in the Boston public schools. He called its curriculum "hollow and condescending" and attributed the academic failure of inner-city students not to their alleged mental disabilities but, rather, to the dilapidated condition of their school facilities.[75] He noted that Operation Counterpoise was "not sufficient to make up for the gross inadequacies of the school building" at his own building, the Christopher Gibson Elementary School in Roxbury, and observed that, based on his brief teaching experience, it seemed clear that poor minority students were capable of at least average achievement—and probably more if they had access to classes with proper desks, chairs, and chalk for the chalkboards.[76]

In June 1965, when Sullivan received Kozol's report and heard of his students' academic success—which disproved the idea that poverty had permanently compromised their learning ability even if it supported the idea that poor minority children learned well in isolated remedial classes—she promptly fired him, ostensibly for insubordination but also for assigning Langston Hughes's militant poem, "Ballad of the Landlord."[77] (Such a move was ironic, given that Operation Counterpoise had encouraged Kozol to use black literature.) Kozol was not alone, however, in his criticisms of Operation Counterpoise. The Lincoln Filene Center for Citizenship and Public Affairs at Tufts University also questioned the educational effectiveness of the program: "Candor and the importance of helping students . . . require us to report that too much of the program consists of old and tired remedies dressed up under new titles, that there is insufficient leadership in the over-all direction of the program, . . . that the teachers in the program are inadequately trained for special compensatory education, and that the total program is inadequate, quantitatively and qualitatively."[78] It was a stinging rebuke. While acknowledging that isolated remedial classes might be helpful for pupils who were truly disabled (and, therefore, fundamentally incapable of average academic achievement), the experts at Tufts argued that isolated classes were not beneficial for students who were *not* disabled but were merely poor or black. In their opinion, special-compensatory programs such as Operation Counterpoise had to distinguish clearly between the educational effects of disability and the educational effects of poverty when it came to minority students. No longer could teachers assume that minority students were retarded simply because of their race or family income.

The Lincoln Filene Center maintained that students who were disadvantaged were not necessarily disabled and did not necessarily require special-compensatory services in isolated remedial classes; instead, the

Center indicated that the best learning environment for poor minority students was a *racially balanced* class. Indeed, by the spring of 1966, more and more experts were criticizing the idea that disadvantaged and disabled students fit into the same general category. Ohrenberger's conflation of cultural disadvantage and cognitive disability had served a useful purpose in 1963 and 1964, when federal support was more readily available for disabled students than disadvantaged students, and it had even found its way into the justification for the ESEA, which implied that disadvantaged students, like disabled students, had special educational needs that responded to carefully targeted (and federally funded) special-compensatory services.[79] Yet, within months of the signing of the ESEA in 1965, it seemed the conflation of disadvantage and disability had fallen out of favor. The assumption that low income led to low achievement was now regarded as discriminatory, and poor minority students were assumed to benefit, first and foremost, from racially balanced schools. This was a seismic shift in contemporary thinking about education and race. *Before* the ESEA, officials had conflated disadvantage and disability to justify the creation of special-compensatory programs in "ghetto" schools. *After* the ESEA, any such conflation was condemned, and policymakers began to suspect that all special-compensatory programs in racially imbalanced schools—even those receiving state and federal grants—perpetuated inequality. Strange as it may sound, the passage of the ESEA coincided with a spreading belief that aid to programs in racially imbalanced schools *caused* rather than *cured* disparities in educational opportunity.

⟡

By the start of 1966, the issue of racial imbalance dominated headlines in Boston. The legislature's decision to withhold funds from racially imbalanced schools, combined with the federal government's decision to withhold funds from schools that were under investigation for discrimination, left the Boston public schools in an increasingly serious predicament. Should the schools defend the existence of racial imbalance, or should they submit to state and federal authorities and concede, in effect, that racial imbalance was always (perhaps by definition) at odds with equal educational opportunities? Should they try to make a case for the value of special-compensatory programs, even if such programs were clustered in racially imbalanced schools—and if they did so, how would state and federal officials react? Would they continue to withhold state and federal grants, or would they resort to other means—such as forced busing—to attain racial balance in the public schools? In January 1966,

Massachusetts governor John Volpe and lieutenant governor Elliot Richardson hosted an informal meeting in Boston to address these and other related issues. Among the guests invited to this conference were Massachusetts commissioner of education Owen Kiernan and Francis Keppel, who had recently been promoted from the post of federal commissioner of education to the newly created post of assistant secretary for education in the Department of Health, Education, and Welfare. In the eight months that had passed since Congress approved the ESEA, Keppel had been traveling the country, explaining the aims of the new law to various state leaders, trying to calm their fears of federal control, and gathering feedback on regulations to guide the use of federal funds. In particular, he had sought to clarify the federal position on racial imbalance in northern schools, and it was for this reason that he had been invited to the governor's conference in Boston.[80]

As a former dean of Harvard's Graduate School of Education, Keppel was well acquainted with Boston's public schools. He assured his colleagues that the federal government had no intention of imposing oppressive rules, regulations, or requirements on local school districts, and his much-anticipated defense of the federal commitment to racial equality and racial integration was surprisingly timid. "The federal government has admittedly changed its role in education," Keppel acknowledged, "not to usurp local authority or impinge upon state operations, but to assume its rightful place in the national educational effort." He went out of his way to emphasize that "the state, for its part, will continue to discharge fundamental legal responsibility for free education. It will supervise the local school boards, maintain educational standards, and train teachers. It will provide leadership for education within its borders and will still continue to be the strategic nexus, the connecting cord, between local and federal interests, the responsible body for state policy in education." This message was not lost on state commissioner of education Owen Kiernan, who held that "the remote position of the federal government should eliminate it, once and for all, from any jurisdictional considerations. Education is a state function, and a state function it must remain." If Keppel disagreed with Kiernan's characterization of the federal-state-local hierarchy, he did not say so at this conference.[81] Instead, he acknowledged that the federal Office of Education was ill-equipped to monitor local compliance with federal rules, and he openly admitted that his staff in Washington would rely on state agencies to oversee the implementation of the ESEA—including its antidiscrimination provisions. With the power to select programs for support and submit evaluations of these programs' success or failure, Keppel conceded, *state* officers would be the gatekeepers of federal aid.

When the Boston public schools obtained nearly $4 million in federal aid during the 1966–67 school year (despite persistent racial imbalance), it became obvious that federal threats of withholding aid until the conclusion of investigations into de facto segregation amounted to a big bark with no bite.[82] In fact, Boston even secured $600,000 under the federal impact-aid program, because in 1966, the eligibility requirement was lowered from 6 percent to 3 percent of local students or parents being connected to federally owned lands.[83] Auditors from the Boston Municipal Research Bureau (BMRB) congratulated the public schools for securing so much federal aid but highlighted areas in which schools could secure even more. According to the BMRB, the city had received only 62 percent of the total aid for which it was eligible in 1966–67. "Of 21 programs now available," the BMRB noted, only "13 are being adequately used."[84] To avoid any lost opportunities in the future, the BMRB assembled a *Catalog of Federal Aids Applicable to Boston* to help administrators maximize their pursuit of funds. "Federal aid programs for cities have been increased vastly in recent years," the BMRB commented. "However, aid programs do no one any good unless their specific availability and utilization to Boston can be determined." Boston was extremely aggressive in its pursuit of federal aid (shortly before the BMRB catalog appeared, the city received an additional $210,000 in Title III aid to plan new programs for the handicapped), but the BMRB warned that the issue of racial imbalance could derail the city's pursuit of *state* aid. According to the BMRB, "one . . . factor may make the entire previous discussion academic—the racial imbalance law of 1965. . . . If this [law] means that the commissioner of education cannot certify anything for Boston [in the way of state aid] . . . , the effects on the city would be crippling."[85] Thus, even as Boston celebrated its receipt of *federal* aid, it continued to worry about the effect racial imbalance might have on its eligibility for *state* aid.

If the state withheld aid from schools enrolling over 50 percent minority students, then Boston's school department might have to distribute the city's minority students to schools in white neighborhoods and duplicate special-compensatory programs it had developed for them—at significant public expense.[86] Louise Day Hicks, as head of the school committee (and holder of the purse strings), insisted that it was far more economical to concentrate special-compensatory programs in the areas where poor minority students lived, areas where studies showed that cultural deprivation led to cognitive deficiency.[87] In her view, the best solution to the problem of educational inequality was not to place all students together in the same schools, pretending that their needs were identical when they were not, but rather, to meet their needs in their own neighborhood schools. The state legislature, however, held that integrated schools were more likely than neighborhood schools to meet the needs of minority students. In March 1966, the legislature made Boston's refusal to integrate less tenable on *financial* grounds by passing a substantial increase in state aid to schools. Working in cooperation with the New England School Development Council (NESDEC), the legislature replaced its old foundation formula with a so-called percentage equalization formula that provided aid to districts on a "sliding scale" so that poorer areas would receive more (relative to their overall tax burden) and wealthier areas would receive less.[88] For the first time, the state aid formula weighed not only a town's *ability* to support local public schools, but also its *effort* to do so. Under the new formula, suburbs with higher property valuations received proportionally less state aid, and cities with lower property valuations received proportionally more, that is, as long as their schools were racially balanced.[89]

The new plan worked as follows. The basic measure of a town's ability to support its schools was its "equalized property valuation per school-attending child." In 1966, the average valuation per school-attending child in Massachusetts was $20,000, so, if a town had precisely $20,000 in equalized valuation, then, under the new law, it was eligible for state reimbursement of 35 percent of its overall school expenditures. If a town had above-average property valuations of, say, $25,000, then it was eligible for state reimbursement of about 18 percent of its total school expenditures. If a town had below-average property valuations of $15,000, then it was eligible for state reimbursement of 51 percent of its school expenditures. The most a town could get in state reimbursements was 75 percent of its total school expenditures (though a hold-harmless clause ensured that each district in the state received at least 15 percent more aid under the new law than it received under the old foundation formula).[90] When it was approved in 1966, the new law represented a major shift in Massachusetts's state aid to schools.[91] Its underlying goal of equalization echoed the rationale for the ESEA, as did its goal of providing incentives to integrate. Yet, at the same time, the new law faced an embarrassing problem: the state lacked the revenues to cover its new commitment to school aid. Under the new law, all state funds for schools were supposed to come from a new sales tax; however, when the sales tax took effect for the first time in the winter of 1966, its revenues fell far short of expectations. Since only 80 percent of the new sales tax was slated for schools, the state school-aid formula was prorated to correspond with sales-tax receipts. In 1966, the law called for $142,312,731 in state aid to schools, but 80 percent of sales-tax revenues yielded only $56,181,693 — that is, 39.4 percent of the required amount.[92] So, under the prorating procedure, each town in Massachusetts received only 39.4 percent of the total state aid it expected for its schools.[93]

This awkward situation improved only slightly the next year, when the new law mandated $173 million in state aid to schools, but sales-tax revenues totaled only $121 million, 80 percent of which was $97 million—or 56.1 percent of the anticipated state aid for education.[94] Thus, Massachusetts's schools received only 56.1 percent of the aid they expected from the state. Over the years, the problems associated with this new law got worse instead of better. In 1966, for example, the city of Boston hoped that 26 percent of its school expenditures would be reimbursed by the state. With a total budget of $54.8 million (or $612.40 per pupil), this percentage implied roughly $14.2 million in state aid. However, since the Boston public schools continued to defy Massachusetts's racial imbalance law, the city forfeited *all* its state aid ($8.9 million).[95] With no state aid, Boston relied heavily on local property taxes to cover school costs—but, in 1966, most of the city's property continued to be underassessed. Even though the state explicitly required municipalities to list properties at full market value, only 25 percent of Boston's taxable properties were actually assessed at full value. Consequently, Boston's city council had to raise the rate at which properties were taxed in order to yield the required funds for public schools. The combined effect of underassessed properties, forfeited state aid, and the ever-growing cost of special services in the inner city put Boston's public schools in a severe financial bind.[96] Complicating this dilemma, the state legislature decided in the fall of 1965 to repeal Chapter 650, its one-year-old program for state aid to special-compensatory classes in low-income areas, because the ESEA was now meeting that need. Repealing Chapter 650 meant federal aid supplanted rather than supplemented state funds (a move explicitly prohibited under the ESEA), but federal monitors failed to catch this change.

The uncertainties of state aid in this period undermined any incentive Boston may have had to integrate. The critical question, however, was not only whether the schools should integrate, but also whether racial imbalance (or de facto segregation) necessarily constituted "discrimination" under the Civil Rights Act. If any school with more than 50 percent minority students was automatically open to charges of discrimination (the exact meaning of which was still not clear), then most schools providing special-compensatory services in Boston risked the inevitable withholding of aid. Yet, if special-compensatory services aimed to meet the "special educational needs" of poor minority students, then it seemed clear that such services would be targeted at racially imbalanced schools. In fact, this concentration of services was intentional, because it seemed the most efficient and effective way to equalize students' opportunities.[97] According to Ohrenberger and Hicks, if the state now withheld funding from special-compensatory services, it would likely put disadvantaged students at even *greater* educational risk and would likely *deepen* existing inequalities in the public schools. Moreover, they argued, a policy that saw racial balance as the only legitimate route to equal educational opportunities ignored the possibility that other priorities—such as more teachers, better facilities, or perhaps curricular reforms—might well do more to improve educational opportunities among poor minority students in inner-city schools. Was racial imbalance *necessarily* indicative of racial discrimination in the Boston public schools? No one knew. As Walter Mode noted at the height of the HEW investigation into de facto segregation in the city's schools in 1965 and 1966, "we want good educational programs run in a non-discriminatory fashion. . . . I don't mean to imply that there is discrimination in Boston. That is what we are trying to determine."[98]

CHAPTER THREE

Aggravating Racial Imbalance, 1966–1968

Before 1966, the federal office of education had focused its desegre-gation efforts on southern schools. Only gradually did its attention shift to northern districts. However, even as it began to investigate charges of "de facto" segregation in cities such as Boston, Chicago, and San Fran-cisco, the Office of Education still lacked a specific legal strategy to pur-sue against northern schools. It had no reliable way to prove discrimi-nation (indeed, it had no consistent definition of *discrimination* as this concept pertained to education), and it lacked the monitoring or over-sight capacity to determine when a school system was, in fact, racially imbalanced. As Harvard's professor Thomas F. Pettigrew commented, "on de facto segregation, . . . the law is only now being formulated."[1] Working to develop an effective framework for northern desegregation were three high-ranking federal officials: Francis Keppel, now assistant secretary of education in HEW; Harold Howe II, who succeeded Keppel as federal commissioner; and John Gardner, the new secretary of HEW, whom President Johnson appointed in 1965 to replace secretary Anthony Celebrezze, who stepped down shortly after the passage of the ESEA. Together, Keppel, Howe, and Gardner hoped to use the ESEA—particularly the financial leverage provided by Title I—to integrate both southern *and* northern schools. Gardner, for his part, had chaired President Johnson's task force on federal aid to public education in 1964 and was deeply committed to the War on Poverty—and, specifically, to the idea that targeted grants to special-compensatory services were the most effective way to meet the needs of socially disadvantaged students. Together with Keppel and Howe, he hoped to make these services available to poor minority students in the inner city without, at the same time, aiding and abetting racially imbalanced schools. It was a difficult goal.[2]

Harold Howe II was particularly attuned to the issue of racial segregation in both southern and northern schools. He had spent his youth in Virginia, where his father was the president of the well-known Hampton Institute, an all-black college with an academic as well as a vocational focus. As a boy, Howe had attended the all-white public school in Hampton for two years, and he later recalled that this school had introduced him to "the South in its segregated condition and probably influenced things I did later in my life." After a stint in the navy during World War II, he had pursued an M.A. in history at Columbia and had then joined the faculty at Phillips Academy in Andover, Massachusetts. In 1950, he became principal of the public junior-senior high school in Andover, but he left that post in 1958 after the passage of the NDEA to become principal of a highly selective, science-oriented public high school in Cincinnati. He returned to Massachusetts in the early 1960s to lead a 3,200-student high school in the Boston suburb of Newton (built when superintendent Gillis was calling for a similar mega-school in the inner city) and, a few years later, became superintendent of schools in Scarsdale, New York. There, he met Scarsdale resident John Gardner and, as he later recollected, "managed to stir the pot by having Scarsdale kids come in contact with kids very different from themselves." Finally, in 1964, he accepted a job as director of the Learning Institute of North Carolina, which sponsored research on improving academic achievement in newly desegregated southern schools. As Howe noted, experiences in all these places showed him how schools—and segregation—operated in the United States. "I gathered a lot of experience dealing with southerners, poor kids, politicians, the legislature, and people in the power system," he noted. "I came to Washington with this background."[3] Above all, he came to Washington with a strong determination to dismantle de facto segregation in northern schools.

Of course, many northern schools, including the public schools in Boston, had stubbornly resisted attempts at racial integration. According to Boston school committee chair Louise Day Hicks, different groups of students had different educational needs, and the best way to meet those needs was to establish different programs in different schools.[4] Moreover, she asserted, the high correlation between racial minorities and urban poverty (as well as the equally high correlation between racial minorities and mental retardation) made it important for schools to place "at-risk" students *together* in special-compensatory programs—preferably in their own neighborhood schools. Fortunately, she noted, Title I grants for disadvantaged/disabled students now supported this approach. As Carl Kaestle and Marshall Smith later wrote in the *Harvard Educational Review*, "implementing Title I . . . required an organizational structure for the delivery of services that was independent of the regular school program. Separate administrative structures were developed [both] in school systems and in schools. Title I personnel were hired and paid for only with Title I funds and were required by law to work only with Title I students even in the halls and in the school yard. In classrooms the segregation of Title I from the regular school [program] was almost as complete."[5] In other words, the "targeted" nature of Title I fostered the de facto segregation of students—segregation that occurred not only at the classroom level, but also at the school level. In Boston, most of the students in Title I–funded programs (including Operation Counterpoise) were minority students, and it was taken for granted that such programs intended to help rather than harm students by providing services tailored to their special needs.[6] Thus protected by their purity of intent, Title I–funded programs avoided charges of discrimination—even if they took place in racially imbalanced schools.[7]

The link between racial imbalance and racial discrimination received considerable scrutiny in 1966, when the Boston school committee was trying to determine how best to comply with Massachusetts's racial imbalance law. In its original form, the law specified two categories of racial identity—white and nonwhite—and stated that any public school with more than 50 percent nonwhite students would be considered racially imbalanced. Hence, when state officials discovered that two Boston elementary schools located in the Chinatown neighborhood—the Josiah Quincy School and the Abraham Lincoln School—had enrollments that were virtually 100 percent Chinese, they declared both schools racially imbalanced.[8] Boston's school committee, however, immediately challenged this decision. Specifically, it hoped that classifying the two schools'

671 Chinese students as white instead of nonwhite would render both schools balanced—and, thus, eligible for state and federal grants. According to Hicks, the term *nonwhite* clearly meant "black."[9] She insisted that the state's racial imbalance law "was drawn specifically for the Negro community" and argued that "there is no justification for including the Chinese with the Negro in this classification of non-white." While it seemed clear to state legislators that Chinese students were nonwhite, Hicks asserted that the purpose of the racial imbalance law was not to guarantee the presence of white students in every classroom in the city but, rather, to improve the educational opportunities of *low-performing* racial minorities. Since Chinese students were not low-performing, she argued, they obviously benefited—or at least did not suffer—from their racially imbalanced schools. In an interview with the *Boston Herald*, Hicks said, "The high academic achievement of the children attending Chinese neighborhood schools is living proof that racial imbalance as far as the Chinese children [are] concerned is not harmful to them."[10]

Throughout the late 1960s, Hicks continued to assert that different groups needed different schools—and others agreed. Teyhi Hsieh, director of the Chinese Philanthropic Service Bureau, endorsed Hicks's reclassification of Chinese students as white and hoped that the residents of Chinatown would be permitted to retain their racially homogeneous neighborhood schools. "There is no such thing as imbalance among the Chinese," Hsieh claimed. "I cannot agree with the state [Department of Education], and I do agree with the school committee. Whatever Mrs. Hicks does, I feel confident she is doing it for the benefit of the Chinese community." Not all Chinese, however, shared Hsieh's favorable impression of Louise Day Hicks. The editors of the *China News* in Taipei, Taiwan, called her reclassification of Chinese students "a sham and deception," but Hicks countered that Chinese pupils in Boston would never actually be *considered* white; instead, they would only be *classified* as white in order to avoid unwanted integration and make their schools eligible for state and federal aid. Hicks assured the city's Chinese parents that they could keep their successful schools separate and that racial distinctions would continue to be upheld: "To say or imply that the Boston school committee called or labeled the Chinese students members of the white race is the grossest form of erroneous and irresponsible reporting," she said. To prove her point, she demanded a new census with three racial categories—white, nonwhite, and Chinese—promising that such a tally would "remove Chinese students from the racial imbalance fray entirely."[11] In short, Hicks commented, "the Chinese were not represented at hearings on the imbalance bill, and they were not considered as being recipients of its so-called benefits."[12] Instead, she insisted, the case of the Quincy and Lincoln schools demonstrated that racial imbalance was acceptable, even desirable, in facilities that met their students' educational needs.

At the core of the debate over the Chinese students in 1966 was a dispute over the meaning of cultural and educational *disadvantage*. According to Hicks (and others who favored Title I–funded programs such as Operation Counterpoise and English as a Second Language), different students from different backgrounds clearly benefited from different programs that served their different educational needs. She saw no inherent connection between racial imbalance and academic failure, just as she saw no inherent connection between racial balance and academic success. She noted that Chinese students were thriving in a racially imbalanced environment and concluded that other minority students could easily do the same. As one of her colleagues on the school committee remarked, "there is no question in my mind that this [racial imbalance] law does not pertain to the Chinese. . . . Their cultural background and self-image is positive, and education in predominantly Chinese schools is excellent." In other words, if the state wanted to improve educational opportunities for truly disadvantaged students, the school committee argued, then it should provide *low-performing* students with more special-compensatory programs and permit *high-performing* students (minority *and* majority) to "stay the course." Despite the protestations of deputy state commissioner of education Thomas Curtin, who claimed that "you can't . . . perpetuate a separate school for a separate group," Hicks responded that racially homogeneous schools were, in fact, the *best* way to help diverse student groups achieve their maximum educational potential. She was not bothered by the fact that Boston's public schools—or special-compensatory programs within those schools—were racially imbalanced; if anything, she asserted, the success of the city's Chinese students indicated that neighborhood schools, combined with well-planned, well-funded, and well-targeted special-compensatory programs, were the most beneficial arrangement of all.[13]

Confronted with this view, federal commissioner of education Harold Howe recruited Professor James Coleman and others at The Johns Hopkins University to conduct a major study on the question of which was more likely to meet the educational needs of poor minority students in the inner city—special programs or racial integration? Coleman's 700-page analysis, *Equality of Educational Opportunity*, was released in 1966 and concluded that racial integration actually did little to boost academic achievement in urban schools. "Our interpretation of the data," Coleman explained, "is that racial integration per se is unrelated to achievement insofar as the data can show a relationship." Coleman added, however, that special-compensatory programs, whether offered in racially integrated or in racially segregated schools, were similarly ineffective in raising achievement levels. As he commented, "differences in school facilities and curricula, which are made to improve schools, are so little related to differences in achievement levels of students that, with few exceptions, their efforts [or the *effects* of different classes and curricula] fail to appear in a survey of this magnitude." At Harvard, a reanalysis of Coleman's data reached similar conclusions, suggesting that the best way to raise academic achievement was neither to integrate students nor to offer special-compensatory programs but, rather, to boost family income. According to sociologist David Armor, "programs which stress financial aid to disadvantaged black families may be just [as] important, if not more so, than programs aimed at integrating blacks into white neighborhoods and schools." Still another study concluded that the "racial composition of the school . . . does not have a substantial effect [on academic achievement]—not nearly so strong as the social class composition of the school."[14] In other words, when it came to improving academic achievement in the inner city, what mattered most was neither special programs nor racial integration, but family background and socioeconomic status.

In light of these findings, the debate over racial imbalance persisted in Boston. If racial balance did not lead to academic achievement, then why should the schools pursue it? On the one hand, Louise Day Hicks held that Boston should devote its limited financial resources to special services designed to meet poor minority students' educational needs. On the other hand, Hicks's critics asserted that such programs did more to harm than help their students. One such critic was Jonathan Kozol, who, in 1966, after his dismissal from Operation Counterpoise, published an exposé on his experiences as a teacher in Boston. In *Death at an Early Age: The Destruction of the Hearts and Minds of Negro Children in the Boston Public Schools,* Kozol lashed out at top education officials, alleging that they failed to see how programs such as Operation Counterpoise were hurting poor minorities in inner-city schools.[15] If such programs consistently failed to raise student achievement, and if their students were poor minorities, Kozol reasoned, then these programs *had* to be considered racially discriminatory (even if they received federal aid and even if teachers in these programs claimed to be helping their students). In Kozol's view, discrimination could not be judged by teachers' *intent;* it had to be judged by students' *results.* Only in this way, he insisted, would it be possible to distinguish the presence of discrimination in a place like the South End—where educational results were far below average—from the absence of discrimination in places such as Chinatown—where educational results were above average. If discrimination were associated not only with racial imbalance but also with substandard achievement, Kozol implied, then it might be possible to criticize the schools that perpetuated low performance while commending schools that promoted at least average gains. "Discrimination" would thus depend not solely on racial imbalance but on a link between racial imbalance and below-average achievement.

Here was a novel way of defining—and dealing with—the issue of discrimination in the public schools, and it was one that even Louise Day Hicks could support. If a given school failed to raise achievement to "average" levels, then (and only then) would a new approach, such as integration, be required. Such a strategy seemed a sensible a way to identify discrimination and, at the same time, to integrate low-achieving minorities into more effective schools. However, this strategy had a hidden flaw: it allowed officials to keep low-achieving students in racially imbalanced schools if they could be diagnosed with "disabilities" suggesting they were fundamentally *incapable* of "average" academic achievement. In other words, it left open the possibility that disabled students—many of whom were poor minorities—could remain in racially imbalanced schools if officials could claim that these schools offered them "appropriate" treatment. This flaw was difficult to dislodge, because disabled students were typically presumed to benefit from specialized services *more* than they would benefit from racial integration. Even the Massachusetts Mental Retardation Planning Project—which, in 1966, encouraged the placement of disabled students in regular classes—kept quiet on the desirability of racial integration for minority students diagnosed as mentally retarded or emotionally disturbed. Its report, *Massachusetts Plans for Its Retarded,* urged teachers to transfer disabled students into regular classrooms whenever possible, but ignored the fact that most schools—and thus most classrooms—in the state's urban areas remained racially imbalanced. Hence, in Massachusetts, grants for special education continued to flow to racially imbalanced schools.

◈

It was not entirely clear what should be done about this dilemma. In Boston, the long-time director of special services for the disabled was Charles Ruddy, who had insisted for decades that different students with different needs required different programs in different settings. Only after Ruddy's death in the fall of 1966 did parents in the inner city begin to challenge his practice of isolating disabled students from their nondisabled peers.[16] In 1967, two groups—the Parents Association for South End Schools and the United South End Settlements—issued a report charging that Boston had misdiagnosed scores of poor, minority, and non-English-speaking pupils as disabled and had relegated these children to isolated remedial classes for the mentally retarded and the emotionally disturbed. The parents' widely distributed report, titled "End Educational Entombment," alleged that virtually all of the students' erroneous diagnoses had occurred without parents' consent, without direct evidence of cognitive or behavioral deficiencies, and without annual reexaminations to see if school psychologists' original diagnoses had been correct.[17] (Such annual retesting was required by Chapter 514 of state law, passed in 1954 when Massachusetts's special commission for the retarded released its first report calling for the integration of disabled children into regular classes.) The South End parents' report was followed by a threat to sue the Boston public schools in federal court if the schools did not promptly retest all children who were placed in special classes. Moreover, the South End parents insisted that, rather than assessing their students' ability on the basis of race, family income, or language background, schools had to assess poor minority students using strictly *academic* criteria. Directly challenging the notion that a "culture of poverty" predisposed poor minority students to mental or behavioral handicaps, the South End parents demanded placements for their children based solely on aptitude tests, which they expected to be racially and culturally neutral.[18]

The South End parents recognized that the only way to discredit the placement of poor minority students in special-compensatory classes for the "disabled" was to discredit schools' testing methods. This endeavor was delicate, however, because tests determined which students needed special-compensatory services, and discrediting the whole system could result in the dismantling of programs that legitimately served student needs. Thus, the challenge was not to destroy all diagnostic and placement methods at once but, rather, to make these methods more precise so that they classified students objectively by ability and not arbitrarily by race, income, or language. (The notion that race, income, and language should be considered "irrelevant" to the diagnosis of disability was itself controversial in the 1960s, when many teachers and parents considered these factors to be intimately related to school performance.) In Boston, assessments of student ability fell under the purview of the Department of Educational Investigation and Measurement. As early as 1956, Gillis had asserted that "standardized tests and materials are used on an individual basis to estimate levels of mental capacity, interest, and aptitude. . . . Individual case studies are made of pupils who manifest some maladjustment, e.g., scholastic failure, [unusual] behavior, truancy, mental and emotional instability, withdrawal, or other irregularities."[19] Gillis was not unaware of the criticisms of standardized tests, but he insisted that they enabled teachers to sort students by ability. "The best achievement and aptitude tests are effective in sorting out students according to their actual and potential performance in the classroom," he asserted. "Much criticism of tests has been made, but it has been proven to be unfair because tests reveal intellectual gifts [and deficits] at every level of the population; they are excellent within the limits for which they were designed."[20]

A decade later, in 1967, Superintendent Ohrenberger agreed with Gillis and noted that the Department of Educational Investigation and Measurement had forwarded exactly 2,936 referrals to the Department of Pupil Adjustment Counseling. "Symptomatically," he explained, "these children may manifest intense anxiety, withdrawal, wide fluctuations in mood, immaturity, hyperactivity, hostility, negative social attitudes, physical neglect, destructiveness, and severe learning problems. The difficulties which they have presented cover the entire gamut of psychopathology."[21] According to Ohrenberger, each of these pupils needed special help, but others dissented from this view. The South End parents, for example, questioned the techniques of the Department of Educational Investigation and Measurement and accused the department of "tracking" poor minority students into low-level classes. As one contemporary noted, "the most important single aspect of the track system is the process by which the school [district] goes about sorting students into the different tracks. This importance stems from the fact that the fundamental premise of the sorting process is the keystone of the whole track system: that school personnel can with reasonable accuracy ascertain the maximum potential of each student and fix the content and pace of his education accordingly. If this premise proves false, the theory of the track system collapses, and with it any justification for consigning the disadvantaged student to a second-best education."[22] Indeed, by 1967, the entire testing (and tracking) process was under close scrutiny. In May of that year, David Goslin of the American Institutes for Research (AIR) issued a study titled *Criticisms of Standardized Tests and Testing* and, a few months later, the powerful College Entrance Examination Board established a National Commission on Tests to investigate testing methods in elementary and secondary schools—particularly in the inner city.[23]

It was in this context that the Parents Association for South End Schools and the United South End Settlements challenged testing and placement techniques in the Boston public schools. When the South End parents learned that the schools were planning to rediagnose students using exactly the same methods that resulted in earlier misplacements, they promptly filed a legal petition to stop the use of "discriminatory" tests.

According to an article in the *Boston Globe*, "one of the major issues raised by [the] petition . . . is that the standardized tests used by the school department to determine a student's learning level discriminate against the poor, the Spanish-speaking, and blacks. . . . The same sort of standardized tests are used by schools to place students in academic 'tracks' according to their performance on them. This use of the tests also has been called discriminatory."[24] In making their case, the South End parents drew heavily on a recent federal district court decision that had been handed down in the nation's capital.[25] In *Hobson v. Hansen*, Judge J. Skelly Wright ruled that the student-placement policies in Washington, D.C.— policies under which all students took IQ and scholastic aptitude tests in elementary grades and were then tracked into remedial, general, regular, or honors classes—violated the equal protection principles of the U.S. Constitution.[26] According to Wright, the use of tracks, combined with the absence of annual retesting to see if students' initial placements were appropriate, effectively blocked students' access to equal educational opportunities.[27] His legal reasoning was complex, but his basic conclusion was clear: the only way to ensure equal opportunities for all students was to ensure that testing procedures assessed abilities using race-neutral methods. The Parents Association for South End Schools and United South End Settlements read Wright's decision closely, then presented an almost identical case in their petition in Boston.

Following Wright, the South End parents held that the use of tracks in the Boston public schools was unconstitutional—not because the schools intended to harm minority students by the use of tracks but, rather, because the tracks effectively classified students by race, and racial classifications tied to unequal treatment were always suspect under the Constitution. Wright had outlined this principle in elaborate detail in *Hobson v. Hansen:* "Orthodox equal protection doctrine can be encapsulated in a single rule: government action which without justification imposes unequal burdens or awards unequal benefits is unconstitutional. The complaint that analytically no violation of equal protection vests unless the inequalities stemmed from a deliberately discriminatory plan is simply false."[28] Thus, it was not necessary to prove that the schools' testing or tracking policy was *intentionally* biased in order to prove that it denied access to equal educational opportunities; it was necessary only to show that the policy imposed unequal burdens on a particular group. Measuring "burdens" on the basis of class sizes, teacher qualifications, and financial resources, Wright found that, even if school officials did not intend to harm minority students, the tracking system under their control imposed unequal burdens on them and was, therefore, unconstitutional. "As the evidence in this case makes painfully clear," he held, "ability grouping as presently practiced in the District of Columbia school system [involves] a denial of equal educational opportunity to the poor and a majority of the Negroes attending school in the nation's capital, a denial that contravenes not only the [due process] guarantees of the Fifth Amendment but also the fundamental premise of the track system itself."[29] According to Wright, any school policy that sent different students to different tracks would face charges of discrimination if such a practice led to racial imbalance on either a school *or* a classroom level.

Wright's decision was a boon to the South End parents, who agreed that Boston's testing and tracking policy had imposed unequal burdens on minorities who had been incorrectly diagnosed as disabled. Yet, Wright's decision was not entirely clear on one crucial point, namely, whether isolated placements based on *nonracial* classifications were necessarily discriminatory. As Wright stated, "it should be made clear that what is at issue here is not whether [schools] are entitled to provide different kinds of students with different kinds of education. Although the equal protection clause is, of course, concerned with classifications which result in disparity of treatment, not all classifications resulting in disparity are unconstitutional. If [a] classification is reasonably related to the purposes of the governmental activity involved and is rationally carried out, the fact that persons are thereby treated differently does not necessarily offend."[30] What made the classification of students unconstitutional in *Hobson v. Hansen* was the finding that these classifications were based on students' *race* rather than their *ability*. If students—including minority students—had bona fide disabilities, then they could be legitimately isolated from their peers without violating the law. The challenge, therefore, was to ensure that schools' diagnostic methods were, in fact, race-neutral—and it was on this point that Wright's ruling hit a snag. According to Wright, even a test presumed to be race-neutral could be exposed as "biased" if it found disproportionate rates of disabilities among minority pupils. "Because of the impoverished circumstances that characterize the disadvantaged child, it is virtually impossible to tell whether [a] test score reflects lack of ability—or simply lack of opportunity," he noted.[31] "When standard aptitude tests are given to low income Negro children, or disadvantaged children, . . . the tests are less precise and less accurate—so much so that test scores become practically meaningless."[32]

As far as Wright was concerned, it was impossible to show that minority students suffered disproportionately from any disability, because evidence to make this point was automatically suspect. Yet, the impracticality of this position in actual classrooms made it easy to ignore—which is exactly what superintendent Ohrenberger did with it in Boston. He affirmed the value of isolated classes for mentally retarded and emotionally disturbed pupils in the inner city (many of whom were poor, minority, or non-English-speaking) and noted in his annual report a year later that Boston had *expanded* its offerings in this area. As he wrote, "assistant superintendents, working with personnel from local mental health centers and family supportive agencies, placed many disturbed and socially maladjusted students in programs designed to enable them to return to a normal classroom situation."[33] Such a statement may have seemed like a change in policy, but, in truth, it entailed no change at all. Boston's programs for emotionally disturbed, socially maladjusted, and mentally retarded students had been operating in the same way since the early 1950s: they were isolated from regular classrooms and, more often than not, they were racially imbalanced. They did not "enable" students to return to regular classes; instead, they separated low-achieving students from their peers on a more or less permanent basis. The only difference was that, after 1967, schools offering these services were able to secure larger amounts of federal aid. Recent amendments to the ESEA had designated 15 percent of all Title III and Title V funds for testing and teaching disabled pupils, and Boston took full advantage of these funds. A year later, Boston also made use of aid provided by the Handicapped Children's Early Education Assistance Act (P.L. 90-538), which, like its predecessors, allowed federal resources to flow in significant sums to disabled students in racially imbalanced schools.

⌀

In June 1967, three days after the *Hobson v. Hansen* ruling, Massachusetts's state commissioner of education Owen Kiernan hosted a meeting of the Council of Chief State School Officers (CCSSO) to discuss Wright's decision. Kiernan was at the time president of the CCSSO, and he invited federal commissioner of education Harold Howe II to bring the nation's state commissioners up-to-date on recent changes in federal education policy. Howe stated that the federal Office of Education did "not immediately have any definitive reaction to the Skelly Wright decision" but assured state commissioners that the decision would not cause a much-dreaded withdrawal of federal grants from special-compensatory programs serving large numbers of poor minority students in the inner city. He promised that such programs—even those in racially imbalanced schools—would not be starved for cash as a way to pressure any school to quicken the pace of integration. As he put it, "it would be a grave mistake to take an 'either/or' position in this realm—insisting that the *only* answer is desegregation or alternatively, that desegregation is not feasible and that the *only* practical answer is compensatory education. The fact is that we need major efforts on both fronts." In other words, according to Howe, the fact that special-compensatory programs served poor minority students in large numbers was not incompatible with the promotion of racial integration over the long run. He therefore stressed the need to continue funding these programs. "Whatever the disagreements about procedures and lines of authority," Howe concluded, "we have more or less buried forever the issue of whether or not there should be federal assistance to education. It is no longer questioned."[34]

If anything, Howe suggested, the government's biggest challenge was to *improve* the flow of federal aid to special-compensatory programs in urban areas with large numbers of poor minority students. "Nowhere are the problems of education more intense or more critical than in the cities," he wrote. "There is considerable well-grounded complaint that in the distribution of education funds within the states, cities are not receiving proportions of money appropriate to their special needs." Moreover, he added, "while education can make a major contribution to the solution of urban problems, the situation obviously goes far beyond education and demands equally vigorous efforts by public and private agencies concerned with housing, transportation, employment and other fundamentals of life in the city."[35] Howe's comments reflected a growing sense that racial integration was not the only solution to educational problems in the inner city. More and more policymakers were calling for additional social welfare services to be concentrated in the nation's most economically disadvantaged and racially isolated areas—and the timing of this call was significant. By 1967, the civil rights movement had split into two halves, one clinging to principles of racial integration while the other pressed an agenda of racial separatism. The Black Panthers, established in 1966 by Stokely Carmichael, Huey Newton, and Bobby Seale, advocated armed zones of community control with independently organized schools. They did not want integration; they wanted racial self-determination. This demand coincided with a subtle turn away from integration in federal education policy. It also coincided with a rise in racial violence in Boston: as one local newspaper observed in 1967, the Solomon Lewenberg Junior High School, on the border between Roxbury and Dorchester, had become a "focal point for racial antipathies. . . . There are rumors, not substantiated, of beatings and knifings on school premises."[36] Indeed, by the fall of 1967, racial integration seemed a rapidly fading ideal.

In April 1967, racial tension in Boston escalated into full-scale violence when a riot broke out in Roxbury just a few blocks from Solomon Lewenberg Junior High. The riot began after a group of black residents staged a sit-in at the city's welfare department. The protesters demanded that city officials include them in welfare-policy deliberations—an idea encouraged by recent federal grants for so-called community action programs intended to aid in the implementation of local welfare projects. When the executive director of the welfare department refused to speak with the protesters, they used bicycle chains to lock themselves—along with several city employees—inside the building. The director then called the police, who cut the chains, forced their way into the building, and started dragging the protesters out. According to a bystander, "several women were beaten severely; others were assaulted without warning. The untrained police managed to club [protesters] and social workers alike, often losing sight of which women were 'hostages' and which ones were protesters. A milling crowd gathered outside, and upon hearing the screams from inside the building began to surge forward. As police called for further reinforcements, the crowd continued to grow in size and hostility. The violence escalated, confrontations between the police and the outraged community members increased, and a riot ensued. Four nights later, over 1,700 police had been mobilized, 75 people had been hospitalized, 60 [others] had been arrested, and the property damage estimates were well into the millions."[37] It was a major conflict, but it was not the only riot to occur in 1967. Six weeks later, a far bloodier melee erupted in Newark, killing 23 and injuring 725. Ten days after that, a huge riot broke out in Detroit, killing 43, injuring 1,200, and involving 7,200 arrests.

Altogether, seventy-five race riots took place in the last six months of the year. By the fall of 1967, many Bostonians began to fear an imminent "race war," and the issue of "community control" took center stage in the mayoral elections that November. Six months earlier, Boston mayor John Collins had announced his retirement after seven years in office. Ten candidates had entered the fall primaries, but only two survived: Massachusetts secretary of state Kevin White and Boston school committee chair Louise Day Hicks. The key difference between the two was that Hicks cast herself as a defender of racial separation while White emphasized the horror of the recent riots and tried to cast himself as a racial conciliator. Hicks promised to protect "neighborhood schools" while White pledged to bring peace back to the streets, build more low-income housing, block a planned highway through the South End, obtain more money for urban-renewal projects, and appoint more minorities to municipal posts. When all the ballots were counted, White defeated Hicks—but only by a margin of 12,429 out of 192,673 votes. Far from a public mandate, the election demonstrated that White needed to work hard to balance the wishes of the city's majority and minority residents. Immediately after his election, he asked one of his campaign staffers, Sister Frances Georgia, to serve as a public relations consultant. An energetic nun connected to the city's Roman Catholic parishes as well as its new immigrant districts, Sister Georgia took it upon herself to "listen" to minority citizens' demands—especially demands related to education. In the winter of 1967, she set out to document the number of minority students throughout the city and, specifically, the number of non-English-speaking immigrant students. Her findings were significant. She discovered that most immigrant parents were less interested in racial integration than in special programs suited to their children's unique educational needs.

The late 1960s saw rapid changes in Boston's immigrant neighborhoods. After the passage of the federal Immigration and Nationality Act of 1965—which eliminated "national-origin quotas" that had been in place for more than forty years—unprecedented numbers of immigrants began to enter the United States, especially from Latin America.[38] By 1966, the Cuban Refugee Center in Boston identified as many as 2,500–4,000 Cubans living in the Brighton and Allston sections of the city. Another 3,000–5,000 Cubans and Puerto Ricans (unaffected by the new immigration law) were living in Jamaica Plain, and 4,800–8,000 Puerto Ricans were living in the South End. By the time Sister Georgia completed her survey, she found an additional 5,000–10,000 Puerto Ricans in houses in Roxbury and Dorchester. Predicting that the Puerto Rican population would increase at a rate of 1,200–1,500 a year, she heard many requests for more Spanish-speaking teachers in the Boston public schools.[39] When she asked, "What do you think is necessary to improve the city's schools?" the most common response from the Cuban parents was "bilingual teachers."[40] Of course, ESL classes with English-speaking teachers had been offered in Boston since the 1960–61 school year. Gradually, however, more and more immigrant parents began to demand Spanish- rather than English-speaking teachers. Superintendent Ohrenberger remarked in 1967, "the large influx of non-English-speaking children into the schools has created problems requiring solutions emphasizing [both] bilingualism and cultural assimilation. During the past school year, Boston's program, English as a Second Language, benefited more than 750 pupils, and approximately 1,400 are expected to use this service in the coming year."[41] But ESL classes were no longer enough: thousands of Spanish-speaking children in Boston were avoiding school altogether because they could not understand the teachers.

By 1968, the urgent question in Boston was not *whether* to add bilingual programs for non-English-speaking students but, rather, *how* to add bilingual programs fast enough. In 1960, Boston had responded to a (much less pressing) influx of non-English-speaking immigrants by appealing for federal aid; now, at the end of the decade, a similar appeal came from both the superintendent and the mayor. The timing of their appeal was not surprising, because, in December 1967, Congress had passed a new law to support the creation of bilingual programs in public schools. The Senate Subcommittee on Education, which included Massachusetts's senator Edward Kennedy, tied bilingual education to President Johnson's continuing War on Poverty and suggested that a lack of proficiency in English deepened the educational disadvantage of immigrant students. "The purpose of this new [bill]," the subcommittee argued, "is to provide a solution to the problem of those children who are educationally disadvantaged because of their inability to speak English."[42] Aimed at immigrant children whose parents earned less than $3,000 a year, the new bill received vocal support from Senator Kennedy, who was mindful of demands for bilingual teachers in Boston—not to mention the city's continuing need for aid. Apparently ignoring the likelihood that bilingual programs would be created in racially imbalanced schools—but expressing, instead, the hope that bilingual classes would improve the educational opportunities and outcomes of non-English-speakers—Kennedy voted to attach a new title, Title VII, to the ESEA. On January 2, 1968, President Johnson signed Title VII, the so-called Bilingual Education Act (P.L. 90-247), into law.[43]

Title VII provided federal funds for "exemplary pilot or demonstration projects in bilingual and bicultural education in a variety of settings," and the Boston public schools immediately applied for this new form of aid. Although Boston was already using federal aid under Title I to support its ESL program, the city successfully applied for a Title VII grant. (Of 300 applications submitted in 1968, fewer than 80 received funding, so Superintendent Ohrenberger was justifiably proud of his success.)[44] Since Title VII was intended to serve children ages three to eight, Ohrenberger directed Boston's initial grant toward ESL programs (rather than bilingual programs) at four elementary schools: Bancroft, Mackey, Winthrop, and Hawthorne, each of which was located in an inner-city neighborhood with large numbers of low-income and Spanish-speaking immigrants. He later used additional Title VII funds to expand the ESL program at Boston's decades-old day school for immigrants.[45] In Ohrenberger's view, Title VII made a welcome addition to the school budget, and he expected it to become a permanent source of support for school programs. Indeed, not long after the passage of Title VII, he established a new office of bilingual instruction at school department headquarters to coordinate applications for Title VII grants. Just the schools had established an Office of Program Development to maximize their eligibility for aid to retarded students in 1963 and had expanded this office in 1965 to maximize aid to disadvantaged students, so, now, the schools created a parallel office to maximize aid to bilingual programs.[46] Within a relatively short period of time, federal aid to special-compensatory programs had become a prominent feature of general operations in the Boston public schools—and most of this aid flowed to racially imbalanced schools.

In 1968, in anticipation of Boston's first federal grant for bilingual pilot programs, Mayor White placed Sister Georgia, along with Rosemary Whiting of the Office of Public Services, in charge of a new initiative to make the city's schools more appealing to Spanish-speaking students in minority neighborhoods. Recalling the destructive riot a year earlier, Whiting noted that "the present structure of the school programs, not being geared to the special needs of the Spanish-speaking, may produce a large number of teenage dropouts within the next three or four years. This [increase in the number of dropouts] can be expected to contribute to Spanish juvenile delinquency and unemployment problems which have now barely emerged." Contending that Boston needed to act fast if it intended to "catch and educate the next wave of impending Spanish-speaking school drop-outs," Whiting recommended the creation of a bilingual *transitional school* where general education would be given in Spanish until the pupils learn enough English to profit by classes conducted in English."[47] Responding enthusiastically to this recommendation, Sister Georgia solicited the premier school consulting firm in Boston, the Education Development Center (EDC), to develop a proposal for so-called bilingual-transitional clusters to accommodate as many as 280 Spanish-speaking middle-school pupils. Operating on a half-day pullout basis, these clusters would teach students in both Spanish and English until they were ready to enter English-speaking classes. EDC asserted that its bilingual-transitional clusters would raise Spanish-speakers' academic achievement and would also prepare them for continued success in upper grades (much as Operation Counterpoise had promised to do five years earlier). EDC demonstrated its confidence in its proposal by offering $60,000 of its own money for teacher training if the schools agreed to cover the remaining $200,000 cost.

◇

Much to EDC's surprise, however, the school committee rejected its proposal and argued that existing services were adequate to meet the demand for bilingual education in Boston. This idea struck EDC as ludicrous. EDC's director pointed out that only 13 percent of the students enrolled in the city's ESL classes were reading at or near grade level. He added that 26 percent of ESL students were one year behind grade level, 25 percent were two years behind, 12 percent were three years behind, and 5 percent were four years behind. At least 8 percent of all ESL students were held back five years or more.[48] Clearly, existing ESL classes were not boosting students' academic achievement. These classes were both de facto segregated *and* academically ineffective (and, thus, it seemed, "discriminatory"). Meanwhile, the city's non-English-speaking population was growing. The Boston Redevelopment Authority, the Cardinal Cushing Center, and the newly created Association Promoting the Constitutional Rights of the Spanish Speaking (APCROSS) showed that the Puerto Rican population included thousands of immigrants living in the South End alone.[49] In 1968, the Harvard-MIT Joint Center for Urban Studies surveyed more than 1,000 Spanish-speaking pupils and found a universal desire for "bilingual-transitional schools" of the very type EDC had proposed.[50] Non-English-speaking students in Boston, it seemed, were not interested in ESL instruction as it was currently structured in the city's schools; instead, they wanted bilingual classes. They were not concerned that bilingual-transitional clusters were likely to be racially imbalanced; rather, they welcomed an innovative program they believed would meet their special educational needs.

At first, it was hard to see why the school committee rejected EDC's proposal. It soon became clear, however, that one reason was a fear of state-aid withholdings tied to racial imbalance.[51] Put simply, the school committee worried that bilingual-transitional clusters established in minority neighborhoods would draw more minority students into these schools and would, in turn, exacerbate rather than alleviate the problem of racial imbalance. Exacerbating racial imbalance would, in turn, lead to further withholdings of aid under the state's racial imbalance law. According to the Boston Municipal Research Bureau (BMRB), the schools' 1967–68 budget was at least $10 million greater than the 1966–67 budget (a 15 percent jump), so any bilingual programs that drew students into racially imbalanced schools would be imprudent if it led to further reductions in aid.[52] This financial predicament showed how different sources of aid could work at cross-purposes with each other. Federal aid under Title VII encouraged the creation of bilingual classes in schools with high concentrations of non-English-speaking students; in fact, once Title VII grants became available, schools had a financial incentive to *maximize* enrollment in bilingual classes (because, as under Title I, more pupils brought more federal aid). Furthermore, by 1968, the Johnson administration had concluded that "concentrated" aid to special-compensatory services in poor minority neighborhoods had a greater impact on student achievement. But maximizing enrollments in bilingual classes involved risks of its own. If administrators accepted funds to add programs in schools with large concentrations of minority students, state funds were likely to be withheld owing to racial imbalance; conversely, if they added programs only in schools that were racially balanced, they might lose the benefits of a carefully targeted effort. With state and federal agencies encouraging concentrated services but also discouraging racial imbalance, local administrators faced a difficult set of choices. These choices were not trivial—nor could they be avoided.

A key question facing the Boston public schools in 1968 was whether maximizing enrollments in special-compensatory programs would ultimately increase or decrease the schools' overall receipt of aid. The new office of bilingual education was, in a sense, responsible for making such calculations—locating the actuarial point at which a decision to add programs might exacerbate racial imbalance and, in turn, give the state department of education a renewed excuse to withhold state aid. Sometimes, these calculations took unexpected directions, as in the fall of 1968, when Superintendent Ohrenberger wanted to secure aid for existing ESL programs (all in racially imbalanced schools) but did *not* want to imply a need for programs that might draw attention to the persistence of racial imbalance in the school district as a whole. Attempting to balance competing objectives, Ohrenberger told officials that public schools in Boston enrolled precisely 2,516 children with Spanish surnames and noted that current ESL programs were sufficient to meet their needs. He failed to mention, however, that up to 5,000 Spanish-speaking children were not in school at all, fearing that additional services for them might worsen racial imbalance. This strategy of underestimating the need for bilingual programs seemed clever at first, but it infuriated Mayor White, who hoped more programs would lead to more federal aid under Title VII.[53] If Title I aid was based on the total number of disadvantaged students in a district, and if Title VII had the potential to grow into a similar categorical program (with aid based on enrollment), then, White argued, it seemed prudent to use the most accurate count of low-income non-English-speaking students. Indeed, if federal aid for the disadvantaged and disabled served as a guide, then, White contended, it might be wise to *exaggerate* the total number of non-English-speaking children in the city in order to maximize the schools' eligibility for aid. At the very least, White argued, the count should reflect Boston's true population of non-English-speaking pupils.

White failed to see, however, that launching bilingual programs in minority areas might bring more students—and more unwanted attention—to racially imbalanced schools. This tension between carefully targeted special-compensatory programs and racial imbalance applied not only to ESL programs but also to many other programs that were designed for minority pupils in the inner city. Included on this list were programs for the mentally retarded and the emotionally disturbed. Should the schools maximize their enrollments in such programs in order to maximize their financial aid, or should they seek racial balance instead? This difficult question came to a head in 1968, when the Boston public schools faced a torrent of criticism regarding the placement of mentally and emotionally disabled students in remedial programs. Between 1948 and 1968, special education enrollments in the United States had skyrocketed from 350,000 to 2,250,000 students—that is, from 1.2 percent to 4.5 percent of all students in the public schools. Yet, in Boston, enrollments in special education had grown even *faster* than this increasing nationwide average. Such a tremendous jump was particularly astonishing given the fact that Boston's most seriously disabled children—those with extreme cognitive disorders or psychiatric problems—were excluded completely from the public schools. As the city's new director of special programs (the successor to Charles Ruddy) explained, her office dealt only with students who had minor illnesses or temporary ailments (in her words, her office "doesn't hear about children who are permanently handicapped. I'm not responsible for that problem").[54] She assumed that such children received instruction at Kennedy Memorial Hospital or perhaps at Boston's Industrial School for Crippled Children, but the Kennedy Hospital offered instruction to only twenty children, and the Industrial School reported only 155 children in attendance, even though it had room for many more.

Apparently, Boston's high enrollments in isolated remedial classes derived from an extraordinary rate of diagnosing poor, black, and Spanish-speaking children with mental retardation and/or emotional disturbance. At a time when the city's most severely handicapped students were shut out of the public schools entirely, remedial classes were overflowing with low-income—as well as low-performing—minority students. As Arthur J. Bindman of the Massachusetts Department of Mental Health explained, "Looking at the normal range of human intelligence, we know that a fixed percentage of a school population will score below a certain point on an IQ test. In Boston, for example, there should be about 1,500 children so retarded that they need special educational services; but [the Boston public schools] have about 4,000 children instead. It's obvious that they've got a lot of children who aren't retarded at all. They have taken kids with a lot of different needs and lumped them all together in these (special) classes."[55] At first, it was difficult to discern the cause of these misplacements beyond racial prejudice—as well as primitive testing procedures or unreliable diagnostic techniques (a problem that grew over time). Yet, starting in 1968, two additional causes of student misplacements came to light, and both were linked to school funding. First, it was discovered that schools placed poor minority pupils in special classes because these classes received state and federal aid based on enrollments: more pupils brought more money, so teachers had a financial incentive to separate low-achieving pupils from their peers in order to receive more "categorical" aid—including aid from Title I, Title III, and Title V of the ESEA.

The second cause of Boston's unusually high rate of diagnosing disabilities was more subtle than the first. In 1968, it was discovered that teachers placed low-performing students in isolated remedial programs in order to mitigate the effects of Massachusetts's racial imbalance law— and their strategy was both legally and financially sophisticated. The racial imbalance law restricted nonwhite enrollment in any school to 50 percent, but a prior law, Chapter 750, required schools to provide "appropriate" classroom placements to children with emotional problems.[56] Teachers found that they could subvert the impact of the racial imbalance law and maintain racially segregated classrooms by diagnosing poor minority students with emotional disturbances and then placing them in isolated programs to which they were entitled under Chapter 750. The subterfuge, however, did not end there. Since none of the Chapter 750 classes were located in minority neighborhoods, minority students diagnosed as "disabled" were bused to all-white schools and placed in isolated—and racially imbalanced—classes *within* otherwise all-white schools. As a result, racial imbalance persisted not only in Chapter 750 classes for the emotionally disturbed but also in regular classes for disabled white students. As one study noted, minorities assigned to all-white schools under the state's racial imbalance law "were being classified as retarded or emotionally disturbed and removed from the classrooms they were [supposed] to integrate."[57] Put another way, "black children . . . are transported out of their own schools and communities because there are too few resources [for emotionally disturbed children] in their neighborhood. This problem, among others, leads to a strong racial imbalance in the operation of the '750' classes in the [otherwise predominantly white] public schools."[58]

By 1968, it was obvious that Chapter 750 and the racial imbalance law worked at cross-purposes and that schools manipulated both laws to ensure racial segregation at the classroom level while also securing aid for disabled students.[59] When J. Edward Conners of the Harvard School of Public Health investigated Chapter 750 in Boston, he uncovered a long list of unsettling trends. He found that 60 percent of the pupils identified as emotionally disturbed came from impoverished, often minority or non-English-speaking, families, despite the fact that minority families accounted for less than 20 percent of Boston's total population. He also found that pupils from poor families were placed in isolated remedial programs at far younger ages—and retained in these programs for much longer periods—than pupils from wealthier families.[60] Moreover, he learned that poor children were more likely to be placed in isolated programs with minimal academic assistance: poor children under age eleven were likely to be relegated to physically isolated classrooms while poor children over age eleven were likely to be consigned to "home instruction."[61] In response to the key question—did poor minority students benefit from their placements or did their placements amount to racial discrimination, Connors answered that racially imbalanced classes were *always* discriminatory and contended that the only way to allay suspicion of discrimination in Chapter 750 was to make the diagnoses of emotional disturbance more reliable (and race-neutral). More reliable diagnoses would enable schools to distinguish pupils who were truly disabled—and who could therefore benefit from isolated remedial programs—from children who were merely below average in academic achievement— and who were thus better off in "regular" classes (located, Connors insisted, in racially balanced schools). Without reliable diagnoses, Connors warned, Chapter 750 programs would continue to fill with children whose only "disability" was their poverty or race.[62]

Yet, reliable diagnoses were not easy to get. Despite an explicit requirement in Chapter 750 to retest all students on an annual basis, schools refused to do so. William Philbrick, the state director of special education, acknowledged the schools' failure to reassess students: "It's against the law," he admitted. "But, . . . When the superintendent of schools and the school committee chairman in Boston swear—under penalty of perjury—that [annual testing] is done, what can you do? They don't re-test them, but they say they do."[63] In 1968, when the Parents Association for South End Schools hired an independent agency to retest their children, they found that more than half of those labeled "retarded" actually had IQ's in the normal range.[64] These results found confirmation throughout the Boston public schools. As some teachers sheepishly confessed, "special classes are used as a 'dumping ground' for children who are trouble-makers in their regular classes. These children often do not have low IQ's. Results of the Stanford-Binet tests are sometimes deliberately rigged."[65] The schools succeeded in this deception, in part, because Chapter 750 required schools to offer "appropriate" services to emotionally disturbed students but did not define the meaning of the term *appropriate*. The ambiguity of this term permitted auditors to look the other way as teachers placed minority students in isolated programs without ensuring that these programs would necessarily raise their academic achievement or facilitate their integration into regular classes. As long as Chapter 750 allowed the removal of low-performing students from regular classes and considered such treatment appropriate, the seemingly intractable problems of racial imbalance and below-average achievement would continue to define the experience of minority students in Boston's public schools. In 1968 it was reasonable to ask which served minority students better—a special (isolated) class in a racially balanced school or a regular class in a racially imbalanced school?

⟡

Complicating the answer to this question was the increasing racial separatism of the late 1960s. In mid-January, 1968, Black Panther cofounder Stokely Carmichael paid an extended visit to Boston to persuade several groups, including black Puerto Ricans and the once-moderate Urban League, to join a black nationalist-separatist coalition dubbed the Black United Front. On April 7, 1968—three days after the assassination of Martin Luther King Jr. in Memphis—this coalition staged a massive protest in Roxbury. The purpose of this rally (which 5,000 people attended) was to mourn King's death and to announce a set of demands for "community control" in Boston's black neighborhoods. Many of the group's demands pertained to the operation of the public schools. For example, the Black United Front proclaimed that "every school in the black community shall have all-black staff, principals, teachers, and custodians. All schools within the black community are to be renamed after black heroes. Names will be selected by the United Front."[66] The United Front expected its racially distinct neighborhood schools to improve the educational opportunities—as well as the academic achievement—of Boston's black students. Moreover, unlike the idea of transitional-bilingual clusters, which promised eventual integration into English-speaking schools, the schools proposed by the United Front were to be *permanently* separated from the white community. Not everyone, however, embraced these proposals. The school committee, for instance, reacted with dismay. Rather than seeing the proposal as an endorsement or an acceptance of de facto segregation in the schools, the committee saw the United Front's initiatives as a direct threat to its own authority. Rather than seeing similarities between the Black United Front's appeals for racial separatism and its own past appeals for "different education for different groups," the committee recoiled at the thought of black-*controlled* schools—even if these schools promised to improve academic achievement.[67]

The school committee much preferred the proposals of another group that was just forming in Boston. Twelve days before the United Front's rally in Roxbury, a new interracial organization, the Boston Urban Coalition, had held its first meeting with 300 of the city's most visible (and politically moderate) leaders in attendance. The members of the Boston Urban Coalition included Robert Slater, president of the John Hancock Mutual Life Insurance Company, Frank Farwell, leader of the Liberty Mutual Insurance Company, Kenneth Guscott, director of the Boston NAACP, Salvatore Carmelio, head of the Massachusetts AFL-CIO, James Killian, president of MIT, and Mayor Kevin White. The Boston Urban Coalition was a branch of the newly formed National Urban Coalition, which had been created in the aftermath of the riots in 1967 "to enlist all elements of the community in opening new opportunities to the poor [by improving] housing, employment opportunities, health [care], education, and other sectors of contemporary urban life." As part of this larger national enterprise, the Boston Urban Coalition aimed to direct the political and financial resources of Boston's civic elite toward urban-renewal programs in ghetto areas such as Roxbury, Dorchester, and the South End. In this effort, the coalition had high-profile support at the federal level. A few weeks before the coalition gathered for its first meeting, U.S. secretary of health, education, and welfare John Gardner announced that he was stepping down from his cabinet post to become the director of the national organization. In March 1968, Gardner cabled from Washington to express his support for Boston's new branch. "I believe Boston can have an outstanding coalition and program of action," he wired in a brief congratulatory telegram. "I wish you every success."[68]

Confidence ran high among the business executives who organized Boston Urban Coalition, yet it was clear from the start that this group did not enjoy the support of Boston's more militant black residents. The *Boston Herald* commented after the group's inaugural meeting that "the Coalition immediately received its baptism of fire. Several Negroes arose at the organizational meeting and accused the sponsors of employing 'the plantation attitude,' and of 'trying to tell the black man what is good for him.'" One black member of the audience told the coalition that "the black man has been lied to and given promises long enough. We are sick and tired of good will. . . . Further, we ourselves want to elect [the] people who will represent us on the coalition committee. We don't want them selected for us." When the coalition pointed to the participation of local NAACP leader Kenneth Guscott in the group, one black woman responded, "I know Mr. Guscott and I respect him, but I'm tired of old people with old ideas telling me what to do." Another black activist warned that "the time has come when one black man can't speak for 10,000. You could have contacted others for this committee." Many black residents in the audience feared that the coalition was "camouflage" for the Johnson administration's National Advisory Commission on Civil Disorders (also called the Kerner Commission after its chairman, governor Otto Kerner of Illinois), established in late 1967 to study the causes of the recent riots. Others worried that the Boston Urban Coalition would function as a mouthpiece for white businessmen. "You got it all laid out," one black man charged. "You've got an established committee that can be counted on, . . . but you can't be telling Roxbury what to do."[69] Calling for direct democracy and community control, radicalized black citizens rebuffed the Boston Urban Coalition and stated their intention to run their own neighborhoods in their own ways—and to achieve better results in the process.[70] Clearly, racial tensions were running very high.

The fact that Boston's Urban Coalition did not enjoy the support of many blacks must have troubled national director John Gardner, who had devoted his last month in the Department of Health, Education, and Welfare to promoting the idea of local participation in the design and implementation of federal urban-renewal projects. In fact, on April 3, 1968—just a day before the assassination of Martin Luther King Jr. and four days before the Black United Front rallied in Roxbury—the Boston school committee had hosted the first of six planned meetings with black parents and community activists to discuss ways of improving education in Roxbury, Dorchester, and the South End.[71] This unprecedented meeting took place under the auspices of a new School-Community Advisory Council, which had, in turn, been created by the federally funded Boston Central City Task Force (created in February 1968, after delegates from Boston attended a school-community-relations seminar that John Gardner held in Washington). In a joint-planning "experiment," Boston's new School-Community Advisory Council decided to try to improve two failing urban schools, the Martin Luther King, Jr., Middle School and the James P. Timilty Junior High School, both of which fell within the boundaries of Boston's Model Neighborhood Area, an area in Roxbury that received federal urban-renewal aid. In the past decade, more than 20,000 white residents had fled this neighborhood, leaving a nonwhite majority and a student population at the King and Timilty schools that was 97 percent black. The schools' achievement levels were extremely low, and their dropout rate was 36 percent higher than the city average. Both schools had reputations as "multi-problem" buildings.[72]

Could a collaborative approach to school improvement—combining local parental involvement with central administrative expertise and concentrated financial resources—have a positive effect on students in a neighborhood as disadvantaged as that of King and Timilty's? According to a School-Community Advisory Council report, "statistics show that many students [in these two schools] do not perform up to the city-wide norms, and do not successfully negotiate the transition to high school. . . . In spite of a recent infusion of specially funded services and a higher per-pupil expenditure rate than in some other areas of Boston, it is clear . . . that a still greater concentration of funds and programs must be marshalled to provide a quality education for these children." With the help of a large federal planning grant under Title III of the ESEA, the School-Community Advisory Council intended to "design programs to attract and concentrate massive resources on these two schools in an effort to improve community/school relations [as well as] the academic achievement of the students." Setting aside concerns about racial imbalance in both schools, officials focused on raising achievement by targeting resources at special-compensatory programs in a single neighborhood: "The comprehensive plan [at King and Timilty] must focus all available community resources on a limited area to the end that a concentration of inputs will strike a telling blow at some of the critical educational problems of [these] inner-city schools." As delegates to the Central City Task Force seminar had discovered, "there is a general feeling that many federally-funded programs, while effective and beneficial in limited areas, have not made a significant impact on the critical educational problems this country faces. Congress will be reluctant to vote additional funds for educational projects unless there is [at least] a 50–50 chance of success; that is, some assurance that the project will make a measurable and significant impact on critical problems, if only in a limited area."[73]

The hope that "a concentration of inputs" would generate "measurable" outcomes attracted no shortage of enthusiasm. The timing, however, was unfortunate. In the wake of Martin Luther King Jr.'s death, the climate for reform had shifted. Appeals for community control and racial self-determination took a confrontational turn in the summer of 1968 — a summer notorious for social and political unrest. Indeed, it would be difficult to overstate the turmoil unleashed in this period: in June, shortly after wining the California Democratic primary, front-running candidate (and Boston native) Robert Kennedy was shot in Los Angeles; in July, a major race riot erupted in Cleveland, leaving several dead; in August, huge protests disrupted the Democratic National Convention in Chicago. Adding to this confusion was a rapidly disintegrating situation in Vietnam: the shocking Tet Offensive in January, followed by revelations of the My Lai massacre in March, had led to mounting student protests at dozens of colleges and universities across the country, including Harvard and MIT. The entire nation seemed ready to explode. Under these increasingly tumultuous circumstances, the seemingly prosaic work of local school reform made little headway. Indeed, any hope for interracial cooperation and shared governance faded as more aggressive leaders seized the upper hand and rejected calls for "collaborative change." Within this context, Boston's fledgling School-Community Advisory Council had no chance, even with the support of high-ranking officials and federal aid. By the time the Boston public schools opened for the fall semester, fear of political mayhem hung in the air, and the dream of partnership between white school officials and black community leaders collapsed.

Despite their apparent differences, however, white school officials and black community leaders pursued much the same goal in 1968: concentrated resources for special-compensatory programs targeting minority students in their own (still racially imbalanced) neighborhood schools. What changed was simply that minorities now expected to control these programs themselves. Not long after the emergence of the School-Community Advisory Council, a parallel body, the Citizens Education Advisory Council (CEAC), formed within Action for Boston Community Development (ABCD), the city's four-year-old federal antipoverty organization.[74] Unlike the School-Community Advisory Council, which had pursued interracial cooperation, the CEAC made no effort to reach out to the all-white school committee—and its militance came through in its rhetoric. "Parent and community participation means in some instances parent control and community control," its chairman noted, adding that, without community control, "there can be no understanding [of] or solution for, the crisis in the school[s]; there can be no remedy—only further entrenchment and bankruptcy of the public school system." Thus, what had begun only a few months earlier as a cooperative movement bringing white school officials and minority community leaders together in a common dialogue about reform now dissolved into a bitterly antagonistic battle for control. The CEAC did not trust the school committee to use resources for effective school programs; instead, it sought to control these resources itself. In August 1968, when Boston secured a new federal grant for $154,000 to promote "concentrated programs serving . . . students in central-city schools," the CEAC immediately assumed that the school committee would squander this money on Operation Counterpoise.[75] School committee chairman Thomas Eisenstadt tried to allay these fears, saying that "a program with some shortcomings is better than no program at all," but William Gaines of ABCD rejected this excuse, responding, "We've been told that for three years."[76]

Amid this mounting crisis, state commissioner of education Owen Kiernan—who had built his reputation, in part, on his ability to secure federal aid for special-compensatory programs in the inner city—resigned. Some saw his departure as a cowardly abdication of his responsibility to solve the growing problems in the state's urban schools. Yet,

Kiernan had seen the writing on the wall. He knew that popular support for integration—or, specifically, for the state racial-imbalance law—was waning among both whites *and* blacks, and he also knew that recent calls for "community control" of special-compensatory programs tended to be at odds with racial integration as an educational goal. Indeed, as journalist and critic Peter Schrag had noted a year earlier in his book, *Village School Downtown: Politics and Education—A Boston Report,* "the conflicting demands for integration and compensatory education . . . batter the schools in an endless series of waves, leaving them in a continuing state of paralytic shock and in postures of administrative defensiveness that have little success either in resolving the political conflicts of the community or in eliminating the educational weaknesses of the classroom."[77] Trapped between demands for racial balance, compensatory programs, and federal aid, Kiernan was at a loss for ways to meet all these demands at once. He realized that compensatory programs were supposed to serve students in concentrated settings, but he also realized that such programs tended to exacerbate racial imbalance in the schools. Unable to resolve this contradiction, he conceded defeat. The contradiction itself, however, did not go away. As Harvard professor Thomas Pettigrew observed at a hearing of the House Subcommittee on Research and Technical Programs, federal assistance had not equalized opportunities in the nation's inner-city schools; instead, the most fundamental problems remained. "By fastening further economic and racial separation," Pettigrew noted, Title I in particular was "contributing directly with federal money to the educational retardation of America's poorest children."[78]

Back in 1965, Francis Keppel, Harold Howe II, and John Gardner had envisioned the possibility of using federal aid to integrate schools, raise achievement, and end poverty all in a single stroke. By November 1968, however, most observers doubted that federal aid could ever accomplish such lofty goals. By the time of the presidential elections that year, even the most basic assumptions surrounding the Great Society had begun to unravel. It was no longer clear that the provision of federal funding for special-compensatory programs was compatible with the pursuit of racial integration, nor was it clear that racial separation necessarily constituted racial discrimination. It was no longer clear that isolated remedial programs imposed unequal burdens on minority students (as Judge Skelly Wright tried to suggest in *Hobson v. Hansen*), nor was it clear that isolated remedial programs perpetuated "educational disadvantage."[79] Given these uncertainties, it was not clear whether the Boston public schools should add programs in the inner city (and risk the withholding of resources due to racial imbalance) or whether the schools should pursue racial balance (and risk losing the advantages of concentrated programs). What *was* clear in November 1968, was the fact that voters were looking for ways to cut educational spending and curtail the kinds of social experimentation that had characterized the War on Poverty. A soon-to-be-identified Silent Majority recoiled from the social welfare policies of the 1960s and sought stability in fiscal conservatism and limited government. Under these conditions, the Republican Party seized the initiative, and, in the presidential race of 1968, Richard Nixon edged past Hubert Humphrey at the polls. While Humphrey attracted 97 percent of the black vote in the hard-fought election, Nixon appealed to white working-class voters who had come to reject Johnson's controversial—and expensive—social-welfare programs.[80]

It was in this complicated political context—with increasingly radical community leaders on the one hand and increasingly conservative national leaders on the other—that the next phase of federal aid to education began to unfold in Boston. After the passage of the Elementary and Secondary Education Act in 1965, dozens of new groups had emerged to lobby for additional aid to special-compensatory services, especially services that fell under the rubric of Title I and Title VII. Such groups included the National Advisory Council for the Education of Disadvantaged Children, the National Association for Administrators of State and Federally Assisted Education Programs, the National Welfare Rights Organization, the National Association for Bilingual Education, the Mexican-American Legal Defense and Education Fund, and—after Nixon pledged in his campaign to significantly cut federal aid to education— the Emergency Committee for Full Funding of Education Programs.[81] What united these groups was not any particular dedication to integrating schools or overcoming the isolation of poor minority students in remedial classes. Instead, what united these groups was a pursuit of special-compensatory services—even if these services facilitated the placement of minority students in racially imbalanced schools. The irony was that both white segregationists *and* black separatists accepted the legitimacy of racially imbalanced schools (albeit for different reasons). The key question was whether racially imbalanced schools could raise students' academic achievement. This question, which echoed the debates of the early 1960s, resurfaced in the late 1960s: if racial imbalance persisted in urban public schools, could these schools somehow become more effective in equalizing educational *outcomes?* Put another way, if racial imbalance was not necessarily "discriminatory," then what sorts of programs would urban schools need to prove it?

CHAPTER FOUR

Seeking Program Effectiveness, 1968–1971

In November 1968, Massachusetts went solidly for Humphrey; in fact, two out of three voters in the state cast their ballots for the Democratic candidate. After the election, however, Massachusetts lost two of its highest-ranking political figures to the new Nixon administration, and their departures changed the state political landscape in important and noticeable ways. In January 1969, Governor John Volpe was summoned to Washington, D.C., to serve as Nixon's first secretary of transportation. Then, a few weeks later, Elliot Richardson (who had recently become Massachusetts's attorney general) went to serve as Nixon's first undersecretary of state. Volpe's replacement in the governor's office was Francis Sargent (who had succeeded Richardson as lieutenant governor when Richardson had become attorney general), and Richardson's replacement in the attorney general's office was Robert Quinn, former speaker of the Massachusetts state legislature. Sargent, a Republican, and Quinn, a Democrat, were soon joined by a new commissioner of education, Neil Sullivan, who replaced the departing Owen Kiernan in February 1969. Taken as a group, Sargent, Quinn, and Sullivan formed a very different team than Volpe, Richardson, and Kiernan had formed. They worked harder than their predecessors had worked to address the enduring issue of racial discrimination in the public schools, and they promised to do everything in their power to equalize opportunities for poor minority children in urban areas. As Neil Sullivan told a reporter shortly after his arrival in 1969, America's 40 million poor "are fed the crumbs of food of education, then forgotten, to be remembered only momentarily as hate erupts and ghettos burn."[1] If the race riots of the previous two years had taught any lesson at all, Sullivan argued, they taught the urgency of ending discrimination in the public schools. The question was how best to achieve this goal in Boston.

According to Sullivan, the way to end discrimination was to ensure racial balance in every school. "More than anything else," the *Boston Globe* noted, Sullivan was "a man personally, emotionally, totally committed to racial integration in the schools[—even] at a time when a lot of respectable educators and a growing number of black parents seem about to give up on the idea."[2] Certainly, Sullivan had a long history of involvement with the struggle for racial integration in the public schools. After receiving his doctorate from the Harvard Graduate School of Education in the late 1950s, he had served as an interim commissioner of education in the state of Maine. Then, in 1963, he had worked with Robert Kennedy and Martin Luther King Jr. on a plan for school integration in the South. Later that year, he served as superintendent of racially mixed "free schools" in Prince Edward County, Virginia—an experience that was particularly formative for him. As he recalled, "police arrested my teachers in one city and someone threw a fire bomb into my house. It was a living hell."[3] He emerged from Virginia more determined than ever to advance the cause of racial integration. In 1964, he moved west to Berkeley, California—where, as superintendent of schools, he not only integrated the district but also served as a regional coordinator in Robert Kennedy's 1968 presidential campaign.[4] After Kennedy's assassination, he returned to Massachusetts as state commissioner of education and began immediately to pursue the same integrationist strategies he had pursued in California. Observing that Massachusetts's racial imbalance law had gone almost entirely unenforced for four years, he boldly proposed to *bus* students to alternate sites until no school in the state had more than 50 percent minority pupils. Opposition to this plan was strong: in 1969, despite voluntary transportation agreements between a few urban and suburban areas, the idea of cross-district busing to achieve racial balance attracted far more criticism than support.[5]

Indeed, when Sullivan first introduced his busing plan in March 1969, he faced outspoken resistance not only in Boston, but also in the new presidential administration in Washington. Throughout his campaign, Nixon had denounced proposals for busing and, as a native Californian, made no secret of his disdain for Sullivan's work in Berkeley. Nixon maintained that busing students from black neighborhoods to white neighborhoods was likely to provoke more violence than it prevented— and once in the White House, he surrounded himself with advisors who shared this view. For example, he chose California lieutenant governor Robert Finch (who had served as his campaign manager in his initial unsuccessful bid for the presidency in 1960) to be his first secretary of health, education, and welfare, and Finch took an outspoken stand against busing. In an interview with *U.S. News and World Report*, published in March 1969, Finch responded to a recent pro-busing decision from the federal district court in Pasadena, California. He held that it was "totally artificial to insist on busing school children if it may be detrimental to the level of education."[6] Much as Louise Day Hicks had asserted in Boston, Finch insisted that there was no inherent link between racial integration and academic performance among poor or minority children in the inner city. He maintained that dedicated teachers, well-designed curricula, consistent discipline at home and at school, and special-compensatory services tailored to meet different students' needs were the best ways to lift academic achievement and equalize educational opportunities. As Nixon himself asserted after the court decision in Pasadena, "Demands that an arbitrary 'racial balance' be established as a matter of fact misinterpret the law and misstate the priorities [of the nation's schools]."[7] According to Nixon—and a growing number of black leaders in the late 1960s—the key to improving inner-city schools was not racial integration but more effective programs.

Shortly after Finch arrived in Washington, he began to search for a commissioner of education. It was a quick search. In February 1969, he appointed James Allen Jr. state commissioner of education in New York, to serve as both federal commissioner of education and as assistant secretary of education—which meant that Allen (yet another product of the Harvard Graduate School of Education) succeeded both Harold Howe and Francis Keppel at the same time. Allen was no stranger to issues of racial discrimination and racial imbalance in urban public schools. In 1963, as New York commissioner he had imposed the nation's first racial-balance plan on the public schools of suburban Malverne, N.Y. (on Long

Island). In defending this action, he had argued that "segregated schools are a deterrent to full equality of opportunity and personally I think [this is] true for white as well as Negro children."[8] Yet, five years later, such a heavy-handed approach to integration was no longer in vogue. In 1968, the New York state legislature responded to racial unrest in New York City by decentralizing the administration of the city's public schools. Emphasizing a need for "community advisory councils" to guide the implementation of school policies, the legislature gave power to a number of locally elected neighborhood boards and made them responsible for promoting more effective programs. By this time, demands for "community control" had outpaced demands for racial balance, and Allen was obliged to soften his appeals for integration. Instead, he encouraged minority parents to run their own local schools. Eventually, federal officials embraced New York's approach and required all Title I schools to incorporate parents "in the early stages of program planning and in discussions concerning the needs of children in the various eligible attendance areas."[9] Ultimately, Allen built his federal commissionership around the goal of making inner-city schools more "effective" *despite* their racial imbalance.[10]

Allen's concerns for the effectiveness of inner-city schools arose, in part, in response to a barrage of criticism that bombarded the federal Office of Education in the spring of 1969. In March of that year, two policy analysts—Ruby Martin of the Southern Center for Studies in Public Policy and Phyllis McClure of the NAACP Legal Defense and Education Fund—released a scathing critique of Title I. Their study, *Title I of ESEA: Is It Helping Poor Children?*, asserted that a number of states, including Massachusetts, had misused Title I funds and, in the process, had undermined the program's goals. They discovered, for example, that Title I funds in Boston had not been equitably distributed to inner-city schools; instead, Title I funds flowed disproportionately to suburban schools.[11] Furthermore, when auditors from the federal Department of Health, Education, and Welfare examined the records of Title I programs in Massachusetts, they found abominable data-collection practices: "inadequate time and attendance records, lack of substantiation of overtime pay to [Title I] teachers, inadequate accounting procedures covering contractual services, inadequate equipment controls and unremitted unused funds."[12] Most shocking of all, Martin and McClure saw no attempt in Massachusetts—or in any other state—to document the connection between Title I expenditures and academic achievement among Title I's poor minority recipients. Since federal evaluation forms did not require schools to show a link between Title I expenditures and classroom instruction—let alone between expenditures and achievement—schools generally did not collect this information.[13] As scholars David Cohen and

Tyll van Geel noted in their own review of Title I grants, "the analysis in the state [program evaluation] report is meaningless . . . because the data it collected could serve no conceivable evaluative purpose. Collecting information was, in the strict sense of the word, futile."[14]

With 466 Title I projects costing $16 million a year, Massachusetts had been very successful in attracting federal resources—but much less successful in documenting the effectiveness of federal programs in raising achievement.[15] For example, when Jerome T. Murphy of the Harvard Graduate School of Education analyzed the annual reports of one school system "in the metropolitan Boston area," he discovered that the "evaluation of its reading program concludes that the overall effect of Title I has been a positive one, citing the fact that fourth-grade Title I children went from 5 months behind non-Title I pupils in September, 1967, to 4 months behind in June, 1968, on a standardized reading test. Examination of the supporting data indicate that the gap did close. The report, however, failed to point out the reason [for the change]: the non-Title I group regressed 2 months in reading during the year, while the Title I group fell back only one month. Although the net result may [indicate] a closing of the gap, these data hardly support the conclusion of positive benefits under Title I."[16] Murphy's patent conclusion was that Title I grants were being wasted on educationally ineffective programs. In fact, when policy makers inquired in 1969 whether Title I had "worked" three years after its passage, they found very little information on which to base such a judgment. Instead, they discovered (belatedly) that Title I had been devised as a financial delivery system: schools were asked to record only how many low-income students participated, how much federal money they had received, how they spent federal grants on special-compensatory programs, and how many more students were expected to participate in these programs the next year.[17] Nowhere on any of the evaluation forms were schools asked to list the academic benefits that might derive from Title I programs. Taking such outcomes for granted, federal agencies focused instead on the delivery of funds to low-income (and, often, racially imbalanced) schools.

To expect academic gains as a direct outcome of Title I was to resurrect a core expectation of the program. The program was created to direct federal funds to low-income students—the assumption being that more funds would somehow facilitate higher achievement—yet, as early as 1967, Robert Kennedy had commented in reference to the ESEA that "I question whether anything is being accomplished in a major way. . . . I also seriously question whether the people in the ghettos feel anything is really being done." Similarly, in 1969, secretary of health, education, and welfare Robert Finch told a congressional budget hearing that "from the massive evidence we have, I do not think we can claim unqualified success [for Title I]. . . . Many curriculum developers are not aware of the best methods of meeting the educational needs of poverty children. Schools and school districts differ greatly in their capacity to provide quality educational programs for disadvantaged children." Likewise, a new National Advisory Council on the Education of Disadvantaged Children examined hundreds of Title I programs and concluded that only 2 percent were successful—where *success* was defined as "measurable gains in language or arithmetical skills." (A year earlier, the National Advisory Council had discovered that "only a small portion [of Title I money] was spent on genuinely new approaches to guiding and stimulating learning.")[18] Yet, four years after the passage of the ESEA, when federal officials looked for a connection between federal grants and academic improvement, they found none. Instead, they found a program exacerbating "de facto" segregation in urban schools and relegating poor minority students to academically ineffective programs. As Harold Howe II confessed, "I doubt that anyone could have dreamed up a series of education programs more difficult to administer and less likely to avoid problems in the course of their administration, but [the] ESEA was not designed with that in mind."[19]

Robert Jeffrey, director of Massachusetts's 400-plus Title I projects, was at a loss to explain these dismal results, but others placed the blame squarely on the *federal* Office of Education. Julie Roy Jeffrey, for example, blamed the federal government for failing to provide states with adequate resources for program administration. "Although Title I set aside 1 percent of the state's Title I grant to pay administrative and evaluation costs," she wrote, "this sum was too small to have real impact on [state] departments of education. In 1968 Massachusetts, for example, received a mere $160,000. The state had only five full-time people working on more than 440 Title I projects. With other duties this staff could not even hope to visit the many projects during the year. It certainly could not do a thorough investigation to see how Title I was working in local communities."[20] In *ESEA: The Office of Education Administers a Law,* Stephen Bailey and Edith Mosher noted that the federal Office of Education had been woefully underprepared to monitor such a large-scale federal aid-to-education program—or even to help states do so. They argued that Title I had no clear objectives beyond the delivery of financial resources, and they criticized the ESEA for failing to make strong connections between financial resources and academic achievement. It was ambiguous, for example, whether Title I was supposed to serve *only* children whose parents earned less than $2,000 annually or whether it could serve those whose parents may have earned more but whose academic achievement was nonetheless below average; often, Title I programs enrolled students who were not poor.[21] Federal auditors found that "Title I benefited a larger number of scholastically able children from economically solid families than disadvantaged children." Similarly, they noted, "in the suburbs, over half of the children receiving Title I services were not disadvantaged."[22]

Evidently, regardless of their intent, Title I programs failed not only to decrease segregation or increase achievement, but also, in many cases, to reach poor students. By the spring of 1969, it was clear that "funds appropriated under the Act [were] being used for general school purposes: to initiate system-wide programs, to buy books and supplies for all school children in the system; to pay general overhead and operating expenses; to meet new teacher contracts which call for higher salaries; to purchase all-purpose school facilities; and to equip superintendents' offices with paneling, wall-to-wall carpeting and color televisions."[23] In Louisiana, schools used Title I aid to install swimming pools, and, in Rhode Island, parents lobbied to use Title I for clothing allowances. In Massachusetts, officials routinely tallied the number of poor children eligible for Title I and then used the money allocated for these children to support academic enrichment programs for students in the suburbs. Thus, even though federal funds were *allocated* to students on the basis of low income, funds were *applied* in classrooms on the basis of low test scores. Of course, children with low scores—those considered to be culturally and educationally deprived—were typically poor, but the ambiguity of the ESEA allowed funds to flow increasingly to low-achieving students who lived in affluent districts. In fact, for several years in a row, Boston actually *returned* aid to the federal government instead of redirecting it to needier areas. As auditors from the Department of Health, Education, and Welfare noted in 1969, "even though the amount of $263,000 was unused by the City of Boston in fiscal year [1968-69], we found that certain eligible attendance areas with high concentrations of children from low-income families . . . were receiving minimal services for meeting the special educational needs of these children."[24] Despite the city's dire need for money, Boston allowed more than $1 million in Title I grants to lapse in 1967, 1968, and 1969.[25]

By 1969, issues of Title I implementation and effectiveness had climbed to the top of the federal education agenda. Calls emerged for a thorough testing of Title I recipients' educational outcomes. The following spring, the *Christian Science Monitor* asked, "Are Boston's Schools Passing Title I Test?" In this article, Daniel Coughlin, staff director of Boston's educational enrichment programs, acknowledged that, four years after Title I's implementation in Boston, test scores had not substantially improved. His explanation for this situation, however, was illuminating. The problem, he insisted, was not that the city's Title I programs were academically ineffective but, rather, that the tests used to evaluate these programs failed to gauge all the ways in which Title I had benefited poor minority students in the inner city. In other words, the fault lay not with the programs but, rather, with the tests. "Coughlin states that this testing does not go far enough in evaluating what real progress has been made in educating a child," the *Monitor* reported. "The tests do not register changes in a child's attitude toward education. And, he says, they are not geared to a child's experience in the inner city." Robert Jeffrey similarly noted that "the biggest battle facing the Title I administration is the development of a diagnostic and evaluative strategy. 'In all of education,' he says, 'nothing is weaker than methods for making clear evaluations about a child's progress. When Title I comes along and demands it [academic achievement as a sign of 'program effectiveness'], communities do not have the facilities to evaluate [other aspects of their Title I programs]. The tests which cities administer [only] register achievement, but attitude, motivation, and the child's self-concept are not really measured.'" Thus, Jeffrey asserted, "complaints that Title I programs are not adequately diagnosing [or improving] academic achievement can be seen as part of a larger problem common to all education."[26] In sum, proof of Title I's effectiveness required different tests.

The issue of evaluating program "effectiveness" had puzzled observers ever since *Hobson v. Hansen* had cast doubt on the validity of standardized tests as a useful measure of performance among inner-city students. If federally funded programs were supposed to raise students' performance, and if standardized tests were not a fair measure of minority students' achievement, then what sort of assessments could officials use to gauge whether federally funded programs had met their primary objectives in ghetto schools? Professor Daniel C. Jordan of the University of Massachusetts-Amherst researched this question in 1969 and 1970. His analysis, "Compensatory Education in Massachusetts: An Evaluation with Recommendations," came up with forty-eight different suggestions. At the top of his list were: "(1) Establish appropriate program objectives, operationally defined, and center all planning on these objectives; (2) Establish sound evaluation components in all Title I projects for use in systematic modifications towards program improvement." As Jordan noted, Title I in Massachusetts was plagued by a lack of consensus about the *purpose* of federally funded education programs. Were they supposed to direct financial assistance to inner-city schools, were they supposed to improve achievement, or were they supposed to facilitate equal educational opportunities in some other way—such as racial integration? In Boston and other cities, Jordan noticed "a growing disillusionment" with Title I.

"The reason for the frustration is clear," he underlined: *"this kind of education is not producing significant results of lasting value in sufficient numbers of students fast enough to deal with a problem [low achievement] that has already reached vast proportions and is still growing at an alarming rate."*[27] According to Jordan, if improving academic achievement was a primary goal of federal aid to education, then Title I needed to do a much better job of meeting that goal in order to justify continued federal support.

⬦

The need for better evidence of program "effectiveness" led federal commissioner Allen, together with New York policy advisor Daniel Patrick Moynihan, to propose a new National Institute of Education to analyze all federal education programs and, specifically, to study the link between federal aid and academic achievement in inner-city schools.[28] Allen also launched a federal Right to Read effort in which he tied federal aid directly to schools' ability to document gains in reading scores. Allen commented, "other commissioners had advocated legislation and money to deal with specific problems, but none had ever taken a particular curriculum area and, setting both the target and the timetable, challenged the country and the educational system to do something about it." This notion of federal intervention in the curriculum, together with the notion of linking aid to achievement, was new in 1969–70. Previous administrations had not required direct evidence of a link between federal aid and student achievement—perhaps because asking for such evidence might lead to requests for resources to *ensure* that all students had sufficient opportunity to reach particular levels of achievement—but Allen had a specific reason for seeking proof of academic achievement: he wanted to show that federal money was not being squandered on ineffective programs. In his words, "with respect to the Right to Read program, the staff of the office of education was enthusiastic and there was an enormous amount of favorable response throughout the country, particularly the private sector. There seemed to be a readiness to accept guidance and leadership in this area, indicating to me that, if the Commissioner of Education spoke out, he could have an influence far beyond the dollars that might be involved." Stressing in particular the need for a link between aid and achievement in poor minority districts, Allen emphasized "the interest of the administration in channeling available funds more in the direction of the disadvantaged."[29]

Allen's initiatives at the federal level were not lost on activists in Boston. In fact, nearly all his ideas, from concentrating resources in urban areas to increasing community participation in local reforms, found support among grassroots organizers in Boston who were already engaged in similar efforts of their own. In early December 1968, and again in late January 1969, a broad-based coalition of urban activists (social workers, lawyers, academics, clergy, and parents) met to discuss the problems confronting Boston's inner-city schools—particularly the need for more "effective" programs for students in ghetto areas. Representatives from dozens of community organizations, including the Urban League, the South End Neighborhood Action Program, the Learning Disabilities Foundation, Inc., the Summer Program for Spanish-Speaking Children, and the Boston Legal Assistance Project, agreed that Boston was not doing enough for poor and minority students. In February 1969, these groups founded a Task Force on Children Out of School to study the need for additional programs in under-resourced schools.[30] It would be difficult to overstate the influence of this Task Force. Over the next three years, it fundamentally reshaped the priorities of education in the city's most disadvantaged areas. Like progressive reformers at the turn of the century, it polled citizens, presented data, and publicized ideas in ways that made its presence hard to ignore. It conducted surveys, coordinated fundraisers, and captured the attention of both the public and the press. It maintained close ties with university and government officials, and it put forward a simple message: Boston's schools were denying thousands of poor minority pupils access to equal educational opportunities and, unless the schools developed more effective special-compensatory programs to meet their needs, the Task Force would file charges in federal court.

The Task Force presented this ultimatum in a manifesto titled *The Way We Go to School: The Exclusion of Children in Boston*. "This report probably will make you very angry," its first line read. "It describes the almost unbelievable experiences that happen every day to thousands of school-age children in Boston. . . . At a time when the public schools must take giant strides to prepare children for today's world, some children are being excluded from school, others discouraged from attending, and still others placed in special classes for the 'inferior.' . . . We cannot overstress our most basic conclusion that the situation we have uncovered presents us with an extreme emergency."[31] With these words, the Task Force launched an attack on the most intractable problems in the Boston public schools: the exclusion of non-English-speaking, disabled, and other "exceptional" students from regular classrooms; the placement of low-performing minority students in programs for the mentally, physically, or emotionally handicapped; the misdiagnosis and misclassification of students with only mild learning difficulties; the use of standardized tests thought to discriminate against racial minorities; and the denial of equal educational opportunities as evidenced by disparate academic outcomes between white and minority students. The Task Force did not focus on the issue of racial imbalance in ghetto schools; rather, it focused on ways inner-city schools could improve educational outcomes among their students—particularly their non-English-speaking and disabled students. This emphasis on improving urban schools *despite* persistent racial imbalance appealed to leaders at both the local and the federal level who no longer saw integration as the only path to effective education for minority students. Rather than promoting racial balance at the school level, Task Force members pursued new programs at the classroom level in hopes that new programs would meet the needs of Boston's most disadvantaged students.

Chairing the Task Force on Children Out of School was Hubert E. "Hubie" Jones, the young black director of the Roxbury Multi-Service Center, an agency created in 1966 with federal aid from the Model Cities Program. The twenty-one member Task Force also included Raquel Cohen of the Harvard Laboratory for Community Psychiatry (an expert on emotionally disturbed children), Phyllis Oram of the department of child psychiatry at Boston University Medical School, Mario Clavell of the Federation of Spanish-Speaking Organizations, and Rollins Griffith of the Massachusetts Negro Educators' Association.[32] The group also included Michael Daly of Massachusetts's state House of Representatives (who chaired the education committee), Stephen Rosenfeld of the Lawyer's Committee for Civil Rights, and two young assistant superintendents from the Boston public schools: Thomas McAuliffe, the director of special education, and Alice Casey, the coordinator of bilingual programs. For obvious reasons, neither McAuliffe nor Casey endorsed the Task Force's manifesto. They maintained that *other* departments at the state level, such as the Department of Mental Health, were responsible for the care of "at-risk" students (including those who were culturally disadvantaged or language deficient) and reminded the Task Force that, in Massachusetts, the Department of Mental Health was, technically, responsible for most special-compensatory programs. The Task Force on Children Out of School, however, sought to end the conflation of disadvantage and disability. It filled its board with mental health professionals who believed poor minority students were failing in school not because they were disabled (and, therefore, incapable of average academic achievement) but, rather, because their schools' programs, while purportedly designed to help, all too often hurt their chances of academic success. Insofar as these programs yielded racially disparate outcomes, the Task Force claimed, they were racially discriminatory.

The psychologists on the Task Force rejected the long-held assumption that poor minority students were disproportionately likely to suffer from cognitive deficiencies and asserted, instead, that public schools were ill-equipped to meet the needs of students who did not fit a traditional white, middle-income, English-speaking, average-achieving norm. Rather than promoting the success of diverse students, the Task Force contended, schools simply labeled poor minority students "retarded" and relegated them to isolated remedial programs (typically funded by state or federal aid). As the Task Force noted in *The Way We Go to School*, "the operation of the school system is predicated on a pupil-excluding definition of normality which affects larger and larger numbers of children. This narrow definition grows from a disease-oriented use of categorical labels which is inappropriate for the education of children. The schools focus almost exclusively on the 'differentness' of certain groups of children—as if being different were indicative of shortcomings in the children [themselves]." The time had come, the Task Force asserted, to hold inner-city schools responsible for the educational success of *all* students—including poor minority students—without identifying them as "disabled" or placing them in remedial classes. "If the schools are to fulfill the public responsibility for the educational development of our children," the Task Force declared, "then they must be organized to do everything in their power to draw children into the educational process. Special services and programs must be utilized to help children remain part of, or return to, the regular school process, instead of being used to remove them from participation."[33] Defining the regular classroom as the normative setting for all students, the Task Force on Children Out of School insisted that in order to avoid charges of discrimination or disparate treatment, inner-city schools had to serve all students together in the *same* learning environment.

Yet, herein lay a dilemma. On the one hand, schools had long been devising new programs to meet the needs of specific groups of educationally disadvantaged or disabled students—generally in isolated settings and often with the help of "categorical" grants. On the other hand, the Task Force hoped to define the regular classroom as the normative environment for every student. Could it work both ways? Could schools demonstrate the effectiveness of special-compensatory programs and, at the same time, place all students in regular classes? The Task Force on Children Out of School thought so. "All children, regardless of differences and abilities, should be encouraged to participate fully in regular school curricula and activities," it contended. "In the educational process, children should neither be excluded from a full educational opportunity nor isolated according to ability grouping. The only rationale for grouping is the provision of *temporary* help to accelerate the development of children with specific needs. As a general rule, children with different abilities should be integrated into the regular school environment. When certain children reach the limit of their abilities to function in that environment, then their specific needs must be identified and met, but not at the cost of excluding them from activities in which they are capable of participating."[34] According to members of the Task Force on Children Out of School, the way to guarantee that all students received an education that was both "effective" and "non-discriminatory" was to provide supplemental services to meet their individual needs and, simultaneously, to integrate these services into a regular classroom environment. In effect, it suggested—perhaps paradoxically—that all students (including those with average or above-average achievement) were entitled not only to supplemental services but also to placement in a regular class. In this way, the Task Force reasoned, the most *inclusive* classroom would also become the most *effective* classroom (or vice versa).

⟡

The Task Force's pursuit of new special-compensatory programs encompassed all poor minority students in Boston, but its agenda for reform centered first on one group in particular: non-English-speakers. The decision to pursue new programs for non-English-speaking students was strategic. In September 1969—less than a month before the Task Force first gathered in Boston—the federal Office of Civil Rights had held a series of congressional hearings to discuss the exclusion of non-English-speaking students from the nation's public schools. These hearings had been organized by J. Stanley Pottinger of the Office of Civil Rights and included, among others, Massachusetts's senator Edward Kennedy. At the hearings, Kennedy called for more federal aid to bilingual programs, stating that the federal government had "a responsibility to fill the vacuum produced by the failure of local and state educational institutions to meet the needs of the limited English-speaking."[35] In the winter of 1969 and into the spring of 1970, as Congress prepared for the first official reauthorization of the Elementary and Secondary Education Act—including Title VII for bilingual education—the idea of increasing federal grants for bilingual programs gained momentum. At the same time, Pottinger used what he had learned from his congressional hearings the previous summer to draft a memorandum on public schools' legal *obligation* to provide bilingual programs for non-English-speaking students. It was this memo, more than anything else, that persuaded the Task Force on Children Out of School to focus its efforts on the needs of non-English-speaking students in Boston. This emphasis was well-timed, but it raised a number of complex issues related to the links between inclusiveness and effectiveness in special-compensatory programs. In the case of bilingual education, it seemed clear that, in order to be "effective," programs for non-English-speaking students had to be *isolated* from regular (English-speaking) classrooms—at least temporarily.

On May 25, 1970, in his memo titled "Identification of Discrimination and Denial of Services on the Basis of National Origin," Pottinger held that a failure to provide equal opportunities to non-English-speaking students—that is, a failure to offer these students effective programs to compensate for their language deficiencies—would be considered a violation of Title VI of the Civil Rights Act, which prohibited discrimination on the basis of "race, color, or national origin." He added that any school found to be discriminating against non-English-speaking (or, specifically, "Spanish-surnamed") students on the basis of their language ability (a proxy for their national origin) would run the risk of losing its federal aid under the ESEA and other programs. He outlined the details of this new policy in four parts: "(1) Where inability to speak and understand the English language excludes national origin–minority children from effective participation in the educational program offered by a school district, the district must take affirmative steps to rectify the language deficiency in order to open its instructional program to these students. (2) School districts must not assign national origin–minority group students to classrooms for the mentally retarded on the basis of criteria which essentially measure or evaluate English language skills. . . . (3) Any ability grouping or tracking system employed by the school system to deal with the special language skill needs of national origin–minority group children must be designed to meet their language skill needs as soon as possible and must not operate as an educational dead-end or permanent track. (4) School districts have a responsibility to adequately notify national origin–minority group parents of school activities which are called to the attention of other parents. Such notices in order to be adequate may have to be provided in a language other than English."[36] Each of these requirements, Pottinger noted, would be effective immediately.

This memo came as a wake-up call to schools throughout the nation and led many non-English-speaking parent groups to file suit against their local schools, demanding the creation of new programs to help overcome their children's language "deficiencies." The most famous of these lawsuits was *Lau v. Nichols,* filed in the spring of 1970 on behalf of Chinese-speaking students in San Francisco, but similar suits soon followed.[37] In Boston, just two weeks after Pottinger sent out his memo, the Massachusetts Commission Against Discrimination (MCAD), a state agency, sued the Boston public schools, citing probable cause that the schools were denying equal educational opportunities to thousands of non-English-speaking students in neighborhood schools. For MCAD, the crucial issue was not that schools were actively *excluding* non-English-speaking students or somehow blocking their access to class but, rather, that schools were *including* these students in classes they could not understand. This sort of inclusion, or linguistic immersion, MCAD argued, was discriminatory, because it failed to make the curriculum comprehensible to non-English-speaking students. Using Pottinger's memo to buttress its argument, MCAD insisted that unlawful discrimination occurred whenever ostensibly equal educational treatment—such as inclusion or immersion in "regular" (English-speaking) classes—resulted in *unequal* educational opportunities (as measured by unequal outcomes). According to MCAD, the policy of including *all* students in English-speaking classrooms offered equal opportunities only to English-speaking students. Based on the large number of non-English-speaking students in Boston who were not in school, MCAD alleged that the city was failing to meet their needs and was, therefore, failing to provide them with an equal—or effective—education. When it came to non-English-speaking students, MCAD argued, "inclusion" amounted to discrimination.

According to MCAD, the only way to ensure equal educational opportunities for non-English-speaking students was to develop *isolated* special-compensatory programs to facilitate the more or less rapid acquisition of English. In his memorandum, Pottinger had implied that bilingual classes, in order to be acceptable, could *not* be integrated into the "regular" English-speaking classroom. If anything, he implied that integrating a bilingual program wholly into a regular classroom would not only limit its effectiveness but would also subject non-English-speaking students to the very same kinds of hazards—linguistic immersion and cultural assimilation—they had resisted in the past. A far better approach, he hinted, was to develop strictly isolated bilingual-transitional classes on a daily pullout basis. In his memo, Pottinger had explained that bilingual programs should facilitate the acquisition of English "as soon as possible" and should not become a "permanent track," but he had *not* stated that bilingual programs for non-English-speaking students should be integrated into regular classes.[38] Instead, in an attempt to avoid discrimination, he implied that bilingual programs must be *isolated* from regular classes. He himself acknowledged that "the classroom separation of non-English-speaking students for educational purposes is not a violation of equal rights as long as it aims at their eventual integration into the regular program and does not last a full day."[39] While Pottinger never specified exactly how long students could be isolated from regular classrooms before their isolation could be considered "discriminatory" (or at least no better than total exclusion from the regular class), he had a clear preference for isolated over integrated bilingual programs. Indeed, in his view, total integration into a regular classroom environment was the very problem bilingual education was supposed to solve.

In a move with profound implications for the future, MCAD accepted Pottinger's preference for isolated bilingual-transitional programs and made the demand for isolated programs a central component of its ongoing litigation against the Boston public schools. This move ensured the support of Pottinger's Office of Civil Rights as well as the federal Department of Health, Education, and Welfare (which housed the civil rights office)—and its timing was propitious. In August 1970, Secretary of Health, Education, and Welfare Robert Finch had resigned and had been replaced by Elliot Richardson, who left his job as undersecretary of state to resume his old connection with HEW. Although Richardson had not been with HEW since the Eisenhower administration, he had stayed abreast of changes in federal education policy—especially the Nixon administration's concern for the effectiveness of federally funded programs. Now, faced with the need to develop programs for non-English-speaking students, Richardson agreed wholeheartedly with Pottinger that an effective bilingual program was one that facilitated the acquisition of English in an isolated classroom setting. Indeed, in the interest of effective education, he readily endorsed the idea of access to isolated bilingual education as a basic *civil right*. The importance of this endorsement could hardly be overstated.[40] For the first time in any federally funded education program, isolation from the regular classroom was defined as a civil right—and Richardson embraced this view. In fact, when the U.S. Supreme Court took up the issue of bilingual education two years later, Richardson filed a brief in amicus curiae to ensure that the court based its decision on the Civil Rights Act and not on the Fourteenth Amendment. His rationale was subtle: the Fourteenth Amendment might have required classroom integration, but the Civil Rights Act permitted isolation so long as it promised better—or more "effective"—results.[41]

By the fall of 1970, the idea of isolated bilingual programs won support not only from federal officials, but also (rather surprisingly) from the Task Force on Children Out of School. It was time, the Task Force concluded, for schools to develop new programs to draw non-English-speaking youth off the city's streets and into the city's schools. If these programs were isolated from regular classes but effective in attracting students to school, then Task Force members showed a willingness to endorse them—and particularly if they improved student achievement. (Apparently, "effectiveness" could trump "inclusiveness.") According to the Task Force, the need for bilingual programs was great. *The Way We Go to School* documented innumerable cases of truancy among non-English-speakers and presented these cases in vivid detail: "A Puerto Rican community worker canvassed his own block in the South End. He found fifteen Spanish-speaking children on that one street who did not go to school. Nuns teaching at an elementary school reported that from their classroom windows, they saw Puerto Rican children each day playing in the streets during school hours. A grocery store manager told of the large number of children he sees regularly in the homes where he delivers food each day. In a short time, he pointed out over eighteen of these homes. . . . Some of these families had six or more children in the them. During the summer of 1969, Spanish-speaking workers conducted a summer program for Puerto Rican and other Spanish-speaking children. Of 400 children who attended, one in eight had never been to school before. Many others had once attended but no longer did so. On the basis of these individual studies and observations, Sister Frances Georgia declared: '. . . by any standards, the fact is incontestable that hundreds and hundreds of Puerto Rican children are not in school at all. They are visibly roaming the streets or just allowed to stay at home.'"[42] It was time, the Task Force argued, to draw these students into school.

To illustrate the need for isolated bilingual-transitional programs, the Task Force asked one of its members, Raquel Cohen, associate director of the Harvard Laboratory for Community Psychiatry and a consultant to the Boston public schools, to verify the precise number of non-English-speaking students who were not in school. Such a verification was important, because Pottinger's memo had been addressed specifically to "School Districts With More Than Five Percent National Origin-Minority Group Children."[43] Thus, in order for federal civil rights provisions to apply in Boston, the city had to find at least 5,000 of its 100,000 students who could benefit from bilingual programs.[44] On October 1, 1970, Cohen led dozens of activists—as well as television and newspaper reporters—on a "walking tour" of the city's Cuban and Puerto Rican districts. Strolling alongside Cohen were a number of prominent federal officials, including Harold Putnam, regional director of HEW; Walter Agnew, regional education commissioner of HEW; and Carmelo Iglesias, a representative from the federal Office of Civil Rights. Putnam (who had replaced Walter Mode as regional director of HEW) called the tour a "showdown" between the school committee and the Task Force on Children Out of School. He told the *Boston Herald* that he and other federal officers wanted to "see for themselves how many school-age Puerto Rican children are not attending school." He asserted that "officials of the Boston school department admit there may be 900, and we have other estimates ranging up to 5,000. We mean to find out the facts and do something about them."[45] The federal officers' presence on this "walking tour" evidently had an effect, because, immediately after it was over, the school committee agreed to a new survey of non-English-speaking children in Boston to determine how many were not in school.[46]

The survey was done by Action for Boston Community Development (ABCD)—and, when its findings were unveiled, it was clear that Boston met the 5,000-pupil cut-off for federally mandated bilingual programs. As the *Boston Globe* noted, "2,500 Spanish-speaking children are enrolled in public schools" and "2,500 Spanish-speaking children of school age are not enrolled."[47] The Task Force brought these figures to the attention of the school committee and warned that a failure to create new bilingual programs in inner-city schools would trigger litigation. The Task Force advised the committee to "officially recognize that an emergency situation exists in the Boston public schools insofar as there are no educational programs for several thousand Spanish-speaking children" and then to "institute emergency action and planning to . . . provide full-time bilingual transitional programs taught by instructors fluent in the children's native language as well as English." The Task Force also suggested that the committee "waive the Boston Teachers Examination and other unnecessary obstacles which might impede the hiring of qualified teachers and administrators," recruit "bilingual parents and community leaders to serve as classroom assistants," and guarantee "counseling and tutoring programs for non-English-speaking children to encourage them to stay in high school." Furthermore, since so many non-English-speaking children were classified as truants, the Task Force urged the school committee to "discontinue the punitive orientation toward children who are truant by: (a) making the services to these children a function of trained counselors who work in the community as well as the school [and by] (b) hiring counselors from lists submitted by community agencies, to reflect an ethnic spread in correlation with sections of the city."[48] Also, in order to foster parent involvement, the Task Force recommended the placement of bilingual clusters in areas with large concentrations of non-English-speaking residents.

At a meeting of the Boston school committee in November 1970, the Task Force reiterated its appeal for more bilingual programs in the inner city but confronted intense opposition from two committee members, Joseph Lee and Paul Tierney, who insisted that existing programs met student needs (the same view that Superintendent Ohrenberger had expressed two years earlier). As the *Globe* observed, "The hearing was marked by heated argument at times, with Tierney and Lee insisting that the problem was not as bad as the Task Force had said." The Task Force on Children Out of School came armed, however, with detailed statistics to support its claims. Larry Brown, a staff researcher employed by the

Task Force, said he knew of "1,000 documented cases of Spanish-speaking children not in school." Yet, when Joseph Lee requested a list of these truants, Brown refused, fearing punishment for truants and saying it was pointless to name these students when the schools had no programs to accommodate them. With more than one hundred children already on waiting lists for existing bilingual programs, Brown asked, "What would you do with 1,000?" Throughout the meeting, the members of the school committee—and Tierney and Lee in particular—maintained that they had done more to help Spanish-speaking students than they had done to help any other immigrant group. According to the *Globe*, "Lee told the group that Puerto Ricans and Cubans in the city should be glad they are getting as much special help as they are. He then listed several other nationalities and said, 'Let the record be clear that we are doing more for you than we've ever done for these others, and actually we have no right to go ahead with these special programs.'" However, Mario Clavell of the Federation of Spanish-Speaking Organizations took umbrage at this remark and "drew applause when he told Lee he was an 'American citizen who wants only equal protection under the law and equal educational opportunity for my people.'"[49]

Clearly, the school committee was not ready to recognize bilingual education as a "civil right," particularly when the committee received only limited financial assistance to cover the costs of bilingual-transitional clusters.[50] According to the *Boston Globe*, Paul Tierney "was distressed by the task force's critical tone. He said the fact that the city will spend about $1 million of its own money this year in addition to $300,000 from federal sources on classes for the Spanish-speaking was 'a great response.'" And, yet, financial excuses did not garner much sympathy after it was discovered that Tierney and his fellow committee members had decided to spend nearly $100,000 the next year on salary increases for dual department heads at the Boston Latin School. As the *Globe* noted, "The Boston school committee pleaded yesterday that it did not have the money to expand bilingual education for Spanish-speaking children who are not in school, then a few minutes later approved spending nearly $100,000 to retain dual department heads at the prestigious Boston Latin School. The members made no connection between these two actions, but together they provided one of the clearest displays to date of the committee's priorities for the city schools. . . . The Latin School vote was taken only a few minutes after committee told representatives from the Task Force on Children Out of School that the major obstacle to expanding bilingual classes is lack of city money and the fact that the state provides no assistance to communities for that purpose. A school official said later that the dual department heads, six of them, will cost about $100,000 a year, enough to provide bilingual classes for an estimated 100 young-sters."[51] Although federal officials had defined bilingual education as a civil right, the school committee nonetheless refused to add bilingual clusters in Boston until the city received more state or federal aid to pay for them.[52]

◈

As it happened, the committee did not have to wait long for aid. The pos-sibility of federal litigation strengthened a movement in the state legis-lature to reimburse schools for the excess costs associated with bilingual programs. In the winter of 1970, Task Force member and state representa-tive Michael Daly had submitted a bill requesting state aid for bilingual programs. This bill passed but received no funding. As the *Boston Herald* explained, "Michael J. Daly (D-Boston), a member of the Task Force, filed a bill which would have supplied from $250,000 up to $4 million statewide over the next five years for bi-lingual education programs, but it never got by the Senate Ways and Means Committee."[53] However, when Daly resubmitted his bill in 1971, it had more success.[54] Among its key supporters were Massachusetts governor Francis Sargent and Bos-ton mayor Kevin White, both of whom had come to recognize the rising demand for bilingual-transitional classes in the inner city. Despite the provisions of Massachusetts's racial imbalance law, both the mayor and the governor supported the placement of new bilingual-transitional classes in areas with large concentrations of non-English-speaking (as well as nonwhite) students. Hoping these classes would foster academic achievement among poor minority students, they convinced themselves that the classroom isolation of non-English-speaking students did not necessarily constitute discrimination. They accepted the idea that differ-ent pupils with different needs required different educational services, and they trusted experts who told them that isolated bilingual programs would facilitate students' rapid acquisition of English. When the state Transitional Bilingual Education Act—also known as Chapter 71A—came up for a vote in May 1971, it passed easily. With Governor Sargent's signature, it became the first state law in the country to *mandate* isolated bilingual-transitional classes for non-English-speaking students.[55]

Chapter 71A required each district in Massachusetts to take a semi-annual census of all children (not just those in attendance) who were non-English-speakers and required any district with at least twenty non-English-speaking students to provide a transitional bilingual cluster. Chapter 71A also included strict enforcement provisions to ensure that schools met the law's requirements. Ernest Mazzone, Massachusetts's state director for bilingual-transitional education, explained that noncompliance with the law would carry the same penalties as noncompliance with the state's racial imbalance law—that is, the immediate withholding of state aid. "We will be watching closely to make sure [that all districts] exhaust every pressure to implement the law," Mazzone told a reporter from the *Boston Globe*. "In the beginning, the [bilingual-transitional] classes are to be taught in the students' native languages then gradually and to an increasing degree, in English. The aim is to develop the oral comprehension, speaking, reading and writing of English."[56] The irony, however, was that the state's new bilingual-transitional clusters—targeted as they were at inner-city schools—were almost *certain* to be racially imbalanced.[57] Thus, schools that hosted these clusters faced a difficult choice. If they accepted state aid for bilingual clusters, they risked aggravating the problem of racial imbalance by drawing non-white students into particular schools; yet, if they did not accept state aid for bilingual clusters, they risked charges of discriminating against non-English-speakers. What, then, was the best way to guarantee equal educational opportunities for non-English-speaking students: to provide them with isolated bilingual programs that would likely aggravate the level of de facto segregation in the city's schools, or to place them in regular (English-speaking) classes in racially balanced schools? By 1971, access to bilingual clusters was considered a civil right—but so, too, was racial balance.[58]

With promises of state aid to cover the excess costs of bilingual education, Boston quickly added bilingual clusters in its inner-city schools. By the fall of 1971, the city had launched six new clusters in the South End and eight in North Dorchester. Superintendent Ohrenberger announced that the new Department of Bilingual Education had "completed its second year of operation by fulfilling its goal of providing all of Boston's non-English-speaking children with full opportunity to receive an education that is both bilingual and bicultural. Services were expanded to embrace 3,500 pupils in 60 schools, including over 800 [students] in bilingual classes in Spanish, Italian, French, and Chinese."[59] The staff administering these programs increased from 92 to 139—an increase of 51 percent—and, with aid from Title I and Title VII, as well as Chapter 71A, clusters proliferated. In 1967, Boston had spent $95,000 on 750 non-English-speaking students; four years later, the city spent $1,803,418 on 3,775 students.[60] The Task Force on Children Out of School saw this rapid growth as a sign of progress. It did not worry that new bilingual-transitional clusters were isolated from regular classes and were housed in racially imbalanced schools—nor did the Task Force worry that students might be assigned to bilingual clusters to *prevent* them from attending otherwise racially balanced schools. Instead, the Task Force trusted Massachusetts's advisory committee to the federal Commission on Civil Rights, which held that Boston's bilingual education programs taught students English "through a bilingual-bicultural program, transferring them to the regular schools when they are able to compete adequately in English with their peers."[61] And, yet, this statement raised more questions than it resolved. For example, how long would it take a bilingual cluster to prepare non-English-speaking students to "compete adequately in English with their peers"—and how long was too long?

Unlike older ESL programs, which pulled students out of regular classrooms for approximately an hour a day, transitional-bilingual clusters pulled students out of regular classrooms—or entirely out of regular schools—for at least a half day at a time, and often for a full day, for years at a time, beginning as early as age three and ending as late as age twelve.[62] Brenda Beelar of Massachusetts's state Bureau of Equal Educational Opportunity noted that "in the past decade, there has been an ever expanding implementation of the bilingual approach for the education of children of limited English speaking ability. In many cases, these classes have been isolated from the regular school program. However, the intent of this isolation, for the most part, is to help the children develop their linguistic capabilities, not as a discriminatory mechanism." Defending Chapter 71A, Beelar insisted that "the intent of the law is *not* to segregate students of limited English speaking ability. The transitional bilingual education classes are required to be located in regular public schools, wherever feasible. Thus, the students can participate with other students in courses which do not require extensive verbalization, such as art, music and physical education. Students of limited English speaking ability should also be given full opportunity to participate in extra-curricular activities." None of these stipulations, however, diminished the fact that non-English-speaking students spent their time in racially imbalanced schools apart from English-speaking peers. Indeed, Chapter 71A gave schools a financial *incentive* to create isolated bilingual clusters that would be eligible for state aid. Even Beelar admitted that "the most pervasive approach to bilingual education seems to be the creation of isolated classes and these programs start in the first grade."[63] Superintendent Ohrenberger echoed this point: "We will continue to expand our programs and hope that next year every child will be in a classroom, and one in which his native language is spoken."[64]

In his annual report for 1971–72, Ohrenberger highlighted the recent opening of the Raphael Hernandez Elementary School in Roxbury. Noting that this new school was "the first ever in Boston to be named for a

Puerto Rican," Ohrenberger explained that the school's "student population was almost wholly Puerto Rican."[65] This announcement was revealing in two ways. First, it indicated that Boston was still engaged in an aggressive school-construction campaign. As Ohrenberger asserted, Boston was "reaping the harvest of what is probably the largest school building program in any of the world's major cities. A dozen new schools have opened within three years as part of a $300 million program in which 37 new schools will be built by 1975."[66] Second, and more importantly, Ohrenberger's admission that the Hernandez School "was almost wholly Puerto Rican" exposed the extent to which racial imbalance still characterized Boston's public schools. While Ohrenberger undoubtedly assumed that his emphasis on the racial composition of the Hernandez School would demonstrate how suitably its bilingual-transitional program served its non-English-speaking students, he overlooked the ways in which it drew attention to the issue of racial imbalance (if not the ways in which racial imbalance often went hand in hand with bilingual programs). Whereas he saw a targeted program and an effort to promote equal educational opportunity with the help of state aid, others saw a clear *denial* of equal educational opportunity due to the persistence of racial imbalance. At a time when bilingual programs and racial balance were both considered to be civil rights and essential to equal opportunity, the question was whether the Boston public schools could meet both requirements at once: could the schools add bilingual clusters in areas with large concentrations of non-English-speaking residents and, at the same time, avoid exacerbating racial imbalance in the inner city?[67]

In 1971, this question led to an awkward pair of investigations. In June 1971—immediately after the passage of Chapter 71A—the Massachusetts Commission Against Discrimination (MCAD) launched an investigation into the need for additional bilingual-transitional clusters in Boston. Five months later, in November 1971, the federal Office of Civil Rights launched an investigation to update information on racial imbalance in the Boston public schools. The question at the heart of both investigations was whether the schools could add bilingual programs without aggravating racial imbalance. The federal investigation was the first to reach an answer. On December 1, 1971, Stanley Pottinger announced he was freezing $10 million in federal aid to the Boston public schools due to persistent racial imbalance citywide. The irony of this announcement was, of course, that Pottinger's own policies with regard to bilingual-transitional clusters had led—at least in part—to Boston's predicament. Pottinger, however, placed the onus of responsibility for racial imbalance exclusively on the school committee. As the *Boston Globe* reported, "A landmark federal finding that the Boston school system is violating the civil rights act by discriminating against minority children is expected tomorrow. . . . J. Stanley Pottinger, head of the HEW civil rights office, will come to Boston tomorrow to brief Boston school superintendent William Ohrenberger on the report." The *Globe* added that "the city is already embroiled in legal actions brought by the state Department of Education and the Massachusetts Commission Against Discrimination. Both these agencies have charged the school system with discrimination. As a result, $14 million in state education aid to Boston has been frozen by court order. Another $30 million in state aid is also at stake [because the] state board [of education] must certify next year's funds by December 31 if Boston is to receive the money."[68]

At issue in these two investigations (one federal, one state) was the very definition of discrimination in the Boston public schools. On the one hand, the federal investigation suggested that the source of discrimination in the public schools was racial imbalance. On the other hand, the state investigation suggested that the source of discrimination for non-English-speaking students was the likelihood of inclusion in English-speaking classes (or, alternatively, a lack of access to isolated bilingual classes). Ironically, Stanley Pottinger found himself on both sides of this debate. In his memo on bilingual education, he clearly implied that it would be discriminatory to integrate non-English-speaking students fully into English-speaking classes before they were ready. Yet, in his decision to withhold money from Boston, he implied that it would be discriminatory *not* to integrate minority and nonminority students into the same—probably English-speaking—schools whenever possible. The pressing issue in December 1971, was whether the schools could continue to place non-English-speaking minority students in bilingual clusters near their homes—even if these clusters were housed in racially imbalanced neighborhood schools. Would Pottinger require Boston to move Puerto Rican students (many of whom were black) into predominantly white schools just to improve the city's overall racial balance—and, if so, would he allow local officials to place these students in isolated (and racially imbalanced) bilingual programs *within* predominantly white schools in order to guard against renewed charges of discrimination on linguistic grounds?[69] Even assuming Boston could persuade a significantly large number of Puerto Rican pupils to attend predominantly white schools (a dubious assumption at a time when racial separatism was growing), which aspect of this arrangement would ensure a nondiscriminatory education: integration into English-speaking schools or isolation from English-speaking classrooms?[70]

In December 1971, Pottinger could not answer this question.[71] Yet, he did not refrain from criticizing the Boston committee. He blamed the committee for "initiating actions which would create segregated schools, and, in effect, operating a 'dual school system.'" Similarly, Charles Glenn of the state Bureau of Equal Educational Opportunities told the *Boston Globe* that "the Boston school department is 'quite consciously' putting black children together in its schools." The number of racially imbalanced schools, including the Hernandez School, had increased by seven within the past year (though neither Pottinger nor Glenn saw the ways in which their own policies had contributed to this problem). By 1971, more than half of Boston's black students attended schools with enrollments that were at least 90 percent black, and that number was growing. School-committee member Paul Tierney pled that it was unfair to expect racial balance when minority students were moving into the city even as white students were moving away: "If the charges are true—and I have my doubts that we are maintaining a dual school system," Tierney argued, then "I know of no conscious act on the part of either the superintendent or the school committee to deprive any child of equal educational opportunity because of race."[72] Indeed, according to Tierney, the best way to guarantee equal educational opportunities in the inner city was not to withhold federal aid but, rather, to concentrate resources on well-designed and well-targeted programs such as the bilingual-transitional clusters at the Hernandez School.[73] It was ironic, Tierney noted, that state and federal officials accused the school committee of intentionally operating a dual school system when, from his perspective, the committee had simply done what such officials had mandated: it had created special-compensatory programs to draw poor minority students off the streets and into local neighborhood schools.[74]

⬡

In December 1971, few noticed the extent to which bilingual programs and racial balance might not be compatible goals, at least not in the immediate future. Based as they were on different conceptions of discrimination and different understandings of the link between "inclusiveness" and "effectiveness," bilingual programs and racial balance were hard to pursue at the same time. Only in retrospect, however, did a reason for their incompatibility become clear. In order for a bilingual program to be effective, its non-English-speaking minority students had to have access to a physically *isolated* class; yet, the pursuit of racial balance required the very same students be placed in *integrated* schools. Likewise, in a bilingual program, inclusion in a regular class was considered to be discriminatory; yet, the pursuit of racial balance made inclusion (or "immersion") in a regular class obligatory. Of course, the pursuit of racial balance on a district-wide basis did not preclude the placement of non-English-speaking minority students in isolated bilingual programs within predominantly white schools, but this approach had two major flaws: first, it was highly unlikely that non-English-speaking minority students would voluntarily attend English-speaking schools; second, if non-English-speaking minority students were required to attend pre-dominantly white schools only to be removed from regular classes, then the essential premise of racial balance as an educational goal—namely, that racial balance *itself* equalized opportunity—would falter, and offi-cials would have to recognize that equalizing opportunity depended not only on racial balance but also (and perhaps more importantly) on the availability of effective (and isolated) compensatory programs. Thus, in the final analysis, the key issue would not be integration or isolation but program effectiveness: if students achieved satisfactory results, then they would not file charges of discrimination—*regardless* of racial bal-ance or imbalance in their schools.[75]

It was Pottinger's job as head of the federal Office of Civil Rights to file charges of discrimination against school systems he thought were failing to provide equal access to educational opportunities. The prob-lem was that "discrimination" took different forms in different circum-stances, and neither the federal Office of Civil Rights nor the federal Office of Education had the resources to distinguish in any detailed manner which local practices actually promoted equal opportunities and which prevented them. In other words, federal officials lacked the capacity to monitor local uses of federal funds and make subtle infer-ences about the enforcement of federal priorities. In fact, Pottinger rarely knew when local school administrators were directing federal aid toward special-compensatory programs that drew students into specific inner-city neighborhood schools while, at the same time, aggravating racial imbalance. As early as January 1970, Professor Jerome Murphy at Harvard noticed that the Nixon administration had "not had enough people to effectively monitor" all the federally funded programs that had been developed in the past five years. He reported that, in "January, 1970, there were some thirty professionals working on all facets of Title I—technical assistance, accounting, program support—[and] . . . only three area desk officers for the entire nation. The one dealing with Mass-achusetts had responsibility for twenty-three other states, the District of Columbia, Puerto Rico, and the Virgin Islands. In addition to his Title I responsibilities, he spent approximately two-thirds of his time working on other projects at the bureau level having practically nothing to do with Title I."[76] Not surprisingly, this overworked bureaucrat expressed little interest in unraveling the subtle contradictions of bilingual programs and racial balance in the administration of federal grants.

Murphy described some of the dilemmas of federal oversight in an article for the *Harvard Educational Review*. The aforementioned bureaucrat, he wrote, "did not want to provide leadership, nor did he view himself as a program 'monitor' in the sense of being an enforcement officer. He readily admitted that he did not have the time to know what was going on in his states, and thus was dependent on information supplied by state officials as to whether they were enforcing the law." Even when such bureaucrats knew that federally funded programs were aggravating racial imbalance, they could not prevent this problem from occurring. As Murphy put it, "It is virtually impossible for USOE [the Office of Education] to cut off funds which the states view as their rightful entitlement under the law. The states know this and so does USOE; thus, orders or demands by USOE are bound to be ineffective since they cannot be backed up with action. Furthermore, demands might alienate the states and result in loss of communication. Since USOE's influence comes mostly from the power of persuasion and since it is presently almost totally reliant on the states for information about local programs, it is absolutely essential that USOE maintain cordial relations with the states. Under these bargaining conditions, the states are in a position to exact a price for their good will. As a result, USOE will be willing to sanction (perhaps covertly) deviations from the statute in exchange for open communications." In other words, the federal government had little leverage with local officials who openly ignored federal priorities. Murphy asserted, "since states receive their full entitlement for mere participation [in federal education programs]—as opposed to producing some specified result, or doing a good job—there are virtually no reasons to follow federal directives. State officials know that there would not be any major repercussions for ignoring federal directives, even with USOE's knowledge."[77]

Thus, the Boston school committee was free to use federal funds to create new bilingual programs in inner-city schools even as it disregarded federal demands to pursue racial balance. Even after Pottinger informed the committee that he would withhold $10 million in federal funds due to the persistence of racial imbalance, the committee did not respond, knowing that the federal Office of Civil Rights lacked the enforcement capacity to follow through on its threats.[78] Moreover, if challenged, the committee was prepared to argue that isolated bilingual-transitional clusters were the most effective way to equalize educational opportunities for non-English-speaking students, a point that Pottinger would have trouble refuting. As Murphy noted, obtaining federal funds did not necessarily mean pursuing racial balance: "not only has the federal thrust toward reform been absorbed by the [Boston] school system, it has been turned to the advantage of Boston to serve Boston's own needs."[79] Indeed, by the early 1970s, it seemed clear that federal aid had not prevented racial imbalance in the Boston public schools; if anything, federal aid had exacerbated the problem.[80] In May 1972, Pottinger himself acknowledged that non-English-speaking students throughout the country were being isolated from their English-speaking peers and were routinely "placed in classes for the mentally retarded because of their limited English-speaking ability."[81] Thus, despite explicit prohibitions against this practice in Pottinger's original memo identifying bilingual classes as a civil right, schools continued to claim that virtually *any* isolated class was acceptable so long as it promised "eventual integration into the regular program and [did] not last a full day." Indeed, as if to thumb its nose at its critics, the Boston school committee did precisely what federal officials—and many local activists—had wanted: it concentrated federal aid in special-compensatory programs in racially imbalanced inner-city schools.[82]

No one was happier about this unchanged state of affairs than Louise Day Hicks, who had long maintained that different students with different needs required different programs in different educational settings. In her view, racial imbalance did not necessarily imply racial discrimination, so the persistence of de facto segregation in the Boston public schools was no cause for concern. Hicks maintained these views throughout the debate on bilingual education—even as she changed political offices several times. In the fall of 1969, when the Task Force on Children Out of School convened for the first time, Hicks gave up her seat on the school committee to run for the city council. Then, in 1970, when the Task Force joined the Massachusetts Commission Against Discrimination in demanding additional bilingual clusters, Hicks left the city council to run for Congress. Campaigning in the heavily Irish-Catholic ninth district, she won a seat occupied for over four decades by John McCormack— who had served most recently as a powerful Speaker of the House. She quickly revealed, however, that she was more interested in Boston than in Washington, and, in the fall of 1971, shortly after the federal Office of Civil Rights reopened its investigation into racial imbalance in the Boston public schools, she launched a second bid for mayor. Her platform had only one plank—opposition to the state's racial imbalance law—and her strategy relied on strong denunciations of Neil Sullivan's busing plans. But Hicks could not defeat Kevin White, whose base of support had become virtually unshakable.[83] After the elections of 1971, she returned to Congress—only to hear Pottinger announce his decision to freeze $10 million in federal aid to Boston's racially imbalanced schools.

Meanwhile, debates in Boston over racial balance and classroom isolation shifted from non-English-speaking students to a different group—the mentally and emotionally disabled. Pottinger's discovery that non-English-speaking students were being placed in isolated programs for the mentally retarded shed light on a problem with a long history in Boston: the use of remedial classes as "dumping grounds" for students who did not fit the average-achieving norm. It was this problem—systematic misplacements and, often, total exclusion from school for various groups of marginalized students—that had spawned the creation of the Task Force on Children Out of School. Between 1969 and 1971, the Task Force's campaign to add new programs for non-English-speaking students had paralleled a campaign to add new programs for disabled students, and the two campaigns had taken very similar paths: a strong emphasis on fully integrated "regular" classes (defined as the only normative and nondiscriminatory learning environment for all students), followed, oddly, by an equally strong emphasis on isolated programs as the best way to provide an effective education for special-needs students. Like the campaign for bilingual education, the campaign for special education overlapped with a fierce debate in federal courts over the relationship between special-compensatory programs, classroom isolation, and racial discrimination. If the creation of isolated remedial classes met the needs of disabled minority students but, at the same time, perpetuated racial imbalance, then what should the schools do? Should they seek to enroll disabled minority students in racially balanced schools—only to place them in racially imbalanced special classes *within* those schools—or should they enroll disabled minority students in special classes regardless of racial imbalance? In the early 1970s, this question was difficult to answer, and Boston's experience with bilingual-transitional clusters offered little guidance.

CHAPTER FIVE

Making "Appropriate" Placements, 1971–1974

W hen the Boston public schools placed non-English-speaking students in isolated bilingual-transitional clusters, teachers were able to justify this practice on legal grounds. They argued that, since language proficiency affected students' learning ability, language *deficiency* constituted a learning *disability*. In other words, they argued, non-English-speaking students belonged to a bona fide "ability group" that could be clearly defined—and diagnosed—and then removed from regular classes on a categorical basis in order to provide "appropriate" special-compensatory educational assistance. This classification of non-English-speakers as members of a bona fide ability group was legally necessary, because it protected schools' isolated bilingual-transitional clusters from charges of racial discrimination. Even when these clusters were filled exclusively with minority students, schools were able to claim that students were isolated because of their disability, not their race. As two civil rights lawyers, Herbert Teitlebaum and Richard Hiller, explained in the *Harvard Educational Review* in the mid-1970s: "A bona fide ability grouping must meet four requirements. First, placement in the group must be based on educationally relevant, non-discriminatory, objective standards of measurement [beyond the mere assessment of language skills]. Second, the grouping must be maintained during the school day for only as long as necessary. Third, it must be designed to meet the students' special needs and to improve academic achievement and performance through specially developed curricula taught by specially trained instructional personnel. Finally, the grouping must be shown through objective testing to be educationally beneficial."[1] Thus, if schools isolated non-English-speaking minority students from their regular classrooms for a substantial part of the school day, they had to show that the policy of isolation was based neither on race nor on language background (that is, on national origin) but, rather, on "disability."

Needless to say, the classification of non-English-speaking students as a bona fide ability group called into question the meaning of the term *disability*—as well as its link to isolation as an educational practice. If disabled students could be isolated for "as long as necessary," then, at what point, if any, could the isolation of disabled students ever really be considered discriminatory—regardless of race or national origin? At what point could the isolation of disabled students ever become legally inappropriate? In Boston, the Task Force on Children Out of School had acquiesced in the isolation of non-English-speaking students, but only on a temporary basis and only until these students were fully prepared to participate in regular English-speaking classes. For non-English-speaking students, the term *disability* did not denote a clinical condition, a cognitive disorder, or some form of mental retardation. Instead, it denoted an easily remediable language deficit: with proper special-compensatory assistance, these students could return to regular classes and could "compete" on equal terms with their native-English-speaking classmates. Indeed, it was the hope that these students would eventually achieve equal outcomes in regular classes that made the practice of isolation tolerable—not only for non-English-speaking students, but for any student with "educational disadvantages."[2] The Task Force on Children Out of School assumed that, with proper access to effective special-compensatory programs, *all* disabilities would be remediable and *all* students could (eventually) be integrated into regular classrooms. The key question was how to tell when students really belonged in an isolated ability group and when they belonged in a regular class. How could schools tell when students were disabled—and, thus, entitled to isolated special-compensatory help—and when they ceased to be so? How could schools tell when isolated classes provided an appropriate education and when they actually provided a discriminatory education? In short, how could schools tell when students were truly disabled?

In Boston, in the early 1970s, these and various other related questions shaped the agenda of the Task Force on Children Out of School. After the passage of Chapter 71A and the provision of state aid for isolated bilingual-transitional clusters, the Task Force turned its attention to other "ability groups"—to students who were mentally retarded, physically or perceptually handicapped, or emotionally disturbed. The challenge in these cases was not unlike the challenge in the case of non-English-speaking students: to secure state funding for new special-compensatory programs while, at the same time, supporting the eventual integration of all students into regular classes. In the fall of 1970, the Task Force listed its goals for disabled students in its report, *The Way We Go to School*. Emphasizing above all the need for accurate diagnoses, the Task Force made several suggestions to improve the educational treatment of disabled pupils. Five stood out from the rest. First, "contract with public and private mental health clinics in the city for the immediate re-evaluation of all children who have been identified as retarded, whether they have been placed in 'special classes' or not." Second, "discontinue the classification of children as 'retarded' and the categorical placements of children in 'special classes' for the 'retarded.' Instead, identify children according to individual abilities and needs (by clinical evaluation), and structure their educational programs accordingly." Third, "provide remedial reading [assistance] to all children having the ability to improve [their] reading skills." Fourth, "provide for an annual psychiatric evaluation of children who have learning disabilities." And, finally, "provide special educational services for children [immediately] when their disability is diagnosed rather than waiting until [they are] at least two years behind academically, as is done now."[3]

According to the Task Force, these changes would guarantee that school programs served all truly disabled students—and served them appropriately. By stressing accurate diagnoses, the Task Force hoped to classify students on the basis of disability and not on the discriminatory bases of race, color, or national origin. As the Task Force argued, "the educational abilities and needs of all children must be determined on an *individual* basis. Presently, children with special needs either are excluded from school altogether, or are inappropriately evaluated and labeled according to what they supposedly are—according to a . . . group stereotype. The labeling of a child as 'mentally retarded' for example, while a convenient stereotype for school officials, does little to enhance the child's educational opportunity. One 'retarded' child may be able to function productively in the regular classroom, while another may require special educational methods. Yet, the present labeling process places them both in the same class as part of a stereotyped group." According to the Task Force, the only way to avoid discrimination was to view every student in every school as a unique individual with unique needs that responded to unique educational treatment. In pursuit of this goal, the Task Force tried to outline a more individualized approach to the assessment of ability. "The evaluation of children must include more than simple testing methods," the Task Force explained. "Evaluation includes psychological testing, pediatric physical examinations, neurological examinations, [tests of] psycho-motor functioning, psychiatric examinations, and more." Above all, the Task Force asserted, teachers should use tests to place students in isolated programs only temporarily: "Because testing in no way measures fixed abilities," the Task Force wrote, "it is useful merely to indicate areas in which children need special attention."[4] Isolated placements were thus permissible, but only if they proved educationally appropriate, beneficial, or effective for specific pupils.

In order to determine when isolated placements were appropriate, it was critical to obtain accurate diagnoses—i.e., diagnoses based not on students' race but, rather, on their individual abilities or disabilities. Yet, obtaining accurate diagnoses was not an easy task. Ever since Judge J. Skelly Wright had issued his decision in *Hobson v. Hansen* in 1967, standardized aptitude and IQ tests had been suspected of racial bias. Hence, whenever minority students received consistently lower scores than white students on standardized tests, their performance could be attributed to "test bias" rather than to individual learning difficulties. The challenge, therefore, was to find ways to diagnose disabilities or learning difficulties in minority students using strictly cognitive rather than cultural criteria. A test that found disproportionate evidence of a certain disability among poor, minority, or non-English-speaking students would be considered unfair. Conversely, a test that found equal evidence of a particular disability distributed uniformly across all segments of the population, regardless of race, income, or language background, would be considered legitimate. Of course, when the measurement of a test's objectivity (or lack of bias) was its likelihood of finding disabilities represented uniformly across the general population, it was difficult—perhaps impossible—to accept the conclusions of any test that found a high concentration of any disability in any social group.[5] A test showing a relationship between race and retardation, for example, would inevitably be suspected of bias; so, too, would a test showing a relationship between low-income and learning disabilities. The key to making appropriate, or nondiscriminatory, placements was, therefore, to find a battery of tests that diagnosed disabilities only where they truly existed.

To help in this search, the Task Force on Children Out of School included several psychiatrists, psychologists, and other mental health professionals—men and women who were well acquainted with the latest techniques for diagnosing disabilities. Indeed, by the early 1970s, cognitive scientists had come to control the field of educational testing and measurement. Using clinical techniques to evaluate students' language usage, phonetic comprehension, visual and aural sensitivity, attention, and memory, cognitive scientists claimed to be able to assess which students' academic difficulties derived from bona fide disabilities—and perhaps warranted isolated placements—and which did not. In Boston, the Task Force on Children Out of School put its faith in cognitive scientists. It asked them to monitor the problem of misdiagnoses and also to study the issue of "inappropriate" classroom isolation. "This isolation happens not only to children whose mental or physical needs require special attention (though even they should not be isolated)," the Task Force contended in *The Way We Go to School*, "it happens to 'normal' children as well—to children whom school officials merely *think* are unusual." Of course, most of the "normal" children incorrectly diagnosed with disabilities in Boston were poor, minority, or non-English-speaking students in inner-city schools. As the Task Force argued, the problem of misdiagnoses had led to "the erroneous labeling of several thousand children as 'mentally retarded' or 'emotionally disturbed.' Meanwhile, many children who actually are retarded or disturbed fail to receive adequate educational programs [to meet] their special needs."[6] For the Task Force, accurate diagnoses were the key to resolving the problem of "discrimination" in the schools: once psychologists made accurate diagnoses, the schools would no longer be able to justify the continued isolation of poor minority students who were not genuinely disabled.

In the fall of 1970, the Task Force set out to determine the number of "truly disabled" students in Boston. Just as the Task Force had tried to gauge the number of non-English-speaking students in the city, so now it tried to gauge the number of disabled students. Yet, unlike the search for non-English-speaking students, in which the aim had been to maximize the estimated number of students in order to qualify for federal civil rights protections as well as state and federal aid for bilingual-transitional clusters, the search for disabled students aimed to tally only students with bona fide disabilities. Because an overrepresentation of minority students might lead to charges of racial bias in its diagnostic procedures, the Task Force tried to avoid all past problems of misclassification to reach an indisputably accurate count of disabled students.[7] In pursuing this objective, the Task Force called on an old state law—Chapter 71, section 46, of the Acts of 1954—which required schools to retest disabled students on an annual basis. The purpose of this law was both to measure students' progress from year to year and to verify that students in isolated programs were, in fact, "still disabled." A decade and a half later, this law gave the Task Force a platform on which to challenge the placements of disabled students in Boston. In September 1970, the Task Force persuaded a federal court to review the schools' placement policies for the mentally retarded; six months later, the court ruled in the case of *Stewart v. Phillips* that Boston's tendency to isolate minority students in classes for the retarded was "irrational" and required immediate revision.[8] This important case (which coincided, ironically, with the Task Force's campaign for more isolated bilingual clusters) set the stage for a major debate over the meaning of educational disabilities and the need for more "appropriate" placements for low-achieving poor and minority students in Boston's public schools.[9]

⟡

The named plaintiff in *Stewart v. Phillips* was Pearl Stewart, mother of one of the South End children who had been "entombed" in a class for mentally retarded students in 1967. The defendants in the case were Boston's Department of Educational Investigation and Measurement (DEIM), represented by its acting director, Agnes Phillips, as well as the state Department of Education and Department of Mental Health. The legal arguments in *Stewart v. Phillips* identified two categories of children: those who had been inappropriately placed in isolated classes for the mentally retarded and those who had been appropriately placed but required additional special-compensatory help. Stewart and her attorneys argued that poorly trained staff using discriminatory diagnostic procedures had misclassified scores of minority children and had denied them access to equal educational opportunities in the Boston public schools.[10] Ruling in Stewart's favor, the court ordered the state to develop new diagnostic procedures, new placement policies, and new training systems for DEIM staff members. (The last time these regulations had been reviewed was in 1955, when Massachusetts's original special commission for the retarded issued its first report calling for the integration of disabled students into regular classrooms.) The new regulations of 1971 stressed the need for more accurate diagnoses as well as more effective programs— programs designed to meet the needs of mentally retarded students and to promote their inclusion in regular classrooms whenever possible. As one scholar later observed, "with their provisions for comprehensive assessment, mainstreaming, parent involvement, and equality of resources, the [new] regulations set forth a radically new format for delivering special education services."[11] Undoubtedly the most important—and ambiguous—aspect of the new guidelines was the definition of "appropriate" placements and "adequate" services for disabled students. What exactly constituted an appropriate or adequate education?

In *Stewart v. Phillips*, the court implied that the appropriateness of each student's classroom placement would be measured chiefly on the basis of the student's educational *benefit*. If the student's placement did not improve his or her educational results, then it could be considered inappropriate and discriminatory; moreover, it could be considered discriminatory regardless of the expressed "intent" of school administrators in making the placement in the first place. According to the court, any intent to discriminate had to be determined retroactively, because, otherwise, school administrators would claim in every case that they intended to help rather than harm students—even when those very students showed a persistent lack of educational progress. The implications of this decision were profound. The court's reasoning took for granted the supposition that all disabilities were, on some level, remediable; if students consistently failed to show academic progress, then the court could attribute their failure to inadequacies in their schools rather than to innate shortcomings in the students themselves. In other words, the court would view failure *not* as evidence of a child's disability but as proof of an inappropriate placement. Conversely, "appropriate" placements could be judged only on the basis of educational success. After *Stewart v. Phillips*, the appropriateness of any educational placement was assessed on the basis of its effectiveness in improving students' outcomes—and the only way for a school to avoid charges of discrimination was to see that *all* students maximized their individual outcomes in their respective classes. Indeed, any hint that superior outcomes might have been attainable in a different class (an integrated class for isolated students or an isolated class for integrated students) might lead to charges of discrimination. However, as Superintendent Haley had observed in the 1950s, it was impossible to gauge *simultaneously* the effect of both integrated and isolated placements on maximizing "potential" benefits.[12]

Stewart v. Phillips set a new standard for measuring the appropriate treatment of disabled students in the public schools, but it was not the only case of its kind to wend its way through a federal court in 1971. In *Pennsylvania Association for Retarded Children (PARC) v. Pennsylvania*, the federal district court in Philadelphia ruled that schools could not unnecessarily isolate pupils on grounds of mental retardation. Going beyond

Stewart v. Phillips, the court in *PARC v. Pennsylvania* required schools to place disabled students in the "least restrictive"—that is, the most integrated—classroom environment. Basing its decision on the Fourteenth Amendment and the idea that "separate educational facilities are inherently unequal," the court ordered schools "to place each mentally retarded child in a free, public program of education and training appropriate to the [mentally retarded] child's capacity, within the context of the general education policy that, among the alternative programs of education and training required by [law] to be available, placement in a regular public school class is preferable to placement in a special public school class and placement in a special public school class is preferable to placement in any other type of program of education and training."[13] The case of *PARC v. Pennsylvania* established two important precedents. First, it required schools to integrate mentally retarded students into regular classes whenever possible. Second, it tied this requirement to the Fourteenth Amendment, implying that integration on both the school *and* the classroom level was legally essential to "equal educational opportunities." And, yet, *PARC v. Pennsylvania* did not deliver the last word on equal educational opportunities for handicapped students in the early 1970s. Between 1971 and 1972, two other cases held that, while classroom integration might be preferable for disabled students, classroom isolation would continue to be permissible so long as it promised to improve educational benefits—as measured by results.

One of these cases, *Mills v. Board of Education,* began in the District of Columbia in November 1971, and ended with a federal district court ruling in August 1972. In this case, Peter Mills joined six other poor black students from the inner city in a class-action lawsuit, contending that "although they [could] profit from an education either in regular classrooms with supportive services or in special classes adapted to their needs, they have been labeled as behavioral problems, mentally retarded, emotionally disturbed, or hyper-active and denied admission to the public schools or excluded therefrom after admission, with no provision for alternative educational placement or periodic review." The school district pleaded that it could not afford the special programs that Mills, his coplaintiffs, and the city's other disabled students required, unless the "Congress of the United States appropriates millions of dollars to improve special education services in the District of Columbia." The court, however, rejected this plea, asserting that "the District of Columbia's interest in educating the excluded children clearly must outweigh its interest in preserving its financial resources. If sufficient funds are not available to finance all of the services and programs that are needed and desirable in the system then the available funds must be expended equitably in such a manner that no child is entirely excluded from a publicly supported education consistent with his needs and ability to benefit therefrom. The inadequacies of the District of Columbia public school system whether occasioned by insufficient funding or administrative inefficiency, certainly cannot be permitted to bear more heavily on the 'exceptional' or handicapped child than on the normal child."[14] In other words, schools had to provide disabled students with "appropriate" services—either in integrated or in isolated classes, depending on recommendations of periodic placement hearings—and financial hardship was no excuse not to do so.

In December 1971, less than a month after *Mills*, a similar class-action case arose in Boston. Originally titled *Association for Mentally Ill Children v. Greenblatt*, the case was later retitled *Barnett v. Goldman*. The three co-defendants in the case were the Boston public schools, the Massachusetts state Department of Education, and the Massachusetts state Department of Mental Health. The plaintiff was Lori Barnett, an eight-year-old girl who had been diagnosed as emotionally disturbed and then categorically excluded from the public schools. Even though Barnett had sought placement in an isolated program for disruptive students and, later, in a state-approved residential program for delinquent girls, the Boston public schools had repeatedly denied her access to all educational placements on grounds of her disability. Since schooling of some kind was legally compulsory in the state of Massachusetts, the attorneys for Barnett asserted that her exclusion from school constituted a denial of due process; in fact, their class-action lawsuit charged that "1,371 emotionally disturbed children, determined to be eligible for special classes, were denied such services" and that this denial of educational services violated both state and federal law. Specifically, Barnett's attorneys argued that the exclusion of disabled children solely on the basis of their disabilities "irrationally denies them a fundamental right to receive an education and to thereby participate meaningfully in a democratic society." This claim was cleverly phrased to combine two constitutional principles, both of which pertained to the placement of different students into different legal categories when applying the equal protection clause of the Fourteenth Amendment.[15] Since the equal protection clause could not be interpreted to mean that institutions of government such as schools had to treat *all* individuals in *exactly* the same way *all* the time, the federal courts used a two-tiered legal protocol to decide when a given classification of students was constitutionally valid.

The first tier of this legal protocol applied the highest constitutional standard—strict scrutiny—to the courts' analysis of such classifications as race, color, or national origin. It held that institutions of government could classify citizens on these bases (and treat them differently) only if such classifications served a "compelling state interest" and did not deny any "fundamental right" guaranteed in the U.S. Constitution. The second tier applied a lower standard—rational basis—to the courts' analysis of such classifications as disability or handicap. Under this standard, institutions of government, including the schools, could classify citizens (and treat them differently) on the basis of disability only if such classifications were "rationally related" to serving some "legitimate state interest." In the past, federal courts had allowed schools to treat disabled and nondisabled students differently, because doing so was thought to serve the legitimate interest of offering both an "appropriate" education. In *Barnett v. Goldman*, however, Barnett's attorneys argued that the separate classification—and subsequent exclusion—of all emotionally disturbed students had no rational basis and served no legitimate state interest; rather, they insisted, such a classification served only to deny emotionally disturbed students' access to equal educational opportunity. Barnett's attorneys then took this argument a step further to say that the right to equal educational opportunity was, in fact, a "fundamental right" implied in the U.S. Constitution itself. This argument was harder to advance. In *Mills v. Board of Education*, the federal court had ruled that all disabled students were entitled to "adequate alternative educational services suited to [their] needs," and Barnett's lawyers interpreted this entitlement as a fundamental right. Yet, without any precise or practical definition of "adequate alternative educational services," the court in *Barnett v. Goldman* was not ready to guarantee such services as a basic right.[16]

Lacking any consistent way to tell when a disabled student's—or any student's—education was, in fact, "adequate," the court bracketed the issue of "fundamental rights" and considered Barnett's case solely on the grounds that her exclusion from school had no rational basis and served no legitimate state interest.[17] Asking whether the Boston public schools could make space immediately for emotionally disturbed students, the court did not specify what *type* of education Barnett should get. It did not say whether she should be placed in an integrated or an isolated class, nor did it say how the "adequacy" or "appropriateness" of her placement should be measured; instead, following the precedent of cases involving non-English-speaking students, it left these decisions to educators who were, presumably, better qualified to make them.[18] Thus, in the wake of considerable litigation, it was still possible for a school to claim that isolated programs were most "appropriate" for disabled students.[19] At the same time, however, isolated placements could be appropriate only if they were made on the basis of a rational classification—that is, a classification unrelated to race, color, or national origin. By emphasizing a rational-basis criterion for classroom placement, the court granted the possibility of classifying (and isolating) students on the basis of disability but foreclosed the possibility of associating disability with race, color, or national origin. If classifications of disability overlapped with classifications of race or national origin, then such classifications would become suspect and would be challenged as "discriminatory." Hence, the only way for a school to *avoid* charges of discriminatory diagnoses or inappropriate placements was to avoid placing too many racial minorities in isolated programs—particularly if those programs did not seem to improve minority students' educational results. The key question thus became, "how many was too many" minorities in an isolated program?

&

By early 1972, the Boston public schools had made substantial additions to their programs for disabled children. Most of the new programs, however, were isolated from regular classrooms. For example, after *Barnett v. Goldman*, Boston doubled its programs for emotionally disturbed students, but each new program took the form of an isolated special-compensatory class. As Superintendent Ohrenberger outlined in his annual report for 1971-72, "additions included eight junior high classes, five elementary classes, and one additional pre-primary group." The aim of these classes was—ostensibly—to prepare disabled students for eventual integration into regular classes. According to Ohrenberger, "new models for educating children with educational handicaps were developed this year by the Department of Special Classes. A project allowed the children to participate in the mainstream of regular education whenever possible and to receive specialized instruction in their areas of handicaps. The title of 'resource teacher' was designated for the teachers involved in the program, and the classrooms in which they based their operations became resource rooms to facilitate integration."[20] Facilitating integration was different, however, from fully practicing it. Many schools hesitated to integrate disabled students into regular classes if it seemed that integration might jeopardize educational outcomes. After all, the courts, despite their calls for integration, had consistently allowed for isolation if isolation promised better results. In *Stewart v. Phillips,* the court implied that the appropriateness of any placement would be judged in terms of its effects, and, in both *Mills v. Board of Education* and *Barnett v. Goldman,* the court, lacking a clear standard of appropriateness or adequacy, declined to make classroom integration a uniform legal requirement. Thus, despite a growing *rhetorical* emphasis on inclusion (or mainstreaming), schools put their *legal* emphasis on isolation whenever isolation promised superior educational gains.[21]

In 1971–72, the Boston public schools acted quickly to create programs for the disabled, and one reason for the schools' alacrity was the prospect of additional state aid. In the fall of 1971, shortly after the passage of Chapter 71A with its pledge of state funds for bilingual programs, a vigorous movement emerged in Massachusetts to grant full state funding to special education for the disabled.[22] One leader of this movement was Jessie Fay Sargent—the wife of Governor Francis Sargent—who directed the state handicapped children's education program task force. This task force worked together with the Task Force on Children Out of School to draft new legislation to increase state aid for special education programs for the disabled. In April 1972, Representative Michael Daly (the same Task Force member who had introduced the bill that became Chapter 71A) joined Representative David Bartley in submitting a bill to revise the state aid formula for special education to help schools meet the standard of "appropriate" treatment that federal courts had set. The Daly-Bartley-Sargent Special Education Act—officially known as Chapter 766—passed in July 1972, by a wide margin. It was a landmark law. It required public schools to offer all handicapped students a free and appropriate education in the least restrictive environment, and it promised full state reimbursement for "excess" costs associated with special education placements. It mandated individualized education plans (IEPs) for each disabled child and gave parents the right to challenge the placement decisions of school officials. Addressing the issue of adequacy, it required schools to help disabled students achieve their "maximum feasible potential" and explained that "until proven otherwise, every child shall be presumed to be appropriately assigned to a regular education program and presumed *not* to be a . . . child requiring special education."[23] In short, the new law promised state aid for the education of all "truly" disabled students.

Although Chapter 766 did not specify how the state would tell when students had reached their "maximum feasible potential," it was the first law in the country to promise state funds in pursuit of that goal. Under Chapter 766, schools had a financial incentive to enroll students who might otherwise have been excluded and to develop new programs to serve their needs. At the same time, schools had to show that their programs served only students who were truly disabled—and served them only until they were prepared to join regular classes. Emphasizing the importance of reliable diagnoses, Chapter 766 pledged to overcome the long-standing correlation between disability and race, a correlation still common in the state's inner-city schools. Indeed, the law endeavored to block any and every possibility of discrimination in the treatment of the disabled. It presumed first, that diagnoses would be accurate and objective; second, that disabilities were evenly distributed throughout the population rather than concentrated in particular racial groups; third, that all truly disabled students, once identified, would be placed only temporarily in isolated programs; fourth, that isolated programs would be designed to facilitate a rapid transition to regular classes; and fifth, that regular classes would be the default placement for all students not found to be disabled. Placements that did not maximize each student's individual "potential" would be judged inappropriate—and, hence, discriminatory.

Passage of Chapter 766 resulted from a combination of legal precedent and local activism. As Milton Budoff, a scholar with the Research Institute for Education Problems at Harvard, asserted, "the main reason for the initial political success of Chapter 766 was that groups and individuals with a relatively diverse set of interests backed a law mandating services to meet the special needs of all children. Compared to this formidable coalition, initial opposition to the bill was feeble and half-hearted. Indeed, a considerable commitment to special education reform has developed." Budoff added, however, that this coalition could quickly dissolve if its members began to doubt the accuracy of disability diagnoses or the appropriateness of pupil placements. He noted, for example, that the coalition had already lost a number of psychologists who refused to place minority students in regular classes when their diagnoses clearly showed that they could benefit from isolated remedial programs. The Massachusetts Psychological Association withdrew from the coalition when it discovered that revised state regulations made it more difficult for psychologists to classify low-achieving minority students as mentally retarded. In Budoff's words, "the professionals became hostile to the reform movement when activities reached the political level"—that is, the level where diagnoses seemed to rely on politics more than science. "It is important to understand whether the timidity of these organizations is endemic to middle-class [professional] organizations, or whether it derived from the professionals' discomfort at taking advocate positions which might be viewed as controversial or compromising to their sense of dignity."[24] Budoff's comments raised an important question: if diagnoses were more political than scientific, then how could the schools know when it was safe to place even *one* minority student in an isolated class, even if the class was likely to be beneficial?[25]

The success of Chapter 766 depended fundamentally on the integrity of diagnostic procedures. If school psychologists found chronically low-achieving minority students to be "normal" rather than disabled, then either these diagnoses would have to be considered correct, in which case these students would not be entitled to isolated remedial classes, or else these diagnoses would have to be considered incorrect, in which case the diagnostic process itself would fall under suspicion as biased or politicized or—at the very least—unable to show a meaningful connection between students' actual ability and the tests used to measure it. In order for parents and the public to trust the validity of diagnoses (as well as the classroom placements and educational interventions that followed from these diagnoses), the tests used to measure disabilities needed to show a more or less transparent connection between students' scores and the treatment they received to improve their performance. When Superintendent Ohrenberger agreed in 1971–72 to retest thousands of students in Boston, he promised to distinguish students with "true" disabilities from students with "false" disabilities and to use these distinctions to place all students into appropriate classes. In each case, he promised that students' placements would facilitate their educational progress, measured in terms of academic achievement. Within this context, it was imperative for psychologists to feel free to place truly disabled students in isolated classes—even when these students were disproportionately minority students—if such placements were most likely to maximize their academic gains. As Ohrenberger recognized, the appropriateness of student placements depended not only on the degree to which they promoted racial balance, but also on the degree to which they maximized results. Reliable diagnoses, appropriate placements, and satisfactory results were, he realized, mutually interdependent.[26]

After the passage of Chapter 766, the Boston public schools created a number of new programs to meet the needs of disabled students—particularly in the inner city. For example, the newly built Joseph Lee Elementary School in Dorchester became a test site for a new program for emotionally disturbed children. The fact that students at the Joseph Lee School were virtually all minorities did not concern the school committee; rather, it praised the concentrated and carefully targeted nature of the school's programs. Most of the students at the Lee School showed persistently low academic achievement and thus received some form of remedial treatment, and a majority had been diagnosed with some form of learning disability that rendered them eligible for programs funded by the state or federal government.[27] Indeed, at the Joseph Lee, special- and compensatory-education programs blended together such that it was difficult to tell where one stopped and the other started; moreover, almost every program served minority students in disproportionate numbers. Yet, herein lay a dilemma: the Joseph Lee was in constant jeopardy of losing its state and federal aid owing to its racial imbalance.[28] Just as the Hernandez School had confronted a dilemma with respect to its bilingual-transitional clusters, so the Lee School confronted a dilemma with respect to its special-compensatory programs. Both schools offered special programs to minority students on a carefully targeted basis, but critics argued that the two schools' racial imbalance automatically undermined students' access to equal educational opportunities. The question was whether minorities could obtain an appropriate education in the Joseph Lee School's special programs or whether they could obtain an appropriate education *only* in a racially balanced school. This question, which had become more and more urgent over time, now came to a head: were racially imbalanced classes or schools inherently incompatible with equal educational opportunities?

At the heart of this question was the enduring controversy over the most effective way to equalize educational opportunities for poor minorities in the inner city. On the one hand, in the years since the passage of Massachusetts's racial imbalance law, the Boston public schools had made very little headway toward the goal of racial integration; if anything, de facto segregation had become even more pronounced. On the other hand, the schools had made a great deal of headway in creating special-compensatory programs to serve diverse groups of students with diverse educational needs. State and federal aid had encouraged the public schools to establish programs for educationally disadvantaged children and to target these programs at schools with large numbers of poor minority students. Various community activists had helped to create new compensatory, bilingual, and special education programs—and they had focused their efforts on programs within racially imbalanced schools. Indeed, the Task Force on Children Out of School had built its entire reform agenda on the notion that new programs could draw neglected students into the public schools.[29] In 1971 and 1972, the Task Force's emphasis on new programs had contributed directly to the passage of Chapter 71A and Chapter 766, and schools had begun to realize that financial incentives associated with special services outweighed financial disincentives associated with racial imbalance; in other words, schools were more likely to gain money for state-mandated special-compensatory programs than they were to lose money for racial imbalance. (Even when the state threatened to withhold aid, it quickly retreated when schools promised to "try harder" to promote integration.) By 1972, it seemed, special-compensatory programs had actually *super-*

seded racial balance as the key to "equal educational opportunity" for poor minority students in inner-city schools.

⟡

Yet, in Boston, the emphasis on special-compensatory programs had a major flaw: despite the dramatic proliferation of new programs in the inner city, the educational *outcomes* of minority students had not significantly improved. Indeed, upon inspection, it seemed that academic achievement within racially imbalanced schools had not improved at all. In the spring of 1972, this uncomfortable and undeniable fact led to an historic lawsuit involving the Joseph Lee School. The lawsuit had extremely complex origins, but it centered on the charge that the Boston school committee had intentionally maintained a racially imbalanced dual school system throughout the city and that this dual system was inherently at odds with equal educational opportunities for black students. The suit held, for example, that, despite promises to make the Joseph Lee School racially balanced, the committee had failed to pursue this goal and, in the process, had deliberately impeded the opportunities of the Joseph Lee's minority students. The committee responded that racial imbalance in the Boston public schools was caused by larger demographic forces beyond its control. Addressing the particular case of the Joseph Lee, the committee noted that the site selected for the school in 1970 had been chosen because of its location on the border between a black neighborhood and a white neighborhood; however, during construction, the supply of federally subsidized low-interest loans had increased, and these loans had attracted large numbers of black residents to the area.[30] As a result, the school committee asserted, the entire vicinity around the Joseph Lee had become de facto segregated, and the school's enrollment had become virtually all black. Some insisted that the committee should have *required* white parents from nearby areas to send their children to the Joseph Lee, but the committee replied that it could not assign students to specific schools solely on the basis of race.[31]

It was at this point that Tallulah Morgan, the mother of three black students at the Joseph Lee, agreed to become the named plaintiff in a federal class-action lawsuit against the Boston school committee, which was, at that time, chaired by James W. Hennigan. In late June 1972, federal district court Judge Arthur Wendell Garrity Jr. heard the opening arguments in the case of *Morgan v. Hennigan*.[32] Morgan's lead attorney, Richard "Nick" Flannery—a Boston native, a veteran of the southern civil rights movement, and a former litigator with the federal Department of Justice—claimed that the school committee had knowingly, deliberately, and intentionally maintained racial imbalance by various means, including dubious site selections, gerrymandered districts, arbitrary student placements, and manipulative transfer policies, and had thereby denied black students' access to equal educational opportunities. Flannery made little effort to explain *why* racial imbalance was inherently at odds with equal educational opportunities for black students (he barely mentioned the fact that 200 black students had staged a sit-in at the Joseph Lee to *avoid* being reassigned to nearby white schools); instead, he focused on the idea that a racially imbalanced dual school system had been intentionally maintained. He noted, for example, that Boston had recently launched three new "bilingual schools," each with 100 percent minority enrollments, and suggested that these schools could not possibly provide equal educational opportunities due to their racial imbalance. He also observed that the city had designated three other schools—the William M. Trotter Elementary School, the George A. Lewis Middle School, and the Copley Square High School—as a model demonstration subsystem for Title I programs and implied that these schools had equalized educational opportunities not by providing special-compensatory programs but, rather, by enrolling a certain number of low-income white students from the suburbs.[33]

By suggesting that racially imbalanced schools never offered equal opportunities, Flannery hoped to make a persuasive case of intentional discrimination on the part of the school committee. Within a constitutional framework, it was not sufficient for Flannery simply to show that the Boston public schools were racially imbalanced; he also had to show that racial imbalance had resulted from intentional "state action" and had done real educational harm to minority students. In other words, he had to show that the committee had, in effect, required most black students to attend racially imbalanced schools *because of their race* and that these schools had produced racially disparate as well as detrimental educational outcomes. The first point was far easier to prove than the second. Flannery cited copious examples whereby the "maintenance of pupil assignment policies, the establishment and manipulation of [school] attendance areas and district lines reflecting segregated residential patterns, the establishment of grade structures and feeder patterns; the administration of school capacity, enlargement, and construction policies, [as well as pupil] transportation practices" had perpetuated racial imbalance in the Boston public schools.[34] Flannery also had data to show that predominantly black schools were more crowded than predominantly white schools and had less experienced instructors. He used this evidence to infer that racially imbalanced schools led directly to unequal levels of educational achievement among blacks and whites. The logic supporting this inference (which rested on a correlation more than a proven cause) was thin, but Flannery's case depended on it.[35] He repeatedly asserted that racially imbalanced schools had promoted unequal opportunities as gauged by unequal resources and results (if resources or results had been equal, then a suit might not have been filed), and he implied that racial balance would, by contrast, yield equal opportunities (again, as gauged by resources and results).

The trial in *Morgan v. Hennigan* lasted only two weeks, but it took Judge Garrity more than two years to sort it all out. Born in Worcester, Massachusetts, in 1920, Garrity had graduated from Holy Cross College in 1941 and from Harvard Law School in 1946 and had clerked for federal district court Judge Francis J. W. Ford before serving as assistant U.S. attorney in Boston from 1948 to 1950. In 1952 and again in 1958, he had worked for John F. Kennedy's senatorial campaigns, and in 1960 he had played an active role in Kennedy's presidential election. In 1961, Kennedy rewarded Garrity for this help by naming him to succeed Elliot Richardson as U.S. attorney for Massachusetts (it was at this point that Richardson served briefly as a special assistant to attorney general Robert F. Kennedy), and Garrity remained in the U.S. attorney's office for five years. Then, in 1966, he was appointed by President Johnson to the federal bench. As a judge presiding over the federal district court in Massachusetts, Garrity was the picture of propriety and judicial diligence. As one author described Garrity in the courtroom, "if anything, he was conscientious to a fault—the smallest procedural matters had to be submitted in writing. Unlike other judges, who delegated heavily to young law clerks, Garrity read everything that crossed his desk, often working twelve hours a day, and such diligence meant that years might go by before he decided a complex case."[36] Certainly, *Morgan v. Hennigan* was a complex case. At its heart was a presumed connection between racial balance and equal educational opportunity. Were racially imbalanced schools inherently incompatible with equal educational opportunity for black students? Flannery thought so—but, given the rapid growth over the past decade of state and federal grants to special-compensatory programs targeted at racially imbalanced schools (and designed to equalize resources as well as results), others evidently thought not.

In 1972, as Garrity reviewed arguments in *Morgan v. Hennigan,* the link between racial balance and equal educational opportunity received significant attention—not only in Boston, but throughout the country. Specifically, the idea of court-ordered busing as a remedy for racial imbalance provoked heated debate. President Nixon made much of this debate in his campaign for reelection in 1972, employing a so-called southern strategy to exploit racial fears and delay school desegregation in the

South as long as possible. When arch-segregationist George Wallace won the Democratic primary in Florida, Nixon quickly urged Congress to impose a nationwide moratorium on local busing plans—and his antibusing platform received vigorous support from Massachusetts's congresswoman Louise Day Hicks. Hicks argued that "President Nixon has taken a forthright and logical position on the question of busing, one that I support and—as Mr. Nixon says—one that is supported by moderate Americans, black or white." Nixon did not receive support, however, from Massachusetts's influential black senator, Edward Brooke III, who, like Nixon, was a Republican. According to Brooke, "quality education must be integrated education."[37] In 1972, both Hicks and Brooke were campaigning for reelection, but, while Brooke won easily with two-thirds of the statewide vote, Hicks lost a close race in the ninth district to former state senator Joseph Moakley, who won by a mere 4,000 of 160,000 votes. Moakley took control of the busing issue by announcing his strong support for racial balance and, at the same time, his strong opposition to court-ordered busing.[38] Meanwhile, in the presidential campaign, Nixon's southern strategy worked. He beat challenger George McGovern in every state except one: Massachusetts. Even in Massachusetts, however, he received 45 percent of the vote—up from 33 percent four years earlier. The election of 1972 left no doubt that racial balance was one of the most contentious domestic issues of the day.

At its heart, the busing controversy involved an important constitutional question, namely, was racial balance constitutionally *required* in public schools? Nixon's secretary of health, education, and welfare, Elliot Richardson, thought not. Recalling the Supreme Court's decision to uphold a busing order in *Swann v. Charlotte-Mecklenburg Board of Education* a year earlier, Richardson noted that "technically, all the Supreme Court held was that the [lower court judge] had acted within the scope of his power. [However], the content of the remedy (busing) was not compelled by the Constitution in those specific terms."[39] Thus, while it was possible for busing to foster equal educational opportunities for black pupils, the Constitution did not necessarily *require* that approach. Although Richardson left HEW in January 1973, to become secretary of defense and, shortly thereafter, attorney general, the busing controversy did not diminish. Instead, it intensified. In June 1973, in the case of *Keyes v. Denver School District No. 1,* the Supreme Court ruled for the first time on the issue of racial segregation in a northern school system—that is, a system with no history of explicit laws requiring the segregation of races in public schools. *Keyes* held that the absence of explicit segregationist laws did not preclude a finding of unconstitutional segregation in a northern school district. It also held that a failure to provide equal educational opportunities to all students, regardless of race, constituted "intentional state action" in violation of the Fourteenth Amendment. By linking racial imbalance to intentional state action, the *Keyes* decision cast what had once been considered de facto segregation as de jure segregation and, in turn, cast local leaders as directly responsible for unequal educational opportunities in racially imbalanced schools. As Justice Douglas summarized, "there is, for purposes of the Equal Protection Clause of the Fourteenth Amendment as applied to school cases, no difference between *de facto* and *de jure* segregation. The school board is a state agency and the lines that it draws, the locations it selects for school sites, the allocation it makes of students, [and] the budgets it prepares are state action for Fourteenth Amendment purposes."[40]

The *Keyes* decision transformed the way Judge Garrity saw the case of *Morgan v. Hennigan* in Boston.[41] Once he was able to discard the distinction between de facto and de jure segregation, he was free to link Flannery's proof of racial imbalance to a case of intentional discrimination.[42] In other words, he was free to infer that racial imbalance, if deliberately maintained, was inherently at odds with equal educational opportunities for minority students. It followed, then, that the only sure way to provide equal opportunities to minority students was to place them in racially balanced schools—by means of court-ordered busing, if necessary. Garrity's decision rested on a conviction that busing would, in fact, provide equal educational opportunities for minority students—not only in the procedural sense of "equal access," but also in the substantive sense of "equal treatment." If it turned out that minorities' educational treatment did not improve in racially balanced schools, then the presumed connection between racial balance and equal opportunities might falter—as would the justification for busing. This point could not be exaggerated. If busing did not boost educational results among minority students, then it would appear that racial balance and academic achievement were not causally related. Garrity's constitutional logic might then collapse. As Elliot Richardson had noted, the Constitution did not require racial balance; rather, since *Brown v. Board of Education*, it required only equal educational opportunities. If Garrity selected the wrong remedy to achieve that aim, his ruling would fail as a matter of both policy and law.[43] Yet, by the fall of 1973, he was convinced that court-ordered busing was the only way to protect minority pupils' rights.[44]

As Garrity moved toward a controversial busing remedy in *Morgan v. Hennigan*, several important events took place in Massachusetts.[45] In June 1973—a week after the Supreme Court released its decision in *Keyes*—Governor Sargent asked the state supreme court for an "advisory opinion" on a bill passed by the state legislature, which would have prohibited busing without parents' permission. Facing an antibusing electorate, Sargent hoped to sign this bill (which represented a retreat from the values that led to the racial imbalance law eight years earlier), but only if the court would deem it constitutional. As it happened, the state supreme court declared the bill *un*constitutional, and Sargent was forced to look for other ways to counter the prospect of busing. His best alternative, he concluded, was to replace his uncompromisingly probusing commissioner of education, Neil Sullivan, with a more moderate figure. He chose Gregory Anrig, director of the Institute for Teaching and Learning at the University of Massachusetts–Boston. Anrig held a doctorate from the Harvard Graduate School of Education and had served as director of the division of equal educational opportunities in the federal Office of Education.[46] He shared his predecessor's support for racial balance, but he did not share his predecessor's zeal for busing. As the *Boston Globe* observed, Sullivan had been "an outgoing, flamboyant figure who came in headlong with a commitment to break patterns of racial segregation in the schools. Anrig is much more low-key and very conscious of the political sensitivity of the racial balance issue. He does not emphasize it, although he says he remains fully committed to seeing black children get equal opportunities in the state's educational system and this means doing what Sullivan set out to do: break the patterns of segregation." What distinguished Anrig from Sullivan was not the aim of equal opportunity per se but, rather, the idea that court-ordered busing was the only—or even the best—way to accomplish this goal.[47]

The selection of Commissioner Anrig followed close on the heels of another major transition in Massachusetts's educational leadership, namely, the departure of William Ohrenberger as superintendent of the Boston public schools. In the summer of 1972—just after *Morgan v. Hennigan* was filed—Ohrenberger had turned his duties over to William J. Leary, a teacher in Boston since 1958 who held one doctorate of education from Boston University and a second from Harvard. In many ways, Ohrenberger's retirement marked the end of an era.[48] When he took office in the summer of 1963, public awareness of the challenges facing inner-city schools was only just beginning to emerge, and the idea of massive state and federal aid for targeted special-compensatory programs was still in its earliest infancy. Yet, over the years, urban renewal aid and impact aid had expanded into a wide array of programs serving a broad range of students: a small set of services for the disabled had grown into a plethora of grants-in-aid, most of which were consolidated in 1970 under the Education of the Handicapped Act (which became part B of Title VI of the reauthorized Elementary and Secondary Education Act); Title I of the ESEA had served larger and larger numbers of low-income pupils; and

Title VII funded more and more bilingual-transitional classes for non-English-speaking students. Over the years, Ohrenberger had ensured that Boston applied for nearly every penny of federal aid for which the city was eligible, and the Boston public schools had collected millions of dollars each year in carefully targeted categorical grants—*despite* the persistence of racial imbalance in the very schools that received the bulk of these funds. When federal aid was combined with state aid under Chapter 71A, Chapter 766, and Chapter 70 (general aid), it was clear that Ohrenberger had overseen a massive expansion of outside financial support for Boston's racially imbalanced schools.

Yet, after *Keyes*, it was clear that Ohrenberger's strategy of applying external aid to special-compensatory programs in racially imbalanced schools was under attack. The courts, observing that externally supported programs had not improved the effectiveness of inner-city schools, had started to demand (in the words of Justice Brennan in his *Keyes* opinion) "compensatory education in an integrated environment."[49] Inasmuch as special-compensatory programs alone had not raised academic achievement, the courts expected a combination of special-compensatory programs and racial integration to do better. In Massachusetts, state officials shared this expectation. In June 1973—four days after *Keyes*—Massachusetts's state board of education adopted a busing plan developed by Professor Louis Jaffe of the Harvard Law School, and, in November, the state supreme court ordered the Boston public schools to implement this plan.[50] The school committee filed a series of legal objections, but by January 1974, the courts had rejected every one. In the meantime, Garrity was putting the finishing touches on his decision in *Morgan v. Hennigan*, and the school committee's latest antics only strengthened his conviction that the committee was determined to maintain a racially segregated system. When he released his 152-page judgment on June 21, 1974, he had no doubt of the committee's guilt: "In view of the plaintiffs' proof of the defendants' pervasive practices which were intentionally segregative and their direct and reciprocal effects, the court concludes that the defendants' actions had a segregative impact far beyond the schools which were the immediate subjects of their actions." He concluded that "the defendants have knowingly carried out a systematic program of segregation affecting all of the city's students, teachers and school facilities and have intentionally brought about and maintained a dual school system. Therefore the entire school system of Boston is unconstitutionally segregated."[51]

It was a momentous ruling. Henceforth, any sign of racial imbalance in Boston's public schools would be attributed directly and exclusively to the intentional action of the school committee. Exonerating both state and federal agencies for any possible role they might have played in perpetuating racial imbalance, Garrity placed the onus of responsibility entirely on local officials. In his view, the intent to segregate (and, thus, the intent to "discriminate") resided solely with the five-member school committee, not with government programs that facilitated racially differentiated residential patterns or funded special-compensatory services that directed poor minority students toward particular schools. Deciding that racially imbalanced schools were, in fact, inherently incompatible with equal opportunities for black students, he ordered the school committee to ensure not only minority students' theoretical access to racially balanced schools but also their actual placement in racially balanced schools—by means of busing, if necessary. It was, of course, this plan for busing that generated the most hostility in Boston, not because this remedy was unexpected (it was not) but, rather, because it seemed extreme, and perhaps even unconstitutional itself. As many antibusing observers noted, the equal protection clause of the Fourteenth Amendment barred school officials from classifying students and assigning them to schools on the basis of race. Yet Garrity's remedy seemed to do just that. It had not eliminated racial classifications; it had emphasized them. It had not ensured equal educational opportunities; it had only ensured placement in racially balanced schools. The flaw in Garrity's remedy, critics argued, was that it pinned equal educational opportunity above all on racial balance and left the most important question unresolved: would racially balanced schools lead to equal opportunity as measured by equal resources and results, or would they—like their racially imbalanced predecessors—merely perpetuate the educational inequalities that led to litigation in the first place?[52]

⬦

After releasing his decision, Garrity allowed the Boston school committee one last chance to suggest an alternative to the busing plan submitted by Louis Jaffe a year earlier. When the committee failed to meet his two-month deadline, however, he ordered Jaffe's plan (which used complicated busing routes to reduce the number of racially imbalanced schools from 68 to 44) to take effect on September 1, 1974. Days later, the fall semester began, and the public reaction was immediate: "School buses were stoned, their windows broken, and some children cut by shattered glass," Garrity wrote. "Angry crowds of white parents and students gathered in front of the schools to protest the entry of black students assigned there. Student boycotts of varying effectiveness were organized. Many students stayed at home or were kept at home by their parents out of fear for their personal safety. Several city high schools were scenes of racially connected fights and incidents. As the school year continued, violence subsided, then recurred."[53] Mayor Kevin White deployed extra police forces to suppress the crowds, and Governor Sargent reassigned hundreds of state troopers to guard the city's schools. More than 300 helmeted officers were stationed at South Boston High School, where the most intense violence occurred: 134 guarded the neighborhood while 166 others monitored the halls and classrooms of the building itself. News broadcasts showed parents escorting their children to class wearing hard hats and carrying baseball bats as if preparing for race war. Photographs of surging mobs appeared on the front pages of dozens of major newspapers, and the violence only escalated as the months passed. When a black student stabbed a white classmate at South Boston High in December, administrators closed the school for an extended winter vacation. With chaos erupting citywide, many began to wonder what the phrase *equal educational opportunity* really meant for students attending newly "balanced" schools.[54]

Opposition to busing was not restricted to white residents of South Boston. It also came from federal and state officials. In February 1974—months before Garrity's ruling in *Morgan v. Hennigan*—the Democrat-controlled Congress had passed a so-called Equal Educational Opportunity Act, which said in part that "after June 30, 1974, no court of the United States shall order the implementation of any plan to remedy a finding of de jure segregation which involves the transportation of students, unless the court first finds that all alternative remedies are inadequate." The law also stated that "no provision of this act shall be construed to require the assignment or transportation of students or teachers in order to overcome racial imbalance."[55] To enforce these stipulations, Congress barred the use of federal monies to pay for court-ordered busing. Then, in July 1974, Massachusetts legislators endorsed this federal antibusing law by moderating their own nine-year-old mandate for all schools to maintain at least 50-percent white enrollments. These changes at both the federal and state level sprang from the conviction that "forced busing" unconstitutionally classified students by race.[56] Garrity rejected this logic, saying that the classification of students for the sake of busing was minor in comparison to the classification (and discriminatory treatment) of students under the old dual school system, but his judgment did little to diminish local resistance to busing. Blacks also resisted busing, asserting that racial balance was not synonymous with quality education. As black activist Malecai Andrews commented, "What you have in Boston is the spectacle of working class people fighting among themselves (black and white) to get into, or to retain schools that everybody knows victimize all students, . . . schools which do little in terms of educating, which are often harmful to any pupil, whatever his race." For Andrews and other black activists by the mid-1970s, "the solution for blacks [was] community control."[57]

Indeed, a revival of "black community control" as a response to busing swept Boston in 1974.[58] "The black community in Boston should know where it's at," said Noel Day, who had helped organize the city's first school boycott more than a decade earlier. "If busing is really just a means to an end—a way of transporting kids to a place where they can get 'quality' education, or at least a better education—then South Boston is not the place to go. More students go to college, for example, from . . . high schools with large numbers of black students than from South Boston High School. The kids in South Boston are as educationally 'deprived' and 'disadvantaged' as the black kids are. If quality education has any meaning, a busing program would be set up to move white kids out of South Boston, too. Instead of pushing for better schools, black people and white people are fighting over who will sit next to whom in some of the worst schools in the nation."[59] According to Day, the key to equal educational opportunity was not racial balance but, rather, new programs and community control. Erika Huggins, the director of a model program for black children in Oakland, California, agreed with Day. "I question whether schools in white communities have the 'quality' of education that black and other minority children require," she noted. "There would be no controversy over quality education in the black community if black people had concrete control of our schools." With independent control over funding and curricula, as well as the hiring of teachers, Huggins asserted, black neighborhoods could improve their schools and raise the achievement of black students *without* busing. "What we must do," Huggins argued, "is stop busing our children from one bad situation to another and start dealing with the real problem—[a need for a] complete overhaul of the structure and philosophy of public education in this country."[60]

Garrity had not anticipated such vehement black opposition to busing, and he was dismayed by the fact that it resurfaced so quickly after his decision in the case of *Morgan v. Hennigan*.[61] Rushing to include more black community leaders in the implementation of his busing decree, he moved in October 1974, to establish so-called racial-ethnic parent councils to "deal with racial tensions and problems at the individual school level."[62] Meanwhile, black parents began to create their own groups to monitor the busing program. As the New Left journal *Ramparts Magazine* noted, "black parents have recently begun to fight for control of the schools in the black community. All year, they have been in the forefront of a referendum campaign to disestablish the school committee and set up a system of community school councils to supervise education in [each of the city's black] neighborhoods."[63] Faced with the loss of their old neighborhood schools, black parents revisited the idea of community control and the idea (first advanced under the slogan "Black Power" a decade earlier) that racial separation did not have to mean racial discrimination. Embracing the once-shunned idea that different students with different needs could benefit from different schools, they turned *Brown v. Board of Education* on its head, asserting, in Huggins's words, that black students bused to predominantly white schools "typically develop feelings of inferiority because *they know* that they are considered 'culturally deprived' individuals who come to [the predominantly white] school for so-called educational, social, and cultural uplift."[64] Indeed, by 1974, many black parents believed that educational opportunity hinged less on racial balance and more on community participation, culturally relevant pedagogies, and carefully targeted programs. As Massachusetts's Advisory Council on Education (MACE) noted, "no minority individual or group has ever been heard to complain about going to a superior school whether or not it was legally balanced."[65]

This focus on community control rather than racial integration found support not only among black residents, but also among other minority residents in Boston—notably Hispanic, Chinese, and other non-English-speaking residents in the inner city. Although the class-action in *Morgan v. Hennigan* had been limited to a class of "all black children enrolled in the Boston public school system and their parents," Garrity had included all the city's minorities in his busing remedy (indeed, the precedent in *Keyes*, which involved not only blacks, but also Hispanics—obligated him to do so).[66] Yet, the decision to integrate non-English-speaking minorities into predominantly white and predominantly English-speaking schools raised difficult questions, not least of which was the question of how best to promote equal educational opportunities for non-English-speaking minorities without placing them in (discriminatory) English-speaking classrooms. This question was particularly pressing in 1974, because, in January of that year, the U.S. Supreme Court ruled in the case *Lau v. Nichols* that a failure to make appropriate classroom placements for non-English-speaking students would constitute a violation of the Civil Rights Act of 1964. In *Lau*—which dated to 1970, when Stanley Pottinger released his memorandum requiring schools to provide isolated bilingual classes—the court held that "there is no equality of treatment merely by providing students with the same facilities, textbooks, teachers, and curriculum; for students who do not understand English are effectively foreclosed from any meaningful education."[67] *Lau* required schools to offer compensatory education not only in an integrated school, but also, whenever necessary, in an isolated class *within* an integrated school.

After *Lau,* access to isolated bilingual programs was a civil right for non-English-speaking students, and Garrity had to accommodate this fact in his rulings. As he wrote in his remedy-phase decision, "El Comite de Padres Pro Defensa de la Educacion Bilingue, representing the class of Spanish-speaking students and their parents, have stressed their right to adequate bilingual education. The remedy accordingly concentrates on providing bilingual schooling for Hispanic students and for others in need of this service. Assignment of bilingual students before others will prevent excessive dispersal. Thus the 'clustering' of bilingual classes will be possible and Boston's schools will be enabled to fulfill the promise of this state's exemplary bilingual education law . . . as well as . . . the requirements of the federal Civil Rights Act of 1964."[68] Many school administrators feared that Garrity might require them to bus non-English-speaking students to new schools and create new bilingual transitional programs throughout the city at considerable public expense, but, as the federal Office of Education revealed, Boston's "bilingual department was able to avoid this outcome by invoking the need to for keeping bilingual students together as a condition of implementing the state law on bilingual education [Chapter 71A]. In 1974–75, the district decided to keep children together for bilingual programs."[69] In other words, when it came to non-English-speaking students, Garrity made an exception to his overall busing plan.[70] He noted that "the Hernandez School, which contains a citywide Spanish-English bilingual program, may enroll a student body up to 65 percent Hispanic," then added that "other minority students will be eligible along with white and black students [for] the remaining 35 percent of school capacity."[71] Accepting the idea that a bilingual program in a racially imbalanced school could, in fact, ensure equal educational opportunities for non-English-speaking students, Garrity exempted the Hernandez School from busing.

The Hernandez School exemption suggested a fundamental contradiction between the two Supreme Court precedents that had informed Garrity's busing remedy in the case of *Morgan v. Hennigan.* On the one hand, *Keyes,* based on the Fourteenth Amendment, had applied strict scrutiny to classifications of both race and national origin and found no compelling state interest in placing *any* minority student in a separate educational setting. On the other hand, *Lau,* based on the Civil Rights Act, had avoided strict scrutiny as it related to race and national origin and had relied, instead, on classifications of language deficiency or disability to find a legitimate state interest in placing non-English-speaking minority students in separate classes and even in separate schools. By exempting the Hernandez School from busing, Garrity's ruling implied that *Keyes* (which ensured placement in integrated schools on constitutional grounds) had perhaps given way to *Lau* (which ensured placement in appropriate or "meaningful" classrooms on civil rights grounds). In *Keyes*, the rationale for desegregation had been the belief that *racial balance* at the school level would end discrimination and equalize educational opportunity; in *Lau*, the rationale for isolated bilingual classes was a belief that *special-compensatory services* at the classroom level would end discrimination and equalize opportunity. In moving from *Keyes* in 1973 to *Lau* in 1974, the court retreated from the presumption that racial integration per se was somehow essential to equal educational opportunity for minority students and hinted that, in cases of language deficiency, isolated special-compensatory programs were best suited to accomplish this goal. In the same way, Garrity's exemption of the Hernandez School from his busing order implied that isolated bilingual programs could, in fact, ensure equal opportunities for national-origin minority students, even if these programs were located in racially imbalanced schools.[72]

Some court-watchers asserted that *Keyes* and *Lau* were not comparable, because *Keyes* had been based on the equal protection clause of the Fourteenth Amendment while *Lau* had been based on the merely statutory provisions of the Civil Rights Act. Yet, less than a month after *Morgan v. Hennigan*, the Tenth Circuit Court of Appeals drew on the Fourteenth Amendment to uphold a "right" of non-English-speaking students in Portales, New Mexico, to isolated bilingual-transitional programs.[73] The lower court ruled in the case of *Serna v. Portales Municipal Schools* that "Spanish-surnamed children do not have equal educational opportunity and, thus, a violation of their constitutional right to equal protection exists." Although the court's ruling was part of a desegregation suit, it focused on the need for bilingual classes. According to the court, "All students in grades 1–3 shall receive 60 minutes per day bilingual instruction. All students in grades 4–6 shall receive 45 minutes per day bilingual instruction." It added that every student "should be tested for English language proficiency and, if necessary, further bilingual instruction should be available for students who [still] display a language barrier deficiency."[74] The ruling in *Serna v. Portales Municipal Schools* came down at the same time as Garrity's ruling in *Morgan v. Hennigan*, but it applied a substantially different standard of equal educational opportunities to non-English-speaking students. Its standard for appropriate or nondiscriminatory placement did not stress classroom integration; it stressed isolated supplemental services to lift academic achievement.[75] In crafting his remedy, Garrity noted that "as we understand *Keyes*, little short of a positive showing that defendants acted with *integrative* intent would suffice to rebut the presumption of segregative intent"; yet, in the case of Spanish-speaking, national-origin minority students in *Serna,* "segregative intent" was not only permissible at the classroom level but *required* in the provision of equal educational opportunities.[76]

Despite Garrity's attempts to desegregate the Boston public schools, the concept of equal educational opportunities hinged on the "appropriateness" of student placements, and appropriateness hinged not just on racial balance but also on the hope that placements would be educationally "adequate" or beneficial. An educationally beneficial placement was not always one that fostered inter-racial contact but, rather, one that raised academic achievement in clearly measurable ways. In the wake of education-related lawsuits in the early 1970s—from *Stewart v. Phillips* and *Barnett v. Goldman* to *PARC v. Pennsylvania* and *Mills v. Board of Education,* from *Keyes v. Denver School District No. 1* and *Morgan v. Hennigan* to *Lau v. Nichols* and *Serna v. Portales Municipal Schools*—the concept of equal educational opportunities had acquired a double meaning. On the one hand, schools could be accused of denying equal opportunities if they failed to foster racial integration. On the other hand, schools could be accused of denying equal opportunities if they failed to raise academic achievement. The question thus remained: was educational opportunity a matter of racial integration, or was it a matter of academic achievement and the services needed to maximize it? In the mid-1970s, the court answered "both," but Boston's public schools were torn—not only because they had resisted racial integration for so long, but also because they had no guarantee that racial integration would finally bring charges of discrimination to an end. Moreover, they lacked the *funds* to add all the new services that Garrity's busing orders demanded. A decade of withholdings tied to racial imbalance had left the schools in dire financial circumstances, and a prolonged recession had only made the situation worse. The critical issue facing the Boston public schools in the mid-1970s was not only how to proceed with court-ordered desegregation, but also how to *pay* for the expansion of services that court-ordered desegregation required.

CHAPTER SIX

Reconfiguring School Finances, 1974–1977

In his remedy-phase ruling (known as *Morgan v. Kerrigan* after John Kerrigan replaced James Hennigan as chair of the Boston school committee), Garrity required every school in Boston to offer special services for disabled and disadvantaged students. His ninety-five-page decision held that "every school facility shall receive and educate mild and moderate special needs students, who will be assigned to schools in accordance with regular assignment procedure. . . . No less than one resource room and one special needs services space shall be set aside in each school. Each school shall have special educators and materials."[1] Garrity did not explain how schools would pay for these resource rooms, teachers, or materials; he simply declared that all these items were mandated by state law. Indeed, in September 1974, just when Garrity's busing plan took effect, Massachusetts's new special education law, Chapter 766, also took effect. The new law, passed two years earlier, required schools to retest all students and place those with diagnosed disabilities in the "most appropriate" and "least restrictive" classroom setting. It made no mention of racial integration on the classroom level; it simply stated that, in order to avoid charges of discrimination and receive state aid, schools had to ensure that disabled students achieved their "maximum feasible potential." Such a mandate, however, presented a dilemma. The simultaneous implementation of Chapter 766 and Garrity's busing order—combined with the ongoing implementation of Chapter 71A for bilingual-transitional clusters—brought a tripartite conflict between racial integration, special-compensatory services, and budget limitations to a head. In the mid-1970s, it was not at all clear that Boston would be able to pursue racial integration on a school level, provide special-compensatory programs on a classroom level, and promise balanced budgets on a district level—all at the same time. It was distinctly possible that financial considerations would derail Garrity's plans.

Under Garrity's busing remedy, each school in Boston was required to matriculate disabled, disadvantaged, and language-deficient students and to place these students in appropriate and effective special-compensatory classes. While these classes were intended to equalize educational opportunity, they were also likely to be racially imbalanced. For minority students in these classes, it was not always clear which aspect of their placement ensured equal educational opportunities: was it placement in a racially balanced school or placement in a racially imbalanced special-compensatory program? Some argued "both," not only because they believed that racially integrated schools were now constitutionally required, but also because they believed that, without racial integration, minority students would lack sufficient financial (and, thus, educational) resources in the schools they attended. It was a common assumption that Boston devoted fewer resources to predominantly black schools than to predominantly white schools and that integration would bring parity to school funding throughout the city. Though this assumption was somewhat misleading (after the growth of special-compensatory services under the ESEA, it pertained to urban-suburban school comparisons more than urban-urban school comparisons), it nonetheless fueled a debate over the relationship between resources and opportunities in public schools. Many hoped that racial integration would lead to equal resources for blacks and whites and that equal resources would, in turn, "close the gap" in academic achievement between the two groups. Implicit in Garrity's busing remedy was his belief that the best way to guarantee equal educational opportunity to all students was to promote racial integration at a school level and special programs at a classroom level—and, in this way, to assure that resources flowed to students on the basis of their needs. He believed that integration would lead to resources; resources would lead to programs; and programs would lead to achievement.[2]

What this plan failed to acknowledge, however, was that *none* of Boston's schools had sufficient resources in the mid-1970s. As black activist Noel Day commented in 1974 after Garrity released his first busing decision, "busing seems to work best where people can afford to be liberal," and Boston did not have the resources to be liberal in its support of schools.[3] Indeed, beneath the din of protests over court-ordered busing in this period, the issue with the most serious and troublesome implications for the future of the Boston public schools was not only racial integration but also school finance. As early as 1969—that is, just when the Task Force on Children Out of School was starting to demand new programs in bilingual and special education—the *Boston Globe* observed that the schools confronted "a long list of problems beginning . . . with money."[4] In November 1969, the Boston Municipal Research Bureau (BMRB) reported that the city's "expenditures for general school purposes have increased almost 25 percent in the past two years," though, over the same period, increases in the cost of living had risen only 10 percent.[5] In May 1970, the BMRB noted that "school budget submissions to the mayor this year came to $93,601,955, an increase over 1969 of $20,718,957 or 28.4 percent."[6] In March 1971, the BMRB held that "substantial borrowing for schools, urban renewal, public buildings, and streets, plus a need to borrow to meet an accelerated school payroll in 1970, indicate that 1971 debt service will exceed $33 million—[or] $20 on the tax rate."[7] By May 1972 (just before the trial in *Morgan v. Hennigan*), the financial situation in Boston had reached a crisis point. According to the BMRB, "the Boston School Department budget for 1972 totals $116.5 million; this is $20.8 million or almost 22 percent above the 1971 appropriation for school purposes. The increased budget, if not cut back, represents a $12.50 jump in the 1972 tax rate."[8] In this financial climate, adding new programs seemed all but impossible.

The fiscal troubles of the Boston public schools stemmed from four factors. The first was the nationwide recession of the early 1970s. Inflation had begun a steady rise as early as 1967, and unemployment had begun to increase in 1969. The expense of the war in Vietnam, combined with the expense of new social programs, had taken a toll on the national economy. Also, federal monetary policy, responding to escalating prices, had moved in the direction of higher interest rates, which, in turn, had caused a gradual contraction in the overall economy. In 1971, the Nixon administration accepted a policy of deficit spending and, for the first time in the nation's history, allowed the U.S. dollar to float on the world market—a policy that permitted larger fluctuations in domestic prices. In 1973, an oil embargo imposed by the Organization of Petroleum Exporting Countries (OPEC) in response to the Arab-Israeli War led to a threefold jump in domestic energy costs, which pushed prices for both manufactured goods and agricultural commodities to record highs. Annual inflation climbed from 3 percent in 1972 to 11 percent in 1974, and purchasing power plummeted.[9] The result was "stagflation," a term invented to describe a situation in which consumer prices and unemployment rose while corporate investments and output fell. Tax revenues shrank and deficits ballooned at the state and local level. As companies shifted industrial plants from the rust belt to the sun belt, many northern cities began to feel a pinch. Boston raised property taxes repeatedly throughout the 1970s to compensate for budget shortfalls, and, over time, taxpayers began to talk of revolt. The fact that middle-class families moved to the suburbs in search of lower taxes and better schools did not help Massachusetts's cities, which spent more on welfare services for the jobless. As one 1970s observer noted, "Massachusetts state and local government is caught in the classic squeeze—an increasing demand for services and declining resources."[10]

The second cause of financial troubles in the Boston public schools was the high cost of new construction. As Superintendent William Leary noted in his annual report for the 1972–73 school year, the city had built twenty-eight new schools in the past three decades and planned to build several more before the 1970s were out. "Boston currently is experiencing the most extensive program for the building of new schools and educational facilities in the city's history," he wrote. "Between 35 and 40 new schools are scheduled to be completed and occupied by 1980 at a cost of over $400 million." Leary explained that the pace of new school construction had increased dramatically in the past three or four years. The city had erected more than a dozen new elementary schools since 1969, including the now-famous Joseph Lee Elementary School in Roxbury, and these schools accommodated more than 12,000 students.[11] The city had rushed to build six of these new elementary schools, as well as a major addition to a junior high school, in 1972 at a cost that exceeded $40 million. Also in 1972, the city completed work on a modern ten-story high-rise to replace the original Boston English High School (the oldest high school in the country, founded in 1821). This structure alone had cost more than $25 million. As Leary explained in the spring of 1973, "fourteen other new schools are scheduled to be built and occupied in the next two years, seven to be ready for occupancy in September, 1975, and seven more in September, 1976." Unlike earlier buildings, these buildings had to meet the requirements of Chapter 766 for handicap accessibility—requirements that added to their cost. Moreover, the city had to retro-fit its existing schools to meet the new standards. In Boston in the mid-1970s, school construction costs quickly exhausted taxpayers' patience and, over time, made it more difficult to raise money for education.[12]

A third cause of fiscal trouble in Boston's public schools was a dramatic rise in teacher salaries. Teachers unions grew rapidly in the early 1970s, even as other unions fell apart. For years, the teachers unions had argued that low pay compromised the supply of new recruits.[13] They insisted that higher salaries would raise both the quantity and the quality of new teachers. In effect, they argued that higher teacher salaries would lead to higher student achievement. In the 1970s, teachers in Boston did win higher salaries, but the link between pay and performance was hard to see. As the BMRB asserted, "teachers' pay scale for bachelor's degree holders rose over the two years [from 1967 to 1969] by 16.7 percent. . . . For those with a master's degree, the two-year increase for the first step was 16.9 percent." The administrative staff also received substantial raises in this period. According to the BMRB, "the assistant superintendents, administrative assistants to the superintendent, personnel relations coordinator, and personnel relations consultant were all increased $3,645 or 19.2 percent in two years. The superintendent received a $5,000 or 15.1 percent hike, while the [six] associate superintendents were raised $3,250 or 13.4 percent." The BMRB could not see any rational justification for these raises—particularly since the schools did not seem to be doing a better job of educating their students. "With the rapid rise in school costs and the important bearing salaries have on these costs, it is no longer acceptable merely to announce to taxpayers what new salaries are going to be each September. The rationale for raises, even those collectively bargained for, must be explained."[14] In fact, much to the chagrin of the BMRB, the teachers in Boston frequently demanded pay increases and then opposed tax increases necessary to fund these raises.[15] In March 1970, teachers seeking higher salaries went on strike (for the first time ever in the city's history), but they did not endorse higher taxes.[16]

The issue of taxes pointed to the fourth cause of financial troubles in the Boston public schools. Starting in 1969, state legislators had begun to make a series of changes to Chapter 70, Massachusetts's formula for distributing state aid to schools. The changes were complex, but they boiled down to a subtle shift from "equalized" toward "general" aid to schools. In 1966, the legislature had linked Chapter 70 aid to "equalized property valuations per school-attending child." This formula was supposed to ensure that Chapter 70 grants reflected not only a town's ability to support its schools but also its effort to do so. If a town had higher equalized property valuations per child—and, thus, an easier time collecting property tax revenues—then the state would contribute proportionally less aid to that town's schools. If a town had lower property valuations per child—and, thus, a harder time collecting property tax revenue—then the state would contribute proportionally more. In theory, this formula was supposed to equalize the burden of supporting public schools in each town throughout the state; in reality, however, while it ensured that towns with low property valuations received more aid in *proportional* terms, it still allowed towns with high property valuations to receive more aid in *absolute* terms. For example, a wealthy suburb with high property valuations and few children attending school could receive more aid *per child* in absolute terms than an urban area with low property valuations and far more children attending school. Under this formula, cities like Boston, with mid-range property valuations and large numbers of students, did not necessarily benefit. Boston's total Chapter 70 assistance increased under the percentage-equalization formula, but it did not increase on a per-pupil basis as much as state assistance to some wealthier districts with fewer students.

Thus, the equalization formula did not actually equalize state aid to students. In a 1970 report to the Federal Reserve Bank of Boston, economist Steven Weiss noted that "the Massachusetts program actually has a slight tendency to yield perverse results—a positive relationship between ability [to pay] and state aid per pupil."[17] Weiss also found that, in trying to keep up with their neighbors, Massachusetts towns with lower property valuations were taxing themselves at much higher rates than towns with higher property valuations. In 1971, the Massachusetts Department of Education created a subcommittee on equal educational opportunities to analyze these disparities. It contrasted the relatively poor town of Oxford with the relatively rich town of Brookline: "Oxford, in 1969–70, had a per pupil cost of $661—$60 below the state average. Yet Oxford's effort ranked second in the state that year with $7.41 [in taxes] per $100 of equalized valuation. Brookline, by comparison, ranked 303 out of the 351 cities and towns in Massachusetts in local effort. Brookline, with its per pupil costs close to $1,300, had almost twice as much to spend on each child and required three times *less* effort, because Brookline's effort is set at $2.30 per $100 of equalized valuation. The principal reason for this difference is found in Brookline's $55,500 equalized valuation per school-attending child, which is $44,000 higher than Oxford's [equalized valuation of only $11,500 per school-attending child]."[18] Thus, even at higher tax rates, towns with lower property valuations could not fund their schools at the same level as towns with higher property valuations. As André Danière, a member of the state Bureau of Equal

Educational Opportunities and an economist at Boston College, observed in a *Cost-Benefit Analysis of General Purpose State School-Aid Formulas in Massachusetts,* the fiftieth town from the bottom of the "valuation" list spent only 70 percent as much as the fiftieth town from the top—at equal levels of tax effort.[19]

⟡

In an attempt to overcome these inequalities, the Massachusetts legislature voted in 1969 to reprioritize its commitment to "general" and "equalized" aid. Whereas, earlier, the state had put equalized aid (based on property valuations) ahead of general aid (based on need), the state now reversed this order and placed general aid ahead of equalized aid. This change benefited the poorest towns, but it had a mixed effect in Boston, which had neither the highest nor the lowest property valuations in the state. Essentially, the revised priorities meant Boston's state school aid remained unchanged. Before the revision, the city received $32,341,687 in state school aid. After the revision, it received $32,664,375. The amount of general aid rose from $14,206,611 to $24,375,000, but the amount of equalized aid fell from $15,673,403 to $5,700,000. As the BMRB reported, "there is no doubt that the new priorities of distribution are more sensible. Phasing out the equalized valuation formula will knock out a formula which does not relate to need. But a more principled method of distribution will not ease the initial shock for Boston of receiving little more in 1970 than in 1969. . . . Thus, the cry from Boston and other cities and towns for additional state aid or [a greater state] assumption of certain local costs will not abate. School and other local costs are growing so fast that the annual increase in the distribution of state-shared taxes is inadequate and a piece-meal approach."[20] Moreover, the revised priorities in 1969 tied any future increases in general school aid to increases in state sales tax receipts, which varied annually. As one Boston policy analyst explained, "the yield of a sales tax is highly elastic, typically fluctuating more than proportionately with changes in general economic conditions. As a result, sales-tax revenue growth did not exhibit any regularity, let alone any significant correlation with the rate of increase in school spending."[21]

Adding to the fiscal crisis of the Boston public schools in this period was the fact that the state distributed aid on a reimbursement basis, which meant that state aid for any program reflected a school's costs not in the current year but, rather, in the *previous* year. Furthermore, when the state determined local-aid distributions in January, it deducted the previous year's state aid—as well as federal aid—from each district's reimbursable costs. As a result, state aid followed what was known as a "yo-yo" pattern: if aid was relatively high in the previous year, then it would be relatively low in the current year, because the state deducted the previous year's higher allocations from the current year's reimbursable expenditures. Even if costs went up, the district would have to accept lower amounts of aid in the current year and wait until state aid caught up to escalating expenses in the next year (at which point aid tied to earlier costs was still unlikely to meet steadily increasing needs). As one observer argued, "since entitlements are determined in part by averages that are unknown until it is too late, no one can make adequate educational plans. Local property taxes [covering the difference between state reimbursements and schools' annual needs] . . . cannot be fully determined until these reimbursements are known. Thus, the current state aid program is especially ineffective as a policy instrument to encourage longer-term educational planning."[22] In Boston, this approach had a serious effect, because the schools relied heavily on state and federal aid, *both* of which were deducted from annual reimbursable expenses. If the schools received more federal aid in a given year, then they received less state aid the next year.[23] Growing school budgets were, thus, in part, a response to volatile reimbursements from the state: by submitting larger-than-necessary budget requests, schools hoped to recoup some of the losses that resulted from deducting their previous year's state and federal aid.

The intricacies of state school aid provoked intense and sometimes bitter debate in the 1970s—a time when many educators believed that equal expenditures promised equal opportunities and must not depend on local wealth. In Massachusetts, some argued that a state-mandated "minimum expenditure" for all schools would ensure equal educational opportunities. In "The State Dollar and the Schools," Charlotte Ryan of the state Educational Conference Board outlined a minimum-expenditure bill drafted by André Danière. "A relatively high *mandated minimum expenditure* was an integral part of the Danière foundation program," she observed, "on the premise that the mandated expenditure ought to provide the desired education for each child." Suggesting that a failure to spend the minimum should trigger a reduction in state aid, Ryan noted that Danière's minimum was high enough to provide a "quality" education to all: "Since the minimum was set as the average of the highest 25 percent of the previous year's expenditures in all school districts, a continuing rise in the standard would be assured." She also asserted that "if the minimum is set at a high level, all but the richest districts [will be] likely to make similar expenditures and thus salary competition will be reduced; communities will be freed from debate on the budget they can 'afford,' and will turn to educational considerations." Of course, one obstacle to this plan was the difficulty of raising enough money at the state level to support a "high" mandated expenditure; another was the difficulty of accommodating the extra needs of urban schools over and above the mandated minimum. Yet, Ryan had solutions to both obstacles. Her solution to the first was a new system of income, sales, and state property taxes, and her solution to the second was a "municipal overburden factor" to compensate cities for any excess costs associated with compensatory, bilingual, and special education programs.[24] Ultimately, she promised, Boston would receive the aid it needed.

Ryan's ideas circulated widely in Massachusetts in 1970 and built support for the hypothesis that equal expenditures would promote equal opportunities in schools. A variation on this hypothesis led to a famous legal decision in 1971 (a year before *Morgan v. Hennigan* went to trial) when California's supreme court ruled in *Serrano v. Priest* that that state's formula for distributing school aid did not equalize school spending and, thus, unconstitutionally discriminated against pupils on the basis of local wealth. In the court's words, "We have determined that this funding scheme invidiously discriminates against the poor because it makes the quality of a child's education a function of the wealth of his parents and his neighbors. Recognizing as we must that the right to an education in our public schools is a fundamental interest which cannot be conditioned on wealth, we can discern no compelling state purpose necessitating the present method of financing. We have concluded, therefore, that such a system cannot withstand constitutional challenge and must fall before the equal protection clause [of the state constitution]." The court's ruling in *Serrano v. Priest* (released four months before the filing of *Barnett v. Goldman,* which tried to extend the notion of education as a "fundamental interest" to disabled students in Massachusetts) worried state administrators, who hurriedly tried to predict how they might have to alter their aid formulas to meet the (apparent) standard of equal educational resources as a fundamental right. The class action in *Serrano* extended the category of "wealth discrimination" to all children in the state except those who lived in the district offering "the greatest educational opportunity of all school districts within California."[25] In this way, it implied that, in order to avoid charges of discrimination, the state would have to aid each school up to the level of the one with the highest expenditure per pupil.

The *Serrano* decision certainly captured the attention of school officials and state legislators in Massachusetts. Shortly after the decision, the legislature's equal educational opportunities subcommittee learned that the National Educational Finance Project placed Massachusetts below California on its most recent ranking of "equity" in state school-aid formulas. "On a scale of 1 to 8.400, Hawaii's state school system rates a perfect 8.400," the subcommittee noted, explaining that Hawaii had collapsed all schools into one district with full state funding. "Massachusetts ranks a poor 33rd with a score of 4.536, slightly behind California's 4.841 but ahead of Minnesota's 4.333." The fact that Massachusetts outranked Minnesota offered little—if any—consolation, however, because, according to the subcommittee, Minnesota's formula for state aid, like California's, had "been found by a federal district court judge to be in violation of the Fourteenth Amendment." After the *Serrano* decision, it looked as though any formula that did not resolve the problem of unequal expenditures at the local level could be deemed unconstitutional. This possibility spurred the Massachusetts equal educational opportunities subcommittee to recommend a number of changes to the state formula. "Our sense of urgency in proposing a course of action results not so much from the California court decision and its sequels as from our awareness of the minimal progress the state has made towards equality of school support, and of the importance of providing for equal educational opportunity. The urgency of this problem requires *immediate* action."[26] The subcommittee's top three suggestions were, first, to detach school aid from sales-tax revenues so that past limitations on aid (due to prorating) could be avoided; second, to require towns to use up-to-date property assessments so that revenues would not be derived from assessments made in 1945; and third, to adopt a municipal overburden factor to compensate urban areas for high-cost special services.[27]

When the state legislature failed to enact any of these changes, several prominent individuals stepped forward to press the issue. In 1972, former Harvard president James Conant, once a leading proponent of local control, recommended full state funding for all schools. In a four-part proposal, he called, first, for a thorough centralization of power in the hands of the chief state school officer (the state commissioner); second, for a uniform schedule of teacher salaries throughout the state; third, for a revision of district borders to reflect "strictly educational considerations" rather than income or property differences; and, fourth, for greater allocations of resources to areas with greater educational needs. "For example," he stated in a lecture at Harvard, "districts which had a larger percentage of disadvantaged children would be entitled to an increase in the teaching staff following guidelines determined by the state as a result of collective bargaining. . . . Construction needs would be determined by state officials after consultation with the chairmen of the local boards."[28] Conant held that the necessary increase in the state budget could come from a "state property tax" (akin to the state property tax Charlotte Ryan had outlined) to replace the traditional local property tax. This concept of a state property tax appealed to Robert Capeless, a member of Massachusetts's special commission to develop a master tax plan (and a former tax commissioner under Governor Furcolo). At a joint meeting of the Harvard Graduate School of Education, the New England School Development Council, and the Federal Reserve Bank of Boston, Capeless argued that a state property tax levied "not on individual property owners but on each city and town according to its equalized valuation" would "eliminate the gross inequities of a large-scale *local* property tax" and, in the process, would ensure equal expenditures—and, thus equal programs and equal opportunities—in every school in Massachusetts.[29]

Capeless estimated that full state funding for local schools would cost about $1.3 billion per year—$800 million more than Massachusetts was already spending on education—and argued that *Serrano* necessitated this huge increase. "After a horrendous interim period of reconciling the differences between high spending–high quality systems and low spending–low quality systems," he held, "this approach should achieve complete equality of educational opportunity or as near thereto as can be achieved. It would mean . . . an end to the absurdity of over 300 independent local systems in Massachusetts, and their replacement by a monolithic central agency or more probably by a system of large, sensibly balanced, and comparatively equal regional groupings. It would mean certainly an end to determination by local or regional groups of their own levels of spending." This proposal would have sounded preposterous a decade earlier, but, after *Serrano*, it seemed the only way to meet the new constitutional standard: "Local autonomy," Capeless wrote, "would be preserved only as to management and spending of funds allocated centrally on an equal basis."[30] Indeed, even the Nixon administration—a long-time proponent of local control—gradually come around to the idea of full state funding for local schools. The *Boston Globe* noted in March 1972, that a National Commission on School Finance had urged the Congress "to supply financial incentives that would make it possible for states to absorb public education costs now borne by localities, so that the fiscal disparity between wealthy and impoverished school districts might be eliminated and property taxes reduced." The *Globe* added that a shift to full state funding had been made "all but inevitable by a series of recent court decisions declaring that the local property tax is an unconstitutional means of paying school costs since it makes the quality of education dependent on the wealth of a district."[31]

The fact that the Nixon administration endorsed full state funding for schools and, at the same time, opposed busing to achieve racial balance indicated that, at least in 1972, the administration saw equalized expenditures as a substitute for racial integration. From Nixon's perspective, equal educational opportunities depended *not* on racial integration but on equal resources for school programs, and the best way to counter lawsuits on behalf of racial balance (such as *Morgan v. Hennigan* in Boston) was to show that racially imbalanced schools could succeed with sufficient infusions of state aid. As policy analyst Paul Cook of MIT argued in a major report, *Modernizing School Governance for Educational Equality and Diversity* (printed under the aegis of the Massachusetts Advisory Council on Education [MACE] in 1972), "the threat of [court-ordered desegregation] has produced friends for educational equality in hardcore poverty areas that such areas never knew they had. Thus, there is growing support for improving quality in the poorest schools as a way of forestalling the alternative." Cook added that "if those who want equality for its own sake are joined by the hypocrites who want it for the wrong reason, [then] a convincing majority should result." Asserting that all "children should have access to approximately the same level of professional and other staffing, support materials and services, and building quality, or at least substantially equivalent combinations of these things," Cook nonetheless warned that equal resources alone might not lead to equal educational opportunities for disadvantaged students in inner-city schools. In his view, truly equal schools—where equality was measured in terms of educational results—would eventually have to "go beyond [equal resources], and attempt to equalize peer group influences by [integrating] student bodies, which is of course a far more explosive issue than mere resource equalization."[32]

◈

The pursuit of equal funds as the key to equal educational opportunities or outcomes lost much of its momentum in the spring of 1973, when the U.S. Supreme Court issued two decisions, which together suggested that, at least from a federal perspective, integration was essential to equal opportunities, but resources were not. One of these two decisions was, of course, the *Keyes* decision, which led a year later to Garrity's busing orders in Boston. The other decision, which preceded *Keyes* by three months, came in the case of the *San Antonio Independent School District v. Rodriguez*. In this case, the court found that the system of state school aid in Texas did not violate the equal protection clause of the Fourteenth Amendment, despite disparities in local school resources and differences in tax effort throughout the state. *Rodriguez*, like *Keyes*, was a closely divided decision, and the combination of the two indicated that the majority was more concerned about racial integration than equal resources in schools (at least as these issues applied to the equal protection clause of the Fourteenth Amendment). Apparently, in the court's view, integrated schools offered equal opportunities *even* if they had grossly unequal resources. As Justice Powell summarized, the Texas system, "by its provision for state contributions to each district, assured a basic education for every child, while permitting and encouraging vital local participation and control of schools through district taxation." Powell added that the Texas system, "which was similar to systems employed in virtually every other state, was not the product of purposeful discrimination against any class, but instead was a responsible attempt to arrive at practical and workable solutions to educational problems."[33] He concluded, therefore, that Texas's formula for state school aid did not violate the basic principle of equal educational opportunity for all students.

The *Rodriguez* decision effectively limited the *Serrano* decision to California (as far as it pertained to state constitutional law) and relegated all cases dealing with state aid to state courts. Moreover, in a rather jarring move, Powell held that, since education was not a fundamental right mentioned either explicitly or implicitly in the U.S. Constitution, federal courts had no method of adjudicating issues of educational spending: "Even if it were conceded that some identifiable quantum of education is a constitutionally protected prerequisite to the meaningful exercise of [either the explicitly enumerated 'right' to free speech or the implicitly guaranteed 'right' to vote], we have no indication that the present educational expenditure in Texas provides an education that falls short. Whatever merit [the plaintiffs'] argument might have if a state's financing system occasioned an absolute denial of educational opportunities to any of its children, that argument provides no basis for finding an interference with fundamental rights where only relative differences in spending levels are involved and where—as is true in the present case—no charge fairly could be made that the system fails to provide each child with an opportunity to acquire the basic minimum skills necessary for the enjoyment of the rights of speech and of full participation in the political process." In other words, as long as each state cultivated "the basic minimum skills" required to participate in a democratic society, federal courts were likely to uphold their systems of school aid as constitutionally adequate.[34] As Powell noted, "at least where wealth is involved, the Equal Protection Clause does not require absolute equality or precisely equal advantages. Nor, indeed, in view of the infinite variables affecting the educational process, can any system assure equal quality of education except in the most relative sense."[35] According to Justice Powell, the quality of education (beyond a basic minimum) was "non-justiciable" at the federal level.

Powell's assertion that the quality of education was ultimately "non-justiciable" at the federal level took the debate over school finances out of federal courts and threw it to state legislatures. It shifted the debate from the legal arena to a *political* arena and forced states to reconsider the link between educational resources and educational opportunities. Recognizing that his decision placed the onus of responsibility on states, Powell offered a "cautionary postscript" to those who would debate this issue: "Some commentators have concluded that, whatever the contours of the alternative financing programs that might be devised and approved, the result could not avoid being a beneficial one. But, just as there is nothing simple about the constitutional issues involved in these cases, there is nothing simple or certain about predicting the consequences of massive changes in the financing and control of public education. Those who have devoted the most thoughtful attention to the practical ramifications of these cases have found no clear or dependable answers and their scholarship reflects no such unqualified confidence in the desirability of completely uprooting the existing system." Noting that inner-city schools were not always located in the poorest districts in their states, Powell warned that revising property tax formulas to benefit poorer areas would not necessarily win votes from property-rich but income-poor cities: "Any alternative that calls for significant increases in expenditures for education, whether financed through increases in property taxation or through other sources of tax dollars, such as income and sales taxes, is certain to encounter political barriers," Powell explained. "At a time when nearly every state and locality is suffering from fiscal undernourishment, and with demands for local services of all kinds burgeoning and with weary taxpayers already resisting tax increases," urban schools, if they wanted resources, would have to explain to the public why their educational programs were worth the expense.[36]

Powell was right. By 1973, the greatest challenge facing urban schools was not a lack of legal protection for equal educational opportunities but, rather, a lack of *political* consensus about the best way to promote high-quality education for all. Schools had to be "accountable" for results, but what was the measure of accountability? Were integrated schools enough if they did not also have better *programs* to improve student outcomes?[37] As early as January 1973 (approximately two months before *Rodriguez*), Joseph Cronin, the state secretary for educational affairs in Massachusetts under Governor Sargent, raised precisely this point. "Rising demands for educational productivity, for accountability and for performance are coming from the people who entrust their children to our educational institutions, and who also foot the bills," he asserted. "Massachusetts is not now geared up to meet these challenges and demands. It is not organized properly to provide quality in a time of scarcity or to widen its understanding of education at a time when education itself is under attack."[38] During the 1973-74 school year, Cronin rallied his colleagues at the state level to construct a "Plan for Advancing Quality and Excellence by the Organization and Management of Public Education," which appealed for increased local accountability. "There is no doubt that there is a substantial and invisible movement toward greater accountability in the schools," the 150-page document explained. "There is an increasing concern on the part of the public about higher educational expenditures and how these increased costs are related to improved programs and services." In response to this concern, the plan outlined "a results-oriented school management system characterized by needs assessment, goal definition, careful consideration and selection of action or program alternatives (so-called program budgeting), long-range planning, opportunity for citizen involvement on a broad scale, and careful evaluation techniques."[39]

In 1973-74, as part of its broad push for accountability, the Massachusetts Department of Education began—for the first time—to collect data on statewide academic achievement. As Cronin summarized, "state evaluation staff members have provided test data and analyses as a first step toward measuring the actual performance in each school system."[40] He added that the state adopted "specific measures for evaluating the progress of each student and the success of each educational program. These accountability gauges shall be systematic and public, and shall make use of standardized measures of progress such as the National Assessment of Educational Progress."[41] By comparing scores from school to school and district to district, Cronin promised, the state would be able to correlate inputs with outcomes (that is, spending with results) and, using these data, would be able to determine whether different students in different schools had, in fact, had access to equal educational opportunities. If test scores were equal, then, it was assumed, opportunities must have been equal, too.[42] "We strongly endorse the building of a statewide program for assessing results," said the governor's staff, adding that assessing results presumed the availability of quality programs to maximize both opportunities and outcomes: "measuring results is an incomplete practice unless one also measures whether or not an organization is really trying (has programs) to pursue these results; and whether or not the appropriate programs are really readily accessible to all students. Without these latter measurements, truly informed decisions cannot be made about what actions might best be taken to achieve better results."[43] Connecting resources to programs, programs to opportunities, and opportunities to outcomes, Cronin held that the way to show taxpayers the value of their educational investment was to show results.[44] As Charlotte

Ryan put it, "unless the end result satisfies the community, school support tends to disappear."[45]

This emphasis on accountability marked a harbinger of things to come, but, after Garrity's busing order in the fall of 1974, the primary measure of accountability was not results per se but racial integration—which Garrity insisted would *lead* to results. And, yet, not even integrated schools could improve results without resources, and it was resources that Massachusetts lacked. In November 1974, in a close gubernatorial election shaped by the related issues of busing and the budget, Francis Sargent lost on both these key issues to Michael Dukakis, a forty-one-year-old state representative from Brookline whose public television talk show, *The Advocate*, boosted his visibility. Dukakis, who had been the Democratic nominee for lieutenant governor in 1970 when his running mate was Boston mayor Kevin White, won the nomination for governor in 1974 by defeating Attorney General Robert Quinn in the primaries. He chose Thomas P. O'Neill III—the son of Congressman Thomas P. "Tip" O'Neill—as his lieutenant governor and ran a skillful campaign against the incumbent Sargent. Amid the tumult of the busing crisis in the fall, Sargent had found himself in a difficult political situation. Branded as the governor who had declared martial law, he alienated many white voters, and Dukakis capitalized on this vulnerability. Promising to restore peace in the state, Dukakis also pledged to balance the state budget with no new taxes. He won the general election with 56 percent of the vote and immediately set out to rebuild Massachusetts's weakened financial base. Inheriting a record deficit as well as record unemployment from his predecessor, he vowed to "put the state's fiscal house in order" and did his part by riding Boston's subway to work. Young and energetic, he led recession-weary citizens to expect "the kind of cool, crisp decision making his media personality seemed to promise."[46] As the *Boston Globe* observed, "the Dukakis administration is demanding efficiency for every public dollar spent."[47]

Dukakis was not, however, Boston's only newcomer. Just after his inauguration in 1975, the Boston school committee replaced forty-four-year-old Superintendent William J. Leary, who had been in office less than three years, with Marion Fahey, an associate superintendent who had been a protégé of William Ohrenberger and who also was the first woman to head the city's schools. Leary, like Governor Sargent, had found himself in an impossible predicament after Garrity's busing order in 1974. "It was a damned-if-you-do, damned-if-you-don't period," he recalled of the months leading up to his dismissal. "I was trying to carry out an order of the court, and the majority of the committee was not in favor of it." In a series of retrospective articles, the *Boston Globe* noted that "for Leary, the busing era was an almost daily delirium of 16-hour work-days, violence erupting in city schools, and, sometimes, angry white residents stoning buses filled with black schoolchildren. On the rare night he got home in time to watch the national network news, he was treated to anchormen intoning, 'Today in Boston chaos reigned.'" Leary was trapped between the rigid expectations of the courts and the equally rigid expectations of the school committee. The court saw busing as the key to equal educational opportunities, but the committee said busing could not work without additional programs funded by the state. "It was rough," Leary recalled of the 1974–75 year. "I thought at forty-one I was a pretty knowledgeable person. . . . Educationally, I was. Politically, I was not. I had to learn things they don't teach you at Harvard."[48] What he learned, above all, was that the pursuit of equal educational opportunity for poor minority students in the inner city was no easy matter; at a time when the federal court was demanding racial integration *and* new programs, it was not obvious that Boston could afford both at once.[49] If nothing else, unprecedented oil prices in 1974–75 made busing far costlier than anyone in the school department had anticipated.

Thus, when Marion Fahey took the chief job in the Boston public schools, she had to consider not only what the courts mandated, but also what the city could afford. Facing the same two challenges her predecessor had faced—busing and the budget—she adopted a strategy that her mentor, Superintendent Ohrenberger, had used: she applied for federal aid to special-compensatory programs. It was a smart strategy for many reasons, and its timing was propitious. In 1974–75, after Garrity's busing order had taken effect, the Boston public schools were eligible for federal aid to a degree that they had not been eligible in over a decade. Also, the amount of aid that was available was larger than ever, because the Education Amendments of 1974—the second reauthorization of the Elementary and Secondary Education Act (the ESEA)—had dramatically expanded the scope of federal support for the public schools. These amendments covered all aspects of federal aid—from compensatory education for the disadvantaged to special education for the disabled—and included funding for the National Defense Education Act as well as the Emergency School Assistance Act, which supported inner-city "magnet" schools to facilitate desegregation. The amendments also aided dropout prevention projects, school health services, gifted children's programs, women's equity programs, career education, arts education, metric education, consumer education, ethnic heritage centers, and federal programs for migratory, delinquent, and Native American pupils. All told, the Education Amendments of 1974 (P.L. 93-380) authorized more than $12 billion over four years to fund categorical programs in public schools—and Superintendent Fahey sought to obtain as much of this aid as possible. Like her mentor, she began to position the Boston public schools to maximize their eligibility for federal aid. And, like Ohrenberger, she did so by expanding special-compensatory programs for the disadvantaged and the disabled.

⟡

This sort of maneuvering to maximize aid was exactly what some federal officials began to fear in 1974-75. Gerald Ford—who signed the new education amendments two weeks after replacing Richard Nixon in the White House—criticized the growth of federal spending at a time of continuing stagflation. The financial uncertainties of the era (the OPEC embargo peaked in 1974-75) made Ford reluctant to sign legislation that sent large grants to local schools without any proof of their effectiveness. In his first presidential address, Ford remarked, "Last week, the Congress passed the elementary and secondary education bill, and I found it on my desk. . . . I must be frank. In implementing its provisions, I will oppose excessive funding during this inflationary crisis." Calling inflation "domestic enemy number one," Ford warned the Congress to beware of "substantially increased federal funding for education, especially at a time when excessive federal spending is already fanning the flames of inflation. . . . I hope Congress will exercise restraint in appropriating funds . . . and will carefully avoid increasing the budget."[50] Congress, however, did not heed this advice. It increased overall authorizations for educational programs by 23 percent—from $2.8 billion in 1974 to $3.5 billion in 1975—and, in so doing, strengthened the idea that carefully targeted categorical programs were essential to equal educational opportunities in the nation's schools. At the same time, however, Congress barred the use of federal money for any purpose related to court-ordered busing, presumably on grounds that busing was *not* essential to promoting equal opportunities. This combination of federal aid to categorical programs and federal opposition to court-ordered busing matched the aims of Superintendent Fahey in Boston. To improve Boston's (now at least theoretically integrated) schools, she held, the city needed more aid for special-compensatory programs.[51]

Fahey's aims were remarkably well suited to the federal education amendments. Following the past precedents of the ESEA, the amendments targeted funds on a categorical basis at programs assisting specific groups of disadvantaged and disabled students. The most prominent of these programs was, of course, Title I, which distributed $1.8 billion, or 51 percent of the total, in 1975. Another increasingly prominent program was Title VII for bilingual education, which distributed nearly $100 million in 1975. Fahey sought as much aid as possible under Title I and Title VII and discovered that, under the new education amendments, federal funds were more accessible than ever. Title VII aid, for example, had originally been linked to the antipoverty rationale of the ESEA, but the new amendments removed the poverty criterion for eligibility, so Title VII aid flowed to non-English-speaking students *regardless* of their family income. In effect, non-English-speaking pupils received federal aid not because of economic disadvantages but, rather, because of linguistic deficiencies. The same principle applied to other groups of disabled pupils, including mentally retarded, physically handicapped, and emotionally disturbed students, all of whom received aid regardless of family income. Indeed, one of the most significant shifts in federal aid after 1974–75 was a subtle shift from poverty-related to nonpoverty-related criteria for eligibility. Increasingly, aid for the disabled was considered a civil right, but aid for the disadvantaged was not. This shift had a major effect on urban schools in the coming years, but it went largely undetected at first. In the meantime, Superintendent Fahey welcomed the tendency to identify "need" on the basis of disability and took it as a cue to initiate special-compensatory programs. She made up for the fact that Boston's public schools could not use federal aid to pay for court-ordered busing by using federal aid to pay for court-ordered special-compensatory programs.

Increases in federal aid for special-compensatory programs came at the right time in Massachusetts. The new state special education law, Chapter 766, took effect just two weeks after the passage of the new federal education amendments, and it did not take Fahey long to realize that federal aid to new special-compensatory programs could defray some of the initial costs of Chapter 766—which, due to state reimbursement procedures, required local districts to cover the full costs of all mandated special education programs in the first year (estimated at $50 million to $100 million statewide in 1974–75) while waiting for state reimbursements the following year. The simultaneous impact of busing and Chapter 766 threatened to send the already overextended Boston public schools into an irreversible financial tailspin unless they received some up-front state or federal aid. Indeed, throughout Massachusetts, many districts hesitated to fulfill the requirements of Chapter 766 until they were sure of receiving state or federal grants; the fact that the state allocated only $26 million in "up-front" aid did not help schools' compliance rate.[52] As the Massachusetts Advocacy Center (MAC)—the newly incorporated version of Boston's Task Force on Children Out of School— noted, first-year compliance with Chapter 766 was poor. "No school system was fully implementing it," the MAC found, and many "failed to implement the most basic new provisions." Surveys revealed that many schools did not retest their students, and some, citing a lack of funds, did not even hire psychologists to do this job. According to the MAC, the Boston public schools were far behind schedule.[53] The *Boston Globe* added that "no Massachusetts city or town is ending this school year [1974–75] confident that it has complied fully with the complicated and ambitious special education legislation known as Chapter 766."[54] Fahey, for her part, blamed Boston's sluggishness not on a lack of resolve but, rather, on a lack of resources.

In June 1975, associate superintendent for special education Alice Casey claimed that the Boston public schools "would have had to have a budget of $25 million, at least," to pay for the city's first-year expenditure under Chapter 766. When the city received less than $4 million in up-front assistance from the state (that is, only half of what the school committee requested), newly elected committee member Kathleen Sullivan, a former special education teacher, condemned what she considered the "failure of both the mayor and the school department to give Chapter 766 high priority."[55] Yet, the mayor and the school department deserved only partial blame for the city's slow start in implementing Chapter 766. As policy analyst Milton Budoff wrote in the *Harvard Educational Review* the state had not been sufficiently prepared to help local schools administer the law. Most glaringly, the law lacked clear procedures for identifying students who might be eligible for special education programs. In its attempt to avoid "stigmatizing" labels, the law had neglected to specify any criteria for schools to use in diagnosing particular disabilities. As Budoff explained, "no definition of the child with special educational needs was ever established. Consequently, the districts had difficulty estimating the numbers of children potentially eligible for services, and they could not project staffing needs for the first implementation year. The final regulations were so late in coming and rumors so rife as successive drafts were produced, that budgets for staff and other contracted costs—which had to be drawn up by district staff and approved by school committees during the year before the implementation date—could not be realistically formulated." In short, the state could not say which students needed placement in special programs, and schools hesitated to make placements until they were sure of state reimbursements.[56] As Superintendent Fahey repeatedly asserted, new programs required dependable resources.

Of course, both programs *and* resources hinged on reliable diagnoses—which, in the absence of clear placement guidelines, were difficult to obtain. Some districts, fearing litigation for over-diagnoses, actually reduced enrollments in special education programs. Other districts, fearing litigation for under-diagnoses, transferred record number of pupils into these programs. At first, diagnoses appeared to lack any pattern. Gradually, however, a subtle design emerged—along with a very subtle explanation. To understand why some districts erred on the side of over-diagnoses while others, including Boston, erred initially on the side of under-diagnoses, it was necessary to grasp, first, the particular formula Massachusetts used to allocate state aid to special- and regular-education programs and, second, the growing expectation in 1975 of a major increase in federal categorical aid for the disabled. In 1969, when Massachusetts's school-aid formula shifted its emphasis from "equalized" to "general" aid—ostensibly to benefit poorer districts—the state legislature, at the same time, shifted the priority it assigned to special and regular education. In keeping with its focus on need, the state put special education *ahead* of regular education in its sequence of distribution; hence, the state met its obligations to special-education programs *before* it met any obligations to regular-education programs. Although intended to benefit inner-city districts with large numbers of students in special education, this reprioritization had an unintended effect after the passage of Chapter 766: since funds for special and regular education drew on the same revenue source (the state sales tax), and since funds for special education were legally guaranteed while funds for regular education were subject to proration, schools had an incentive to move expenses (that is, enrollments) into special education programs. In other words, after Chapter 766, schools could maximize state aid by maximizing special education enrollments.[57]

This incentive to maximize special education enrollments applied to all districts, but it applied especially to affluent districts that stood to receive more aid under Chapter 766 than they received under Chapter 70 (i.e., equalized aid).[58] As one analyst explained, wealthier districts "artificially inflated their reported special education spending in 1972-73 and 1973-74 in the hope of increasing their state aid for special education in the crucial 'base-line' hold-harmless year, 1974-75. This was particularly true in districts with higher-than-average taxable property wealth per pupil, which generally fared poorly under the state's equalizing Chapter 70 school aid program." From 1972 until 1975, "the growth of special education programs fed a tendency among school districts to withdraw resources from children in regular day programs in an attempt to limit the growth in overall school budget[s]."[59] This tactic was widespread. As the Institute for Governmental Services (IGS) at the University of Massachusetts–Amherst noted, "it is no secret in the Commonwealth that wealthier communities increase state aid by identifying and serving more children in special education programs. They increase their state aid by shifting expenditures to the more lucrative Chapter 766 formula for reimbursement. Wealthier communities expend more per pupil on special education programs and are reimbursed by the state at a rate they would not qualify for under Chapter 70 for regular education expenditures."[60] The effect of this strategy was clear: both enrollments and expenditures in special education skyrocketed in affluent areas in 1974–75. As long as state aid to special education came "off the top" of the general education budget, wealthier districts transferred students into special education programs. Indeed, suburban communities welcomed state aid for their special education programs—and were happy to remind critics that recent court rulings (*PARC v. Pennsylvania*, for example) construed access to these programs as a constitutional right.[61]

This situation was fraught with historical irony. For years, poor minority students in the inner city had been over-diagnosed as mentally retarded and emotionally disturbed. Boston had been under court pressure for half a decade to *reduce* enrollments in special classes. And, yet, urban schools had succeeded in curbing their diagnoses just when state and federal agencies started to direct financial resources to the disabled. Indeed, it was in 1969—the very year South End parents sued to "end educational entombment" in isolated classes (a lawsuit the parents later won in *Stewart v. Phillips*)—that special education had been placed ahead of regular education in Massachusetts's state budget priorities. As soon as state and federal aid was available to reimburse schools for costs associated with special education, suburban schools seized the opportunity to place more students in aid-eligible programs.[62] Resource rooms in suburban schools filled with affluent white students who claimed access to isolated remedial classes as a civil right, even as resource rooms in urban schools continued to face charges of "discrimination" for disproportionate enrollments of poor minority students. Of course, suburban students were legally eligible for special education as long as they were learning disabled—a classification applicable to nearly any student whose academic record was below average. The presumption was that learning difficulties in the suburbs were just as "disabling" as learning difficulties in the inner city. In effect, then, the important factor in diagnosing disabilities was no longer poverty, but performance, and, despite attempts to steer financial resources toward urban districts, suburban districts managed to secure larger and larger reimbursements for their disabled— though not disadvantaged—students. In this context, the often-decried characterization of "disadvantage" as a form of "disability" took on new meaning, and with resources for special-compensatory services for poor students on the line, perhaps even some appeal.[63]

Superintendent Fahey was well aware of the fact that schools in affluent suburbs were expanding high-cost programs in an effort to maximize categorical reimbursements under Chapter 766.[64] The Huron Institute in Cambridge, Massachusetts, found that nearly every suburban district around Boston was making use of state grants for resource rooms, early-childhood programs, vocational-education centers, audiovisual equipment, reading specialists, hearing experts, psychologists, and computer information systems for keeping student records.[65] Indeed, suburban schools were much savvier than urban schools about expanding special education programs, which they defended as a civil right. According to analysts at the Institute for Governmental Studies, "wealthier communities have more sophisticated resources ([both] programs and personnel) to take advantage of the services provided by state agencies. State employees more readily respond to school systems that have the expertise to demand responses and underserve those who do not."[66] This flow of aid to suburban districts occurred *despite* the fact that urban districts were presumed to have more students who were "truly" disabled and, thus, in need of special-compensatory services. According to the state Department of Education, "the special learning problems of pupils in older, larger central cities necessitate higher levels of per pupil expenditure if [such pupils] are to have the same 'educational opportunities' offered pupils living elsewhere."[67] Yet, in the initial years of Chapter 766, state aid for special education programs flowed *away* from Boston. A combination of vague diagnostic criteria and long-standing suspicions about "test bias" and over-diagnoses of poor minority students enabled suburban districts to outpace urban districts in the development of programs eligible for reimbursement. In this way, the suburbs gradually but legally siphoned resources away from inner-city schools.[68]

What to do, then, about Boston's public schools? How could they, too, maximize their eligibility for state aid to special education? In the spring of 1975, John Heffley, a policy analyst with the Massachusetts Advisory Council on Education (MACE), observed that suburbs were outpacing cities in the identification and placement of the "disabled" and advised the state legislature to reverse the priorities it assigned to Chapter 70 and Chapter 766 so that urban districts could receive their "fair share" of state aid. Heffley wrote that "children with special learning deficiencies caused by social or cultural deprivation or mental or physical incapacities cannot always be served well in traditional school programs. And, the school programs geared to the needs of these students cost more than regular programs geared to [the needs of] students without any particular learning problems." In his report, Heffley outlined three ways in which inner-city schools could receive more state aid for "high-cost" students. First, he proposed that disabled or disadvantaged students could be "identified according to some clearly defined categories" and supplemental resources could be "provided through the general aid fund" according to a "system of pupil weighting or through some process of per pupil stipend." Second, he recommended a set of categorical aid programs to "reimburse school districts at some pre-determined percentage amount for legitimate expenses incurred in high cost programs." Third, he suggested that the state could "recognize the extra cost aspect of such programs and assume the costs for properly identified students and programs."[69] Each of these ideas, he asserted, would tie state aid to local expenses for disabled and disadvantaged students and would benefit urban districts such as Boston, which, given financial incentives, were likely to find more low-achieving students who could be placed *legitimately* in high-cost special-compensatory programs.[70]

Heffley's ideas made rapid headway in Massachusetts.[71] In June 1975—just after associate superintendent Casey called for more aid to expand special education programs in Boston—the state board of education sent a "pupil-weighting" bill to the legislature. The bill recommended that "the added costs of providing special programs for students in bilingual education, special education and vocational education [be] recognized through a system of pupil weights. A pupil's time in special programs will be given added weight based on the relative cost of such a program across the state. A small additional weight [will also be] given for disadvantaged students in recognition of the added cost of providing quality education to such pupils." The board specified pupil weights as follows: regular students received a weight of 1.0; disadvantaged students a weight of 1.2; non-English-speaking students a weight of 1.4; disabled students in "regular" classes a weight of 2.5; and disabled students in isolated classes in regular schools a weight of 3.5. This system seemed a fair way to compensate schools for high-cost pupils. Yet, it had hidden dangers based on the relative accuracy of the weights. On the one hand, if a weight exceeded the true added cost of a special program, then schools would have an incentive to overenroll students in that program in order to obtain extra funds. On the other hand, if a weight fell short of the true added cost of a special program, then schools would have an incentive to underenroll students in that program. The only way to make a pupil-weight system work was to see that reimbursements *exactly* reflected the true costs of special programs—and the only way to guarantee precise reimbursements was to adopt a fool-proof method for diagnosing students. Without strict methods for monitoring eligibility and supervising enrollments, schools would use their categorical programs not to maximize "appropriate" placements for disabled students but, rather, to maximize financial reimbursements.[72]

⟡

By June 1975, special education enrollments and expenses had climbed to record heights in Massachusetts. This exponential growth in special education programs derived not only from the perverse incentives of Chapter 766, but also from the prospect of larger *federal* grants. The new education amendments (scheduled to take effect in the fall) had boosted federal spending on special education from $100 million in 1974 to $660 million in 1975—and these grants flowed to districts regardless of their wealth. Moreover, in the summer of 1975, Congress was on the verge of passing an historic increase in federal aid to special education programs. More than three and a half years earlier, Senator Hubert Humphrey (D-Minn.), whose granddaughter had Downs Syndrome, had introduced a bill to increase categorical aid to the disabled. Using the civil rights language that had played a role in such cases as *Barnett v. Goldman* in Massachusetts, Humphrey had argued that "every child—gifted, normal and handicapped—has a fundamental right to educational opportunity." A year later, Senator Harrison Williams (D-N.J.), who sat on the Senate's Labor and Welfare Committee with Massachusetts senator Edward Kennedy, presented a similar bill, calling it the Education for All Handicapped Children Act. Together, Senators Williams and Kennedy had sponsored hearings on this bill in Massachusetts, New Jersey, Pennsylvania, and Washington, D.C. Their choice of locations was strategic; at the time, these places had generated the most prominent special education lawsuits, and, in the wake of these suits, states such as Massachusetts and Pennsylvania had written the nation's most progressive special education laws. As Kennedy asserted at the time of the legislative hearings on the Education for All Handicapped Children Act, "court actions and state laws throughout the nation have made it clear that the right to education of [all] handicapped children is a present right, one which is to be implemented immediately."[73]

Boston watched carefully as Kennedy guided the Education for All Handicapped Children Act through Congress. After more than twelve years in office, Kennedy—whose mentally retarded sister, Rosemary, had motivated his brother's earlier work on behalf of the disabled—exercised tremendous influence over federal education policy and, as chair of the Senate Subcommittee on Education, used his power to advocate for categorical aid to special education programs. He agreed with his fellow subcommittee members that, "the Congress of the United States has a responsibility to assure equal protection of the laws and thus to take action to assure that handicapped children throughout the United States have available to them appropriate educational services."[74] In this endeavor, he had the support of several major interest groups, including the National Association for Retarded Children (NARC), the Council for Exceptional Children (CEC), the National Education Association (NEA), the National Association of School Boards (NASB), the Committee for the Full Funding of Education (CFFE), the Council of Chief State School Officers (CCSSO), the Council of Great City Schools (CGCS), and others.[75] In 1975, he also had the support of the Ford administration. President Ford's first commissioner of education, Sidney Marland (who replaced interim commissioner Terrell Bell, who, in turn, had replaced James Allen), made categorical aid to special education his top legislative priority. "The right of a handicapped child to the special education he needs is as basic to him as is the right of any other young citizen to an appropriate education in the public schools," Marland commented. "It is unjust for our society to provide handicapped children with anything less than a full and equal educational opportunity they need to reach their maximum potential and attain rewarding, satisfying lives."[76]

On June 18, 1975—six days after associate superintendent Casey in Boston asked for more state aid to cover special education programs (and thirteen days after Judge Garrity had announced that every school in Boston must accommodate "mild and moderate special-needs students")—the Senate, with Kennedy's guidance, passed its version of the Education for All Handicapped Children Act by a vote of 83 to 10. A few weeks later, the House passed its own version by a vote of 375 to 44. The chief difference between the two versions had to do with the number of students in each local district who could be classified as "disabled." The Senate put a strict 10-percent cap on the number of students (between ages three and twenty-one) who could be classified as disabled, while the House put a slightly more lenient 12-percent cap on the number of children (between ages five and seventeen) who could be so classified. The Senate version put no limit on the number of students who could be placed in any given category of disability, but, in an effort to keep the costs of the legislation under control, the House limited the number of students who could be placed in the vague category of "learning disabled" to 2 percent. In conference, the House generally prevailed, which meant the 12-percent limit on overall disabilities and the 2-percent restriction on learning disabilities stuck. Neither the House nor the Senate specified any diagnostic criteria for disabilities covered under the bill (which varied from mental retardation and emotional disturbance to dyslexia), but both incorporated the due-process guarantees that had emerged from recent court decisions to ensure "appropriate" placement in the "least restrictive" classroom—at least for pupils who were truly disabled. Both the House and the Senate paid lip service to the principle of mainstreaming, but neither indicated that classroom integration should take precedence over classroom isolation if isolation promised better educational results.

On November 29, 1975, President Ford signed the Education for All Handicapped Children Act (P.L. 94-142) into law. Reflecting many of the innovations of Chapter 766 in Massachusetts—and, thus, the imprint of Senator Kennedy—the new law dramatically increased the federal commitment to categorical aid to special education. With a price tag of $3 billion to $4 billion over five years, it authorized funds to cover "excess" costs associated with special education on a steadily increasing annual basis, from 5-percent reimbursements in the first year to 10-percent in the second year, 20-percent in the third year, 30-percent in the fourth year, and 40-percent in the fifth and all subsequent years. It made big promises; indeed, in Ford's view, at a time of rising inflation, it promised far more than the federal government could ever deliver: "Even the strongest supporters of this measure know as well as I that they are falsely raising the expectations of the groups affected by claiming authorization levels which are excessive and unrealistic," he stated. "Despite my strong support for full educational opportunities for handicapped children, the funding levels proposed in this bill will simply not be possible if federal expenditures are to be brought under control and a balanced budget achieved over the next few years." In the end, Ford worried, P.L. 94-142 would simply become another "unfunded mandate" with legal obligations that outstripped its financial means. "It establishes complex requirements under which tax dollars would be used to support administrative paperwork and not educational programs," Ford said. "Unfortunately, these requirements will remain in effect even though the Congress appropriates far less than the amounts contemplated in [the law]." By the time P.L. 94-142 took effect in 1977, Ford warned, Congress would have to trim both its financial promises *and* its regulatory requirements; otherwise, he said, "its good intentions could be thwarted by the many unwise provisions it contains."[77]

After the passage of P.L. 94-142, classroom teachers in the Boston public schools did not hesitate to place more disabled students in federally funded special-compensatory programs. As one policy manager in Boston reported, in 1973-74, the last year before Chapter 766 was implemented, head count enrollments in special education accounted for 1.9 percent of total public school enrollments; by 1977-78, this figure had increased to 14.0 percent. At a time of continuing financial strain, this rapid rise in enrollments had a dramatic effect on special education budgets at both the local and the state level. Between 1973–74 and 1976–77, total state and local spending for regular education programs increased from $1.2 billion to $1.6 billion—a jump of 35 percent—but, over the course of the same period, state and local expenditures for special education programs grew by 130 percent. (Meanwhile, state and local expenditures for bilingual education programs grew by 158 percent.)[78] In Boston, special education placements increased most rapidly among poor and minority pupils. In a report, "Double Jeopardy: The Plight of Minority Students in Special Education," the Massachusetts Advocacy Center (MAC) demonstrated that, in Boston (and elsewhere), black students in primary grades were "commonly overenrolled in Chapter 766 [i.e., special education] programs compared to their white peers" and were "far more likely than their white counterparts to be placed out of the regular classroom in restrictive in-school programs."[79] The U.S. Commission on Civil Rights made a similar point with reference to the national scene, reporting that "in desegregated school districts throughout the Nation, [isolated special education] classes often are composed of students of one racial or ethnic group or vary considerably from the racial composition of the [rest of the] school. . . . The most common cause of classroom segregation is the educational practice of ability grouping."[80]

The fact that grouping by ability seemed to overlap with grouping by race was, to some extent, unsurprising—particularly in urban schools. Yet, the possibility that such an overlap would be considered "discriminatory" was ever present. Despite rhetorical efforts at both state and federal levels to avoid the stigmatizing effects of classifying students as disabled, students in special education programs nonetheless continued to be identified—and often isolated—as a legally distinct group. In a *Harvard Educational Review* article titled "Student Classifications, Public Policy, and the Courts," sociologist David Kirp explained that the legality of classifications and placements for disabled students depended not on the degree to which they facilitated racial integration (on either a school level or a classroom level) but, rather, on the degree to which they facilitated educational progress. In Kirp's words, "School sorting practices, unlike explicitly racial classifications, cannot be condemned as inherently harmful. Some classification is clearly necessary if schools are to cope with the bewildering variety of talent and interest that characterizes children. Whether certain classifications are harmful, and hence equality-depriving, is essentially an empirical question."[81] What mattered in the placement of the disabled, therefore, was not evidence of integration (racial or otherwise), but evidence of educational gains. Even if a placement turned out to be physically isolated and racially imbalanced, it was presumed to derive from an intent to help—rather than harm—the student. The historical irony here was sharp. Prior to racial desegregation in the Boston public schools, racially imbalanced special education classes were suspected of being discriminatory, but, with court-ordered busing, due-process provisions, and much-improved funding as well as promises of better diagnoses, better materials, and better results, charges of discriminatory intent in racially imbalanced isolated remedial programs had become much harder to sustain.[82]

Indeed, the practice of isolation itself was harder to criticize—not only because an isolated student now seemed more likely to be accurately diagnosed, but also because the best way to assess the "effectiveness" of a special education program for accountability purposes was to pull disabled students out of regular classes and gauge their progress in a physically isolated setting.[83] When disabled students were mainstreamed, it was hard to tell which aspect of their experience—classroom inclusion or special help—caused their success or failure. Also, the isolation of disabled students occurred for reasons tied to the particular—and conflicting—accounting methods that governed federal and state grants. On the one hand, *federal* accounting methods identified special education students using a categorical approach, whereby specific appropriations reimbursed specific programs for specific groups of handicapped students. On the other hand, *state* accounting methods in Massachusetts eschewed the categorical approach in favor of a more "general" approach that lumped groups together and distributed aid in block grants to each school (by minimizing group differences, the state sought to eliminate stigmatizing labels as well as the tendency to place disabled students in isolated settings). The federal Bureau of Education for the Handicapped was aware of these accounting differences but insisted that categorical procedures were preferable.[84] Granting that Massachusetts faced "a real problem because they've been trying to move away from that kind of accounting," the bureau held that "what [such] states should do is to accommodate [federal methods] by counting children by categories . . . but [also] continue to develop instructional programs noncategorically." As one bureaucrat said, "you don't have to organize the instructional programs in the same way you count the children."[85] Many schools, however, found it easier simply to place disabled students in isolated categorical programs.

In 1977, a focus on categorical programs found its way onto the agenda of newly elected President Jimmy Carter, who pledged to create a new cabinet-level department to oversee all federal education policies. It was unclear how such a department would affect federal aid to local schools, but it was obvious that the new department would confront an extraordinarily complex set of administrative issues. In the 1970s, the debate over special education coincided not only with a major debate over court-ordered busing but also with a major debate over school finance reform. The task in these years was to decide not only how to provide equal educational opportunities to many diverse groups of students, but also how to pay for all the new programs that equal opportunities demanded. When Judge Garrity issued his busing order in Boston, he assumed that racial integration would lead to more resources, more resources would lead to better programs, and better programs would lead to superior outcomes. Unfortunately, this assumption was hard to justify in practice. Integration seemed to have no inherent connection to school resources or student outcomes—and, by the time Garrity issued his ruling in *Morgan v. Kerrigan,* other federal courts had issued a string of opinions excluding both resources *and* outcomes from judicial consideration at the federal level. Despite Garrity's sincere aim to "eliminate segregation and the effect of discrimination in the public schools" and, in the process, to "lay a basis for improving the quality of education for the total city," other federal courts, including the U.S. Supreme Court, were adamant in the view that the judicial system could not guarantee the quality of education "except in the most relative sense."[86] It was likely, then, that, even with the best of legal intentions, a citywide system of court-ordered busing to facilitate racial integration would ensure only that: a citywide system of court-ordered busing to facilitate racial integration. Educational opportunities and educational outcomes hinged on what happened *next*—with individual students and their individual placements in local classrooms.

CHAPTER SEVEN

Evading Local Accountability, 1977–1980

By the time P.L. 94-142 took effect in the fall of 1977, special education referrals had increased at an astounding rate nationwide. Before passage of the law, less than 5 percent of the nation's school-aged population had been diagnosed with disabilities; after federal aid became available, the number exceeded 9 percent. In Chicago, the figure stood at 11.7 percent; in Philadelphia, 12.4 percent; in Baltimore, 14.9 percent. In Boston, the number climbed to 18.4 percent—more than twice the national average and more than six times the city's average three years earlier.[1] Some contended that, with improved diagnostic techniques and due-process protections, Boston's figures represented an accurate picture of disability in the inner city. Others, however, noted how arbitrary the diagnostic process could be.[2] As policy analysts Richard

Weatherly and Michael Lipsky argued in "Street-Level Bureaucrats and Institutional Innovation: Implementing Special Education Reform," published in the *Harvard Educational Review* in May 1977, referrals under Chapter 766 often had little to do with bona fide disabilities. "The chances of a child's being referred, evaluated, and provided with special education services were associated with presumably extraneous factors: the school system and school attended, the child's disruptiveness in class, his or her age and sex, the aggressiveness and socioeconomic status of the parents, the current availability and cost of services needed, and the presence of particular categories of specialists in the school system." Weatherly and Lipsky discovered that "teachers referred (dumped) students who posed the greatest threat to classroom control or recruited those with whom they were trained to work." They added that "in many instances, those doing the screening were actually referring children to themselves."[3] High enrollments were most common among pupils diagnosed with mild handicaps such as speech impairments or learning disabilities, which together accounted for more than 60 percent of all special education referrals in Massachusetts.[4]

Without doubt, this rapid increase in special education enrollments put a strain on school finances.[5] In the spring of 1977, editorialist Warren Brookes of the *Boston Herald* wrote that "this state is now embarked on a special education spending spree that boggles the mind and threatens the taxpayers, regular students, and teachers." Citing data from the state Department of Education, Brookes noted that one out of every four districts in the state was spending at least $10,000 a year for each student in special education, and some were spending far more (for example, suburban Wellesley spent, in some cases, over $30,000 a year for pupils in special education—at a time when parents could enroll their daughters at Wellesley College for less than $6,000 a year, including expenses).[6] Between 1974 and 1977, the number of regular education teachers in Boston fell by 350 even as the number of special education teachers *grew* by 187. Meanwhile, parents of more than 1,000 students in the state held due-process hearings to obtain special education placements for their children, often in isolated classrooms or residential facilities.[7] School officials found that Chapter 766 did not discourage such placements if they met the standard of "appropriateness"—a standard which, for funding purposes, was far more important than the standard of "least restrictiveness." When it came to Chapter 766, schools had little to lose: the law promised up to 110 percent of the state average excess costs for "instruction, training, and support, including the cost of special personnel, materials, and equipment, tuition, transportation, rent, and consultant services [for all] children in special classes, instruction periods, or other programs."[8] Thus, a district that spent $1,000 per student in regular education and $5,000 per student in special education could expect reimbursements up to $5,400 per student in special education—so long as state funds were actually available.[9]

By 1977, all districts endeavored to maximize their eligibility for state and federal aid to special education—and they persisted even when this process became complicated, as it did for students whose disabilities were eligible for private insurance or for Medicaid coverage. Particularly after Governor Dukakis cut funds to human services to save money, school officials had to find other ways to offer mandated—but often unfunded—assistance. As one policy analyst explained, "When Governor Dukakis's austerity budget for fiscal year 1976 cut back spending by various state human service agencies and medical facilities, the resulting withdrawal of state-provided services and resources increased the demands being made on local public schools by the families of children with special needs. . . . An unknown number of these children had formerly received services, however minimal, from the state's human services agencies, public hospitals, and 'custodial' institutions. Due to the budget cutbacks, [however,] a number of these institutions simply eliminated or greatly reduced services, referring children to local public schools instead." It was at this point, the analyst noted, that "private insurance companies, including Blue Cross/Blue Shield, which had formerly covered the costs of providing services to handicapped children, now refused to continue funding those services. Most cited a clause in their policies which absolved them of any financial responsibility for services which were by law the responsibility of state [or] local government agencies. This [tactic] led federal officials to warn [states and insurers] that the 50 percent federal Medicaid reimbursement for medical and social services rendered to eligible special needs children might be withdrawn since Medicaid was intended only as a 'last resort' funding source. Many school district administrators, unaccustomed to providing and paying for services which they had always considered to be the responsibility of medical or custodial care institutions, felt overwhelmed."[10]

At a time of skyrocketing demands for services and shrinking financial resources, no agency wanted to be left with the responsibility for treating high-cost disabled students. And, yet, with federal agencies bickering about the coverage of specific programs under Medicaid or P.L. 94-142, state agencies fighting about the coverage of services under the Department of Education or the Department of Mental Health, and local agencies trying to decide whether to pursue funds under federal or state programs, it was hard for schools to know which source of funds would provide the most aid (let alone which source would provide the most benefit to disabled students). What schools *did* know was that all disabled students were entitled by law to special education services to meet their needs. Both P.L. 94-142 and Chapter 766 entailed "zero-rejection" clauses, which meant that all disabled students, regardless of their degree of disability, were fully entitled to placement in special education programs unless they explicitly opted out. Every school had to test every student for any sign of disability—from hearing impairments to visual handicaps to physical deformities to speech troubles to emotional disturbances to mental retardation to mild learning problems—and every student discovered to have a bona fide disability was entitled to every service that might ensure "adequate" treatment, which, in Massachusetts, meant a service designed to help a student reach his or her "maximum feasible potential." The zero-rejection clause was designed to ensure that no disabled student would be denied services to which he or she was entitled. Yet, such a clause was useful only if diagnostic processes were absolutely reliable. If schools assigned to special education students who were *not* disabled, then the idea of "serving all disabled students" would lose credibility. Instead of upholding civil rights by making "appropriate" placements, the schools would be suspected of undermining civil rights by making "discriminatory" placements.

Everything hinged on reliable diagnoses. Yet, as many educators acknowledged, reliability was rare in the diagnosis of disability. In 1977, the Stanford Research Institute (SRI) investigated 400 analyses of the "prevalence" of different categories of disability in the general population and found that "no single set of prevalence figures can be accepted as fact."[11] Scholars attributed disparities in diagnosis rates to four factors: the ways states defined categories of disability, the ways professionals screened groups of children, the ways schools located potentially handicapped children, and, perhaps most important of all, the ways in which states distributed financial reimbursements. Each of these factors contributed to a situation where the very same student could be diagnosed with a particular disability in one state but not in another. For example, during the third year of the implementation of P.L. 94-142, the highly ambiguous category of "learning disabled" accounted for 19 percent of the total population of disabled students in New York but 63 percent of the total population of disabled students in Hawaii. It was unlikely that pupils in Hawaii were three times more likely to be learning disabled than pupils in New York (if anything, psychologists who tried to attribute learning disabilities to purely cognitive rather than cultural, environmental, or socioeconomic causes insisted that the prevalence of learning disabilities should be uniform across the entire human population); instead, it turned out that New York diagnosed more of its academically low-performing students as "mentally retarded" or "emotionally disturbed." New York, like Massachusetts, placed approximately 18 percent of its disabled students in each of these categories, which involved more intensive (and expensive) services that garnered more state and federal aid. Thus, teachers in New York routinely diagnosed academically low-performing students as mentally retarded rather than learning disabled.[12]

Similarly, in Boston, decisions to diagnose borderline students as either mentally retarded or learning disabled hinged on financial more than pedagogical factors. So, too, did choices between isolated placements (which tended to be more costly) and integrated placements. Moreover, the state *encouraged* these calculations. In 1977, anticipating the arrival of federal aid for isolated categorical programs, the state legislature decided to tie all reimbursements under Chapter 766 to the amount of time disabled students spent *outside* the regular classroom. Further, in an effort to increase federal aid (and decrease state aid) to "learning disabled" pupils, legislators voted to tighten the diagnostic criteria for this disability by adjusting the IQ cut-off from 85 down to 79 (that is, from one down to two standard deviations below the mean). This shift instantly—and arbitrarily—reduced by 80 percent the total number of pupils who were considered to be learning disabled and, at the same time, ensured that those who remained in this group were likely to be "disabled enough" for placements in relatively expensive programs that were likely to obtain larger federal reimbursements. (Students with mild learning difficulties who were unlikely to require federally funded services were simply considered "cured.")[13] In this way, state and local officials tailored diagnostic criteria to fit available resources—a practice that not only cast doubt over the validity of diagnoses but also confirmed public suspicions that the aim of many diagnoses was not to make appropriate placements but, rather, to secure financial reimbursements.[14] If a student was only "mildly" disabled, then what services was a school obligated to provide? If such a student was entitled to services *regardless of cost,* then when, if ever, could a school claim that he or she had received "sufficient" or "adequate" help?

The answer to this question depended in part on the definition of *mild disabilities* and in part on the particular educational "treatments" that such disabilities might require. In the past, the term *disability* had referred to mental, physical, or emotional handicaps that rendered pupils fundamentally incapable of average academic achievement (though some handicapped pupils might reach average levels of achievement with supplemental help). By the late 1970s, however, the meaning of the term *disability* had changed. It had come to encompass a much broader spectrum of educational difficulties, particularly at the mild end of the continuum where the line separating disabled and nondisabled students blurred. If a given student posted below-average achievement, then he or she could, at least potentially, be considered mildly disabled. At the same time, however, this label no longer implied that such a student was fundamentally incapable of average achievement; by the late 1970s, the prevailing assumption was that *all* students—even those identified as "mildly disabled"—were capable of average achievement with appropriate help. Indeed, an a priori assumption that a student was incapable of average achievement could constitute proof of discrimination if it resulted in a denial of services.[15] The task, therefore, was to distinguish low-achieving students who were not disabled—and, thus, not entitled to special help—from low-achieving students who were, in fact, disabled—and, thus, entitled to help up to the point of attaining their "maximum feasible potential." Any student whose academic achievement was below average (that is, below the average of a class, a school, a district, or a state) was a candidate for a disability diagnosis and, hence, a candidate for special services.[16]

Of course, the only way to distinguish the disabled from the nondisabled student was to apply absolutely reliable diagnostic methods to both. Since reliable diagnostic techniques did not exist in the late 1970s, schools typically made distinctions on other grounds—most often, on the basis of money. If more financial resources were available, then more students were likely to be placed in special education classes; if fewer financial resources were available, then fewer students were likely to be placed in special classes. The linkage between financial and educational considerations pervaded the implementation of Chapter 766 and P.L. 94-142 in Boston. Yet, at a time of fiscal crisis, such a linkage generated continual debate. Some insisted that marginally disabled students were entitled to special services as a civil right. Others believed that marginally disabled students were entitled to special education only if their diagnoses were absolutely reliable (that is, based on clinical rather than financial considerations). Still others held that marginally disabled students were entitled to special education only if schools could show that supplemental services would produce gains in academic achievement commensurate with a service's costs. According to school-finance expert Bruce Perlstein, schools brokered continuous debates between "parents of special needs children, on the one hand, and school committee members and municipal officials on the other. The former shared a common perception of the problem as one of securing [local] compliance with what they felt was a civil rights law for a shamefully and badly neglected and politically powerless group of children and their families, often in the face of stubborn local resistance. Municipal officials and school committee members, on the other hand, often found themselves being forced to raise local taxes [to pay for services], something for which they would undoubtedly be held politically accountable."[17]

◈

In the absence of reliable diagnoses, schools faced public criticism no matter what they did: if special education enrollments rose, then the public criticized schools for their exorbitant cost; if special education enrollments fell, then the public criticized schools for their failure to protect disabled students' rights. The issue of rights was perhaps most sensitive when it involved minority students in special education—and, specifically, the alleged overenrollment of black students in physically isolated, racially imbalanced classes. While white parents expressed less concern about the enrollment of their children in isolated programs and occasionally *preferred* isolated placements in the hope that such placements would yield superior outcomes, black parents tended to pay close attention to the enrollment of their children in isolated programs and often feared that such programs would yield *inferior* outcomes. Based on previous experience, white parents trusted their children's diagnoses and attributed them to clinical factors; black parents distrusted their children's diagnoses and attributed them to racial factors.[18] Certainly, in the late 1970s, it was no secret that minorities were placed disproportionately in isolated classes. In 1976–77, black students comprised 15 percent of the nation's total school enrollments but 21 percent of special education enrollments and 38 percent of enrollments in classes for the educable mentally retarded. In 1978–79 (the year after federal grants for special education programs first became available under P.L. 94-142), black students comprised 17 percent of the nation's total enrollments but 23 percent of special education enrollments and 41 percent of enrollments in classes for the educable mentally retarded. Wilbert Cheatham, deputy director of the federal Office of Civil Rights, asserted that high enrollments of minority students ought to "be considered a positive trend since it suggests that school districts are evaluating the educational needs of minority students with greater accuracy and sensitivity than in the past."[19] Others, however, believed that high enrollments of minority students resulted directly from racial discrimination.[20]

In 1977–78, the Massachusetts Advocacy Center (MAC) launched a full-scale investigation of minority enrollments in special education programs in the Boston public schools. Hubert Jones, former chair of the Task Force on Children Out of School, led the year-long inquiry. "While disproportionate rates do not absolutely prove that racial discrimination exists in special education in Massachusetts," Jones admitted, "they do constitute serious prima facie evidence of discrimination." The MAC discovered that, in Boston, "all groups of students, including whites, were substantially overplaced in restrictive programs compared to state-wide rates." In 1975-76, isolated programs enrolled 41.9 percent of white special education students, 44.2 percent of black special education students, and 46.4 percent of Hispanic special education students. Two years later, isolated programs enrolled 41.3 percent of white special education students, 47.1 percent of black special education students, and 48.6 percent of Hispanic special education students. Moreover, the MAC contended, "discrimination in individual classrooms and in program administration is far worse than [these] . . . data indicate." The MAC "witnessed substantially separate programs in Boston that are comprised entirely of black students. In addition, in the Boston cases received by the Center, a disproportionate number of black students have been cited for disciplinary problems and eventually placed in 502.4 programs [i.e., programs isolating students for more than 60 percent of the school day] for emotionally disturbed children. This is reminiscent of the 1970 finding by the Task Force on Children Out of School that a disproportionately high number of black students were placed in classes for the emotionally disturbed."[21] To the MAC, the evidence of discrimination in Boston's special education programs was clear.[22]

To Boston's school officials, however, the evidence was far less clear. School officials reminded the MAC critics that financial considerations were also involved. Under the state's school-aid system, the way to increase funding was to increase special education enrollments: if Boston chose not to increase its enrollments, then suburbs less averse to special education placements would continue to claim larger portions of the state's school-aid budget. Given the widespread view that Boston was not getting its fair share of state aid, officials did not apologize for using special education enrollments as a way to increase reimbursements—nor did they apologize for the disproportionate enrollment of poor minority pupils in isolated programs.[23] Pointing to the enduring link between disadvantage and disability among poor minority students in the inner city, they rejected the notion that disabilities were distributed uniformly across the total population and cited "poverty, transiency and cultural differences as the reasons for the generally higher rates of placement of minority students in special education."[24] Sensing that any rate of placement of minority students in special education was susceptible to criticism for being either too high or too low—and discriminatory in both cases—administrators built their special education strategy around the goal of maximizing state and federal aid. From their point of view, what mattered in special education was not racial balance but financial reimbursement—and the likelihood that reimbursements would improve both opportunities and outcomes for poor minority students. Reiterating a principle that had guided categorical aid for special-compensatory education for over a decade, school officials in Boston argued that different students with different needs could benefit from different programs in different classroom settings.

This principle of "different programs for different students" had had remarkable staying power, and the reason for its longevity was that, in subtle ways, it served both sides of the debate over equal educational opportunities in the schools. On the one hand, different programs for different students in different settings could promote isolation; on the other hand, different programs for different students with different needs could foster academic achievement. The decisive issue was the point at which different educational needs actually *warranted* different classroom settings and the point at which different classroom settings actually *ensured* greater gains in achievement. Some argued that integrated settings were *inherently* preferable to isolated settings, others that integrated settings were preferable only to the extent that they ensured better results than isolated settings—that is to say, integrated settings lost their preferability at the exact moment that an isolated setting could ensure greater gains. What distinguished these two positions was the relative value that each assigned to integration versus achievement. Despite strong rhetoric to the contrary, neither goal had "inherent" value, and neither had the final say in matters of equal educational opportunity. Put simply, equal educational opportunity was in the eye of the beholder: if a school program was racially imbalanced but educationally effective (that is, if it produced optimal gains in achievement), then charges of discrimination were unlikely, but if a program was racially imbalanced and educationally ineffective, then charges of discrimination were virtually certain. As with programs for non-English-speaking minority students (whether Hispanic or Chinese), what led to charges of discrimination was not imbalance but ineffectiveness.[25]

Indeed, judgments about the overenrollment or underenrollment of non-English-speaking minority students in special education in Boston depended not on racial balance but, rather, on the relative effectiveness of each student's placement in boosting academic achievement. As the Massachusetts Advocacy Center noted, "overenrollment of Hispanic students in Chapter 766 programs often results from mistaken identification of language needs as special education needs or placement of bilingual students in Chapter 766 programs as an excuse for not developing adequate language programs. Also some schools may automatically be passing bilingual children into special education programs without adequate evaluations when their three years in the transitional bilingual education programs have expired." Similarly, the MAC commented, "underenrollment of Hispanic students commonly results from [schools'] failure to identify legitimate special education needs because tests for bilingual students are nonexistent or are improperly administered and interpreted by English-speaking evaluators. Even when the special education needs of Spanish-speaking students are accurately identified, schools usually have too few, if any, bilingual/special education personnel (e.g., psychologists, teachers, social workers) to serve the children adequately."[26] While both bilingual- and special-education programs for non-English-speaking minority pupils were likely to be racially imbalanced, the MAC accused schools of overenrollment in special education only when it felt non-English-speaking pupils could attain superior results in regular (or bilingual) classes, and it accused schools of underenrollment when it felt non-English-speakers could achieve superior results in special education.[27] In both cases, the ultimate measure of "appropriateness" in any student's placement was neither classroom integration nor racial balance but academic achievement.

⟡

The emphasis on academic achievement was not limited to students in bilingual or special education; in the late 1970s, it also extended to students in regular education. The reason for this focus on achievement was a sudden sense of crisis about falling scores on standardized tests. In the fall of 1977, the College Board assembled an expert panel to investigate a steady drop in SAT scores over the past fourteen years. Between 1963 and 1977, average mathematics scores had fallen 32 points, while average verbal scores had fallen 49 points—half a standard deviation. The College Board attributed these declines to its perception that more minority (and female) students were taking the test, but, when Massachusetts ran its own study, it reached a different conclusion. In "Declining Test Scores: A State Study," policy analyst Janice Weinman of the state Department of Education observed that, following the rapid growth of special-compensatory services in the 1960s, the dropout rate had begun to decline, and more low-achieving students remained in school: "The increased number of students remaining in school (partly as a result of the emphasis on drop-out prevention in the late 1950s and early 1960s) may have resulted in administrators, counselors, and curriculum specialists switching their attention and services from college-bound students to the low-achievers. The present college-bound students thus may not be receiving the same intensity or level of education as did students attending school at a time when the dropout rate was higher." In other words, greater commitment to compensatory, bilingual, and special education kept low-achievers in school and pulled resources away from high-achieving, college-bound students. Thus fewer students now posted high scores on the SAT. It was therefore necessary, Weinman argued, for the public schools to refocus their efforts on higher academic achievement, specifically in basic skills such as reading and mathematics.[28]

In the fall of 1978, a special advisory committee to Massachusetts's state board of education rolled out a comprehensive policy on "basic skills improvement." The policy (spurred by promises of federal aid) called on the state board to "mandate assessment of basic skills achievement at the earliest grade levels feasible and at each appropriate grade level thereafter to (1) monitor individual achievement and progress, (2) provide early instructional help to pupils with diagnosed needs, (3) evaluate the effectiveness of the curriculum and instruction, and (4) make appropriate changes and improvements in the total educational program." The policy also called on the state to require local districts to "provide assurances that instructional services and programs leading to the achievement of the competencies are available to all students." By testing students' basic skills, the state hoped to be able to assess the overall effectiveness of the public schools. Yet, the new policy harbored a contradiction. On the one hand, it promised that results from basic skills tests would help schools "evaluate the effectiveness of the curriculum" and "make appropriate changes and improvements in the total educational program." On the other hand, it maintained that "minimum competency tests" should assess general skills but should not be attached to any specific or state-mandated curriculum. According to the special advisory committee, the way to resolve this contradiction was to use local curriculum-based tests rather than statewide basic skills tests. In its words, "the use of curriculum-based diagnostic achievement tests rather than 'competency tests' would provide a better means of earlier identification for students in need of additional basic skills development."[29] Emphasizing curriculum-based tests did not, however, clarify whether persistently low scores (i.e., incompetencies in core subjects) would point to shortcomings in specific pupils or in the curriculum itself. The key question was: should low scores be attributed to students, or their schools?

If the aim of basic skills competency testing was, indeed, to measure competency in basic skills such as reading, then one of the ironies of this movement in Massachusetts was that it coincided with the end of the federally funded Right to Read program in the state. As program director Joseph Tremont noted in his final report, "the last year of the Right to Read Effort . . . will coincide with planning for the basic skills emphasis." After seven years in operation (the program was the brainchild of federal Commissioner of Education James Allen in 1969–70), the program had produced rather disappointing results. Between the time of Massachusetts's first state reading assessment in 1974 and its second in 1978, average reading achievement for nine-year-olds and seventeen-year-olds had not improved at all; indeed, achievement had *declined* as students passed through the upper grades. According to Tremont, "the cause [of] this decline remains to be known, since the statewide assessment measured only the results, not causes. Meanwhile, it is open season for finger-pointers to guess at why gains appear to be dissipated as the students proceed through the junior high and senior high school." Conceding that schools were "not using the results of the statewide assessments as a springboard for revising teacher practices in reading," Tremont admitted it was not entirely clear whether the Right to Read effort was really supposed to change instructional methods or promote curricular reform. Moreover, he added, even if a basic skills approach replaced the Right to Read approach, higher test scores among disadvantaged pupils could not be guaranteed. "The assumption . . . is that our children are being taught more by better teachers, better schools, [and] better materials," Tremont said of the various high-profile, high-cost reform movements of the 1970s (in fact, Right to Read itself had emerged in response to the failure of earlier Title I programs). "It has been and continues to be a dangerous assumption."[30]

In the late 1970s, Tremont had plenty of reasons to believe the basic skills competency movement was no more likely to raise academic achievement than Right to Read had been.[31] In 1977, the highly respected American Institutes for Research (AIR) reported in a three-year, $1.8 million study for the federal Office of Education that "innovative programs" in public schools had had no discernible effect on academic achievement over time. As the *Washington Post* commented, "most of the highly touted innovations of the past 20 years produce little substantial improvement in standardized reading and math scores. Open classrooms, team teaching, individualization of instruction, increased classroom democracy, multimedia emphasis, volunteer aides, [and] student selection of materials—none of these things seems to matter very much, the researchers found. And sometimes their effect is negative." For example, AIR found "no clear evidence" that levels of innovation or degrees of individualization ensured gains in reading, and it found that levels of innovation and degrees of individualization were, in fact, "negatively, rather than positively, related to growth in arithmetic achievement." Echoing some aspects of the Coleman Report a decade earlier, the AIR researchers warned that their study's findings "should serve as a reminder to educators—as well as to parents and legislators—that educational innovation per se will not necessarily produce dramatic effects on student achievement."[32] Massachusetts, however, did not listen. In 1978, with promises of federal aid, the state legislature required every school to devise a "basic skills improvement plan" in the next year. "Evaluation of student achievement of minimum standards is obviously necessary in order to know how students are doing and whether or not they have achieved minimum standards," the state Department of Education noted, implying that a test to see how students were doing was the first step toward a program that might help students—especially poor minority students in inner-city schools—actually learn.[33]

In Boston, the shift to basic skills and curriculum-based testing coincided with a rather abrupt shift in the superintendent's office. After three years in office, Marion Fahey turned her duties over to Robert Wood—the city's third superintendent in six years. Wood was a distinguished figure in Massachusetts's education circles. A former professor of political science at MIT and a former president of the five-campus University of Massachusetts System, he had also served as federal secretary of housing and urban development in the last days of the Johnson administration. "I am an urbanist," the fifty-four-year-old Wood declared after his arrival in the superintendent's office. "The schools are the future of the city. As the schools go, so goes the city."[34] When the school committee hired Wood (and sent Fahey to the intergovernmental relations office), it hired its first superintendent from outside the system in more than seventy years. In so doing, it hoped to find a leader who could manage the transition to state-mandated basic skills competency testing and, at the same time, face the busing and budget challenges that had faced his predecessors. For Wood, these three key issues—basic skills, busing, and the budget—were intertwined with a fourth issue: accountability. His top priority as superintendent was to show that racially integrated schools in Boston could be academically effective *and* financially efficient at the same time. Before accepting the superintendency of the city's public schools, he had led the Citywide Coordinating Council, the organization responsible for supervising court-ordered busing. Now, as the first superintendent to serve after compensatory education, bilingual education, special education, and racial integration were all in place for (ostensibly) equal educational opportunities, he told the city's residents they could finally expect *results,* or at least accountability for results, in their public schools.[35]

⬦

In his push for accountability, Wood had the full support of the state legislature, which passed two important laws shortly before his appointment. The first, Chapter 333, called for a far-reaching administrative reorganization of the Boston school department. It gave the superintendent blanket authority to dismiss senior administrators at will and also gave the superintendent broader authority over the school department's budget decisions. As Wood remarked, "for the first time the superintendent had oversight over the business operations of the school department as well as academic activities. The superintendent was to function as chief executive officer of the entire department."[36] The second reform at the state level was a major reconfiguration of Massachusetts's school-aid law.[37] Using the idea of a "pupil-weighting" system that John Heffley had developed a year earlier, the new formula owed its passage to the skilled politicking of state commissioner of education Gregory Anrig and his newly appointed deputy, Michael Daly (former representative and member of the Task Force on Children Out of School). Anrig and Daly worked with the governor to make state aid to schools a top legislative priority, and they pushed especially hard for aid to urban areas. As one scholar noted, Dukakis "attempted to favor the state's older urban areas in every way possible which did not conflict with his policy of fiscal austerity. His 1974 electoral victory had been due in large part to sizable majorities in the larger cities, a pattern he said that he hoped to repeat in 1978." Adding momentum to this process was a lawsuit filed in state court alleging—à la *Serrano*—that unequal school funding violated students' constitutional rights. According to Bruce Perlstein, "the specter of possible court intervention was frequently cited by reform proponents as a major reason for the legislature to enact . . . reform. With the history of the court-ordered desegregation of the Boston public schools fresh in the minds of most legislators, [this] argument was quite persuasive."[38]

When the legislature approved the new aid formula in July 1978, Superintendent Wood looked forward to a large increase in aid to the Boston public schools—and several features of the formula encouraged such a hope. First, it combined all state aid to schools, including state aid to special education and bilingual education, into a single "equalizing" formula. Second, it assigned weights—ranging from 1.0 for students in regular education programs to 6.3 for students in residential special education programs—to all students in the public schools based on the relative costs of their instruction. Third, it set a statewide minimum expenditure *requiring* all localities to spend at least 85 percent of the state average on education. Fourth, it ended delays in reimbursements by tying reimbursements to current enrollments. Finally, it linked payments to local property valuations per capita rather than local property valuations per child, thus benefiting cities with larger populations. By far the most important aspect of the new law was its "pupil-weighting" feature. Schools were permitted to count students enrolled in multiple programs according to the category with the highest weight, and each low-income pupil "counted as one full-time equivalent pupil in whatever program or programs he or she is enrolled *plus* an additional FTE [full-time equivalent] pupil weight of 0.2."[39] As Perlstein explained, "the July 1978 school-finance reform obviously was most favorable to the state's largest cities, especially Boston: whereas in fiscal year 1978 Boston had received $55.5 million, or 8.8 percent of total school aid statewide, in fiscal year 1979 Boston received $84.7 million, or 13.4 percent [of the statewide total]. In terms of both [a] municipal overburden equity standard and Dukakis's re-election campaign strategy, the reform . . . appeared to be a success."[40] Also, in directing aid to urban schools, the new law held these schools "accountable" for the efficient and effective use of funds in raising academic achievement.

The new state-aid formula seemed, at first, to be a great political victory for Anrig and Dukakis—but it had major costs. For starters, the new formula brought only minimal increases in aid to 244 out of 351 towns in Massachusetts. While these towns were small, rural, and, together, contained less than half the state's population, their political influence was great, and they felt betrayed by a policy that directed more aid to the cities.[41] These towns had their revenge in the fall of 1978, when Dukakis ran for re-election as governor. His opponent in the Democratic primary was Edward King, once a professional football player and, more recently, director of Massachusetts's Port Authority and president of the New England Council, a coalition of business, academic, and policy leaders committed to regional economic development. King mounted a strong campaign against Dukakis in the primaries. He noted, in particular, that, despite explicit promises, the governor had raised taxes several times to pay for new social programs. As the *Boston Globe* reported, King ran a "pocketbook-oriented" campaign touting a "supply-side" strategy to end stagflation by cutting taxes as well as spending to spur private investment and create jobs. According to one analyst, King's platform indicated "that there are a large number of voters . . . for the candidate of the moderate or moderate-conservative philosophy."[42] In the Democratic primary, King cast himself as a conservative on most issues, including support of "capital punishment, of mandatory prison sentences for drug dealers, of raising the drinking age to 21, . . . of building nuclear power plants, and of downplaying environmental concerns to spur economic growth."[43] He eventually defeated Dukakis by a wide margin and went on to challenge state legislator Francis Hatch in the general election. Endorsed by both Senator Edward Kennedy and Representative "Tip" O'Neill (whose son was the incumbent lieutenant governor) as well as Superintendent Wood, King won with 50.4 percent of the vote.

The election of 1978 was humiliating for Dukakis, who lost in small towns as well as urban centers, including Boston. Evidently, his oft-repeated dedication to urban areas—and, specifically, to urban schools—did not help him at the polls. Superintendent Wood publicly identified him as "short-sighted about education," and the new school-aid law failed to win support from Mayor Kevin White, who, owing to subtle machinations of his own, refused to give the governor credit for directing funds to the city. At first, it was hard to understand White's opposition to the new aid law, but it soon became clear that it stemmed from an intricate behind-the-scenes struggle for political control of the local school budget. In particular, White's opposition to the school-aid law derived from a position he took in a prior mayoral campaign, when, in a close race against Louise Day Hicks (his rival in both 1967 and 1971), he joined Hicks in attacking "court-ordered busing as the cause of the high cost of [the] Boston public schools." After his victory, he pledged to fix the schools' fiscal problems once and for all by raising property taxes from $19.67 to $25.59 (per $100 of valuation)—a 28.6 percent jump. In response to public furor at this proposal, he vowed to leave taxes static until the next mayoral elections in 1979. This promise, however, created a dilemma when the state legislature devised its new school-aid formula, because state law required municipalities to use all new state aid to *reduce* existing local tax levies. White did not want to lower the rates he had just raised; thus, he opted to withdraw his support from the aid law. This withdrawal puzzled many, because it implied that White not only opposed a formula designed to benefit the Boston public schools, but also favored higher taxes. Yet, several commentators argued that White planned to horde revenues from the high local tax rate while accepting more state aid so that, in a flourish of (false) political generosity a year later, he could lower the city's taxes just in time to secure his own reelection.[44]

If the school budget was subject to so much political intrigue, then, Superintendent Wood noted, it seemed unfair to hold him personally responsible for the success or failure of the system. Indeed, if public schools had inadequate resources due primarily to political in-fighting, then perhaps the politicians—not the educators—should be held accountable.

This idea came to the fore in 1979–80, when, despite the advantages of the new school-aid law and the significant increase in local property taxes, Boston's public schools *still* accumulated a deficit of $10 million (including $1 million for unanticipated busing costs and $1 million for private residential special education facilities).[45] By 1980, the issue of annual school deficits had escalated into a huge political imbroglio involving the superintendent, the mayor, the city council, and the school committee. Tempers flared when the mayor and the city council finally tried to halt rising deficits by rejecting the school committee's budget. As Wood explained, "the committee is empowered to appropriate a budget for any fiscal year that is equal to the budget of the preceding year; but if additional funds are desired, the mayor and the city council must concur." When city and school officials disagreed on the expense of teacher contracts—which lay at the root of ongoing deficits—open conflict erupted. "The city maintained control over the payroll process," Wood remarked, "and the annual deficit was usually determined and reconciled by subterranean transfers among accounts that took place well after the close of the fiscal year. Whether it would be the city or the school department that assumed . . . school expenses or was credited with overhead from federal grants [for mandated programs] was a matter of backroom, closed-door negotiations at middle management levels."[46]

In 1980, however, backroom, closed-door negotiations came to an abrupt end as city and school officials tried to pin responsibility for persistent deficits on each other. As Wood later recounted, "early in 1980, I publicly informed the school committee of an impending deficit. (This was the first time the school administration was technically capable of projecting its expenditures [because the new state aid law finally resolved the problem of reimbursement lag].) The school committee failed to take timely and decisive action. From all sides, there was the predictable outcry: accusations, counteraccusations, and confrontation. The public was conveyed a picture of the city as prudent taxpayer, the school department as wasteful spender."[47] Wood tried to convince the mayor and the city council that his budget, while large, nonetheless made significant cuts in administrative costs. For example, he abolished forty-five jobs in the central office and one hundred jobs for transitional aides hired to ease the process of racial integration in various schools. Yet, when the Boston Teachers Union heard of this 40-percent reduction in transitional aides, it warned of "unrest and disruption" throughout the city. "These are the people who have spent long hours and time keeping disruption at a minimum in our schools," commented Kathleen Kelley, president of the teachers union (an organization which, only a few years earlier, had vehemently opposed the desegregation of the schools but now defended the additional jobs it had created). Despite the fact that Wood himself had chaired the council in charge of desegregation and now considered these aides to be superfluous, he could not reduce their number. Similarly, his attempt to cut the position of "recruiter" for bilingual classes met a torrent of protest from APCROSS, the Association Promoting the Constitutional Rights of the Spanish-Speaking, which cautioned that any such move "could result in a civil rights lawsuit against the school system."[48]

In crafting a $228 million school budget, Wood repeatedly discovered that legally mandated services were immune to all cuts.[49] "In explaining the new budget figures," the *Boston Globe* stated, "Wood said that $205 million is the result of legislative mandate—for such services as special education and bilingual [education]—or double-digit inflation." In Boston, by 1980, bilingual education programs enrolled more than 5,000 students, and special education programs enrolled more than 12,000. These programs were inordinately expensive owing to their smaller class sizes, their need for special teachers and materials, and their overhead expenses.[50] In a $228 million budget, local outlays for special education salaries were $38 million—up from $12 million before the mandates of P.L. 94-142—and the only way to cut these costs without dismissing teachers (and, thus, risking legal action for breaking teacher contracts or infringing student rights) was to cut administrative jobs. In March 1980, the *Boston Globe* summarized Wood's proposal for "a staff reorganization that will affect teachers and administrators who have been working with special needs programs for many years in the Boston schools. Some would continue in the same positions with new titles, others would have more clearly defined responsibilities, and still others would be shifted to new agencies. Wood would abolish 17 jobs, including those of senior advisor for special services, director of special schools and programs, a number of program specialists and the clerical supervisor. Fifteen other positions would be converted to new functions, and nine new jobs would be authorized with a net loss of 25 positions. Other special education staff, including school psychologist, liaison teachers, and speech and language teachers, would be among those transferred to district offices."[51]

Yet as Wood discovered, accountability for school budgets was difficult whenever it touched on teacher contracts or teacher responsibilities. Teachers' salaries were by far the largest item in the school budget, and the superintendent had very little power to adjust this amount. In talks with the mayor, Wood begged for flexibility in contract negotiations, arguing that "the basic contracts with the unions prescribe and restrain professional behavior, sharply limiting if not replacing management direction. Grievance and arbitration procedures challenge managers' decisions at every level: the performance of individual teachers, the use of sick and vacation leave, the deployment of specialists, [and] the development of curricula."[52] At the very least, Wood pleaded, the school department ought to adopt a system of teacher evaluations to gauge the effectiveness of school personnel—a suggestion that had the full support of a state committee on educational personnel, cochaired by Gregory Anrig and Michael Daly. In their words, "effective and equitable evaluation of educational personnel is important at any time. It is especially important at a time of . . . growing budget constraints, and public questioning of the quality of education." It was no surprise, however, that Wood's proposal for personnel evaluations met stiff resistance from the union, which suspected that evaluations would affect hiring and firing decisions. As the Anrig-Daly committee noted, frequent use of the phrase "'reductions in force' . . . created an atmosphere of tension and suspicion over evaluation policies."[53] Indeed, firing teachers was almost impossible: when the Boston school committee proposed to cut faculty at underenrolled magnet schools, the courts balked, but when the committee suggested it might have to cut faculty at high schools, parents complained. Wood could not trim personnel costs even when he tried. As the Boston Municipal Research Bureau observed, "parent pressure may come to bear on other reduction items, i.e., the termination of all bus monitors."[54]

The idea of terminating bus monitors was as much a rhetorical suggestion as a realistic one: if legally mandated programs and negotiated contracts were immune to cuts, Wood asked, then what else was left? Each line in the budget had some connection to the idea of equal educational opportunity, and it was hard to find exceptions to this rule. After big cuts in administration, Wood had no patience for those who sought more cuts in this area. As he explained to the *Boston Globe*, "the fallacies of this proposition are two: the dollars spent in administration are quantitatively insignificant as a percentage of the budget and the consequence of elimination is the abandonment of . . . essential services," such as payroll and facilities planning.[55] Indeed, it was this second area, facilities planning, that was among the most "essential" in 1980, when Judge Garrity required the immediate closing of thirteen schools to compensate for steadily declining enrollments. As early as 1977, the Boston Municipal Research Bureau had noticed that "10,699 elementary school seats, or 26.0 percent, are empty—and this problem is expected to worsen as total school enrollment is projected to decline an additional 19.7 percent by 1981."[56] Predicting that, by 1982, the city would have to close twelve *more* schools, Garrity implemented "a major reshuffling of students" to ensure that all remaining schools would be racially balanced. These orders, however, unleashed a surge of vituperation across the city. As the *Globe* reported, "Garrity is once again the center of a storm of protests. But this time there is a difference. . . . For the outcry is now coming not just from hard-line foes of busing, but from many of his former supporters." Jane Margulis, chairwoman of the Citywide Parents Advisory Council (which Garrity had created), called the decision "devastating." Mary Ellen Smith of the Citywide Educational Coalition echoed this view: "Basically I had been supportive of the court's orders. . . . But this one just blows my mind."[57]

⟡

Garrity's decision to close up to twenty-five schools over the course of two years stemmed from declining enrollments, which, in turn, stemmed largely from declining numbers of white students in the public schools. One study explained that "in every year since 1964 the white student population has dropped. In 1964 there were 70,703 white students and by 1974 there were 57,623. This decline resulted even though Catholic schools were closing, thus adding more (largely white) students to the public school system."[58] In 1964–65, Boston's public schools had enrolled nearly 95,000 students. In 1974–75 (the first year of court-ordered busing), the public schools enrolled approximately 75,000, with an overall racial composition that was 52 percent white, 36 percent black, and 12 percent Hispanic, Asian, or other minority. In 1980–81, however, the schools enrolled only 63,000 students, with a racial composition roughly 35 percent white, 46 percent black, and 19 percent Hispanic, Asian, and/or other minority. When Garrity issued his busing order, he explicitly limited his plan to Boston alone, which meant that desegregation had to occur entirely within the confines of the city itself (with this ruling, Garrity anticipated the decision of the U.S. Supreme Court in *Milliken v. Bradley,* which reversed a so-called metropolitan solution for racial segregation in Detroit). Under Garrity's plan, the composition of each school in Boston could not deviate from the composition of the district as a whole by more than 10 percent. So, technically, if a district had 45 percent black students and 20 percent "other minority" students, a school could be considered desegregated—and legally compliant—with 55 percent black students, 30 percent other minority students, and only 15 percent white students. Such was the situation in Boston in 1980: legally, any public school in the city could be considered desegregated even if it had only 15 percent white students.[59]

When Garrity ordered Boston to close thirteen schools and to plan for the closing of twelve more, he did so in an effort to spread white students more thinly across the district and, in the process, increase the number of desegregated schools. To his great surprise, however, the most vociferous objections to this decision came not from white parents but, rather, from minority parents. Immediately after Garrity made his ruling, a group of black parents requested a hearing to ask "that no schools be closed pending a detailed survey of educational programs that might be jeopardized."[60] Joining in this request was El Comite de Padres Pro Defensa de la Educacion Bilingue, along with the Boston Teachers Union and the Boston Association of School Administrators and Supervisors. These groups held that racial composition was not the only factor to consider in judgments concerning equal opportunity in the schools: the court also had to consider the quality and continuity of the educational programs in which students participated. According to black parents, educational quality, continuity, and stability increased both the efficiency and the effectiveness of local schools—and state education commissioner Gregory Anrig echoed this view in a personal letter to the court. Anrig urged Garrity to adjust his ruling in a way that would offer parents "the predictability they desire regarding student assignments in the future" and implored Garrity to act soon to avert "a serious breach that appears to be developing" between the court and the public. Superintendent Wood was more blunt. In a speech to the Tri-Lateral Council, a court-appointed group of business, community, and school leaders, Wood accused the court of "unwarranted judicial intervention" and of "failing to understand the complexities" of educating poor minority children in the inner city.[61] In Wood's view, the federal court had assumed the role of an urban school administrator but had not accepted the burden of *accountability* for the schools' outcomes or results.

Garrity's ruling was particularly upsetting to Wood because, a few months earlier, the judge had pledged to pull back from his involvement in the day-to-day operation of schools, and, from Wood's perspective as superintendent, the time had definitely come for Garrity to loosen his grip. "Throughout the 1970s, federal and state courts were trying to cope with obvious violations of constitutional rights by public agencies," Wood wrote. "Class action suits were on the rise, and cease-and-desist orders or the award of damages no longer sufficed to right wrongs. As a result, [the] courts were moving first to oversee institutional behavior on a day-to-day basis, and then to intervene directly in the affairs of internal management." Gradually, however, both the number and scope of judicial actions had exceeded the limits of the courts' expertise. "In the Boston case," Wood commented, "well over 200 court orders to the school department are outstanding, ranging from major efforts at planning to the repair and maintenance of individual classrooms. When I once asked an able department counsel whether we were inadvertently in contempt of court in any major way, he shrugged his reply, 'Who knows—it's hard enough to count the orders, let alone read them.'" In Wood's view, the massive scale of federal legal involvement in the schools had distorted the meaning of the term *accountability* in school administration. As he remarked, "each of the courses of intervention the courts chose interjected new patterns of administrative complexity and made accountability next to impossible. . . . Court orders for the most part have been indifferent to the problems posed by austerity; unions have exacted their concessions in work rules; [and] parents have acted like any consumer without a direct user charge."[62] By 1980, Wood held, it had become impossible to determine who was accountable for school failure: the administrators, the teachers, the parents, the mayor, the city council, the state legislature, or even the federal court itself.

For instance, if the schools obeyed desegregation orders but continued to fail, then why not hold the court accountable for a lack of equal opportunities as measured by student outcomes, Wood asked. Some insisted that the courts were not responsible for educational outcomes but only for racial integration.[63] Others held that the issue of "accountability" could not be decided until the court's remedy had been fully implemented. Still others argued that it was unfair to expect a direct correlation between racial desegregation and student achievement—that, legally, the issue of desegregation was an issue of racial classification, not an issue of the educational *effects* of racial classification. Yet, herein lay a basic dilemma. It was incongruous for the court to claim that its involvement in minority student placements, once engaged, had no bearing on educational outcomes or results, because this claim would absolve the court of any responsibility for the effects of its own actions. Further, while it may have been true that the constitutional framework for adjudicating racial segregation under the equal protection clause of the Fourteenth Amendment hinged on the suspect nature of all racial classifications that did not serve a "compelling state interest," the widespread assumption was that racial classifications leading to segregated placements were unjust *because* they led to disparate opportunities as measured by disparate effects or outcomes. Indeed, the very concept of discrimination hinged on assessments of deleterious effects among an injured class, and the acceptability of busing as a remedy for racial segregation in Boston hinged on the view that busing would heal this injury by fostering better results. As Wood asserted, however, his "central problem [as superintendent was] to cope with different claimants who assert they have an equal if not superior legitimate right to decide [how the schools should be run], but who accept no responsibility for the outcome."[64]

One of the ironies of this dilemma was that Garrity, in his push for integration and accountability, believed he was acting in the interests of the original plaintiffs in *Morgan v. Hennigan*—the class of "all black children enrolled in the Boston public school system and their parents"—when, in fact, many of the city's black and other minority residents no longer believed that racial integration was the key to equal educational opportunity. Indeed, in a truly uncanny reversal of roles, many black residents urged the school department *not* to obey the court's order to close facilities that were admitted to be racially imbalanced, even as the superintendent felt intense pressure to appease the court. Amazingly, the black parents found themselves aligned with the conservative wing of the Boston school committee, led by John McDonough, Gerald O'Leary, and Elvira "Pixie" Palladino, an outspoken critic of busing who held that, under the court's supervision, "the system has gone right down the drain."[65] The black community and the school committee both wanted to keep the city's racially imbalanced schools open—even if they had different motives for their seemingly unified position. The black parents, on the one hand, hoped that racially imbalanced neighborhood schools would offer high-quality programs to black pupils. The school committee, on the other hand, hoped that racially imbalanced neighborhood schools would attract more federal aid. In July 1980, in a note to the newly created federal Department of Education to support its application for desegregation funds, the school department identified not 25 but 114 out of 150 schools as noncompliant with federal desegregation orders. By placing as many schools as possible under the heading of " noncompliance," the committee hoped to maximize Boston's receipt of aid under the Emergency School Assistance Act (ESAA), which funded integration efforts. In other words, making the city's plight seem even worse than it was, the committee hoped to obtain more aid.[66]

Yet, if Boston could deliberately perpetuate racial imbalance as a way to maximize federal aid at a time of ongoing budgetary strain, then which party was ultimately accountable for this behavior? Was it the federal legislators who created incentives for the city to overstate its number of imbalanced schools, or was it the diverse state and local officials whose own prior actions strained budgets in the first place? It came as no surprise that the school committee had one answer to this question while the mayor, the parents, the teachers, and the court had others. As Wood commented, "it may be that the concept of a partnership between teacher and parent pursuing in common the good of the child was always a fantasy: but there have been times and places in which common bonds have linked most parents. Now they are fractionalized: special needs parents, bilingual parents, regular education parents, examination school parents, advanced standing parents. Each has a different perspective and different priorities, and each asserts special claims on resources. Finding common ground with the [entire] school community—finding [any] community at all—is increasingly uncertain." Recalling his own experiences during the optimistic days of the Johnson administration (he had been present at the creation of both Title I for low-income students and Title VII for non-English-speaking pupils), Wood now bemoaned the extent to which federal aid to categorical programs had fragmented the schools and had lifted public expectations to stratospheric heights—*despite* the fact that achievement had not improved among poor minority students in the inner city. "Expectations have been raised to unrealistic levels," he now lamented, "creating aspirations . . . that are well beyond the power of any system to deliver."[67] Within this context, Wood maintained, it was unfair to hold superintendents personally accountable for student results when so many others controlled school budgets.

⬦

By August 1980, Wood's "inability" to gain control of the budget had affected the school committee's estimate of his performance as chief executive—and, in a surprise move just two weeks before the start of the fall semester, the committee voted to terminate his two-year-old contract. Citing negligent administration and an $18 million deficit, the committee also identified "poor handling of standardized reading test results this year" and irritation over "the continued jurisdiction of the federal court" as reasons for its three-to-one decision. McDonough, Palladino, and O'Leary voted against Wood; newly elected committee member Jean Sullivan McKeigue, the sister of former member Kathleen Sullivan Alioto, voted for him; and John O'Bryant, the committee's only black member, refused to vote, saying "I do not choose to be present at a lynching." According to the *Boston Globe*, Wood's dismissal "prompted numerous expressions of shock," not least because it indicated the failure of his campaign for administrative accountability and the return of a patronage-based system unlikely to restrain costs.[68] "Wood angered and worried many old-time school personnel with his affirmative action hiring and plans to evaluate staff," the *Globe* noted. "Brought in with a promise of strong and comprehensive executive power in 1978, he found himself in a new arena in 1980. Ultimately, the newly elected school committee, which balked at granting Wood the mandate allowed under the 1978 administrative reform, turned around and used that same reform legislation to fire the superintendent." At the core of the vote to fire Wood was the issue of accountability and the desire to fix blame for the schools' ineffectiveness and inefficiency. Yet, as the *Globe* put it, "while the committee may have regained a measure of control over the day-to-day administration of the Boston school system, it may well have lost the larger battle and, in the process, thrown into serious question its credibility with the court."[69]

In short, by firing the superintendent, the school committee would have to accept responsibility for improving the system itself. If it did not, then the court might place the entire system into receivership (as a federal district court judge had done in Cleveland a week earlier).[70] Wood's dismissal thus put the burden of accountability on the committee and its choice of his successor. It was a grievous burden. The man who replaced Wood as superintendent was Paul Kennedy, acting deputy superintendent for academic affairs (and a finalist for the top job in each of the last two searches which hired Fahey and Wood). A former teacher and Title I director, the fifty-two-year-old Kennedy had served as head of collective bargaining and personnel before ascending to the superintendency. However, he had no interest in reform or continuing his predecessor's reorganization effort. In fact, immediately after his arrival in the school department, he began to undo most of the personnel changes his predecessor had made.[71] As the *Globe* noted, "at least four administrators hired by Wood . . . are expected to be dismissed or at least displaced as part of the recommended changes." He appointed Edward Lambert to fill the position of deputy superintendent for academic affairs and Victor McInnis to be deputy superintendent for management. Both men lived in the suburbs—as did Kennedy himself, who commuted from Quincy. He also sought a replacement for Bernice Miller, the school department's senior officer for curriculum and competency, who not only was responsible for state-mandated basic skills competency testing but also was the highest-ranking black woman in the public schools.[72] Kennedy claimed to be creating a new team of administrators that would be more accountable to public demands—and in this endeavor, the *Boston Globe* explained, he had "the respect and confidence of many of the old timers who resented Wood and his promises of reform."[73]

Kennedy upheld his predecessor's nomination of Robert Peterkin—who was also black—to head the new Hubert H. Humphrey Occupational Resource Center in Roxbury, but many black leaders criticized his unwillingness to include more black educators in his inner circle. In their view, the call for greater accountability in the public schools implied greater black influence over school policies and budgets. "It's one thing to have a job; it's quite another to have a role," argued one unnamed black school employee. "I don't think blacks will have effective roles or exert any influence over [this] superintendent."[74] When Kennedy announced that six out of twelve administrative promotions would go to blacks, school committee member John O'Bryant responded that promoting six blacks "doesn't mean anything if the six have no real power or influence."[75] Noting that the federal court had required the schools to increase minority employment to 20 percent system-wide and that the system had only recently achieved this goal, O'Bryant stated that the presence of minority administrators in the schools had to be "meaningful"—and, in his view, the only way to tell if minority representation had, in fact, been meaningful was to see its effect on specific policies the department pursued.[76] Put another way, the test of an "effective role" was to see whether minorities had "real power or influence," and the test of real power or influence was to determine whether minorities at school headquarters actually *set* policy. Ignoring the question of whether minorities within the school system shared a common perspective on any given policy issue—for example, the merits of integrated and isolated programs for disabled students, an issue that had generated disagreement not only among black but also among white and non-English-speaking parents for years—O'Bryant held that hiring black educators was meaningful only if they had a clearly discernible effect on school policies and budget decisions (though he did not say what this effect might be).

Certainly, it was the budget—the subject that had so vexed his predecessors—that was Superintendent Kennedy's foremost concern in the fall of 1980. The day after he arrived in office, he received a message from Mayor White saying the schools' budget would remain static at $195 million—$33 million less than the $228 million budget that Wood had requested. William Sinich of the mayor's budget staff told Kennedy that, despite a reduction from 8,100 to 7,100 school employees in the past year, salary costs actually *grew* by $20 million due to teacher raises.[77] It was time, Sinich argued, to put an end to the continuous escalation of school expenses. "The only thing we can control is the bottom line," Sinich informed the *Boston Globe*. "Holding them to what they are statutorily allowed to spend, if nothing else, creates the incentive for management at the school department to shut the door on the trend of increasing deficits and to hold the line on costs." Kennedy, however, was dismayed. "I have come to the conclusion that in no way can we live with $195 million. I hope [the mayor] can be convinced to reassess his thinking in order to meet the needs of [all] the schools relative to a quality education." Even the Boston Municipal Research Bureau (BMRB), usually supportive of budget cuts, observed that $195 million was too little to run the schools. Samuel Tyler, the executive director of the BMRB, noted that the mayor himself regularly exceeded his *own* budget: "Preliminary figures indicate that the mayor's city budget spent over $20 million beyond appropriations last year, but he recommended an increase of $57 million, or 18 percent, for this year's budget." If the mayor constrained school budgets in order to accommodate his own spending, then, Tyler feared, the whole process of school budgeting might fall to the court. In his words, "I am afraid the result of the mayor's action is to invite the courts to determine what the proper level of school spending is."[78]

Surely, *someone* had to determine a "proper level of school spending." Yet, with so many different parties involved in making this determination, the proper level—that is, the level most likely to ensure equal opportunities for all students—was anyone's guess. For example, it did not help local schools in Boston when federal aid for special education under P.L. 94-142 failed to keep up with federal legal mandates. By 1980, federal aid was supposed to cover 30 percent of special education costs, but actual appropriations covered only 10 percent. As Carol Kervick, state director of special education, stated, "we're not seeing as much federal money coming into the state as was initially promised. Therefore, some school systems have had to cut back on what they perceive as nonessential services to special-needs students."[79] Cutting back on services to disabled students, however, carried legal risks. As Paul Cox of Boston College noted, "local educational authorities were caught in a two-pronged legal [bind]. They could be sued for not providing services even when no more funds were available, and they could be sued for spending money which was not legally budgeted."[80] Indeed, the prospect of legal action was at least partly responsible for the fact that new jobs in special education continued to appear even as jobs in regular education disappeared.[81] Making the budget dilemma all the more perplexing was the fact that, despite much litigation, many disabled children *still* did not receive services to which they were entitled. Even after Boston hired a monitor "to oversee the [school] department's special education programs and to make a detailed analysis of the bureaucratic problems within the programs aimed at suggesting systematic reforms," officials could not explain "why . . . student evaluations are still not made in a timely fashion; why special needs services are still not provided when they are due; [and] why transportation is periodically unavailable [to disabled students]."[82]

If school accountability hinged on public trust, then, by October 1980, the Boston public schools were teetering on the brink of an accountability disaster—and the situation only got worse. The crisis focused, in part, on the aforementioned issue of transportation. In one of his last acts as superintendent, Wood had approved a $40 million contract with Philadelphia-based ARA Services, Inc., for the schools' busing needs, including door-to-door shuttles for 2,500 disabled students.[83] Boston's annual busing contract was second only to the annual teachers contract in size—and it was similarly vulnerable to abuse. Not long after Wood's dismissal in August 1980, school committee member Gerald O'Leary was indicted for extorting $650,000 from ARA Services, Inc., in exchange for the busing contract.[84] It was a devastating blow to the schools, but it was not the end of the turmoil. A few weeks later, the state Department of Education issued a scathing audit of the city's special education services. It cited "flagrant violations in accountability" and "disorderly and haphazard" administration. As chief auditor Gail Enman asserted, "it was impossible to figure out where the money (including more than $5 million in federal funds channeled through the state in the last four years) [was] going." When Gregory Anrig received the state's report, he was livid. "Personally, I've never been more discouraged about the Boston schools," he told the *Boston Globe*. "We've had points of conflict with the Boston school system before . . . but now [it has] built up to a growing disenchantment and resentment." State board of education member James Green echoed this view: "This isn't the first time state funds have not been used in the way they were originally intended in Boston," he fumed, "and I'll be damned if this board is going to continue to be compromised by the Boston school system."[85] Thus, even when the pieces for equal educational opportunities were seemingly all in place, Boston's schools were still a long way from realizing that goal.

The public, for its part, blamed the schools' troubles on managerial incompetence and rarely saw its own demands for services as a source of budgetary strains. Few noticed that rapid growth in school programs had outpaced any public willingness to foot the bill. Yet, as Susan Thompkins of the Massachusetts Taxpayers Foundation noted in the fall of 1980 at a meeting to debate the efficiency and effectiveness of public schools, "the good time of essentially unlimited resources is over." She added that public "expectations were too high and the record was not too good, and to some extent there is a kind of disillusion in the land."[86] While some of the programs that had emerged from citizens' demands for services may have benefited otherwise neglected students, their cost—mandated or not—exceeded available resources. As James McGarry of Massachusetts's state Department of Education noted of Chapter 766 and P.L. 94-142, "educators, parents, and members of the general public bitterly resented the cost involved in one or more individual cases."[87] In fact, as budget woes persisted, these laws drew hostility to the very students they aimed to help.[88] It rarely, if ever, occurred to taxpayers that rising costs for special education in Massachusetts derived not from a few extreme cases of severe disability but, rather, from the innumerable cases of mild disability across the state—chiefly in the suburbs—

and from the vast array of services mandated to ensure they reached their maximum feasible potential as measured by their academic achievement. Undoubtedly, budget difficulties in Boston owed much to mismanagement and the problem of unfunded mandates at both state and federal levels. Far more serious for the future, however, was the spreading conviction that equal educational opportunities should be gauged in terms of equal educational *outcomes* in the public schools. By 1980, citizens demanding accountability began to embrace two interconnected (though perhaps also contradictory) ideas: tax cuts and testing. In a sense, the public asked schools to produce superior results with fewer resources—that is, to do more with less.

CHAPTER EIGHT

Compelling Better Results? 1980–1985

On October 1, 1980, Superintendent Kennedy informed Mayor White and the city council that he required $46 million to cover special education expenses in the 1980–81 school year and would file charges if the city failed to provide the resources necessary to meet civil rights mandates.[1] The mayor countered with a threat to file charges against the school committee if it overspent its budget, which was legally restricted to the previous year's allotment of $195 million. State commissioner of education Gregory Anrig warned that such a limited budget would force the schools to close in mid-March of the following year, and city auditor Newell Cook calculated that the schools would run out of money by mid-February. Adding tension to this budget standoff was an historic tax proposal listed on the ballot for November 1980—a voter initiative known as Proposition 2½ that would slash municipal property tax rates throughout Massachusetts to a maximum of 2.5 percent of assessed valuations. At a time when the state's average property tax rate was 8 percent and Boston's local tax rate approached 26 percent, such a draconian tax cut portended drastic reductions in public services, including public schools: "Classes will be bigger," the *Boston Globe* stated. "Courses that used to be routinely available will no longer be offered at some schools. Interscholastic athletics will be cut back and swimming pools closed. Gone will be many of the aides who are relied on for everything from discipline to counseling to processing student records." Some asserted that schools would no longer be able to serve meals to low-income pupils; others insisted that schools would have to lay off coaches, librarians, and nurses.[2] If voters approved Proposition 2½, Commissioner Anrig warned, then Massachusetts schools—which absorbed 60 percent of property tax revenues statewide—would suffer huge losses. Moreover, the commissioner stressed, "average" children, unprotected by legal mandates, would suffer the most.[3]

Yet, few listened. The idea behind Proposition 2½ originated in 1978 when voters in California sanctioned a similar property tax cut known as Proposition 13.[4] Three days after Proposition 13 had passed, conservative legislators in Massachusetts had introduced their first version of Proposition 2½.[5] This initial measure faded after the state passed its new school-aid formula using "pupil weights," but it did not disappear entirely. A later year, a group of property owners calling themselves Citizens for Limited Taxation (CLT) joined the Massachusetts Taxpayers Foundation (MTF) and several other groups to rally support for a major property tax cut.[6] They collected the 56,000 signatures necessary to place an initiative on the legislative docket, but the legislature failed to enact any sort of tax reform in its 1979–80 session. CLT therefore gathered additional signatures and registered Proposition 2½ on the November ballot.[7] The election took place at the height of the school budget fiasco in Boston, and many citizens had lost their patience. Lawrence Susskind, a distinguished professor of urban planning at MIT, noted that "on election day, voters were asked to choose between Proposition 2½ and the status quo. Several opinion polls showed that voters supported the initiative because they felt property taxes were too high, not because they wanted smaller government or fewer services. More importantly, when given a choice, a majority preferred a more moderate alternative that restricted the growth of property taxes or slightly lowered them. But, [this sort of] alternative was not on the ballot, and in the three years prior to the election the legislature demonstrated that it would not enact such legislation."[8] So, by a two-to-one margin, citizens across the state (including Boston) approved Proposition 2½. In so doing, they brought three decades of escalating property taxes and expanding public services to an end.[9]

Of course, the election that put Proposition 2½ on the books in Massachusetts also put Ronald Reagan in the White House. A landslide victory handed Reagan 90.9 percent of the electoral vote (indeed, he even carried Massachusetts, a Democratic stronghold, by 2,421 ballots). In crafting his extremely successful campaign, Reagan took full advantage of his opponent's difficulties: an Islamist revolution in Iran that led to a year-long hostage crisis and a failed rescue attempt, a near-doubling of gasoline prices, and an inflation rate near 13 percent. Though Carter defeated Massachusetts's senator Edward Kennedy in the spring primaries, he was unprepared for the groundswell of fiscal and social conservatism that swept Reagan into office. As a former two-term governor of California, Reagan had favored Proposition 13, and, in his race for the presidency, he promised to deliver similar tax cuts at the federal level. He kept this promise. A few months after his inauguration, he persuaded both houses of Congress to pass a sprawling five-year tax cut worth more than $750 billion, including a 25 percent reduction in personal income taxes and a lowering of the top marginal rate from 70 to 50 percent. David Stockman, who ran the Office of Management and the Budget (OMB) under Reagan, admitted the cuts benefited the rich but argued that consumer spending would gradually stimulate the economy. Inflation did fall during Reagan's first year in office, but, at the same time, unemployment flared to 10 percent. Despite supply-side theories holding that corporate investment would lead to job growth, poverty jumped dramatically, especially among minorities. At least 36 percent of all black families and 30 percent of Hispanic families sought assistance—even as benefits were shrinking due to state-level cuts. Certainly, in Massachusetts, the most urgent topic of political debate in 1981 was the crisis of Proposition 2½.[10] How, officials asked, would public services—including public schools—handle such huge cuts?[11]

Scheduled to take effect on July 1, 1981, Proposition 2½ precipitated massive cuts in local budgets. If a town's property tax rate was higher than 2.5 percent (as most were), then the law mandated annual spending cuts of 15 percent to bring local budgets into line with the revenues that would be generated by a (maximum) 2.5 percent rate. The law also restricted local tax increases to no more than 2.5 percent per year, regardless of growth in population or real property values. As one commentator observed, "Proposition 2½ turned the entire budget process upside down." Rather than seeing how much a local budget demanded and then setting the tax rate accordingly, "the tax rate was fixed *first*."[12] In Boston—where 63.7 percent of local property comprised tax-exempt buildings such as churches, synagogues, hospitals, colleges, universities, and government offices—the law had a devastating impact. As Gregory Anrig asserted, Proposition 2½ affected "most heavily our largest and poorest communities. . . . Boston's budget, for instance, if you use the current recommended property valuations and the current year tax levy, would have to [be reduced] . . . by 70 percent."[13] Faced with such numbers, the various departments of city government had to make difficult choices. Indeed, the Boston school committee had to make some of the most difficult choices of all. First, the school committee had to decide which legislative mandates to obey and which to ignore: the new budget simply would not support compliance with them all. Second, the committee had to decide which sorts of cuts would minimize the legal backlash schools would inevitably confront: both the courts and the public would scrutinize every cut the committee made to assess its effects on "equal educational opportunities." Third, the committee—once it had made these preliminary calculations— had to decide whether its first round of cuts should hit programs or personnel, or both. No matter what, bitter controversy was inevitable.[14]

Adding to the difficulty of these decisions was the fact that, in January 1981, the Boston school committee was embroiled in the push-and-pull of selecting its next leader. After the indictment (and eventual conviction) of committee member Gerald O'Leary the previous fall, Kevin McCluskey, the sixth-highest vote-getter in the last citywide election, had taken his seat. McCluskey, an outspoken twenty-six-year-old recent Harvard graduate and youth counselor, had grown up in a federal housing project in the ghetto neighborhood of Columbia Point. He now held the swing vote in the contest for leadership between John O'Bryant (who, if elected, would become the first black member to occupy the chair) and Jean Sullivan-McKeigue (the daughter of New England Patriots football team owner William Sullivan and the sister of former school committee member and chair Kathleen Sullivan-Alioto). "I spent a sleepless night before making my decision," McCluskey told the *Boston Globe*. "There is no secret that my vote is the key." Acknowledging that his vote would likely determine the schools' direction in the wake of Proposition 2½, McCluskey weighed his options carefully. He eventually chose O'Bryant based on O'Bryant's slight seniority over Sullivan-McKeigue: "To have denied John the position would have been to say that rules of seniority and succession apply except when it comes to black people," McCluskey later commented, adding that O'Bryant was "a powerful voice" for minorities in the city. Indeed, Joseph Feaster of the Boston chapter of the NAACP was delighted by O'Bryant's selection. "John O'Bryant has the sensitivity and capability to carry out this task," Feaster commented in an interview with the *Globe*. "We may [finally] have crossed the bridge toward having a responsive school committee in the City of Boston."[15] And, yet, O'Bryant faced a daunting task. In order to rebuild public support for the schools, he needed, first, to reduce costs to fit the limits of Proposition 2½ and, simultaneously, to improve student results. He needed, in other words, to do more with less.

Recalling his recent appeal for more black influence over school policy, O'Bryant now had the power he wanted, and he felt a great deal of pressure to use it wisely. As the *Boston Globe* reported, "O'Bryant is moving into the school committee's most influential seat at a time [when] the system is beset with problems. The committee is fighting in the courts to force Mayor Kevin H. White to have the city help pay its [mounting] bills. Meanwhile, the combination of the city's fiscal problems and the new state tax initiative, Proposition 2½, is expected to force the closing of more than 20 schools and the dismissal of 1,000 to 2,000 school department employees."[16] Indeed, after O'Bryant's election, Superintendent Kennedy immediately asked the school committee to authorize nearly 900 administrative and instructional layoffs to avert the immediate shutdown of all the schools. According to the *Globe*, the proposed cutbacks threatened to "strip the nine district offices of most of their employees and virtually wipe out two departments at school headquarters," including the Department of Intergovernmental Relations, which monitored state and federal grants. When O'Bryant learned that Kennedy's layoffs included black teachers, however, he said he would not support any request that violated court-ordered affirmative action personnel guidelines. Kennedy maintained that, in urgent matters of hiring and firing, the operative principle should be seniority (the same principle that McCluskey had used to cast his vote for O'Bryant)—not race. Further, Kennedy held, "the advantages of keeping the schools open for the remainder of this school year outweigh . . . the disadvantages that will be caused by the severity of reductions that are being recommended."[17] But O'Bryant refused to budge. When it came to equal educational opportunity for black students, he insisted that additional black teachers were ultimately more important than additional school days.

◇

Evidently, this row with O'Bryant was too much for Kennedy to bear: a few weeks later, he suffered a coronary embolism and died while driving to attend a meeting in South Boston. "Kennedy literally gave his life to the system," O'Bryant told a reporter from the *Boston Globe* after receiving the news. "He worked day and night for the Boston public schools and at all times gave his best for the system. . . . He obviously worked very hard and was very dedicated. All of us have been under a lot of pressure. He internalized a lot of things."[18] Kennedy's sudden death threw Boston's school committee into an extended period of confusion and turmoil. Facing imminent budget cuts linked to Proposition 2½, the committee's highest objective was to find a new superintendent who could reduce school expenses and, at the same time, rebuild public trust by responding to local demands and raising student achievement in measurable ways. It was an extraordinarily tough job (though it attracted scores of eager applicants). Finally, in June 1981, the committee picked Robert "Bud" Spillane as its next superintendent: its seventh in nine years. Formerly a deputy state commissioner in New York, the forty-six-year-old Spillane was a native of Lowell, Massachusetts, but grew up in Hartford, Connecticut. He had been the youngest principal in Connecticut when, in 1960, at the age of twenty-five, he had served in the small rural town of Chaplin. He later served in Darien and Trumbull, Connecticut, before accepting three superintendencies: first, in Glassboro, New Jersey; second, in Roosevelt, New York; and, finally, in New Rochelle, New York. After the reelection of New York governor Hugh Carey in 1978, Spillane went to Albany as deputy state commissioner of elementary and secondary education. In that capacity, he quickly distinguished himself as a "risk-oriented" administrator who made hard decisions in a period of severe budget cuts. He was, it seemed, a perfect fit for Boston.[19]

Spillane's ability to run a statewide organization with 83 divisions and a budget of $11 billion impressed the Boston school committee, but it was his work in New Rochelle that clinched the deal. "He arrived in New Rochelle to find the system in debt and immediately reduced staff," the *Globe* noted in a profile of the new superintendent. "At 46, Spillane is a self-assured and experienced educator who was not afraid to take on the teachers' union when he had to lay off staff."[20] This readiness to "take on the teachers' union" was precisely the quality Spillane needed in Boston. As he began to review the schools' payroll, the first step was to announce that, in cutting staff (a necessity), he would honor all court orders—including the order that 20 percent of school positions must go to black candidates. The union opposed this announcement, but the *Bay State Banner*, a black weekly published in Roxbury, called it a victory for black teachers, nine out of ten of whom had been hired in the seven years since the court's initial decree. The editors of the *Banner* explained that, if layoffs followed seniority, then three-quarters of the city's black teachers would lose their jobs, and their proportion of the staff would drop from 20 to 5 percent.[21] To prevent this outcome (and to keep the court from placing the entire system into receivership), Spillane terminated the contracts of 1,300 tenured white teachers. This move was strategic on two fronts: it avoided the wrath of the federal court and it also eliminated teachers with high salaries. Simply put, by dismissing tenured white teachers, Spillane was able to save money. In this way, he showed the public that he would make decisions not only to please the federal court, but, above all, to protect the budget and to make schools accountable to the taxpayers they were supposed to serve.[22] "Accountability must start at the top," Spillane told a reporter shortly after his arrival—and his controversial personnel decisions proved it.[23]

Spillane repeatedly emphasized the need to make the schools more accountable to taxpayers. "After only six weeks on the job," the *Boston Globe* reported, "Spillane said last night he has school department management problems 'by the throat' and is ready to focus on improving accountability." By accountability, the *Globe* implied, Spillane meant that schools would seek to maximize the educational benefit of every dollar they received and would show their efficiency and effectiveness in concrete terms: "As part of his push for accountability," the *Globe* noted, "Spillane said he would make unannounced visits to Boston schools weekly to see what's going on."[24] These visits, he promised, would form the basis of a new personnel evaluation system that would review all school employees—both teachers and principals—on the basis of their students' academic achievement. More specifically, he explained, all personnel would be reviewed on the basis of their students' scores on the citywide Individual Criterion Reference Test (ICRT), a standardized test of basic reading skills.[25] Spillane won immediate and enthusiastic public support for his new personnel evaluation policy—but a furious Boston Teachers Union threatened to walk out in protest. Spillane brashly replied to this threat by calling the union's bluff: "If the union really wants to blow itself out of the water [in terms of public support, then] call a strike," he goaded. "It will absolutely destroy it."[26] This standoff marked a significant moment in Spillane's push for greater accountability in the Boston public schools. In effect, he made teachers' jobs contingent neither on race nor on seniority but, rather, on competence as reflected in student performance on standardized tests. In so doing, he took seriously the assumption that court-ordered affirmative action hiring policies would foster educational opportunities that could be measured in terms of students' educational outcomes.[27] If this assumption was incorrect, he calculated, then blame would fall on the court, not on himself.

Spillane was not alone in emphasizing "outcomes" as the key to accountability in the public schools. His decision to utilize the Individual Criterion Reference Test (ICRT) was—in part—a response to a new set of accountability requirements at the state level. In the summer of 1981, the state Department of Education began to require all districts receiving aid to give basic skills competency tests in reading, writing, and mathematics at three points in each student's years in school—elementary, middle, and high school. The aim of this requirement was to generate consistent, uniform, and reliable information on statewide achievement over time. The requirement, however, had a flaw: in an effort to make its rapid implementation as palatable as possible, the state permitted each district to choose its own test. Some districts chose the Iowa Test of Basic Skills, others chose the California Test of Basic Skills, and still others chose local tests that fit local curricular priorities. State commissioner of education Gregory Anrig hoped schools would be able to use local test data to identify curricular problems and "tweak" classroom programs for specific pupils. He did not say exactly *how* basic skills tests should alter the curriculum; he simply hinted they *would*. As the *Globe* noted, "the first statewide testing program to measure student abilities in the basic skills was launched . . . under a deliberately flexible program that gave local school districts some control over the grades to be tested, the instruments to be used and the standards for pass and fail."[28] The paper added that Commissioner Anrig had adopted a new testing requirement only "reluctantly in response to a growing demand for 'accountability.' He hoped they would remain diagnostic tools for individual school systems and not become a standard for making 'invidious comparisons' about the relative effectiveness of different school systems."[29]

Despite such warnings, basic skills competency testing expanded rapidly in the early 1980s and fueled the idea of developing a statewide assessment policy for *all* public schools. "Competency testing," the *Boston Globe* commented, "has acquired the aura of a consumer/accountability movement which may [eventually] make the adoption of some statewide testing program politically necessary." As one editorialist observed, "the mere appearance of the 1981 scores has apparently been enough to generate an irresistible pressure to go statewide with a mandatory testing system."[30] And, yet, the prospect of a statewide testing system did not win universal support. For each proponent, several detractors stood ready to identify serious problems with the idea. Foremost among these problems was the lack of alignment between standardized tests and local curricula. As the *Globe* explained, "There often is no relationship between what skills are taught and what skills are tested. The skills that are tested in the third grade in one school might differ significantly from the skills tested in the same grade elsewhere, even within the same school." Curriculum specialist Ronald Edmonds of the Harvard Graduate School of Education noted that "if you don't have [just one] curriculum to go by, [then] . . . you have a standard of progress that obtains in one part of the city [but] not in another, or a standard of progress that obtains for blacks

and not for whites, or for Hispanics and not for blacks." In Boston, however, the lack of a unified curriculum stemmed directly from a court order: five years earlier, Judge Garrity had moved the school department's
curriculum developers "from the central office to the nine school districts throughout the city"—a move that had had the effect of encouraging different curricula at different schools around the city.[31] Yet, with no
clear ties between local curricula and state-mandated tests, it was impossible to collect comparable data on student achievement—let alone
on the particular school programs that fostered it.[32]

Despite these and countless other problems, basic skills competency
tests soon became a permanent feature of Massachusetts education policy. The instigator of this policy, state commissioner Gregory Anrig, did
not, however, remain in office long enough to guide the early development of statewide testing. Instead, in 1981, after nearly a decade of service,
he accepted a job as president of the Educational Testing Service (ETS) in
Princeton, New Jersey. Anrig was eager to accept this new post. In his last
interview with the Boston Globe, he remarked, "The last few months have
probably been the most unhappy professionally for me. I don't like the
recommendations I've had to come up with in cutting back programs because of Proposition 2½. I'm not getting any satisfaction out of it."[33] Happy
to avoid the implementation of statewide competency testing in Massachusetts, Anrig left this difficult task to his successor, John Lawson, formerly superintendent of schools in Lexington, Massachusetts. A native
of Gloucester, he had earned his Ed.D. at Boston University in 1958 and
had served as superintendent in Hamilton-Wenham and Hingham, Massachusetts, before moving to Shaker Heights, Ohio, a wealthy suburb of
Cleveland. There, he had launched a voluntary urban-suburban busing
plan modeled on the Metropolitan Council for Educational Opportunity
(METCO) program in Boston. Returning to Massachusetts to accept the
superintendency in Lexington in 1975, he had faced severe budget cuts
and declining student enrollments but had quickly won a reputation as
"a solid financial manager." As one school committee member explained, "when it came to closing five schools here because of declining
enrollment, he carried the ball. . . . he was . . . conscious of waste and
was not averse to consolidating."[34] Perhaps not surprisingly, Massachusetts's new commissioner also favored statewide basic skills competency
tests as a way to foster increased accountability in local schools.[35]

⬦

Lawson believed that, if local schools could show a link between financial inputs and educational outcomes, they would be able to secure

public trust—and, hence, public funds. Consequently, when he rose to the commissionership in 1981, he lobbied strongly for a unified testing system across the state. "I am interested in having information that will permit comparisons," he insisted. "I would like to see some state norm established so local school systems can match scores up to that."[36] Lawson recognized that the only way to make schools accountable to the same standard was to achieve comparability across districts, and the only way to achieve comparability was to use a uniform statewide test. His challenge, therefore, was to convince local officials of this view. Over the course of the 1981–82 school year, he developed close ties with Superintendent Spillane in Boston. Both agreed that Boston's public schools needed to rebuild public trust, and both agreed that doing so would require a concerted effort to hold schools accountable for student performance.[37] As Rosemary Rosen, deputy superintendent for financial administration, noted, it was imperative for Boston to show taxpayers a "link between the performance of educational programs and the dollars that are spent on them." What the schools needed, therefore, was an information-management system that helped observers see the connection between financial inputs and educational outcomes, preferably in one large spreadsheet. In the spring of 1982, thanks to innovations in the fast-growing computer industry, Superintendent Spillane was able to obtain software that integrated (for the first time) the schools' data on personnel, payroll, and programs. This new computerized budget system enabled the central office to compare payroll and personnel data for each school and—by feeding test scores into the analysis—to compare the efficiency and effectiveness of specific programs citywide.[38]

The new budget management system appealed not only to Commissioner Lawson and Superintendent Spillane, but also to local business leaders who, in 1981–82, began to express greater interest in the schools. Spillane actively recruited business executives to become involved in educational reforms—and, strategically, used their involvement as a way to hold them jointly accountable for the success of the city's most at-risk students. "I wanted them to form a part of the effort to improve the Boston schools," he asserted, "so that if, for example, the school committee [or the mayor or the city council or the voters who endorsed Proposition 2½] were to say, 'Cut the budget by $20 million,' it would be a real slap in the face to the business community."[39] Spillane recognized that his survival as superintendent, as well as the survival of the Boston public schools, hinged on his ability to create a broad network of supporters, each with a clear stake in high-quality education. Business support was especially crucial at a time when—according to a survey conducted by a consultant to Mayor Kevin White—fewer than 12 percent of taxpayers in

Boston had children in the public schools, and those with children in the schools tended not to be politically active. As one commentator put it, "the student population is predominantly black and other minority and has a constituency which is far less politically sophisticated. It has, therefore, become expedient for the politicians to appeal to the growing majority of citizens who do not use the public schools and who resent paying for them. The most obvious of these politicians has been the mayor of this city who has carefully polled the voters and [has] come to the conclusion that public education in this city is no longer in vogue."[40] Given this reality, Spillane returned to an idea that the old Boston Urban Coalition had framed years earlier—namely, the idea that business support for high-quality schools in ghetto areas could foster the social and economic well-being of the city as a whole.

In the summer of 1982, Spillane teamed up with Boston's most ambitious business-school partnership to date—an arrangement called the Boston Compact. Featured in dozens of newspapers (as well as *Rolling Stone*), the Boston Compact seized national attention. One reporter described it as "an alliance between the schools and major area businesses designed to guarantee high school graduates jobs in exchange for continued improved performance on the part of the school system."[41] Under the agreement, local business leaders promised to hire 1,000 high school students for summer jobs as well as 1,000 high school graduates for entry-level jobs at three hundred area companies. School officials, in turn, pledged to reduce absentee and dropout rates by 5 percent a year and to guarantee each graduate's basic competency in reading, writing, and mathematics.[42] In addition, local trade unions promised to reserve 5 percent of their apprenticeships for qualified students, and local colleges and universities agreed to admit more graduates from the Boston public schools and give them generous financial aid.[43] William Edgerly, chair of the State Street Bank and head of the Boston Private Industry Council, said of the new compact, "You had an evolution from concern about the school system to concrete action toward improving the schools. . . . There was an act of commitment by large employers to get involved with the schools."[44] Edgerly also recognized the critical role that federal job-training grants had played in the early stages of the Boston Compact. His own group, the Boston Private Industry Council, had been created in 1977 to coordinate applications for job-training grants under the federal Youth Employment Demonstration Project Act—part of the Comprehensive Employment Training Act (CETA)—and, from 1978 to 1980, federal agencies had sent $40 million to Boston-area businesses to create summer jobs for inner-city students.[45] In 1982, the Boston Compact built on this existing federal program.

By the end of Spillane's first year in office, with federal help, the Boston public schools participated in dozens of business-school partnerships. For example, the Bank of Boston sent tutors every afternoon to assist students at Josiah Quincy Elementary School, John W. McCormack Middle School, and Hyde Park High School. In a similar program, the John Hancock Mutual Life Insurance Company offered periodic seminars on résumé preparation, job-hunting, and interview techniques to seniors at English High School. The Gillette Company and the Federal Reserve Bank of Boston ran a collaborative project at South Boston High School, and the New England Telephone Company and the University of Massachusetts–Boston sponsored a project at Dorchester High School (a venture begun in 1969 and a model for the federal court-ordered Tri-Lateral Council in 1974). These projects gave businesses a way to train future employees, and they also gave executives a glimpse into urban schools. As Frank Morris, president of the Federal Reserve Bank of Boston, remarked, "people coming into the labor force from the schools were often functionally illiterate. The school system was not doing its job."[46] The business community *had* to act, Morris held, in order to protect its own interests. This reasoning was, of course, precisely the kind of reasoning Superintendent Spillane had sought to cultivate among business leaders. His development of business-school partnerships was part of a comprehensive strategy to build community support for the schools— and, slowly, his strategy worked. "There is a general assessment that the schools have settled down," the *Globe* reported at the end of Spillane's first year. "In place now is a rating process for the appointment of new principals and headmasters, a personnel evaluation system, improved budget and personnel management, the inauguration of a citywide curriculum, the beginnings of a system-wide testing program and a new alliance between the schools and business."[47] Boston's public schools, it seemed, were improving.

Perhaps the most notable feature of new business involvement in the schools was the near-total absence of emphasis on racial integration. With a public-school population in Boston that was nearing 47 percent black, 31 percent white, and 22 percent Hispanic, Asian, and other minority, the pursuit of integration (by means of court-ordered busing) gave way in the early 1980s to a renewed focus on educational *quality* in neighborhood schools. Ruth Batson, professor of community psychiatry at Boston University's School of Medicine, former director of the Massachusetts Commission Against Discrimination, founder of the METCO program, and veteran civil-rights activist who had organized one of the first boycotts of Boston's public schools in the 1960s, expressed the views of many black parents who rejected busing in the 1980s. "We talk about a commitment to educating children," she asserted. "What we had [instead] was [the] assignment of children on buses without caring what happened to them. What was never achieved was the improvement of the educational lot of those children."[48] Agreeing that federal court orders had not led to high-quality schools for poor minority students in neglected inner-city neighborhoods, Larry Johnson of the Harvard Center for Law and Education (the lawyer who represented the class of black plaintiffs in the city's ongoing desegregation lawsuit) decided in the fall of 1982 to withdraw from ongoing negotiations in the decade-old case. He told the Black Parents' Committee he would no longer support Judge Garrity's student-assignment plan but would, instead, "work with black parents on a broader plan that gives parents freedom to send their children to the schools of their choice."[49] This emphasis on "school choice" appealed to many black parents. A *Boston Globe* survey in March 1982, found that "80 percent of black parents in the city favored freedom of choice."[50] Evidently, choice had replaced integration as the key to quality education in the eyes of many black parents.

A focus on choice and quality resonated not only with black parents, but also with administrators who believed it was time for the court to end its micromanagement of the schools' daily operations. (Indeed, even Garrity himself seemed increasingly eager to cut the cord: "This is a case that started in 1972, and it is going to end in 1982," he claimed at one point from the bench.[51]) The federal court's departure was briefly delayed, however, by a dispute involving the choice issue. In the fall of 1982, the school committee had endorsed a plan to allow the Maurice J. Tobin Elementary School in Roxbury to develop an experimental fine-arts curriculum for kindergarteners through eighth-graders. The plan enjoyed broad community support, and school administrators promised it would improve both racial balance and test scores at the inner-city school. Garrity, however, hesitated to endorse the plan on grounds that a new program at the Tobin School might undermine the overall structure of racial balance (such as it was) in the rest of the city. He asserted that a new curriculum—and grade range—at the Tobin School might draw students out of other schools and thereby disrupt the racial balance on which "equal educational opportunities" (supposedly) depended. His inclination, therefore, was to block the reforms. Yet, the case raised three important legal questions. First, was the federal court empowered to render judgments about educational innovations specifically intended to improve school quality? Second, was the federal court empowered to prevent innovations at one school whenever such innovations threatened to draw students away from another school (even within the same district)? Third, was a federal court empowered to prohibit the public from choosing schools they believed would provide the best education for children? If so, then it seemed that parents would have to accept whatever programs the court approved, and the court, in order to preserve racial balance, would approve only those programs that posed no threat of drawing students away from other schools.[52]

As far as the Boston school committee was concerned, any such judicial meddling would make a mockery of the schools' pursuit of "equal educational opportunities"—and particularly so, when the priorities of the court differed so dramatically from the priorities of parents. "We took the initiative, got people excited, got them to think about improving education for kids in that school," Spillane asserted. "Innovative programs and personal enthusiasm cannot be imposed. . . . But where they arise, they must be supported." Contending that parental support was "the most important factor" in the general success of inner-city schools—even more important than racial balance—Spillane argued that "grassroots initiatives such as the one at Tobin . . . must be nurtured and supported where they grow or they will not grow at all."[53] The court, he insisted, was not equipped to ensure school quality; only the schools themselves could do so: "You cannot manage a school system from afar, especially from a court," he asserted. "The intrusions, I think, are inhibiting better ways to desegregate the district and improve programs."[54] Over time, Spillane (who reminded the court of his own meticulous cooperation with all its previous rulings and orders) became less and less patient with the court's involvement in the schools, and his criticisms grew less restrained: "I would have the judge butt out on anything that's an educational decision," he snapped in a particularly unguarded moment. "Let not my cool demeanor . . . hide the frustration and anger . . . and the seething discontent we [in the superintendent's suite] have toward the federal court."[55] Though he later apologized for this comment, it evidently had its desired effect: in the fall of 1982, Garrity turned responsibility for monitoring school desegregation plans over to Commissioner Lawson and the state board of education.[56]

⬦

Garrity's first tentative step back from the schools coincided with a pair of related political events: first was the election of Jean McGuire, longtime director of the METCO busing program, as the newest black member of the Boston school committee; second was the return of Michael Dukakis as governor with substantial black support. Both events reassured Garrity that blacks were politically represented at the local and the state level. Dukakis—who had spent the last four years as a lecturer at

Harvard—ousted Ed King in the Democratic primaries in 1982. Calling the incumbent a "Reagan Democrat," he cast King as a wolf in sheep's clothing who not only endorsed Proposition 2½ but also pushed for the rapid dissolution of state social-welfare programs to the disproportionate harm of racial minorities. "Reaganomics," he alleged, "with its supply-side mythology, has given this nation its highest unemployment [rates], its highest interest rates, and its highest peacetime deficits since World War II."[57] Observing that unemployment in Massachusetts had doubled on King's watch and had hit minorities especially hard, Dukakis won endorsements from the Massachusetts Commission Against Discrimination as well as the United South End Settlements, which represented Boston's still-growing Puerto Rican population (his fluent Spanish certainly helped).[58] He also emphasized public education in urban areas, promising state aid for the construction of a new $30-million campus for Roxbury's community college and pledging increases in school aid. "We need first rate schools and state colleges and universities now more than ever," he asserted. "For make no mistake about it, this state's economic future depends on its reputation for educational excellence—now and in the decades to come."[59] In campaign speeches, Dukakis promised "computer literacy drives" in libraries and said he would "pay special attention to older, urban school systems such as Boston's."[60]

Promises like these gave Dukakis a comfortable victory over King in the primary, and he went on to defeat Republican challenger John Sears in the general election with 59 percent of the statewide vote. It certainly helped Dukakis to have endorsements from both the Massachusetts Teachers Association and the Boston Teachers Union—endorsements he gained by stating his vehement opposition to competency tests for teachers. "Anybody who thinks that the way you test a teacher for competency is to give him or her a written exam doesn't understand teaching," Dukakis told reporters at a press conference staged at the still-predominantly black James P. Timilty Middle School in Roxbury. "As somebody who has taught fairly recently and had to learn that profession from the ground up, let me tell you that if someone had given me a written examination as the basis for testing my competency, I probably would have flunked."[61] Despite his opposition to competency tests for teachers, however, the governor gave his wholehearted support to Massachusetts's new statewide basic skills competency tests for students. In so doing, he received approval from Commissioner Lawson and from Superintendent Spillane, both of whom agreed that local schools would regain public trust only by demonstrating "accountability" in terms of student achievement. Dukakis, Lawson, and Spillane all held that schools' accountability depended principally on test scores—or, more specifically, on schools' ability to show direct connections between financial inputs and educational outcomes—and their focus on tests garnered widespread public support. For example, when the governor asserted that "certain types of standardized tests are necessary" to measure efficiency, effectiveness, and equity in schools, most parents concurred.[62]

The fact that state leaders such as Dukakis seized the initiative for school reforms heartened officials in the Reagan administration, who began in 1982 to shift a broad array of responsibilities in education back to states. Remembering a campaign promise to devolve financial and regulatory powers to state and local agencies whenever possible, Reagan persuaded the Congress to cut not only the amount of federal aid to education but also the extent of federal regulation in the schools. The most drastic cuts accompanied the so-called Educational Consolidation and Improvement Act (ECIA), part of the Omnibus Budget Reconciliation Act of 1981 (P.L. 97-35).[63] Taking effect in June 1982, the ECIA represented the latest reauthorization of the Elementary and Secondary Education Act of 1965 (ESEA)—and it substantially altered the original law. It changed the name of Title I to Chapter 1 and collapsed twenty-nine smaller categorical programs into block grants, which it identified as Chapter 2.[64] All told, the ECIA cut federal aid to schools by more than $1 billion, or 15 percent, in its first year (1982–83), and it specified larger cuts for the future.[65] After several decades of steadily expanding federal aid to schools, the ECIA marked a sudden federal retreat—and its effect was dramatic. Unlike the original ESEA, which federal officials had used, in part, to promote compliance with civil rights statutes and desegregation guidelines, the ECIA pulled back from these priorities and insisted that local officials were best suited to solve local problems. Reflecting an "anti-centralization" ideology that had guided Republican politics for decades (indeed, ever since Eisenhower compared the New Deal and the Fair Deal with socialism), the ECIA emphasized smaller government and local authority—a message flexible enough to win support not only from whites advocating "local control" but also from blacks advocating "community control." The purpose of the ECIA was, in short, to return "control" to people closer to schools.[66]

The centerpiece of the ECIA—the piece that most directly fostered the devolution of power away from the federal government—was Chapter 2, with its block grant to each state. Under Chapter 2, the federal Department of Education allotted a lump sum to each state, which then parceled this sum out to local schools. The amount of each state's block grant was set according to a "pupil-weighting" formula much like the one Massachusetts used to distribute its own state aid. (If a state had more students in high-cost or heavily weighted programs—that is, programs for low-income, non-English-speaking, or disabled students—then it received a larger Chapter 2 block grant.) However, once a state received its Chapter 2 grant, it was under no obligation to use this grant for programs that served high-cost students; indeed, each state was free to use its entire Chapter 2 block grant in any way it wished. Policy expert Milbrey McLaughlin of the Rand Corporation noted that "although [each state's] Chapter 2 formula must include a factor for high-cost children, neither Congress nor . . . Department of Education (ED) regulations specify what these high-cost factors should be. Thus it is possible for a state to devise a formula that includes multiple and exclusive high-cost factors—such as students who are educationally disadvantaged, gifted and talented, bilingual, or who live in sparsely settled areas—that are evenly distributed throughout [the whole state]. Consequently, in practice the Chapter 2 formula could track general enrollment."[67] Whereas the aim of the original ESEA had been to target federal resources at categorical programs serving educationally disadvantaged (that is, high-cost, at-risk, or "neglected") students, Chapter 2 of the ECIA allowed states to decide for themselves how best to use federal aid. On the one hand, this flexibility allowed states to meet the educational needs they considered most pressing. On the other hand, it allowed funds to bypass students from politically marginal groups.

One consequence of this system was that urban schools with large enrollments of high-cost students helped their states obtain large Chapter 2 grants but did not themselves receive large amounts of aid. Indeed, most urban districts received comparatively small allocations under Chapter 2, which "consolidated" (that is, eliminated) many of the categorical programs that previously distributed aid to high-cost students in the inner city. The most publicized example of this process involved the Emergency School Assistance Act (ESAA), which funded urban desegregation efforts. (It was this program that Boston had exploited by overcounting segregated schools.)[68] When the ESAA was consolidated under Chapter 2, it vanished as a discrete program, and states were free to move its funds into other programs. In the year before the ECIA, the ESAA had distributed more than $1 million to each of seventeen large urban districts; after the ECIA, the entire $150 million budget of the ESAA dissolved into Chapter 2, and states immediately shifted these funds into nonurban programs. Policy analysts Richard Jung and Michael Tashjian commented that most districts "operating under court-ordered desegregation plans— the same districts that had usually received sizable ESAA grants—took larger proportional cuts under the block grant than did those districts that were operating under voluntary desegregation plans or that had no desegregation plan."[69] Of course, the consolidation of the ESAA did not alter the legal requirement to desegregate: urban districts simply had to obey the court's orders with less federal aid. If a state failed to supply the resources needed to meet a court order, then its schools would face litigation (a very real prospect, because, ever since *San Antonio Independent School District v. Rodriguez,* federal jurisprudence required schools to protect civil rights but took no responsibility for school finance; hence, schools losing civil rights cases might nonetheless be *politically* unable to raise the resources needed to comply with court-ordered reforms).

Herein lay the dilemma of Chapter 2 block grants. The goal behind Chapter 2 was to give state and local administrators more freedom to decide how to meet the educational needs of students in public schools. Yet, a block grant program itself could not reduce the overall level of federal regulation or control in schools—for the simple reason that block grants had no effect on the *legal* requirements that defined students' "rights." If anything, block grants made it harder for urban schools (which were at greater risk of civil rights lawsuits) to secure the funds they needed to provide supplementary (and often court-ordered) programs to various "high-cost" students. In other words, block grants left urban schools with mandates they could not afford to meet. As one principal said, "There is such a . . . hands-off approach from the federal government [under Chapter 2] that some of us are suspicious that we'll be asked for information about [block grants' efficacy] that we're not prepared to provide."[70] In urban schools with large enrollments of high-cost students, administrators feared that Chapter 2 would leave them without the funds they needed to offer "equal educational opportunities"—even as federal courts held them to unbending legal standards. "We don't object to being held accountable," a second principal asserted, "but we believe that we have to have the benefit of appropriate guidance and clear authority from the outset. We are afraid that too little regulation might be almost as bad as too much."[71] Neither a lack of federal resources nor a lack of federal regulations absolved the public schools of the need to meet *legal* expectations concerning equal opportunity—expectations that extended from racial desegregation to special and bilingual education. If schools did not meet these expectations with federal grants from the ECIA—under Chapter 1, Chapter 2, or other nonconsolidated programs—they would have to get the necessary funds from state and local sources, even if taxpayers were loath to pay.

Even apart from the courts, the Reagan administration had expectations of its own regarding the educational impact of the ECIA. Inasmuch as the ESEA had been criticized as a mere financial delivery system that asked schools only to record how much aid they received and how many students they served but not whether achievement had improved, it seemed unlikely that the ECIA would be so lax in assessing educational "effectiveness." Especially at a time when schools were being asked to do more with less, it seemed inevitable that federal officials would, at some future date, require local schools to verify the ECIA's outcomes or results. The expectation that block grants would lead to superior outcomes (measured by standardized test scores) was nowhere explicitly stated in the ECIA itself; nonetheless, it pervaded the Reagan administration's rhetoric on education and education policy—most conspicuously, its often-repeated pronouncements regarding "excellence," "quality," and "standards" in the schools. The chief spokesperson for such ideals was federal secretary of education Terrel Bell (former state commissioner of education in Utah and interim federal commissioner during the Nixon administration). One of the first projects Bell undertook as secretary in the early 1980s was the creation of a National Commission on Excellence in Education, the goal of which (at least according the Heritage Foundation, which actively shaped the commission's agenda) was to review "best practices" leading to high achievement in the public schools. Among these practices were "a school-wide emphasis on basic skills; teachers that demand high standards; and a system of monitoring pupil performance."[72] Even if federal expectations for results were vague in the language of the ECIA, local administrators anticipated that federal officials would eventually ask for proof of *measurable* gains in achievement.[73]

In April 1983, Secretary Bell himself affirmed the emphasis on achievement in an influential report titled *A Nation at Risk: The Imperative for Educational Reform*. Printed under the auspices of Bell's National Commission on Excellence in Education, this report used standardized test scores to paint a bleak picture of performance levels in the schools: "Average achievement of high school students on most standardized tests is now lower than 26 years ago when *Sputnik* was launched," the report claimed. "The College Board's Scholastic Aptitude Tests (SAT) demonstrate a virtually unbroken decline from 1963 to 1980. Average verbal scores fell over 50 points and average mathematics scores dropped nearly 40 points. . . . Both the number and proportion of students demonstrating superior achievement on the SATs (i.e., those with scores of 650 or higher) have also dramatically declined." Muffling the fact that such declines coincided almost exactly with the period of expanding federal aid to education, the report implied that schools in recent years had prioritized access over achievement—equity over excellence—and had thereby shortchanged the students who most needed high standards. "Our society and its educational institutions seem to have lost sight of the basic purposes of schooling, and of the high expectations and disciplined effort needed to attain them," it commented: "In some metropolitan areas basic literacy has become the goal rather than the starting point." Calling for a renewed commitment to schools "of high quality throughout the length and breadth of our land," *A Nation at Risk* also called for a nation-wide system of standardized tests. "Standardized tests of achievement . . . should be administered at major transition points from one level of schooling to another and particularly from high school to college," it noted. "The tests should be administered as part of a nationwide (but not federal) system of state and local standardized tests."[74]

This call for a nationwide system of tests marked a new era in federal educational policy—an era in which "equal opportunity" would be measured not so much in terms of financial resources, special programs, or even racial desegregation but, rather, in terms of student test scores. As policy analysts David Clark, Terry Astuto, and Paula Rooney noted in the journal *Phi Delta Kappan* in the fall of 1983, this federal emphasis on standardized tests reoriented the basic aims of public education in the United States. In their words, the focus on standardized tests "altered the semantic structure" of the schools, "changing, for example, need and access to ability and selectivity, equity and compensatory education to excellence and standards of performance, intervention and diffusion of innovations to exhortation and information sharing, common schools to parental choice, and federal initiatives to state and local initiatives."[75] In short, the new focus on standardized tests marked a shift in emphasis from low-*income* to low-*achieving* students, from a definition of unequal opportunities that stemmed from poverty (or racism) to a definition that stemmed from below-average educational performance. In the future, it appeared, the concept of educational "need"—or disadvantage or disability—would apply to students *not* on the basis of their income or race but, rather, on the basis of their scores on standardized tests. Indeed, any students at risk of below-average scores (regardless of race or income) could now be construed as educationally "disadvantaged," and students with average or above-average scores could not. The importance of this shift was great. After the publication of *A Nation at Risk*, equal educational opportunity hinged not on school expenditures or compensatory programs or classroom integration or racial balance; these factors mattered only insofar as they contributed to satisfactory gains in academic achievement.

This shift in the meaning of educational disadvantage had important implications for federal policy. As secretary Bell put it, he and his colleagues in the Reagan administration had a "commitment to the disadvantaged [and] to the handicapped. . . . But there is also reason for concern about how 'disadvantaged' and 'handicapped' are defined."[76] By the early 1980s, the definition of such key concepts as educational disadvantage and disability depended above all on academic achievement. Even the courts began to adopt this view. For example, in 1982, the U.S. Supreme Court heard an important case directly concerned with the definition of educational disability and students' "right" to federally funded services to boost their academic achievement. In *Board of Education v. Rowley*, a first-grader named Amy Rowley, who suffered from a hearing deficiency, requested a sign-language interpreter as part of her individualized education plan (IEP). Her attorneys maintained that such an interpreter was necessary to guarantee her a "free and appropriate education" as mandated by the federal Education for All Handicapped Children Act (P.L. 94-142). The court, however, rejected this claim. Emphasizing that Rowley's academic achievement was already well above average, even without an interpreter, the court ruled that schools had no constitutional obligation to maximize students' educational outcomes (or to ensure that students reached their "full" potential). Chief Justice William Rehnquist wrote the majority opinion in the case. The Education for All Handicapped Children Act, he noted, was intended "to make public education available to handicapped children. But in seeking to provide access to public education, Congress did not impose upon the states any greater substantive educational standard than would be necessary to make such access meaningful. . . . Thus, the intent of the Act was more to open the door of public education to handicapped children on appropriate terms than to guarantee any particular level of education once inside." In sum, Rehnquist wrote, a student whose achievement surpassed that of her classmates was *not* entitled to extra services: "Whatever Congress meant by an 'appropriate' education, it is clear it did not mean a potential-maximizing education."[77]

In drafting his decision, Rehnquist went to great lengths to explain why the public schools were not obligated to maximize students' educational outcomes even if they *were* obligated to offer an education that was both appropriate and meaningful. "Implicit in the congressional purpose of providing access to a 'free appropriate public education' is the requirement that the education to which access is provided be sufficient to confer some educational benefit upon the handicapped child," Rehnquist asserted. The key question was how to discern when students had received "sufficient" benefits. "The determination of when handicapped children are receiving sufficient educational benefits to satisfy the requirements of the Act presents a more difficult problem," Rehnquist acknowledged. "It is clear that the benefits obtainable by children at one end of the spectrum [of disabilities] will differ dramatically from [the educational benefits] obtainable by children at the other end [of the same spectrum], with infinite variations in between. One child may have little difficulty competing successfully in an academic setting with nonhandicapped children while another child may encounter great difficulties in acquiring even the most basic of self-maintenance skills." Ultimately, Rehnquist held, the determination of "sufficient benefit" hinged (at least for students with a chance to be mainstreamed) on evidence of progress from grade to grade with passing marks. "When the handicapped child is being educated in the regular classes of a public school system," Rehnquist noted, "the achievement of passing marks and advancement from grade to grade will be one important factor in determining educational benefit." In other words, if students placed in regular classes received passing marks, then, in the court's view, their education was legally sufficient, regardless of disabilities. Similarly, if students placed in regular classes earned failing marks, then it was possible a claim of insufficient education could be made (at least for students diagnosed with "disabilities").[78]

Defining a sufficient education as one that ensured passing marks for students placed in regular classes was a dubious standard (at best), but what about students *not* enrolled in regular classes? What constituted a sufficient—or appropriate or meaningful or beneficial or effective or adequate or reasonable—education for students who spent a major portion of each school day *isolated* from their peers? What standard would the court use to gauge the legal acceptability of *their* educational opportunities? This question was important not only for students with more serious cognitive deficiencies but also for students with, say, language deficiencies—students whose isolation from regular classes was construed as a civil right. In *Board of Education v. Rowley,* it was unclear what distinguished a hearing-deficient student who needed a sign-language interpreter to render education meaningful from a language-deficient student who required a bilingual instructor to render education meaningful. Yet, the courts treated hearing- and language-deficient students differently. Language-deficient students (even if they had no cognitive handicaps) were entitled to isolated placements to improve their educational opportunities (and outcomes); hearing-deficient students (unless they had serious mental handicaps) were not. Why? The court did not explain this discrepancy; indeed, the court did not even seem to notice it.[79] Yet, by using different standards of educational benefit for different groups of students, the court left schools to ask which services were legally sufficient to help which groups attain which levels of academic achievement. If the sufficient-benefit standard depended on passing marks in regular classes, would *all* students, even those *not* in regular classes, be expected to reach such a level? In other words, if sufficient benefit relied on passing marks, would students who did *not* reach such a level be inclined to accuse their schools of "discrimination"?[80]

◈

In a way, such questions were especially urgent in Massachusetts—where Chapter 766 still required schools to provide all possible assistance to help disabled students reach their "maximum feasible potential" and Chapter 71A still obligated schools to place non-English-speaking students in isolated bilingual transitional clusters until they were able to "compete effectively" in regular classes with native-English-speaking peers.[81] The issue in Massachusetts was how the benefits of such programs would be assessed: in a nutshell, would students in special education and bilingual education be expected to reach average scores on standardized tests, or would these students be exempt from standardized tests—even if such tests were part of a state accountability system? To make matters more complex, in Boston, special education programs enrolled fully 18 percent of students (in the public schools), and bilingual education programs enrolled 13 percent—and most of the students in *both* programs were racial minorities.[82] If schools exempted more than 30 percent of students from standardized tests (or made some other accommodation for them), and if large numbers of exempt students were racial minorities, then it would be difficult if not impossible for leaders at the local or state level to know if racial minorities were receiving a "sufficient" education or were, instead, continuing to receive treatment that was somehow inappropriate or discriminatory. Without uniform tests to measure educational benefit across programs or groups, it would be impossible to know if urban minority students in special and bilingual education programs were receiving greater or lesser "benefit" than minority students *not* enrolled in these programs; in other words, it would be impossible to know if *all* minority students were, in fact, receiving "equal" (albeit different) educational opportunities as measured by their outcomes.[83]

The hazards of racial discrimination seriously complicated the use of standardized tests. While some argued that standardized tests were the only way to know if all students had, in fact, had access to equal educational opportunity, others asserted that standardized tests were, by their very nature, racially biased. The federal Department of Education itself had once stated that "where present testing and evaluation materials and procedures have an adverse impact on members of a particular race, . . . additional or substitute materials and procedures which do not have such an adverse impact must be employed before placing such children in a special education program."[84] Or, as the state Department of Education in Massachusetts put it (even as it called for mandatory uniform statewide testing), "the practices and procedures which cause a school system to address the testing of minority children from the point of view that such procedures should be no different than they are for white children reflect a lack of awareness which can negatively affect [minority] children."[85] And, yet, if the only fair or valid tests were ones that had no adverse impact on any identifiable group of students, and if the only way to avoid charges of bias or discrimination was to show equal—or at least randomly distributed—scores on all tests, then standardized tests would be useless for comparing educational opportunities across racial groups. If schools gave all their students the same test and minority students received disproportionately lower scores, then schools could be accused of "biased" tests; yet, since it was obviously discriminatory to give different tests to different students, the only way to avoid such accusations was to show racially equal scores. (This rather absurd line of reasoning would, similarly, make it impossible to accept test scores that suggested a narrowing racial "gap" in achievement: a test generating higher scores for minorities or lower scores for whites could easily be construed as racially slanted or skewed.)

In the early 1980s, school officials in Boston generally ignored accusations of test bias and, instead, stressed rising scores: "Between 1981 and 1984," the *Globe* noted, "the focus on teaching math and reading paid off in higher scores. By the last round of testing, Boston students topped national averages in reading in four grades, matched them in one, and fell below in six. In math, results were better, with eight grades hitting above national averages and three below." Moreover, the *Globe* noted, academic achievement seemed to be improving faster over time. "Student test scores," the paper reported, "have risen from below national averages to above at every single grade level from, 1983 to 1984."[86] These congratulations, however, did not last. In 1984, the schools admitted that, even as student test scores had risen, so had student dropout rates. "For the first time, we are seeing high school dropout rates increasing," former state commissioner of education Gregory Anrig told a large audience at Harvard during a discussion of school accountability and the dangers of linking teacher evaluation to student performance. "Does this mean we are getting higher standards, or does the threat of tests encourage teachers just to get rid of kids who might not pass—in other words, are we having more pushouts? And doesn't that tend to hurt minorities?"[87] By 1984, the high school dropout rate in Boston exceeded 40 percent of all students. "The dropout problem is an extremely serious matter," the *Globe* reported, "particularly since most of those who quit do so during the freshman or sophomore year. Students who quit school having completed only the ninth or tenth grade are, in economic terms, worthless. Their prospects of finding any kind of work are dismal, and their chances of finding a good job with a chance for advancement are beyond remote. What do these young people do? Some find jobs at the bottom of the economic ladder. Some do nothing. Some have children and go on welfare. Some steal, rob, assault."[88]

The (apparent) link between standardized tests and dropout rates did not convince policymakers that schools gave students too many tests; rather, it convinced policymakers that schools needed more resources to help students *pass*. By 1984, officials at both the state and the federal level began to emphasize the need for supplemental aid to help students meet higher academic standards. In his State of the Union message the year before, Reagan even went so far as to propose a new categorical program to improve students' achievement in mathematics, science, and technology, and he proceeded to give more than fifty school-related speeches in the months leading up to the elections of 1984. As secretary of education Bell asserted, "Reagan was spending much of his time speaking on the topic of education reform. And just as suddenly, it was no longer a propitious time for slashing funding for education or for proposing to banish education from the [federal] scene. . . . If one looks at President Reagan's willingness to act on the nationwide need to strengthen math, science, and technology education, one must conclude that he is willing to provide federal funds . . . to meet an emerging crisis in education."[89] Two years earlier, Massachusetts senator Edward Kennedy had dubbed the Reagan administration the most "antieducation, antiteacher, antistudent administration in our national history," but this criticism fell flat in 1984 when Reagan won 97.6 percent of the electoral vote.[90] Stressing "achievement" and "accountability" as prerequisites for government aid, Reagan carved a niche for himself as a leader in educational reform. He made eligibility for aid contingent on disadvantage (cast as low achievement), but he also made *continuing* eligibility for aid contingent on rising test scores. If schools did not produce higher scores, they would lose federal aid. According to Reagan, this expectation of rising test scores was the only way to prevent schools from prolonging their eligibility for aid by perpetuating low scores.

Yet, expectations of rising scores on standardized tests had unintended—and often counterintuitive—effects. For example, some teachers artificially inflated scores to make themselves seem more effective and, thus, to receive better personnel evaluations (a practice especially tempting among teachers of slow-to-improve remedial students). However, by inflating test scores, many teachers unwittingly compromised their schools' eligibility for aid targeted at programs for low-scoring students. Put simply, if fewer students posted low scores, then such programs would lose enrollment—and, in turn, aid. In *The Federal Role in Education: New Directions for the Eighties,* policy analysts Harriet Bernstein and David Merenda asserted that some urban school districts with large numbers of high-cost students actually had a *disincentive* to improve student achievement on standardized tests: "Since eligible children within individual schools are chosen on the basis of low achievement (and [since] the law encourages that only those with the greatest need be served), there is an additional financial disincentive to expect much and achieve well. If all the children in a Title I school were to miraculously start achieving on grade level, the school would lose its extra positions and materials."[91] Moreover, the constantly growing pressure to show higher and higher scores on standardized tests particularly harmed underachieving students, because the distorted test scores made them ineligible for remedial programs they would otherwise be entitled to. So, despite the hope that standardized tests would lead to higher achievement, it was conceivable that schools, in order to retain their grants for remedial programs serving "high-cost" students, might actually keep scores low—or *low enough* to maintain eligibility for aid. At the very least, schools with large numbers of low-scoring students faced the question: was it wiser to pursue high scores or low scores when both outcomes could result in lost aid?

To avoid such paradoxical incentives, Massachusetts took a different approach to the idea of linking aid to achievement. In 1984, at a gathering of the Citywide Education Coalition in Boston, Governor Dukakis and his staff introduced the Public Schools Improvement Act, or Chapter 188, to "provide supplementary funds for school districts spending proportionately less than school districts of comparable size; and require schools to meet measurable performance standards to remain eligible for state aid."[92] Officials in the state Department of Education insisted that Chapter 188 would "increase the accountability of teachers and students, finance creative educational improvements, and provide resources to equalize educational opportunities."[93] The legislation earmarked funds for urban schools with large numbers of low-achieving students. In Boston, these schools included the Raphael Hernandez School, the Martin Luther King, Jr., Middle School, and South Boston High School. To help these schools increase student test scores—without increasing dropout rates—Chapter 188 later added "challenge" grants to reward inner-city schools for higher scores on statewide basic skills competency tests. "Among the proposals being considered," one *Globe* columnist noted, "is one dubbed REACH (Rewarding Educational Achievement) that would provide bonuses to schools and school districts that show measurable improvement in meeting board-of-education goals. There would be awards for teachers [and] principals and other staff as well as additional money for school improvement councils for increasing student performance." The legislature also promised funds "to schools where there is a 5 percent jump in the [absolute] number of students passing basic skills tests."[94] At the same time, however, Chapter 188 permitted schools to exempt students in special or bilingual education from tests (this exemption, in turn, gave schools an incentive to move additional students at risk of low scores into these programs.)[95]

Money for Chapter 188 came from state revenues that had increased rapidly in the period since governor Dukakis's return to office. Taking credit for a high-tech boom that observers later called the Massachusetts Miracle, the governor used tax revenue from fast-growing computer hardware and software companies to revive various public services—including public schools. By 1984, the Massachusetts High Technology Council (established seven years earlier) had a roster of more than 120 companies, which, together, employed nearly 115,000 people and conducted nearly $11 billion in annual business.[96] Corporate leaders, recognizing their need for well-trained workers, supported Chapter 188, which distributed $11,688,451 in extra state aid to the Boston public schools. The bulk of this amount came in the form of equal educational opportunity grants, which the law designated for districts that spent less than $2,890 per student per year. (Technically, this criterion did not fit the Boston public schools. As Superintendent Spillane commented, "about $4,000 annually is spent on each of Boston's 58,000 students, but the actual figure is closer to $2,000 if one discounts the money expended on special educational programs and students with special needs.")[97] Besides equal educational opportunity funds, Boston also secured $235,000 in dropout prevention funds, $500,000 in remedial education funds, and $928,240 for school improvement councils that awarded $10 per student to cultivate alternative education programs, cultural education programs, community or parent involvement programs, and business-school partnerships.[98] Reviving an idea that had lain dormant since the 1960s, school improvement councils rested on the principle that community involvement—along with financial aid from the state—would improve academic achievement in neighborhood schools, even if those schools were (still) racially imbalanced. In fact, underlying Chapter 188 was the idea that ghetto schools, given proper resources, could produce better results.

Paving the way for this new emphasis on high-quality neighborhood schools was the gradual withdrawal of the federal court from its daily supervision of the system. In 1984 Superintendent Spillane told interviewers, "I can only hope that, after 10 long, and in some cases, desperate years, Judge Garrity understands that the people of Boston want him out of the case and want the school committee and its superintendent to manage the affairs of the school system. I believe the last three years have shown unquestionable progress in student achievement and in giving the Boston public schools national credibility and access for all students. I certainly hope he chooses to leave gracefully."[99] And, indeed, he did. Over the course of the 1984–85 school year, Garrity slowly brought his involvement with the schools to a close. First, he pulled away from special, bilingual, and vocational education and returned to school officials the authority to decide when placements in these programs were or were not discriminatory. Next, he pulled back from student discipline, safety, and transportation and gave school department personnel the responsibility for busing. Then he withdrew from the areas of enrollment and facilities management and gave the superintendent the power to regulate school closings and pupil transfers. Last, he relinquished control of teacher contracts, affirmative action, and the pairing of schools with businesses, colleges, and universities. By the end of the 1984–85 school year, he even sanctioned a modified school-choice plan that allowed 7,000 elementary students—nearly half the city's total—to select the facility they would attend from a list of five schools in Roxbury, Dorchester, Mattapan, Roslindale, and Hyde Park (although he placed an 80 percent maximum on the proportion of students of any race who could attend any one school). Declaring—without a hint of irony—that "the court regards the adversarial judicial process as inhibitive of an ideally functioning school system," Garrity finally left the system to run itself.[100]

Garrity's departure marked the end of an era in more ways than one. In the midst of his withdrawal from the schools, his leading critic, Superintendent Spillane, announced his own resignation and his acceptance of the superintendency in affluent Fairfax County, Virginia. Spillane left Boston with mixed emotions but also with a sense of confidence in the future of the city's schools. "Spillane, by most accounts, has restored professionalism, optimism, and credibility to the Boston public schools," the *Boston Globe* noted. "He leaves with a national reputation as a born leader, an instinctive politician, an accomplished administrator, and an engaging speaker. And he takes with him, too, credit for developing what some expected would be impossible—a renewed school system."[101] Spillane's replacement was forty-nine-year-old Laval Wilson, superintendent of schools in Rochester, New York, and formerly superintendent in Berkeley, California. Wilson had Spillane's personal recommendation (and had, in fact, applied for the post in Boston in 1981 when it went to

Spillane). What made Wilson's election notable, however, was the fact that he was black. Characterizing him as a "qualified, urban educator who has already demonstrated his competency in [both] Berkeley and Rochester and who happens to be black," John O'Bryant was especially gratified by Wilson's appointment, which he hoped would expand black influence over the schools.[102] Others stressed Wilson's qualities as a leader. "The first thing people . . . say about school superintendent Laval S. Wilson is not that he has raised student test scores and cut suspensions and absenteeism," the *Globe* noted. "The first thing people [in Rochester] say about Wilson is that he has, through the force of his personality and his use of the media, totally changed the image of [the] public schools. Through well-planned educational innovations, stiff discipline, and decisive and visible leadership, he has carried out the school board's mandate to 'sell the schools' to a city that five years ago seemed resigned to their continuing deterioration."[103] Wilson had, in other words, won the public's trust.

Shortly after his arrival in Boston, the new superintendent reached out to the public by attending a "Town Meeting on Race and Class in Boston," hosted by the John F. Kennedy Library. The meeting was held in conjunction with the publication of J. Anthony Lukas's award-winning book, *Common Ground: A Turbulent Decade in the Lives of Three American Families*, which chronicled the desegregation controversy from the passage of the state's racial-imbalance act in 1965 through the federal court orders of 1975. In a discussion of the book, Lukas, who attended the meeting, hinted that busing might have been more successful if the court had required suburbs to enroll students from inner-city schools. "The consequences of limiting school desegregation to the city proper were grave," he told a crowd filled with suburbanites. "It meant that the sons and daughters of metropolitan Boston's businessmen, engineers, lawyers, physicians, professors, accountants and journalists were, with few exceptions, exempted from Garrity's orders."[104] This argument drew polite nods from listeners, many of whom agreed in principle that transcending district borders and transferring responsibility to the state would equalize both opportunities and outcomes for poor minority students from the inner city. Wilson listened quietly to Lukas and other community members in the room. It seemed clear to him that metropolitan desegregation was, at best, only a partial fix. It could not reduce the rising costs of special-compensatory programs or resolve the issue of discriminatory classroom placements; it could not guarantee efficient management or curb unfunded legislative mandates. If anything, it risked *jeopardizing* the participation of minority parents in their children's neighborhood schools. As the meeting drew to its end, he rose from his chair and shared his own view on the subject of equal opportunity in the public schools. The "single factor that can overcome the handicaps of both race and class," he declared, was measurable "academic performance," and it was this goal, even beyond the (unrealized) goal of racial integration, that he "pledged to bring to Boston's schools."[105]

✧ CONCLUSION ✧

The Complex History of American School Reform

A t first, it appeared that Superintendent Wilson might fulfill his promise to raise the level of academic achievement in Boston's public schools. From 1986 to 1989, student performance on standardized tests increased at a rate of seven points a year. More than 70 percent of the city's students posted scores either at or above the national average. Encouraged by these results, the school committee rehired Wilson in October 1989, for another four-year term. A few months later, however, things changed. Test experts found that, even if 70 percent of students in Boston scored above the national average on standardized tests, more than 90 percent of students across the country were able to make the same claim. National test averages had been "normed" eight years earlier (in 1981, at the beginning of the test craze that followed the passage of the ECIA) and, since then, had not been adjusted to gauge current achievement levels; moreover, test monitors discovered that schools in Boston had been reusing the same tests to coach their students and boost their scores. So, while scores in Boston had increased, they had increased only relative to an outdated norm. If anything, they had increased *less* than scores in the rest of the nation's schools.[1] In light of these revelations, Superintendent Wilson faced mounting criticism from the school committee. Despite his success in balancing the budget, reducing the dropout rate, and clarifying the schools' "guidelines for accountability," the committee eventually voted in February 1990 to fire its first-ever black superintendent for not improving academic achievement enough. As one angry (as well as racist) committee member asserted, "the whole system has been held hostage because of the color of a man's skin. Laval has had a $100 million increase in the budget in the time he's been here, and he hasn't done anything with it."[2]

By 1990, the pressure to raise test scores was intense, and it affected virtually all aspects of the public schools.[3] Holding students to higher standards meant that roughly 10 percent of all students in Boston were held back at least one grade, not only so they could acquire the skills needed to advance, but also so the effects of their low scores on school accountability measures could be controlled. (Scores of students retained in lower grade levels were less likely to harm the overall average of those grades than scores of students prematurely rushed into higher grades.)[4] While some observers lamented the dangers of "social promotion" among low-achieving students in urban schools, most administrators looked aggressively for ways to improve their achievement profiles—and made decisions about student promotion or retention accordingly. Indeed, the overwhelming compulsion to post high scores on standardized tests derived not only from pressure at the local level, but also from new pressures at the federal level. Two years earlier, the Hawkins-Stafford School Improvement Amendments of 1988 (P.L. 100-297, named for cosponsors Augustus Hawkins [D-Calif.] and Robert Stafford [R-Vt.]), had increased appropriations for Title I/Chapter I of the ECIA by $500 million on the condition that local schools document measurable gains in achievement in order to remain eligible for aid. Under these amendments, every school receiving Chapter I aid had to show that test scores—or other measures of achievement—increased each year for educationally disadvantaged children participating in Title I/Chapter I programs. If participants in a given school showed no improvement in the first year, then the local district had to work with the school to improve its Title I/Chapter I program. If participants still showed no improvement in the second year, then the state Department of Education had to work with the local district to review the school's program.[5]

The Hawkins-Stafford amendments did not say what might happen if, after three years, participants in a Title I/Chapter I program still showed no improvement; it was simply assumed that extra attention from state officials as well as extra resources from the federal government would produce results. To encourage new approaches to instruction, the Hawkins-Stafford amendments increased allocations for "schoolwide reforms"— that is, reforms unrelated to any specific category of students (such as disadvantaged, disabled, or non-English-speaking students) but designed to raise the academic achievement of *all* students in the Title I/Chapter I school. Modifying the notion of loosely regulated block grants that had guided the ECIA, the idea of schoolwide grants exchanged one set of regulations (associated with schools' allocation of funds) for another set of regulations (associated with schools' accountability for performance). As Ellin Nolan, staff director for Senator Stafford, noted, "no one talked about block grants" in the legislative meetings for the new amendments; "instead they talked about targeting resources" to areas with large concentrations of low-achieving students.[6] Defining educational disadvantage implicitly in terms of below-average achievement, the Hawkins-Stafford amendments codified an idea that had been lurking beneath federal educational policy for several decades, namely, the idea that aid should be tied directly to achievement. Henceforth, the federal commitment to facilitating equal educational opportunities in the public schools would be tied directly to evidence of improvement on standardized tests. It was a pivotal moment in the history of the federal role—and it raised difficult questions. For example, if test scores remained low among disadvantaged students in urban areas, who would be held responsible for this situation: the students, the schools, the states, or the federal government itself?[7]

History suggested that blame for low scores would fall *not* on students and *not* on state or federal officials but, rather, on schools.[8] And, yet, when scores rose or fell, were schools entirely responsible for this result? Did scores accurately reflect the educational effectiveness of a school? Did a low score mean that a school was ineffective or that a particular student was less able? Did a low score mean a particular student required more help or just a different kind of help? Ever since the late 1960s, when effectiveness became the watchword of public education, standardized tests had raised at least as many questions as they had answered. While standardized tests may have measured student outcomes, it was not always clear what *caused* particular outcomes to occur. Was it a school program, or was it, perhaps, some nonschool factor such as income, parenting, family structure, nutrition, or some other factor over which schools had no control? For every school that was eager to take credit for its students' high scores—attributing its success to well-funded programs, well-designed curricula, well-prepared teachers, or well-equipped classrooms—another school was eager to avoid castigation for its students' low scores—attributing failure to poorly funded programs, poorly designed curricula, poorly prepared teachers, poorly equipped classrooms, or, above all, "hard-to-teach" students, many of whom were poor minority students from ghetto areas. The focus on standardized tests as the measure of school effectiveness did very little to clarify the link between inputs and outcomes in individual classrooms; if anything, it led to a single-minded fixation on scores as a way to hold particular schools responsible for particular students' "results."

Holding schools accountable for students' results was not the same, however, as actually *reforming* schools. As the case of Boston illustrated, when it came to improving scores, the range of possible reforms was almost infinite. Some argued that low-scoring students needed integrated classroom placements, others that low-scoring students needed isolated classroom placements. Some insisted that low-scoring pupils likely suffered from learning disabilities, others that low-scoring pupils were susceptible to misdiagnosis if they were racial minorities. Some maintained that low scores were linked to racially imbalanced schools, others that low scores had less to do with racial imbalance than with hidden racial bias in the tests. Some asserted that low scores derived from culturally "irrelevant" pedagogies, others that low scores derived from inadequate budget resources. As the history of reform in Boston showed, these issues were endlessly debatable—and, in every case, *both* sides of each debate used standardized test scores to validate their respective views. Yet, neither could use scores to argue definitively for a particular course of action, and the reason for this stalemate was clear: while tests measured outcomes directly, they measured inputs (and their relative impact) only indirectly. A test of academic achievement, by itself, gave only hints about the relative effectiveness of the diverse inputs that *contributed* to achievement, such as specialized programs, racial balance, or budgetary resources. Since, in a large urban school district, it was impossible to control for all these inputs simultaneously, it was difficult to ascertain which school (or nonschool) factor had the greatest impact on students' outcomes, either positively or negatively. For policymakers who sought "accountability for results," the limitations of standardized tests were undoubtedly frustrating—but they were also unavoidable.[9]

The limits of standardized tests did not, however, forestall their growing use. In the 1990s, tests became a ubiquitous feature of educational policymaking at both the state and federal levels. In 1993, the state legislature in Massachusetts passed a so-called Education Reform Act, which not only directed more funds to low-spending districts, but also held each local district accountable for high scores on a new, statewide, curriculum-based exam known as the Massachusetts Comprehensive Assessment System (MCAS). According to one observer, "the MCAS would be a truth teller. Results would enable us to track reform progress for each district each year." Robert Gaudet, a research analyst at the University of Massachusetts, explained that "the theory behind this effort was that, if [low-spending and low-performing] school districts were given more money, and if there were a way to measure progress, then the districts would spend that money in productive ways . . . so that students could meet the new high standards."[10] A year later, in 1994, Congress used this same theory when passing the Improving America's Schools Act (P.L. 103-382, which reauthorized the ESEA) and the Goals 2000: Educate America Act (P.L. 103-227). Both steered aid to poorer districts, but neither was able to increase test scores or narrow the achievement gap between white and minority students.[11] In 1999, 44.6 percent of white tenth-graders in Boston earned "high" scores on the reading portion of the MCAS, while only 9.9 percent of black tenth-graders and 10.3 percent of Hispanic tenth-graders did so. On the math portion, 35.8 percent of whites received "high" scores, but only 6.0 percent of blacks and 6.4 percent of Hispanics did so.[12] These statistics were especially alarming when one realized that, by 1999, blacks and Hispanics comprised *75 percent* of Boston's public school enrollments, and many of these students— particularly those whose scores were likely to be lowest—either dropped out before the tenth grade or continued to be put in special and bilingual classes that were exempt from the MCAS.[13]

The gap in test scores between whites and minorities persisted in Boston despite an increasing emphasis on high achievement.[14] In 1998, a nationwide survey of 800 black and 800 white parents asked, "What should be a bigger priority for your own children's schools?" and gave respondents two options: "to focus on raising academic standards and achievement" or "to focus on achieving more diversity and integration." More than 80 percent of both groups chose achievement, and less than 10 percent of both groups chose integration. When asked "Do you think that kids get a better education in a racially integrated school, that the education they get is worse, or that it makes little difference?" more than 70 percent of white parents thought it made little difference, and more than

50 percent of black parents agreed. When presented with the following statement, "I do not care about the race of the kids in my children's schools, so long as they come from good, hard-working families," 55 percent of white parents said they "strongly agreed," and 61 percent of black parents shared this view. In *Time to Move On: African-American and White Parents Set an Agenda for Schools*, the pollsters who conducted this survey argued that, even while "blacks and whites believe in integration," it was very clear that "black parents put academics first and are willing to set racial issues aside to achieve that goal." Perhaps taking such findings as a cue, the Boston school committee voted in 1999 to end the use of race in making student assignments—a change that several recent federal court rulings endorsed. In a system where minorities were now the overwhelming majority, the pursuit of integration gave way to a renewed emphasis on achievement, and the timing of this shift was poignant.[15] In September 1999, just two weeks after this latest return to neighborhood-based school assignments, Judge Garrity died.[16]

The end of race-based assignments brought an expansion of the "modified school choice" plan that Superintendent Spillane had initiated and Garrity had approved more than a dozen years earlier. The expansion of choice was, in fact, one more indication that academic achievement had become a higher priority than racial integration in judgments of educational "quality" or "adequacy" in Boston. If all schools in the city had produced equal levels of academic achievement among all students—regardless of race—over the past five decades, then perhaps integration efforts may have had more success. However, the persistence of unequal academic achievement between races severely hampered the process of racial desegregation in the city. While some argued that persistent racial imbalance had, either directly or indirectly, hindered minority students' progress toward equal achievement, this claim rested on still-unproven claims about a causal relationship between academic performance and racial balance. If parents were, in fact, truthful when they said they wanted high achievement for their children, regardless of the racial composition of schools, then, it seemed, the best way to facilitate desegregation was to produce high academic achievement among *all* students in *all* schools and wait for parents to "keep their promise" to choose any school that showed results. Racial desegregation would then occur naturally. Those who insisted that racial desegregation had failed because it was never given a "fair chance" to succeed overlooked an important historical lesson, namely, that parents of all racial backgrounds—black, white, Hispanic, Chinese, and others—repeatedly expressed a commitment to "equal educational opportunities" but, more often than not, measured this goal in terms of academic achievement. Throughout the

1950s, 1960s, 1970s, and early 1980s, racial integration competed with *alternate* conceptions of equal educational opportunity in the schools.[17]

◈

A return to neighborhood schools in Boston did not produce a surge of rising test scores among poor minority students across the city. Instead, as subsequent results on the MCAS indicated, scores in the inner city remained appallingly low. In a sense, persistent low scores among "at-risk" students were not surprising, because this group was *defined* by its low scores (thus, a process of identifying at-risk students was a sort of tautological process of identifying the very students whose scores "had not been raised").[18] Yet, at the same time, the failure to narrow the gap between low-scoring and high-scoring students was also attributable to other—perhaps less obvious—causes. In particular, the failure to narrow this gap could be attributed to a system of federal aid that delivered resources to students chiefly on the basis of below-average academic achievement. Over time, federal aid had supported the development of hundreds of programs for low-achieving students. Students participated in these programs not because they were poor or because they were minorities (the classifications traditionally associated with federal aid) but, in most cases, because their achievement was below average. Yet, the flaw in this system was that it gave schools dependent on aid incentives to *maintain* their enrollments of low-achieving students—that is, to show that large numbers of students were, at all times, "still eligible" for grants to at-risk groups.[19] For aid-dependent schools, the financial risks of raising achievement "too much" for "too many" students could be great. As one journalist put it, "the leaders of these schools share the goal of improvement, [but] their students benefited from increased state [and federal] attention by staying on the list" of failing schools. Since rewards for raising achievement often fell short of the resources the schools received for remedial programs (especially if these remedial programs were ineffective enough to keep students enrolled for long periods of time), local officials faced "a complicated decision."[20]

In effect, the basic structure of federal aid to education had produced a system in which superintendents pledged to raise achievement even as they continuously bolstered enrollments in aid-eligible programs for low-achievers. While individual teachers may have been unaware of this situation (excepting those who pursued ever-larger enrollments in remedial classes), the rapid proliferation of new programs receiving categorical grants in the 1960s and 1970s indicated that state and local administrators saw clear advantages (perhaps some educational advantages but principally, it seems, financial advantages) in placing as many students as possible in specialized programs. Moreover, these programs, which typically served different students in different settings, perpetuated the notion that "separate" could, in fact, be "equal."[21] Despite much-vaunted rhetoric on behalf of racial integration and classroom inclusion in these decades, federal programs (unintentionally) perpetuated the idea that different students with different needs benefited from different placements in different environments—and, slowly but surely, these programs drew both students and resources away from regular education.[22] Between 1967 and 1991, the share of total school expenditures flowing to regular education decreased from 80 percent to 59 percent nationally while the share to special education increased from 4 to 17 percent. In Boston in 1991, special and bilingual programs enrolled fully 35 percent of all students and consumed 41 percent of the budget; regular education consumed only 23 percent.[23] Inasmuch as special programs stood a better chance of financial reimbursement, prudent administrators, facing pressure from local taxpayers to maximize external grants, placed increasing numbers of students in these programs. Indeed, they continued to make these placements even *after* it became clear that federal aid—along with state aid—would not meet their skyrocketing cost.[24]

The continued placement of students in special classes even after it became clear that state and federal aid would not fully cover their cost was puzzling until one realized that regular education was even *less* assured of receiving sufficient aid. This situation—whereby specialized programs came to "outrank" regular education in their eligibility for aid—was arguably the single most important development in public school finance in the 1950s, 1960s, 1970s, and 1980s. Yet, the specific causes of this overriding emphasis on specialized programs remained, for the most part, hidden from policymakers' view. (Indeed, the cause of the rapid growth of special programs went largely undetected, or at least unappreciated, in scholarly circles, too.) Of course, the rise of specialized programs had many causes—ranging from a federal preference for "categorical" over "general" aid to an enduring belief in the efficacy of isolated classes to meet "special needs"—but these programs would not have attained their dominant place in schools without a complex web of *legal* protections at the federal level to support their privileged claim on resources. To understand the federal role in public schools over the past half-century, it is imperative to understand how the federal courts have defined the phrase *equal educational opportunity* differently for students in special and regular education. Put simply, while the students in special education were able to use the concept of civil and constitutional "rights" to secure financial assistance, students in regular education were not. Moreover, while the federal courts measured the adequacy of special programs in terms of their "appropriateness" or "meaningfulness" for their students, the courts did not use these same criteria to measure the adequacy of regular education. Over time, it seems, this differentiated legal approach to special and regular education subtly but significantly affected the organization and the operation of public schools.[25]

To understand the criteria federal courts used to judge the quality or adequacy of special and regular education, one must look back to a series of three Supreme Court rulings in 1973 and 1974. In 1973, in the closely divided cases of *Rodriguez* and *Keyes*—both based on the equal protection clause of the Fourteenth Amendment—the court ruled that, under the Constitution, students did not have a right to equal school funding but *did* have a right to racially integrated school assignments. The court reconciled these rulings, in part, on grounds that, in education, student classifications based on race were "suspect" under the Fourteenth Amendment but student classifications based on income (or wealth) were not. Thus, equal treatment was required for all racial groups but not for all income groups—at least not as far as federal constitutional law was concerned. In 1974, however, this framework for judging equal treatment in education under federal law took a critical turn. In the case of *Lau v. Nichols*, the high court addressed the issue of equal treatment for national origin-minority group children with language deficiencies. In this case (and, in fact, in all subsequent cases involving linguistic minorities), the court opted to rule *not* on the basis of the equal protection clause of the Fourteenth Amendment—which, under *Keyes*, would have prohibited the intentional segregation of any national origin-minority group students unless their segregation promoted a compelling state interest—but, rather, on the statutory basis of the Civil Rights Act—which, according to the court, required the schools to provide special programs for "language-deficient" students and permitted these programs to be isolated from the regular classroom (albeit "temporarily") as long as they fostered students' acquisition of English and, in turn, their overall academic achievement in some measurable way.[26]

Lau was pivotal for educational decision-making at a classroom level. In a sense, it allowed the Fourteenth Amendment, with its emphasis on desegregation, to defer to the Civil Rights Act, with its emphasis on nondiscrimination, in certain aspects of education law. In the process, it placed academic achievement *over* racial integration as the key to equal educational opportunity—at least for students with language deficiencies. It made the provision of special accommodations for these students a legal requirement, ordering schools "to establish [programs] to deal with the language problems of non-English speaking ... students."[27]

Most important of all, it mandated such programs (and the resources needed to provide them) *not* because of these students' race or national origin or family income but, rather, because of specific deficiencies that rendered them unable to "compete effectively" in the schools' regular classroom program. It was a crucial ruling in the history of federal education law. In *Rodriguez*, decided a year earlier on the basis of the Fourteenth Amendment, the court had accepted the legal argument that "by assuring teachers, books, transportation, and operating funds, [public schools in Texas] endeavored to 'guarantee . . . that all people shall have at least an adequate program of education'"; yet, in *Lau*, decided on the basis of the Civil Rights Act, the court found that "there is no equality of treatment merely by providing students with the same facilities, textbooks, teachers, and curriculum, for students who do not understand English are effectively foreclosed from any meaningful education."[28] In *Rodriguez*, the court explicitly declared issues of educational quality nonjudiciable at the federal level; however, in *Lau*, the court implicitly defined educational quality in terms of "meaningfulness," which, in turn, it associated with clear evidence of language proficiency leading to overall academic achievement. Apparently, even if the Fourteenth Amendment did not entail a federal right to education of a certain quality, the Civil Rights Act did.[29]

The contrast between the court's decisions in *Rodriguez, Keyes,* and *Lau* raised a series of important questions. First, how exactly *did* the court measure the "quality" of education for language deficient students? Second, would the court extend the criteria of quality or adequacy it used for language deficient students to all other students, including those who did not fall into special ability groups? Third, if the court measured the quality or adequacy of education for any group of students in terms of academic achievement (or some proxy for achievement), how exactly would the court prioritize this goal *vis à vis* other goals, such as racial integration, on either a school or a classroom level? Fourth, if the court measured the adequacy of education in terms of achievement for any group of students—or, indeed, for *all* students—and if the court ranked this goal high on its list of legal priorities (perhaps even higher than racial integration), would the court also require schools to "establish programs" to help all students *meet* such a goal? Fifth, if the courts required schools to establish programs to foster students' academic achievement—again, in order to ensure the adequacy (or meaningfulness or appropriateness) of their education—would the courts also require local or state agencies to provide the resources to *fund* such programs? Sixth, if a federal court required local or state agencies to provide the resources to operate such programs, would the court find that such resources had been spent equitably only when students' achievement was "equal"? Finally, if the court did not associate equitable spending with equal achievement, how exactly would the court know when local or state agencies had demonstrated a "sufficient" commitment to providing equal opportunities for all students? Would the federal courts apply one standard of adequacy to students in special education and a different standard to students in regular education?[30]

This line of questioning showed quite clearly that federal courts had used different standards to measure the adequacy of education for different groups of students depending on their placement in special or regular education. It also showed why federal courts had *not* used academic achievement to gauge the adequacy of education for all students.[31] The concomitant demands for resources were (politically) unsustainable when applied to all students. Moreover, using academic achievement to gauge the legal adequacy of education meant that any student whose test scores fell below average was a potential litigant in a discrimination suit against the schools. For these reasons, a *right* to adequate education measured in terms of achievement (as well as the resources needed to provide it) was applied to students in special education but not, it would appear, to students in regular education. The ironies of this legal framework were twofold. First, it implied that "adequacy" would be measured in terms of achievement for the very students whose placement in special classes derived from a diagnosed *inability* to achieve average test scores.[32] Second, it implied that a federal "right" to adequate education hinged not on a finding of educational disadvantage linked to race or poverty but, rather, on a finding of disadvantage linked to *disability*.[33] Under this framework, it was no wonder that schools in both urban and suburban areas placed so many students in special education: resources for special education were protected by the federal courts, whereas resources for regular education were subject to highly politicized battles not only in Congress, but also in state legislatures and local school committees. Even when state courts ordered more resources to local schools—as Massachusetts's supreme court did in 1993 in *McDuffy v. Robertson,* the case that led to the Education Reform Act and the MCAS—aid for regular education was still limited to funds *left over* from special and bilingual programs.[34]

⟐

As the 1990s unfolded, enrollments in specialized programs in the Boston public schools continued to grow.[35] Fully one-third of the city's student population was enrolled either in special education or in bilingual education, and the costs of these programs were staggering.[36] Despite repeated attempts to refine eligibility guidelines, placements seemed all but impossible to control.[37] More and more schools were placing more and more students in more and more specialized classes.[38] State and federal reimbursements did not, however, keep pace with these rising enrollments, and local taxpayers grew increasingly upset with the ballooning expense. Finally, in the year 2000, the system began to buckle. In the fall of that year, the state legislature voted to abandon its commitment to help all disabled students reach their "maximum feasible potential." The legislature adopted, instead, the federal standard that required schools to offer "appropriate" services (which the Supreme Court had defined in *Rowley* as services necessary to help mainstreamed students progress from grade to grade with passing, or even average, marks). This standard was still high, but it was lower than the standard that had distinguished Chapter 766 for nearly three decades. Moreover, the new standard gave local schools permission to begin shifting resources from special to regular classes. This shift was important, because new statewide placement guidelines rendered 30,000 "mildly," "moderately," or "marginally" disabled students ineligible for special education and forced them back into regular classrooms.[39] The only question was whether regular classes would have sufficient resources to handle them or whether these recently "cured" students would find themselves in the same predicament as all the other students in regular education, a predicament in which they no longer had legal guarantees of "adequate" resources to help them meet achievement standards that officials at the state level—and, following the passage of the No Child Left Behind Act (P.L. 107-110) in 2001, also at the federal level—expected them to reach.

The contraction of services in Massachusetts extended beyond special education to include bilingual education as well. Just as enrollments in special education had grown dramatically over the course of the 1990s, so, too, had enrollments in bilingual education. Moreover, students were remaining in bilingual classes for longer and longer stretches of time. In one study, Massachusetts's state Department of Education found that, in Boston, "a substantial number of Hispanic students remain in the program for six or more years without—according to the data available—achieving the working knowledge of English which would permit them to take advantage of the educational and career opportunities in the Boston area."[40] The department also noted that exempting non-English-speaking students from state-mandated tests prevented officials from measuring the "effectiveness" of bilingual classes. Nonetheless, by the late 1990s, the Boston public schools were offering bilingual instruction to 10,000 students (approximately 15 percent of the total school population) in an impressive variety of languages, including Spanish, Chinese,

Haitian-Creole, French, Italian, Portuguese, Greek, Khmer, Somali, Vietnamese, and Hmong, although the achievement levels of these students continued to disappoint.[41] In 2000, shortly after the diminution of state requirements for special education, a movement emerged to reduce state requirements for bilingual education. Coordinated as well as bankrolled by California entrepreneur and Harvard graduate Ronald Unz, this movement led, in 2002, to a ballot initiative that gave voters a chance to replace three-year bilingual-transitional programs with one-year English-immersion programs. Promising to lower costs and raise achievement, this initiative passed overwhelmingly with 70 percent of the vote, including large majorities in Boston's immigrant areas. Three decades after the passage of Chapter 71A, bilingual education in Massachusetts was on the wane for not producing "results."[42]

It was, however, up to the federal courts to decide whether English-immersion programs met the standard of a "meaningful" or "adequate" education for non-English-speaking students.[43] In considering this issue, the courts would have to specify what role academic achievement would play—if any—in determinations of educational quality or adequacy in the public schools. Given the danger of creating an "injured class" out of all students with below-average scores on standardized tests, it seemed likely that the courts would declare academic achievement—together with various attendant factors, such as funding, curriculum, and instruction—nonjudiciable at the federal level. And, yet, the implications of such a ruling would be profound. If the courts decided that judgments of educational adequacy could not be based on academic achievement for one group of students, they would have to apply the same approach to all groups. They could not require the public schools to "establish programs" to help one group of disadvantaged students improve its academic achievement without requiring the public schools to help *all* students do the same. It could not make the provision of specialized programs a civil right for some but not for others—lest the entire legal framework of "equal educational opportunities" collapse. Despite the federal courts' repeated insistence that state and local agencies set their own standards for adequate education, it had became increasingly clear that federal courts were the final arbiters of equal opportunity in the schools.[44] It was, therefore, incumbent on the courts to resolve the lingering ambiguities that surrounded this ideal; more specifically, it was incumbent on the courts to clarify the legal importance of pursuing adequacy measured, either directly or indirectly, in terms of academic achievement. The courts, having created a confusing standard, had a responsibility to fix it.

If and when the courts undertake this process, considerable wisdom and patience will be required. After all, as this book has tried to show, resolving all the contradictions of public school policy is like trying to solve a Rubik's Cube. Every part of the system is linked to every other part, and, while the system must, in the end, form a coherent whole, the process of bringing all the pieces into alignment so each serves its legitimate purpose without disrupting the others can seem impossible. Indeed, one is often tempted to cheat (as many frustrated Cube-solvers have) by simply disassembling the entire apparatus and *forcing* the pieces into their intended places. Unfortunately, any organizational system as complex as the public schools cannot be taken apart—yanked, as it were, from history—and then rebuilt from scratch. Reforms of the future must somehow come to terms with the bewildering variety of specialized programs that have, it seems, irreversibly reshaped the public schools. Indeed, one of the most confounding aspects of school reform between 1950 and 1985 has been the way in which an ever-widening matrix of specialized programs have secured federal aid, consolidated political support, and then proceeded to work at cross-purposes with one another in the schools. Policymakers of the future will have to deal with this profoundly complicated and contentious system. They will have to work hard to see the entire system of school policy as one entity in which all the parts work toward the same goal. They cannot "tinker" their way toward utopia; they must see the system—as well as the vast social, political, cultural, legal, and economic context that surrounds it—whole. This book, structured as an historical case study, has attempted to describe the multilayerd complexity of the public education system, a system that lies at the heart of the nation's democratic experiment. If the federal role in the public schools is, in fact, analogous to a Rubik's Cube, then perhaps this study has filled in two or three sides of the puzzle.

NOTES

Introduction

1. For a daily summary of the events following the court's busing order, see J. Michael Ross and William M. Berg, *"I Respectfully Disagree with the Judge's Order": The Boston School Desegregation Controversy* (Washington, D.C.: University Press of America, 1981).

2. See Gerald N. Rosenberg, *The Hollow Hope: Can the Courts Bring About Social Change?* (Chicago: University of Chicago Press, 1993).

3. For an introduction to the historiography on *Brown v. Board of Education,* see Richard Kluger, *Simple Justice: The History of* Brown v. Board of Education *and Black America's Struggle for Equality* (New York: Alfred A. Knopf, 1976); James T. Patterson, Brown v. Board of Education: *A Civil Rights Milestone and Its Troubled Legacy* (New York: Oxford University Press, 2001); and Jack M. Balkin, ed., *What* Brown v. Board of Education *Should Have Said: The Nation's Top Legal Experts Rewrite America's Landmark Civil Rights Decision* (New York: New York University Press, 2001).

1. For more information on the Boston Association for Retarded Children, see Massachusetts Mental Retardation Planning Project, *Massachusetts Plans for Its Retarded* (Boston, 1966), 137.

2. Dennis Haley, *Annual Report of the Superintendent* (1950), 35–36; see also 7. Haley was proud of Boston's path-breaking tradition in public education. As he wrote, "Beginning with the first Latin grammar school, Boston has established an impressive list of 'firsts,' of which the first English high school, the first girls' high school, the first kindergarten, the first music education in public schools, and the first efforts in vocational guidance are but a few."

3. The Massachusetts Association for the Retarded was not the only organization of its kind in New England. See Barbara Bair, "The Parents Council for Retarded Children in Rhode Island, 1951–1970," *Rhode Island History* 40:4 (1981), 145–59.

4. "Class for Blind in Hub Planned," *Boston Post* (September 1, 1952). See also "Boston Board Considers School for Blind Children," *Boston Globe* (June 18, 1952). "Dr. Frederick J. Gillis, assistant superintendent of the Boston public schools, said last night the Boston school department is making a study to determine the need to include as part of their program the teaching of Braille to blind children. . . . Gillis also said the Boston system is making a survey to determine the need for classes for children afflicted with cerebral palsy."

5. Dennis Haley, *Annual Report of the Superintendent* (1953–54), no page numbers.

6. See Dennis Haley, *Annual Report of the Superintendent* (1952), 21. As Haley explained, "the work of educating mentally retarded children in the Boston schools has grown so extensively that today there are over 130 specialists serving some 1,700 backward children in 125 special classes and follow-up groups."

7. See Massachusetts General Laws, chapter 77 of the Resolves of 1952.

8. The rapid organization of special education advocates was not unique to Massachusetts. See Bair, 145–59.

9. Massachusetts Legislative Documents, 1954, House no. 2279, quoted in Nicholas Michael Balasalle, "A History of Public Policy for the Education of Handicapped Children in Massachusetts" (Ed.D. dissertation, Harvard Graduate School of Education, 1980), 145–48. The emphasis on community-based mental-health services increased in the 1950s as more professionals began to criticize the institutionalization of the mentally retarded and the mentally ill. These criticisms were not unwarranted in Massachusetts, where the Walter E. Fernald School cooperated in the 1950s with researchers at Harvard and MIT who conducted experiments on the effects of radioactive tracers in the human body. The tracers were added to the milk and cereal of 125 retarded children without their knowledge and without their parents' consent. Many of these children died as a result of their involvement in these experiments.

10. Balasalle, 148 (emphasis in original), 149.

11. Both of these laws were technically part of chapter 514 of the Acts of 1954, passed on May 28, 1954. See Massachusetts Mental Retardation Planning Project, *Massachusetts Plans for its Retarded* (Boston 1966), 137; and Massachusetts Legislative Documents, 1954, House no. 2270, quoted in Balasalle, 151.

12. Dennis Haley, *Annual Report of the Superintendent* (1955), 48.

13. At a time when the concept of universal public education was just beginning to extend to the high school level, Haley stressed that different students required different services—and not everyone needed to attend high school. See Dennis Haley, *Annual*

Report of the Superintendent (1950), 11. "In high school there have been changes grow-ing out of the more recent concept of the secondary school. It is the policy of educators, at present, to make such a level of instruction available to everyone, even to those who formerly would not have been deemed mentally capable of it. That all may attend high school and eventually graduate, it has been necessary to adjust not only the course of study but also the point of view underlying it. Since the high school is no longer an in-stitution for the select few, subjects and courses suited to the ability and needs of all must form an important part of the curriculum."

14. See Leon Friedman, ed., *Argument: The Oral Argument Before the Supreme Court in* Brown v. Board of Education of Topeka, *1952–1955* (New York: Chelsea, 1969).

15. *Brown v. Board of Education,* 349 U.S. 294 (1955).

16. Massachusetts Legislative Documents, 1955, House no. 2580, quoted in Bal-asalle, 157.

17. See Massachusetts Mental Retardation Planning Project, 140.

18. Services for emotionally disturbed and socially maladjusted students grew over time. In 1945, the Boston public schools created a Division of Juvenile Adjustment— later called the Division of Pupil Adjustment Counseling—and this division expanded rapidly. See Dennis Haley, *Annual Report of the Superintendent* (1958), 59. "Operating with a head of division, 10 counselors, and two assigned psychologists, the Division of Pupil Adjustment Counseling handled 1,144 individual cases of disturbed children. Of this group, 461 were given various types of psychological tests to determine causes of maladjustment and to provide analyses and interpretations to assist counselors in con-ferences, guidance, and referrals for treatment. Nearly all children tested were seriously disturbed emotionally, pre-delinquent, or delinquent. Others gave evidence of potential maladjustment and needed long-term study and therapy."

19. In 1956, Congress passed P.L. 84-922 to pay for instructional materials for the blind. See James J. Cremins, *Legal and Political Issues in Special Education* (Springfield, Ill.: C. C. Thomas, 1983), 8.

20. See "Special Services in the Boston Public Schools," 4, 18. Assistant superin-tendent Frederick Gillis described the procedure for placing a student in special educa-tion. "The procedure followed is that each retardate is studied by a member of the De-partment of Educational Investigation and Measurement, a complete social case study is made, and later a conference is held with the parent and principal concerning the pupil before placement in the special class suited to his ability level. The special educa-tion program planned for the retarded child in the 50 to 80 I.Q. group begins at age seven when the pupil first enters the special class and is continued through the ele-mentary and junior high schools and culminates in job placement and follow-up of the pupil on the job. When these educable pupils are twelve years of age, they are advanced to the junior high school program. At this level, there is greater integration with the regular classes than at the elementary school level. The pupils attend the special class for their academic subjects and participate with the regular pupils in such subjects as art, music, home economics, shop, and physical education."

21. Herein lay Haley's distinction between disabled and nondisabled children in a classroom setting. If a child was capable of average achievement *only* with special ser-vices, then he or she was legitimately disabled. If a child was capable of average achievement *without* special services, then he or she was not legitimately disabled (at least not in an educational sense). If a student was legitimately disabled, then, Haley be-lieved, he or she should receive special assistance *outside* the regular class, but Haley did not believe any student should be allowed to claim a right to special services *within* a

regular class, because, if such a claim were honored, then *every* student within a regular class would claim a right to special services.

22. See Susan Moore Johnson, *Declining Enrollments in the Massachusetts Public Schools: What It Means and What to Do* (Boston, 1978), 7.

23. The need for new school buildings arose even before the full effects of the baby boom were clear. See "Induction of Dr. Dennis Haley as Superintendent of Schools," School Document 11 (1948), 11. The Massachusetts state legislature passed Chapter 645 of the Acts of 1948 to provide financial aid for school construction. This law was amended by Chapter 528 of the Acts of 1950, by Chapter 389 of the Acts of 1952, and again by several subsequent laws.

24. Dennis Haley, *Annual Report of the Superintendent* (1955), 11.

25. Dennis Haley, *Annual Report of the Superintendent* (1957), no page numbers.

26. Dennis Haley, *Annual Report of the Superintendent* (1955), 11. As Haley explained, his building plans emphasized schools to serve "new centers of population which have been established because of private and public housing developments."

27. President Eisenhower was disturbed by the rapid increase in federal aid allocated under P.L. 83-815 and P.L. 83-874. See Don T. Martin, "Eisenhower and the Politics of Federal Aid to Education: The Watershed Years, 1953-1961," *Midwest History of Education Journal* 25:1 (1998), 7-12; James L. Sundquist, *Politics and Policy: The Eisenhower, Kennedy, and Johnson Years* (Washington, D.C.: Brookings Institution, 1968); and Iwan W. Morgan, *Eisenhower versus "The Spenders": The Eisenhower Administration, the Democrats, and the Budget, 1953-1960* (New York: St. Martin's Press, 1990).

28. See Massachusetts Department of Education, "Public Laws 815 and 874: Their Effects on the Cities and Towns of Massachusetts through April 1, 1963" (Boston, 1963).

29. "U.S. Aid Due Hub Schools?" *Boston Globe* (January 8, 1964).

30. See Barbara Barksdale Clowse, *Brainpower for the Cold War: The Sputnik Crisis and National Defense Education Act of 1958* (Westport, Conn.: Greenwood Press, 1981). See also Earl McGrath, "Sputnik and American Education," *Teachers College Record* 59 (April 1958), 379-95; Frank J. Munger and Richard F. Fenno, Jr., *National Politics and Federal Aid to Education* (Syracuse: Syracuse University Press, 1962); Sidney Sufrin, *Administering the National Defense Education Act* (Syracuse, N.Y.: Syracuse University Press, 1963); James R. Killian, Jr., *Sputnik, Scientists, and Eisenhower: A Memoir of the First Special Assistant to the President for Science and Technology* (Cambridge, Mass.: MIT Press, 1977); Robert A. Divine, *The Sputnik Challenge* (New York: Oxford University Press, 1993); and John L. Rudolph, *Scientists in the Classroom: The Cold War Reconstruction of American Science Education* (New York: Palgrave, 2002).

31. For a pre-*Sputnik* article on gifted students, see Harry Passow, "Talented Youth: Our Future Leaders," *Teachers College Record* 55 (1955), 164-71. Harvard president James Conant echoed the themes of the NDEA in his widely read book, *The American High School Today* (New York: McGraw-Hill, 1959), which urged a differentiated curriculum and stronger programs in science, math, and foreign languages, especially for gifted students.

32. Eisenhower quoted in Clowse, 16; columnist quoted in Clowse, 15.

33. See Rufus E. Miles, Jr., *The Department of Health, Education, and Welfare* (New York: Praeger, 1974).

34. Clowse, 94-95.

35. Clowse, 119. For several years, starting in 1956, Representative Adam Clayton Powell (D-N.Y.) added antisegregation amendments to virtually every bill proposing

federal aid to education. These amendments predictably killed each bill to which they were attached.

36. Quoted in Clowse, 119, 129.

37. Quoted in Clowse, 138.

38. Quoted in Clowse, 141.

39. See Sevan G. Terzian, "Indiana and the National Defense Education Act of 1958," *Midwest History of Education Journal* 24 (1997), 6–12. According to Terzian, "the major proponent of the bill [NDEA] in the House, Alabama Democrat Carl Elliott, writes in his memoirs that the bill was intended to establish a precedent for further federal aid to education: 'Of course I couldn't admit it at the time.'" See also Carl Elliott, Sr., and Mike D'Orso, *The Cost of Courage: The Journey of an American Congressman* (New York: Doubleday, 1992).

40. Quoted in Clowse, 55.

41. See Dennis Haley, *Annual Report of the Superintendent* (1958), 26, 7–11.

42. See Dennis Haley, "Science and Mathematics in the Boston Public Schools" in *Annual Report of the Superintendent* (1958), 7–11. "During the past year, American education at all levels has been widely subjected to critical analysis by many writers and speakers alarmed by the scientific accomplishments of the Russians and eager to contribute to the improvement of the schools and colleges of our nation. . . . Although all aspects of American education have received careful scrutiny, public attention has been principally directed toward the teaching of science and mathematics and the selection, encouragement, and development of pupils of superior ability."

43. Dennis Haley, *Annual Report of the Superintendent* (1958), 13, 12; see also 31–32. More than 160 students attended the Science Institute for Able Learners, which involved weekend and after-school lecture-demonstrations given by high school faculty. Haley also mentioned the introduction of accelerated classes for elementary school students, first organized on a pilot basis and later incorporated into full-time classes. "One day each week these ten pupils whose I.Q.'s range from 150 to 170 meet in the Robert Treat Paine School. . . . Members of the advanced work class show great enthusiasm for their new work and carry this program and their regular work with ease. A noticeable improvement in the quality of arithmetic and written composition work of these students is evident in their regular classroom situations."

44. Dennis Haley, *Annual Report of the Superintendent* (1959), 24. For more on the embrace of these new federal funds, see Haley, *Annual Report of the Superintendent* (1951), 9. The emphasis on mathematics and the natural sciences received a significant boost with the opening of Boston's new Museum of Science in 1951.

45. See, for example, Frederick J. Gillis, *Annual Report of the Superintendent* (1961), 31–32. See also Frederick J. Gillis, *Annual Report of the Superintendent* (December 1962), 91: "Advanced work classes, first mentioned in the June, 1958, report from this office, have expanded notably. Whereas these classes were organized at first on a pilot basis in five sections of the city to meet only one day a week, they are now a full-fledged part of elementary education in Boston."

46. Dennis Haley, *Annual Report of the Superintendent* (1952), 9; (1955), 18.

47. Dennis Haley, *Annual Report of the Superintendent* (1960), 26.

48. See Frederick J. Gillis, *Annual Report of the Superintendent* (1963).

49. For more on Kennedy's failure to pass a "general aid" bill, see Hugh Douglas Price, "Race, Religion, and the Rules Committee," in *The Uses of Power: Seven Cases in American Politics*, ed. Alan Westin (New York: Harcourt, Brace, and World, 1962), 2–71;

George A. Kizer, "Federal Aid to Education, 1945-1963," *History of Education Quarterly* 10 (Spring 1970), 84-102; Hugh D. Graham, *The Uncertain Triumph: Federal Education Policy in the Kennedy and Johnson Years* (Chapel Hill: University of North Carolina Press, 1984); and Lawrence J. McAndrews, *Broken Ground: John F. Kennedy and the Politics of Education* (1991).

50. In 1963, Kennedy signed the National Education Improvement Act into law.

51. See Edward Shorter, *The Kennedy Family and the Story of Mental Retardation* (Temple, Penn.: Temple University Press, 2000).

52. Chapter 750, signed on November 1, 1960, amended Chapter 71, section 46, of 1954 (which was passed in its original form in 1919). See Frederick J. Gillis, *Annual Report of the Superintendent* (1961), 45. "Next year by law the department will be enlarged to take over the instruction of mentally [i.e., emotionally] disturbed children. By provision of the Acts of the General Court of the Commonwealth in 1960 the Boston public schools will be reimbursed for 50 percent of the cost of instruction of all physically handicapped children. This portion of the act became effective in November, 1960. When the instruction of mentally [i.e., emotionally] disturbed children becomes effective in January, 1962, the state will reimburse us for 100 percent of these costs."

53. Frederick J. Gillis, *Annual Report of the Superintendent* (1961), 47, 95.

54. See Frederick J. Gillis, "Special Classes, Elementary Level," School Document 8 (July 5, 1960), 1-2. "The pupil with non-remediable defects must be helped to understand his limitations and aided in developing his optimal potentialities. Expectations of pupil achievement should always be in harmony with the individual's ability and growth."

55. Gillis had high hopes for the Juvenile Delinquency and Youth Offenses Control Act of 1961. See Frederick J. Gillis, *Annual Report of the Superintendent* (1963), 47-49. "Our concept of the Juvenile Delinquency and Youth Offenses Control Act of 1961 is that it places the heaviest onus upon education. The act suggests a new long-range approach which attempts to search out and remedy the grassroot causes of delinquency, especially among the culturally disadvantaged." See also James Gilbert, *A Cycle of Outrage: America's Reaction to the Juvenile Delinquent in the 1950s* (New York: Oxford University Press, 1986).

56. John S. Dooley, Director of Audio-Visual Instruction, *Annual Report of the Superintendent* (1960-61), 78. The use of audiovisual equipment in the Boston public schools was not new in the early 1960s. See, for example, Dennis Haley, *Annual Report of the Superintendent* (1950), 28-30.

57. See John H. Fischer, "Educational Reform in Other States," in Jamieson S. Reid, ed., *Proceedings of the Massachusetts Governor's Conference on Education* (January 27-28, 1966), 17. Gillis especially invested in televisions. As he explained in his annual report for 1962, "widespread use of television in classroom instruction has grown to the extent that eighty more television sets are being installed throughout the school system to make as much advantage as possible of the instruction (especially [in] science and languages) offered by '21-inch classroom' broadcasting." See Frederick Gillis, *Annual Report of the Superintendent* (1961-62), 78.

58. Frederick J. Gillis, *Annual Report of the Superintendent* (1961), 24-25.

59. See Frederick J. Gillis, *Annual Report of the Superintendent* (1963), 23, 86. "The school year now closing showed an increase of 1,000 pupils over the school year 1961-62, with the greatest percent of increase found in the elementary grades. With in-migrants moving into Boston every month from the deep South, with a continually expanding birthrate—particularly in the Roxbury and North Dorchester areas—plus

transfers from the parochial school system, this rising population trend will continue for some time to come. It predicates more schools, and more teachers. Where to build these schools and find the teachers to staff them is no small problem." Gillis also explained that "in October, 1962, there was established at the Abraham Lincoln School an upgrading class for in-migrant pupils from rural areas of the South. Of junior high school age, and transferred from the South to upper grades of our elementary and junior high schools, many of these in-migrant pupils were found to be so far below seventh-grade standards in reading and arithmetic that they could get little or nothing from junior high school instruction. In fact, some in-migrants had scarcely attained first-grade ability in reading and arithmetic. With the purpose of upgrading the abilities of the most backward in reading and arithmetic, it was decided to establish an upgrading class." See also Nicholas Lemann, *The Promised Land: The Great Black Migration and How It Changed America* (New York: Alfred A. Knopf, 1991).

60. See Gerald Gamm, *Urban Exodus: Why the Jews Left Boston and the Catholics Stayed* (Cambridge, Mass.: Harvard University Press, 1999), 224-27, 240-43, 262-63, 273-77.

61. These population estimates are derived from the comments of Noel Day in "Busing—A Symposium," *Ramparts* 13 (1975), 38-48. See also Center for Law and Education, *A Study of the Massachusetts Racial Imbalance Act* (Cambridge, Mass.: Harvard University, February 1972), 11-12. "In 1960, 2.2 percent of the state's residents, and 3.8 percent of the state's total school population was black. Of the state's blacks, 63,165 (56.3 percent) lived within the city of Boston. Data from 1964 revealed that 21,097 of the state's black children (59 percent) attended Boston schools. Moreover, the black population of Boston was rapidly growing. It jumped from 20,000 in 1940 to 40,000 in 1950 to 63,000 in 1960. The trend was to continue; by 1970, blacks were to number over 127,000 in Boston. Over the same period, Boston lost 13 percent of its population (more than 100,000 residents), many of whom were white families moving to the suburbs. . . . In Boston, by 1964, black children constituted 23 percent of the total public school enrollment." See also Frederick J. Gillis, *Annual Report of the Superintendent* (1963), 20. "We do not have a head-count of any minority group in the City of Boston; nor, for that matter, do we need, or want, one."

62. See the U.S. Department of Justice, *Annual Reports of the Immigration and Naturalization Service* (Washington, D.C., 1953-77).

63. Frederick J. Gillis, *Annual Report of the Superintendent* (1962-63), 91. See also Gillis's 1960-61 *Annual Report*, 283: "During the year, a class was organized in the John J. Williams School to teach the young Puerto Rican children the English language. Children are taken out of their regular classes in groups of twelve. Each group receives eighty minutes of instruction five times a week. The scheme is working out very well. In the George Bancroft School Puerto Rican children go to a first-grade room at reading time. This method also seems to be quite effective."

64. Frederick J. Gillis, *Annual Report of the Superintendent* (1962-63), 91.

65. Frederick J. Gillis, *Annual Report of the Superintendent* (1962), 15-16, 18.

66. See Boston Municipal Research Bureau, "A Closer Look at School Spending," (March 31, 1963).

67. See Gamm, *Urban Exodus,* 276.

68. See Frederick J. Gillis, *Annual Report of the Superintendent* (1963), 16. "A renaissance, as it were, is occurring in Boston. People who had gone to the suburbs are moving again into the city; coming back to dwell in new high-rise apartments, returning to live in a New Boston, a Boston being refurbished under a Federal Urban Renewal Plan. Slum clearance is progressing. Relocation of underprivileged families and the con-

struction of modern school plans to replace old and worn-out buildings are integral parts of the over-all Urban Renewal Program."

69. See Frederick J. Gillis, *Annual Report of the Superintendent* (1962), 13.

70. See "New Dimension in Education," *Boston Herald* (September 20, 1962) and "Major School Advance," *Boston Herald* (February 13, 1963).

71. "How Federal Funds Would Aid Schools," *Boston Globe* (September 30, 1962).

72. See "Unshackling a School System," *Boston Herald* (September 15, 1962). According to this editorial, "the alternative to the implementation of the Sargent plan is intolerable—a city condemned to both physical and human blight through its continued failure to provide first-rate educational facilities for children of all economic and social strata, and of all degrees of academic potential. The report's recommended school closings are, of themselves, a tragic indictment of this and past school administrations. It is no accident that not a single school in prosperous West Roxbury is archaic enough to warrant abandonment, while in slum-ridden Roxbury alone there are 18 such schools which, in the words of the report, are 'crowded, ill-heated, dark, odorous, and with cramped sites, as well as below today's standards of fire safety.'"

73. See Boston Municipal Research Bureau, "School Consolidations Still Possible" (September 15, 1960).

74. See "Mayor Links Boston's Rebirth to Program," *Boston Globe* (September 14, 1962). "'By coordinating this program with urban renewal,' the report states, 'it is possible to effect substantial economies. Indeed, it is not to much to say that the schools of the city need urban renewal and, conversely, that urban renewal needs the schools.' . . . 'It's amazing,' remarked Dr. Gillis, 'how much Dr. Sargent's recommendations agree with our own projected program for buildings within the next 10 years.'"

75. Frederick J. Gillis, *Annual Report of the Superintendent* (1962), 16. Gillis requested federal assistance but also demanded local control. "When federal monies do become available," he wrote, "hopefully, local autonomy will not be destroyed by overzealous federal supervision."

76. Frederick J. Gillis, *Annual Report of the Superintendent* (1962), 16-18, 62.

77. Frederick J. Gillis, *Annual Report of the Superintendent* (1962), 16-18. For more on the discussion of the role of public schools in preventing urban decay, see Gamm, *Urban Exodus*, 224-27, 240-43, 262-63, 273-77.

78. Gillis tried to describe the ways in which the culture of poverty affected children in Boston's ghetto areas. See Frederick J. Gillis, *Annual Report of the Superintendent* (1962), 17. "Money is always in short supply, the furniture is poor, beds are inadequate, food very often takes second place to the purchase of intoxicating liquors, and clothing and the way of wearing one's hair is apt to be bizarre. In this home books are not read; sometimes not even a newspaper is available. Self-expression and comprehension are below average, and inward stress and tensions of all kinds are present. The environmental pattern here predicates endless talk, fighting, child bearing, and moving from place to place to escape payment of rent. When the boy or girl comes to the public school from this kind of home, where the culture is several cuts below average, the school, more than ever, must adjust to the needs of this child. If anyone in the world needs love and kindness, sympathetic understanding, and personal guidance, it is the boy or girl who lives in this type of neighborhood."

79. See, for example, Massachusetts Commission Against Discrimination, *Route 128: Boston's Road to Segregation* (Washington, D.C.: U.S. Commission on Civil Rights, January, 1975).

80. Michael Harrington, *The Other America: Poverty in the United States* (New York: MacMillan, 1962).

81. Frederick J. Gillis, *Annual Report of the Superintendent* (1962), 17-18.

82. See Massachusetts Advisory Council on Education, "The New Massachusetts Program of State Aid to Education" (July 31, 1967).

83. See Richard H. DeLone, *Massachusetts Schools: Past, Present, and Possible* (Boston: Massachusetts Advisory Council on Education, 1972), 13. "When the foundation plan was passed in 1948, state support for public schools increased from approximately five percent to some fifteen percent of the total. By 1964, however, the state total had slipped back down to nine percent. This happened because the [legislature] did not act to keep the formula updated as school costs escalated across the nation and the state."

84. Massachusetts Advisory Council on Education, "The New Massachusetts Program of State Aid to Education" (July 31, 1967).

85. Some attributed legislative action to the publication in 1962 of a seven-part series in the *Boston Globe* by Ian Menzies and Ian Forman titled "The Mess in Bay State Education." See, for example, DeLone, 3.

86. Massachusetts Advisory Council on Education, "The New Massachusetts Program of State Aid to Education" (July 31, 1967).

87. For Gillis's reflections on his retirement, see Frederick J. Gillis, *Annual Report of the Superintendent* (1963), 22-23, 57.

Chapter Two

1. See Edward Shorter, *The Kennedy Family and the Story of Mental Retardation* (Philadelphia: Temple University Press, 2000).

2. Ohrenberger first suggested the idea of including more students in isolated remedial classes two years earlier—when he was deputy superintendent. See Frederick J. Gillis, *Annual Report of the Superintendent* (1961), 240.

3. See Frederick J. Gillis, *Annual Report of the Superintendent* (1963), 88. "Aimed at a target area where the incidence of school dropouts is markedly above the city average, Operation Second Chance was established upon a pilot basis in the seventh grade of the Donald McKay School in East Boston. . . . Upon a basis of at least low-normal intelligence, and a record of school failure with two nonpromotions as well as frequent absence, truancy, tardiness, and evidence of poor conduct and effort marks, twenty sixth-grade boys were selected [for participation in Operation Second Chance] in June, 1962."

4. Ohrenberger's predecessor, Superintendent Gillis, had also found ways to increase Boston's receipt of federal aid for the mentally retarded. See Frederick J. Gillis, *Annual Report of the Superintendent* (1963), 84. "It is noteworthy to mention that, from [the] first special class offering a differentiated type of education to a small group of retarded pupils, the instruction has grown over the years to 105 classes with an enrollment of nearly 2,000 children. This increase has not occurred without experiencing growing pains, since in the early days even educators were wary of the salutary effects of these classes, and parents too were loathe to have their children designated 'special.' With time this type of education proved itself and was ultimately accepted wholeheartedly by both administrators and parents."

5. For more on the characterization of poverty as pathology in the 1950s and 1960s, see James T. Patterson, *America's Struggle Against Poverty, 1900-1994* (Cambridge, Mass.: Harvard University Press, 1994). See also August B. Hollingshead and Frederick

C. Redlich, *Social Class and Mental Illness* (New Haven: Yale University Press, 1958); Frank Riessman et al., *Mental Health of the Poor: New Treatment Approaches for Low-Income People* (New York: Free Press of Glencoe, 1964); and Robert Coles, "What Poverty Does to the Mind," *Nation* 202 (June 20, 1966). See also Kenneth Clark, *Dark Ghetto: Dilemmas of Social Power* (Middletown, Conn.: Wesleyan University Press, 1965), 81: "The ghetto [is] institutionalized pathology; it is chronic, self-perpetuating pathology . . . one kind of pathology leads to another."

6. The connection between medical and educational assistance for mentally retarded children remained a subject of intense debate for many years. See Barbara Bair, "The Parents Council for Retarded Children in Rhode Island, 1951-1970," *Rhode Island History* 40:4 (1981), 146-47. "In the 1950s, mental retardation—like death or old age—was virtually dismissed as an irreversible or minimally treatable condition. The focus in teaching and training was on the curable and reversible, the acute condition and not the chronic. . . . Thus the field of mental retardation was avoided as an area of medical failure, full of uncertainties and limited possibilities for professional intervention. . . . Physicians who had learned little information about retardation in medical school tended to share the popular prejudices and misconceptions about retarded people that were prevalent in the population at large. One such misconception was the old idea, popularized at the turn of the century by Henry Goddard and other Social Darwinists, that retardation was somehow associated with degeneracy or a low income, and thus it was the parents' way of life or socioeconomic standing that was to blame for the child's condition."

7. See Harriet T. Bernstein and Daniel W. Merenda, "Categorical Programs: Past and Present," in *The Federal Role in Education: New Directions for the Eighties,* ed. Robert A. Miller (Washington, D.C.: Institute for Educational Leadership, 1981), 57-58. "The language used to anticipate the interplay between specialists and teachers was borrowed from medicine—pathology, diagnosis, prescription, treatment, remediation—suggesting that the deficiencies were to be found in the heads and bodies of individual children and their parents, and not in the teacher, the school, or the curriculum. This way of looking at things tended to result in children with various problems being separated out from others just as ill people are hospitalized for treatment. The medical model, as applied to education, can be seen as a metaphor for the worldview of the 1960's poverty warriors. . . . Poverty was the generic disease, but the diagnosis involved various manifestations of the disease—'emotional disturbance,' 'hyperactivity,' 'perceptual deficits,' or immaturity."

8. See William H. Ohrenberger, *Annual Report of the Superintendent* (1964), 6-8. For a thorough description of Operation Counterpoise, see Frederick J. Gillis, *Annual Report of the Superintendent* (1963), 51-55.

9. Cultural deprivation was sometimes considered to be inherited from parents, especially among black children. See Frederick J. Gillis, *Annual Report of the Superintendent* (1963), 54; see also 18-19. "Negro parents lacking aspirational goals cannot be expected to offer incentive to their children. If the home is without reading materials, if there is no discussion of current events, if there is no quiet corner where a child may study, then the role of the school in the life of children from such homes must differ in curriculum, in terms of expected educational outcomes, and final success. The school by itself cannot overcome insurmountable obstacles. So we predicate that first of all something must be done about some Negro parents, because a richer home life is a *sine qua non* if the status of Negro children is to be improved."

10. Mary Martin, assistant principal of the Henry L. Higginson Elementary School,

quoted in "School Problem Attacked," *Christian Science Monitor* (n.d.); newspaper clipping in the files of the Beebe Communications Library, Boston University.

11. See "'Operation Counterpoise' Aids Disadvantaged Boy," *Boston Globe* (December 22, 1963).

12. William H. Ohrenberger, *Annual Report of the Superintendent* (1964), 6.

13. "School Problem Attacked," *Christian Science Monitor* (n.d.).

14. See Lucia Mouat, "Schools Experiment," *Christian Science Monitor* (November 16, 1964). According to the *Christian Science Monitor,* Operation Counterpoise was "an intensive effort to upgrade reading and arithmetic skills. Phonics is used in the introduction of reading, and in all 'Counterpoise' primary grades. Schools in the program now use beginning reading texts which have Negro as well as white children in the illustrations. . . . One aim of 'Counterpoise' is to group the children into smaller classes by ability. Participating schools have 'junior grade 1's' and an in-between third and fourth grade class called 'operation recap' for children not quite ready for the next grade. In grades 4, 5, and 6, youngsters are grouped across grades according to reading ability for lessons in that subject. Rollins Griffith, assistant principal of David A. Ellis school, says that regrouping as a practice is on the increase in his school. . . . Mr. Griffith, as a veteran of almost two years experience with the 'Counterpoise' program, says . . . 'We've been thrilled with the results and the progress that we've seen.'" Griffith later became president of the Massachusetts Negro Educators Association.

15. Frederick J. Gillis, *Annual Report of the Superintendent* (1963), 19.

16. See Lucia Mouat, "Schools Experiment," *Christian Science Monitor* (November 16, 1964).

17. See Center for Law and Education, *A Study of the Massachusetts Racial Imbalance Act* (Cambridge, Mass.: Harvard University, February 1972), 19. According to Ruth Batson, a civil rights activist in Boston, "the average per pupil expenditure for Boston was $275.47, while in black schools the average was only $228.98."

18. See "School Problem Attacked," *Christian Science Monitor* (n.d.).

19. See the comments of Noel Day, the director of St. Mark's Social Service Center in Roxbury and one of the leaders of the school boycott, in "Busing—A Symposium," *Ramparts* 13 (1975), 41. "In 1963, the Congress of Racial Equality (CORE) conducted a survey of Boston's schools. The findings of that survey indicated that about 7,000 black children were enrolled in schools that were 90 percent or more black and that another 7,000 black children were in schools that were 50 percent to 85 percent non-white. The data cited in CORE's survey, drawn in large part from the Annual Report of the school committee's business manager, also showed that per pupil expenditures in the seven predominantly black school districts in the city were as much as 27 percent lower than average per pupil expenditures in the rest of Boston. CORE's study also pointed out that there were no Negro principals or other top administrators in the Boston public schools and that less than 40 of the more than 3,000 teachers in the system were black. At the time, about 10 percent of Boston's population was black. Incredibly, in the face of this evidence, the Boston school committee refused to admit the existence of '*de facto* segregation,' 'racial imbalance,' or even '*de facto* segregation resulting from residential concentration.' Within a week after the school committee's denial the first of two school boycotts was held in Boston. . . . The black community held a week-long 'sit-in' at the school committee's offices, picketed the building for over two months, and in early 1964 held a second, and larger, school boycott. About 14,000 black students participated and several thousand white students from suburban schools attended the 'freedom schools' that were set up in the black community."

20. See Jonathan Kozol, *Death at An Early Age: The Destruction of the Hearts and Minds of Negro Children in the Boston Public Schools* (Boston: Houghton Mifflin Co., 1967), 51–52.

21. Frederick J. Gillis, *Annual Report of the Superintendent* (1963), 55, 28.

22. Robert L. Levey, "Counterpoise Program Seen As Helping Youngsters," *Boston Globe* (October 25, 1964).

23. See Center for Law and Education, *A Study of the Massachusetts Racial Imbalance Act* (Cambridge, Mass.: Harvard University, February 1972), 16. See also Peter Schrag, *Village School Downtown: Politics and Education—A Boston Report* (Boston: Beacon Press, 1967), 8: "Mrs. Hicks is not a fluke, an accident of the electoral process. She is what Boston wants, and now—having just completed one campaign—she has become so important that she is being mentioned as a possible candidate for mayor, as the putative leader of a national campaign against school integration, and as America's foremost crusader for neighborhood schools."

24. In the spring of 1964, Hicks considered the expansion of Operation Counterpoise a higher priority even than salary raises for teachers. See "Teacher Pay Hike Refused," *Boston Herald* (April 3, 1964).

25. William H. Ohrenberger, *Annual Report of the Superintendent* (1964), 6. ABCD was established in 1962 with funds from Kennedy's Juvenile Delinquency Act. After the passage of the Equal Opportunity Act in 1964, it became Boston's official antipoverty agency. See Stephan Thernstrom, *Poverty, Planning, and Politics in the New Boston: The Origins of ABCD* (New York: Basic Books, 1969).

26. See Massachusetts Mental Retardation Planning Project, *Massachusetts Plans for its Retarded* (Boston 1966), 141.

27. See Massachusetts State Board of Education, *Because It Is Right—Educationally: Report of the Advisory Committee on Racial Imbalance and Education* (April 1965). The advisory committee that produced this report was chaired by state commissioner of education Owen Kiernan and was called the Kiernan Commission. The Kiernan Commission Report grew out of the Interim Report on racial imbalance released by the Massachusetts State board of Education on July 1, 1964. See Center for Law and Education, *A Study of the Massachusetts Racial Imbalance Act*, 43: "On June 14, 1965, Superintendent Ohrenberger released a 61-page reply to the Kiernan Report in which, for the first time, he publicly acknowledged the existence of racial imbalance in some Boston schools. Nevertheless, he disputed the Kiernan Committee's conclusion that such imbalance was of itself, educationally harmful."

28. See Massachusetts Board of Education, *Because It Is Right—Educationally*, 4, 22. Answering the question, "Wouldn't Compensatory Education Be More Helpful Than Racial Integration in the Schools?" Massachusetts's Advisory Committee on Racial Imbalance and Education replied that "the effects of racial imbalance are so damaging that they cannot be counterbalanced by compensatory education programs alone. . . . We have stated our belief that there is no conflict between compensatory educational efforts and racial balancing or that the two policies conflict with each other in any way."

29. See Massachusetts Board of Education, *Because It Is Right—Educationally*, 20.

30. For more information on the evolution of federal education policy in 1964, see Hugh Davis Graham, "Short-Circuiting the Bureaucracy in the Great Society Policy Origins in Education," *Presidential Studies Quarterly* (Summer 1982), 407–20.

31. The first laws Johnson signed as president were the Vocational Education Act and the Higher Education Facilities Act of 1963. For more on the passage of the Civil Rights Act of 1964, see Charles and Barbara Whalen, *The Longest Debate: A Legislative History of the 1964 Civil Rights Act* (Cabin John, Md.: Seven Locks Press, 1985).

32. Stephen K. Bailey and Edith K. Mosher, *ESEA: The Office of Education Administers a Law* (Syracuse, N.Y.: Syracuse University Press, 1968), 35. See also Edith Green, *Education and the Public Good: The Federal Role in Education* (Cambridge, Mass.: Harvard University Press, 1964); Eugene Eidenberg and Roy Morey, *An Act of Congress: The Legislative Process and the Making of Education Policy* (New York: Norton, 1969); Christine Elizabeth Dietrich, "Francis Keppel and Lyndon Johnson, Unique Collaborators in the Struggle for Federal Aid: ESEA, 1965" (Ph.D. dissertation, Lehigh University, 1994); and Edward Miech, "The Necessary Gentleman: Francis Keppel's Leadership in Getting Education's Act Together" (M.A. thesis, Harvard University, 2000).

33. Julie Roy Jeffrey, *Education for Children of the Poor: A Study of the Origins and Implementation of the Elementary and Secondary Education Act of 1965* (Columbus, Ohio: Ohio State University Press, 1978), 38.

34. See Bailey and Mosher, 26–35.

35. Quoted in Jeffrey, 69.

36. Jeffrey, 71.

37. See Bailey and Mosher, 39–45.

38. Jeffrey, 71. For implications of the Civil Rights Act on Keppel's bill, see Jeffrey, 107.

39. See Jeffrey, 76, 86.

40. The scholarly literature on ESEA is vast. Besides Jeffrey, op cit., one might start with Milbrey Wallin McLaughlin, *Evaluation and Reform: The Elementary and Secondary Education Act of 1965, Title I* (Cambridge, Mass.: Ballinger, 1975), and John F. Jennings, ed., *National Issues in Education: Elementary and Secondary Act* (Bloomington, Ind.: Phi Delta Kappa International, 1995).

41. "$5 Million Sought for Schools," *Christian Science Monitor* (May 15, 1965). Observing the rapid expansion of the office of program development, the *Monitor* noted that "the prospect of federal funds for Boston schools speeded its founding."

42. See William H. Ohrenberger, *Annual Report of the Superintendent* (1966), 22.

43. "Battle On to Bring Federal Funds to Hub Schools," *Boston Globe* (May 8, 1966).

44. See "$5 Million Sought for Schools," *Christian Science Monitor* (May 15, 1965), "'There is no excuse for our not getting all that we're eligible for,' says Joseph Slavit, ABCD's executive director. 'The community is going to be asking us some pretty tough questions if we don't.'"

45. See "Boston Schools Today," *Boston Globe* (December 19, 1965).

46. Quoted in Jeffrey, 107.

47. William Fripp, "Halt to Hit 5 Projects," *Boston Globe* (June 20, 1965).

48. Some thought Kiernan withheld federal aid not because of racial imbalance but simply because Boston's special-compensatory programs needed more fine-tuning before they merited aid. See Robert L. Levey, "1.2 Million in Federal Aid Withheld from Hub Schools," *Boston Globe* (December 27, 1965).

49. See "School Probe On in D.C.," *Boston Globe* (October 11, 1965).

50. See "Boston School Funds in Trouble," *Boston Herald* (August 24, 1966).

51. "Mrs. Hicks 'Sure' Hub . . . [?]," *Boston Traveler* (October 7, 1965); newspaper clipping in the files of the Beebe Communications Library, Boston University.

52. "Halt to Hit 5 Projects," *Boston Globe* (June 20, 1965).

53. "Ohrenberger Confident Hub Will Get U.S. Funds," *Boston Globe* (June 22, 1965).

54. "School Probe on in D.C." (October 11, 1965). In fact, the Civil Rights Act of 1964 may specifically have *excluded* federal aid for programs designed to promote racial balance in northern school systems. See Massachusetts State Board of Education, *Because*

It Is Right—Educationally, 17: "Title IV of this act allocates $3,000,000 to assisting lo-
cal communities with problems related to promoting racial balance in the schools. Although it specifically *excludes* support for planning the racial balancing of northern
schools, it includes support for certain phases of the execution of plans devised under
other auspices."

55. See "Ohrenberger Confident Hub Will Get U.S. Funds," *Boston Globe* (June 22,
1965).

56. "$2 Million U.S. Aid Lost for Counterpoise Plan," *Boston Herald* (April 14, 1966).
Remedial reading programs were not unknown in Boston in the 1960s; they had been
in place in elementary schools for at least a decade. See Dennis Haley, *Annual Report of
the Superintendent* (1956), 25–26. See also William H. Ohrenberger, *Annual Report of the
Superintendent* (1966), 16: "In cooperation with Action for Boston Community Development, reading consultants are functioning presently in three junior high schools. It is
hoped that funding under the Elementary and Secondary Education Act will make reading consultants available to at least three other junior high schools."

57. "Mrs. Hicks 'Sure' Hub . . . [?]," *Boston Traveler* (October 7, 1965).

58. See http://163.238.8.169/users/seeley/KEPPEL.HTM.

59. *Briggs v. Elliott*, 132 F. Supp. 776, 777 (1955). By 1965, the reasoning used in this
case was being reconsidered in the fifth and eighth circuits. See *Kemp v. Beasley*, 8 Cir.,
352 F.2d 14 (1965) and *United States v. Jefferson County*, 5 Cir., 372 F.2d 836, 847 (1967).

60. Title VI of the Civil Rights Act of 1964 suggests three ways to identify discrimination. The first is "disparate treatment"; the second is "disparate impact"; the third is
"denial of equal participation." In the 1970s, the U.S. Supreme Court gradually decided
that the second category—disparate impact—did not require litigants to prove "intentionality" on the part of defendants, but this framework was at first applied only to employment discrimination and not to educational discrimination. Litigation under the
equal protection clause of the Fourteenth Amendment, however, always required proof
of intentionality. See *McDonnell Douglas Corporation v. Green* 411 U.S. 792 (1973);
Guardians Association v. Civil Service Commission 463 U.S. 582 (1983); and *St. Mary's
Honor Center v. Hicks* 509 U.S. 502 (1993).

61. "Mrs. Hicks 'Sure' Hub . . . [?]," *Boston Traveler* (October 7, 1965).

62. Superintendent Gillis had implemented an "open enrollment policy" in the
summer of 1963. Although such policies were later struck down—first in the South and
later in the North—they were legally accepted in the mid-1960s. See Frederick J. Gillis,
"Statement of Administrative Policy," *Annual Report of the Superintendent* (1963), 29–55.

63. "Battle On to Bring Federal Funds to Hub Schools," *Boston Globe* (May 8, 1966).

64. Robert C. Wood, "Professionals at Bay: Managing Boston's Public Schools," *Journal of Policy Analysis and Management* (1982), 459. At-large elections for school committee and city council members were part of the good-government reforms of the first
half of the twentieth century and were supposed to counteract the corrupt machine politics that relied on easily manipulated ward-based elections.

65. See "The Racial Imbalance Bill in the Legislature" in *A Study of the Massachusetts
Racial Imbalance Act*, 38–55.

66. See Frank Levy, *Northern Schools and Civil Rights: The Racial Imbalance Act of
Massachusetts* (Chicago: Markham Press, 1971).

67. See "Hub Bids for $1.4M School Cash," *Boston Globe* (May 3, 1966).

68. Under the assumption that racial balance would improve academic achievement
for inner-city minority students, a voluntary program of cross-district busing had begun
in the fall of 1965. See "Boston, Newton Swap," *Boston Globe* (December 23, 1965).

69. See J. Anthony Lukas, *Common Ground: A Turbulent Decade in the Lives of Three American Families* (New York: Vintage Books, 1985), 228–29.

70. Bryant Rollins, "Why Doesn't Ted Speak Up," *Boston Globe* (June 12, 1965), "Kennedy has indicated [that] he is strongly in favor of this kind of economic sanction against stubborn southern school authorities. Since he supports this kind of economic sanction in the South . . . , there is some confusion as to his silence on a bill to impose similar economic sanctions in his own state."

71. See Kozol, *Death at an Early Age*, 133–45.

72. See "$2 Million U.S. Aid Lost for Counterpoise Plan," *Boston Herald* (April 14, 1966).

73. Kozol, *Death at an Early Age*, xi.

74. "Teacher Critical of Counterpoise," *Boston Globe* (June 13, 1965).

75. Kozol, *Death at an Early Age*, 34.

76. "Teacher Critical of Counterpoise," *Boston Globe* (June 13, 1965).

77. Ibid. One of Kozol's fellow teachers noted that "this young man has proved it is possible for Negro children to perform at high levels with proper teaching."

78. "$2 Million U.S. Aid Lost for Counterpoise Plan," *Boston Herald* (April 14, 1966). In 1966, Operation Counterpoise reached a total of seventeen districts and 13,000 students.

79. In 1966, Congress added Title VI to the ESEA, which created a bureau of education for the handicapped within the federal office of education. See Edwin W. Martin, "Breakthrough for the Handicapped: Legislative History," *Exceptional Children* 33 (March 1968), 493–503.

80. Reid, *Proceedings of the Massachusetts Governor's Conference on Education*, no page numbers.

81. Ibid.

82. William H. Ohrenberger, *Annual Report of the Superintendent* (1967), 33–35.

83. See Boston Municipal Research Bureau, "Bureau Brief" (January 21, 1966), 2.

84. "Federal Funds Go Begging," *Boston Globe* (June 26, 1966).

85. See Boston Municipal Research Bureau, "A Catalog of Federal Aids Applicable to Boston" and "Millions for Boston at Stake" (December 1966), 3; and "4 Schools Allotted U.S. Funds," *Boston Globe* (April 19, 1966). For more on the origins of the Boston Municipal Research Bureau, see Boston Urban Study Group, *Who Rules Boston? A Citizen's Guide to Reclaiming the City* (Boston: Institute for Democratic Socialism, 1984), 53–54.

86. The school committee was somewhat disingenuous in its claim that duplicating special-compensatory services would be too expensive, because, in certain cases, the committee readily accepted the expense of duplicating whole buildings in order to maintain the separation of races. See Kozol, *Death at an Early Age*, 34–35.

87. See Boston School Committee, "1966–1967 Plan Toward the Elimination of Racial Imbalance in the Public Schools" (1967).

88. Chapter 14 of the Acts of 1966 was signed on March 2, 1966. It amended Chapter 70 and was known thereafter simply as Chapter 70. See Robert T. Capeless, "Tax Equity and Educational Equality" in Federal Reserve Bank of Boston, *Financing Public Schools: A New England School Development Conference Held in Cooperation with the Harvard Graduate School of Education and the Federal Reserve Bank of Boston* (January 1972).

89. For more on the origins of Chapter 70, see "Lyman Ziegler, 71; Father of Laws on Massachusetts Taxes, Schooling, and Arts," *Boston Globe* (December 12, 1983).

90. See Massachusetts Advisory Council on Education, "The New Massachusetts Program of State Aid to Education" (July 31, 1967). See also Charlotte Ryan, "The State

Dollar and the Schools: A Discussion of State Aid Programs in Massachusetts and Promising Reforms" (Boston: Massachusetts Advisory Council on Education, 1970), 7: "The foundation plan adopted by Massachusetts in 1948 was badly handled," Ryan asserted. "Not only were the proposed grants diminished by half; it was provided that the $130 set as the required per-pupil expenditure would increase in proportion to increasing valuations each time the legislature sanctioned the updating of equalized valuation figures. Since this never occurred, . . . school costs increased faster than state aid, so that the proportion of general school aid fell by 1964 to less than 9 percent of school operating expenditures."

91. The idea of an equalization formula arose in Boston as early as 1963. See Boston Municipal Research Bureau, "Boston and Equalized Valuations" (July 1963).

92. See Bruce William Perlstein, "Taxes, Schools, and Inequality: The Political Economy of The Property Tax and School Finance Reform in Massachusetts" (Ph.D. dissertation, Brandeis University, 1981), 400.

93. The sales tax had been under consideration for at least seven years by the time it became law in 1966. See Boston Municipal Research Bureau, "Sales Tax a Must for Boston" (February 1, 1960). "A few simple facts show why Boston needs considerable relief immediately from its staggering property tax burden. During the past 10 years, the city's property tax levy has skyrocketed by 50 percent. Property owners are now paying almost $50 million more a year in property taxes than in 1950. . . . The city's tax rate has increased at an even greater clip than the property tax levy. This is due to the continuing erosion of the tax base. The shrinkage in assessed valuations during this 10-year period amounts to $105 million. The present system of state aid has failed completely to provide dependable and substantial relief to cities and towns."

94. See Massachusetts Advisory Council on Education, "The New Massachusetts Program of State Aid to Education" (July 31, 1967). The percentage equalization formula was largely the work of Charles Benson at Harvard (and, later, the University of California-Berkeley) and Thomas James of Stanford. See Charles S. Benson, *The Economics of Public Education* (Boston: Houghton Mifflin, 1961). See also Joel S. Wineberg, *State Aid to Education in Massachusetts: A NESDEC Research Report on Existing Conditions and Recommended Change* (1962).

95. See Schrag, 127. According to Schrag, the state Department of Education in 1966 "froze another installment of funds designated for the Boston schools, bringing the total withheld to approximately $16 million. (Massachusetts Commissioner of Education Owen Kiernan estimated that the figure would reach $32 million before the end of 1966.)"

96. See Boston Municipal Research Bureau, *Special Report* (May 1966).

97. See Harriet T., Bernstein and Daniel W. Merenda, "Categorical Programs: Past and Present," in *The Federal Role in Education: New Directions for the Eighties*, ed. Robert A. Miller (Washington, D.C.: Institute for Educational Leadership, 1981), 55. "The direct beneficiaries of Title I funds—administrators at the state, local and building level, teachers, aides, specialists, and members of parent advisory councils—soon became a powerful constituency for the idea that money, kept strictly targeted for the benefit of eligible children and no others, was the prime factor in achieving educational equality for disadvantaged children. That constituency would fight many battles to keep monies targeted and prevent federal resources from being spread over the whole school population. Strict targeting of money (and, as a consequence, the increasing segregation of the children and their teachers and aides), was linked to the idea of remediation for past inequality, which was in turn linked to 'compensatory' programs, parent power, and jobs

for minority parents. Education, *per se,* was not the focal point of their struggle; the proper direction of money was. Just as the initial impetus for Title I was essentially political and not strictly educational, so also was the animating force that shaped the program's evolution in its first years. It now appears in retrospect that everyone was assuming that money would lead to results."

98. "Mrs. Hicks 'Sure' Hub . . . [?]," *Boston Traveler* (October 7, 1965).

Chapter Three

1. Thomas F. Pettigrew and Patricia J. Pajonas, "Social-Pyschological Considerations of Racially Balanced Schools" in Massachusetts Board of Education, *Because It Is Right—Educationally* (Boston: April 1965), 87–88. Pettigrew explained that "a recent Illinois state statute prohibits imbalanced schools; and a recent decision of the highest state court of California favored the creation of balanced schools in a case that did not involve prior acts of explicit discrimination by the school board. These laws and decisions do more than clear the path toward racially integrated education." See also Beryl A. Radin, *Implementation, Change, and the Federal Bureaucracy: School Desegregation Policy in HEW, 1964–1968* (New York: Teachers College Press, 1977).

2. See "Boston School Funds in Trouble" *Boston Herald* (August 24, 1966), "U.S. Commissioner of Education Harold Howe said Tuesday that his office is exploring the possibility of withholding federal funds from the Boston school system because of its inability to comply with the state racial imbalance law. Howe said that the federal government is 'looking into the possibility at this point' and 'exploring the legal posture. It's a complicated matter,' he added." The issue was complicated, in part, because it was not clear whether the federal government could withhold *federal* funds in support of a *state* law. According to the *Herald,* "Massachusetts commissioner of education Owen B. Kiernan . . . explained that the federal withholding action could be a completely separate action, based on the findings of the investigative team from the Department of Health, Education, and Welfare now studying discrimination in the Boston schools. If the team found the city schools to be discriminatory, the school department would be violating the 1964 Civil Rights Act, and funds would be withheld under that statute."

3. See Mark Goldberg, "An Interview with Harold 'Doc' Howe II: 'Stirring the Pot,'" *Phi Delta Kappan,* http://www.pdkintl.org/kappan/kgol0010.htm.

4. See William H. Ohrenberger, *Annual Report of the Superintendent* (1966), 27. "Marked differences in abilities and attitudes are apparent in children attending the Boston public schools. These differences reflect the economic status of the family, the cultural advantages or disadvantages of the home, and the nature of the parent-child relationship. Because an increasing number of children enrolling in the Boston public schools come from disadvantaged homes, and because the physical, emotional, social and intellectual development of many of these children has suffered as a result of their disadvantaged background, measures must be taken to compensate for these disadvantages. . . . Under Title I of the Elementary and Secondary Education Act of 1965, funds were made available for further expansion of compensatory programs, and in February, 1966, [Operation] Counterpoise was expanded to include five additional districts."

5. Carl Kaestle and Marshall Smith, "The Federal Role in Elementary and Secondary Education, 1940–1980," *Harvard Educational Review* 52:4 (1982), 384–408. For a concise statement of this issue, see Peter Schrag, *Village School Downtown: Politics and Education—A Boston Report* (Boston, Beacon Press, 1967), 169–70: "Compensatory education, it is said, strikes at the very heart of the problems of the disadvantaged child. It

provides the special services, the special attention he needs. It is tailored for his condition. But compensatory education also implies—almost as a necessity—some degree of segregation, either within schools or between schools, since those who are now being called 'non-disadvantaged' children presumably don't need it."

6. In urban areas, many—perhaps most—of the nation's federally funded special-compensatory programs were located in de facto segregated schools. See Julie Roy Jeffrey, *Education for Children of the Poor: A Study of the Origins and Implementation of the Elementary and Secondary Education Act of 1965* (Columbus, Ohio: Ohio State University Press, 1978), 156. "In its survey of thirteen cities between 1965 and 1967, [a federal civil rights] commission discovered that in a majority of cases, ESEA funds set up compensatory programs in schools whose student bodies were 50 percent or more black."

7. See Schrag, 170. "Almost all the existing preschool programs—programs like the federally financed Head Start—are premised on concepts of cultural deprivation. . . . But all these programs tend to segregate. Tracking segregates. Remedial reading segregates. Special schools segregate." See also Frank Riessman, *The Culturally Deprived Child* (New York: Harper, 1962); Martin P. Deutsch, *The Disadvantaged Child* (New York: Basic Books, 1967); and Kenneth Clark, *The Educationally Deprived: The Potential for Change* (New York: Metropolitan Applied Research Center, 1972).

8. See "State May Kill Census Listing Chinese 'White'" *Boston Globe* (October 19, 1966).

9. The issue of racial classification later applied to students of Hispanic background. See Massachusetts Advisory Committee to U.S. Commission on Civil Rights, "Issues of Concern to Puerto Ricans in Boston and Springfield" (Boston: February 1972; written in May 1971), 7. "Community leaders also point out . . . the classification of Puerto Ricans either as 'black' or 'white.' Such a classification is necessary under the state racial imbalance act, although the state has not determined how to classify Puerto Ricans. Thus, some school departments lump the Puerto Ricans with 'whites' while others place these students with nonwhites. In no case are Puerto Ricans classified as Puerto Ricans or with other Hispanic groups."

10. "Mrs. Hicks: Chinese Prefer Imbalance," *Boston Herald-Traveler* (October 26, 1966).

11. "Mrs. Hicks: Chinese Prefer Imbalance," *Boston Herald-Traveler* (October 26, 1966); "'We Didn't List Chinese As White' . . . Mrs. Hicks," *Boston Herald-Traveler* (November 2, 1966); "Mrs. Hicks to Push Plan for Chinese Pupils," *Boston Herald-Traveler* (November 18, 1966).

12. "Mrs. Hicks: Chinese Prefer Imbalance," *Boston Herald-Traveler* (October 26, 1966).

13. "Mrs. Hicks to Push Plan For Chinese Pupils," *Boston Herald-Traveler* (November 18, 1966).

14. All quoted in Jeffrey, 154, 148, 151. See also James S. Coleman, et al. *Equality of Educational Opportunity* (Washington, D.C.: Government Printing Office, 1966). The Coleman Report was federally funded under the Civil Rights Act of 1964.

15. Kozol, *Death at an Early Age,* 98-99, 237-38.

16. See William H. Ohrenberger, *Annual Report of the Superintendent* (1967), 10.

17. See Parents Association for South End Schools and the United South End Settlements, "End Educational Entombment" (1967).

18. See Burton Blatt and Frank Garfunkel, *Massachusetts Study of Educational Opportunities for Handicapped and Disadvantaged Children* (Boston: Massachusetts Advisory Council on Education, January 1971), 4-5.

19. "Special Services in the Boston Public Schools," School Document no. 1 (1956), 26–27. See also Frederick Gillis, *Annual Report of the Superintendent* (1961), 234, 238: "The department offers an over-all testing plan which provides for two phases of testing: (1) the all-school program, the September Achievement Testing day, which includes tests which are administered to all students, and (2) a supplementary program in which a variety of tests for special evaluation are administered to students in certain grade or class groups, or individually." Gillis added that "some are recommended for kindergarten or grade placement; others are recommended for either special or subspecial classes; others who cannot be included in either of these groups are recommended for state institution consideration. Keeping these children who cannot profit from training out of our schools means a saving of many tax dollars."

20. Mary B. Cummings, "Report from the Department of Educational Investigation and Measurement" in Frederick J. Gillis, *Annual Report of the Superintendent* (1961), 233.

21. William H. Ohrenberger, *Annual Report of the Superintendent* (1967), 32.

22. *Hobson v. Hansen* 269 F. Supp. 401 (D.C.D.C., 1967). For an example of the use of tracks in Boston, see Schrag, 94.

23. See *Hobson v. Hansen* 269 F. Supp. 401 (D.C.D.C., 1967). According to Judge Wright, "One area being given close attention [by the College Entrance Examination Board National Commission on Tests] is the testing of the culturally disadvantaged and members of distinctive cultural groups."

24. "Aid to Handicapped Pupils to Be Probed," *Boston Globe* (December 25, 1969). The South End parents' petition eventually led to a lawsuit, *Stewart v. Phillips,* Civil No. 70-1199-F (D. Mass., February 8, 1971); reprinted in Harvard University Center for Law and Education, *Classification Materials* (Cambridge, MA: Author, 1972), 234. For more on *Stewart v. Phillips,* see chapter 5.

25. *Hobson v. Hansen,* 269 F. Supp. 401 (D.C.D.C., 1967). The named defendant in this case was Carl F. Hansen, the superintendent of schools in Washington, D.C.

26. See *Hobson v. Hansen,* 269 F. Supp. 401 (D.C.D.C., 1967). As Wright noted, "the track system is by definition a separative device, ostensibly according to students' ability levels. However, the practical effect of such a system is also to group students largely according to their socio-economic status and, to a lesser but observable degree, to their racial status." Wright claimed that he could "not ignore the fact that of all the possible forms of ability grouping, the one that won acceptance in the District [of Columbia] was the one that—with the exception of completely separate schools—involves the greatest amount of physical separation by grouping students in wholly distinct, homogeneous curriculum levels. It cannot ignore that the immediate and known effect of this separation would be to insulate the more academically developed white student from his less fortunate black schoolmate, thus minimizing the impact of [racial] integration [which was required in Washington, D.C., under *Bolling v. Sharpe,* 347 U.S. 497, 74 S. Ct. 693, 98 L. Ed. 884 (1954), the companion to *Brown v. Board of Education,* 347 U.S. 483, 74 S. Ct. 686, 98 L. Ed. 873 (1954)]. . . . To this extent the track system is tainted."

27. According to Wright, it was not entirely clear in 1967 whether de facto segregation in public schools necessarily violated the Constitution. "As every student of the Constitution knows, the intense debate over racial segregation in the schools has clustered around two seminal concepts: de jure and de facto segregation. The first of these, as already indicated, adverts to segregation specifically mandated by law or by public policy pursued under color of law; this is the segregation unequivocally denounced by Bolling and Brown. School segregation is de facto when it results from the action of pupil assignment policies not based on race but upon social or other conditions for

which government cannot be held responsible; whether segregation so occasioned does fall within Brown's proscription the Supreme Court has not yet considered or decided." See *Hobson v. Hansen* 269 F. Supp. 401 (1967).

28. See *Hobson v. Hansen* 269 F. Supp. 401 (D.C.D.C., 1967). "The court does not . . . rest its decision on a finding of intended racial discrimination. Apart from such intentional aspects, the effects of the track system must be held to be a violation of plaintiffs' constitutional rights."

29. Ibid. Since the District of Columbia is not a state, cases involving the principle of equal protection in the District use the Fifth rather than the Fourteenth Amendment as the basis for their judgments and remedies.

30. *Hobson v. Hansen,* 269 F. Supp. 401 (D.C.D.C., 1967). Since classifying students by ability was not necessarily unconstitutional, Wright scrutinized the de facto racial segregation of the public schools on different grounds. "Taking what has been called 'a "new" approach to litigation over racial imbalance,'" he wrote, "the court considers whether these documented inequalities in the predominantly Negro schools deny the children who are assigned . . . to attend them equal educational opportunity and equal protection of the law. However the Supreme Court ultimately decides the question of a school board's duty to avoid pupil-assignment policies which lead to *de facto* segregation by race and class, it should be clear that if whites and Negroes, or rich and poor, are to be consigned to separate schools, pursuant to whatever policy, the minimum the Constitution will require and guarantee is that for their objectively measurable aspects these schools be run on the basis of real equality, at least unless any inequalities are adequately justified." It was not entirely clear what Wright meant by the "real equality" of schools' "objectively measurable aspects," nor was it clear what he might consider adequate justification for any "inequalities."

31. *Hobson v. Hansen,* 269 F. Supp. 401 (D.C.D.C., 1967). When it came to the idea of race-neutral testing, Wright advocated tests based on each student's "local culture": "Two techniques have been cited by plaintiffs that might help give a more accurate estimation of the ability of the disadvantaged child. One of these is the development of a locally standardized test. The principle is the same as that applied to the nationally standardized test, except that the test questions are made appropriate to the students being tested and the norm is ascertained from a group of similarly situated students—that is, those students within the local school system at the appropriate age levels." Wright's use of the phrase *similarly situated* was legally important, because the constitutional principle of equal protection applies to classifications of people who are "similarly situated." Wright extended the meaning of this phrase to include not only the race but also the socioeconomic status of inner-city students. In his view, standardized tests could pass constitutional muster only if they were given to students who were similarly situated in terms of both race and class. "The purpose of the local norm is to produce test scores that will reflect what the child has had the opportunity to learn and to compare his achievement with that of others who have had comparable opportunities," Wright wrote. "Another method of establishing a local norm is to use the standard aptitude test but to restandardize the median score according to local performances." Wright's reasoning, however, was deeply flawed. The notion that tests, in order to be constitutional, had to be given only to "similarly situated" students undercut the notion that tests should facilitate comparisons among *differently* situated students. If Wright's principle of "local tests" were followed to its logical end, then ghetto students would probably receive high scores on ghetto tests, but it would be impossible to determine if ghetto and nonghetto students had, in fact, had "equal" educational opportunities.

32. *Hobson v. Hansen,* 269 F. Supp. 401 (D.C.D.C., 1967).

33. William H. Ohrenberger, *Annual Report of the Superintendent* (1967), 15. Despite Judge Wright's recommendations in *Hobson v. Hansen* regarding the adoption of locally standardized tests, Ohrenberger noted that "a change in the testing procedure will be effected in September, 1967. A standardized test in reading geared to the various grade levels will be given to all pupils, Kindergarten through Grade VIII. This uniform procedure will provide a more accurate evaluation of reading achievement throughout the city. It is also more in agreement with the testing conducted by other large school systems, thus enabling more precise comparisons to be made with both local and national norms."

34. Council of Chief State School Officers, "Development of Special Conference Report" (June 22–24, 1967), 12.

35. Ibid.

36. Quoted in Gerald Gamm, *Urban Exodus: Why the Jews Left Boston and the Catholics Stayed* (Cambridge, Mass.: Harvard University Press, 1999), 274.

37. Anthony D. Perez, "Media Coverage of Collective Violence: An Analysis of Description Bias in the 1967–1972 Race Riots" (unpublished paper, Undergraduate Research Opportunities Program, University of Notre Dame, Fall 2000), 5. For more on the community action programs of the late 1960s, see Daniel Patrick Moynihan, *Maximum Feasible Misunderstanding: Community Action in the War on Poverty* (New York: Free Press, 1969).

38. To some extent, the migration from Latin America to Boston antedated the passage of the Immigration and Naturalization Act of 1965. See Dennis Haley, *Annual Report of the Superintendent* (1956), 71.

39. See William H. Ohrenberger, *Annual Report of the Superintendent* (1966), 12; and William H. Ohrenberger, *Annual Report of the Superintendent* (1968), 30.

40. Rosemary Whiting, "An Overview of the Spanish-Speaking Population in Boston" (August 1969), cited in Task Force on Children Out of School, *The Way We Go to School: The Exclusion of Children in Boston* (Boston 1970), 23.

41. William H. Ohrenberger, *Annual Report of the Superintendent* (1968), 10.

42. Quoted in Susan Gilbert Schneider, *Revolution, Reaction, or Reform: The 1974 Bilingual Education Act* (New York: Las Americas Publishing Company, 1976), 23.

43. See James Crawford, *Bilingual Education: History, Politics, Theory, and Practice,* 4th ed. (Los Angeles: Bilingual Education Services, Inc., 1999), 37. "From its outset, federal aid to bilingual education was regarded as a 'poverty program,' rather than an innovative approach to language instruction. This decision would shape the development of bilingual programs, and the heated ideological battles surrounding them, over the next three decades."

44. See Maria Eugenia Matute-Bianchi, "The Federal Mandate for Bilingual Education" in *Bilingual Education and Public Policy in the United States,* ed. Raymond V. Padilla (1979), 19.

45. See Brenda Beelar, "Schools for the City: The New Bilingual Law—and Beyond" *Model Cities Bulletin* 2 (Massachusetts Department of Education, Bureau of Equal Educational Opportunities, January 1972). Of 150 Title VII programs funded in 1971, Massachusetts had 4.

46. One major problem with bilingual education in the late 1960s was a paucity of qualified teachers. See Gerald C. Cumner and Peter W. Greenwood, "Bay City" in *Federal Programs Supporting Educational Change, Vol. III: The Process of Change, Appendix C. Innovations in Bilingual Education;* R-1589/3-HEW (April 1975), sect, 4, 53.

47. Rosemary Whiting, "An Overview of the Spanish-Speaking Population in Boston" (August 1969).

48. Ibid., 21.

49. See "Language Barrier in Schools," *Boston Globe* (October 20, 1970).

50. One year later, in 1969–70, Ohrenberger reluctantly agreed to test EDC's proposal on a limited basis but, citing the schools' financial inability to sustain such a program over time, he did little to support it. He refused to provide classrooms for the bilingual clusters, leading Sister Frances Georgia to ask Denison House, a social settlement in the South End, to rent space to EDC. As a result of this arrangement, the bilingual-transitional clusters occupied space isolated from regular schools. See Task Force on Children Out of School, 21–23.

51. Massachusetts Advisory Council on Education, "Massachusetts and Its Support of the Public Schools" (April 1, 1968), *v.*

52. See Boston Municipal Research Bureau, "Special Report: Boston's 1968 Financial Woes Mount" (January 1968).

53. See Task Force on Children Out of School, 15.

54. Anne Fontaine, Director of the Department for Physically Handicapped Children, Boston School Department, in testimony before the Task Force on Children Out of School (November 26, 1969), cited in Task Force on Children Out of School, 28–29.

55. Task Force on Children Out of School, 38. Boston's high rate of placement in special classes was partly attributable to the fact that Massachusetts set a higher IQ cut-off score than other states (79 compared to 70 or 75), which meant that children with higher IQ's were nonetheless placed in special classes. Arthur J. Bindman's statement that "the normal range of human intelligence [shows] that a fixed percentage of a school population will score below a certain point on an I.Q. test" was telling. To say that a normal (i.e., bell) curve places a certain proportion of students in the low range says little about intelligence per se; instead, it simply describes the nature of a normal curve. The number of disabled students in a given population depends ultimately on the definition of *disability* itself—that is, on the cut-off line that separates "disabled" from "nondisabled" test scores. This line has no objective meaning; it simply reflects the imagined relationship between student ability (as measured by tests) and curricular demands. Only when parents trust the connection between test scores and classroom placements can different students receive different placements without provoking accusations of discrimination or unequal educational opportunity.

56. The issue of "appropriateness" applied to special-compensatory programs for all students presumed to have special educational needs. See Schrag, 171: "If the civil rights leadership insists that Negro children are no different from all others, and that Negro families, though poor, are just as interested in [the same kind of] education as their white counterparts across town, then it cannot demand anything more than integration and equality. Given these premises it cannot argue that education in the [predominantly white] public schools is irrelevant for Negroes (without arguing that it is also irrelevant for whites) and it must then produce the motivated children, the clean clothes, the decent behavior, and the bourgeois aspirations on which the public schools have always relied. If, on the other hand, it insists that, because of historic deprivation and existing inequities, Negroes have special problems, then it must be willing to accept—or even demand—some sort of special treatment for their children, treatment that inevitably implies segregation or differentiation."

57. Alicia Caban Wheeler, "Public Policy Formulation: Chapter 766, Education of the Handicapped Act" (Qualifying Paper, Harvard Graduate School of Education, June 1980), 25. Boston's Chapter 750 classes were investigated for possible malfeasance in 1968. See William H. Ohrenberger, *Annual Report of the Superintendent* (1968), 10.

58. Task Force on Children Out of School, 49. See also Wheeler, 12: "In spite of the good intent behind the development of Chapter 750 and its regulations, an examination of political and social history, including data from the Project 750 follow-up study, reveals that Chapter 750 was used to: a) misclassify and exclude minority and bilingual children [from regular classes], b) perpetuate racial segregation, and c) discriminate by race and social class."

59. Herbert J. Hoffman, *Take a Giant Step: Final Report of Evaluation of Selected Aspects of Project 750* (Boston: Massachusetts Advisory Council on Education, September 1969), 1, 20-21. As Hoffman noted, "the present regulations and forms [governing Chapter 750] make no provision for recording the child's color. This is understandable in terms of accepted philosophies and practices at the time the regulations were developed in the early 1960s. Times, philosophies and concerns have changed. Events in the black communities over the past five years (black-white confrontations and several federal promulgations) have [now] made it [necessary] for responsible public officials to know what the distribution of clients and employees is by color."

60. See Massachusetts Institute for Governmental Services, *The Children's Puzzle: A Study of Services to Children in Massachusetts* (February 1977), 7.

61. Quoted in Wheeler, 9.

62. Not everyone agreed that better diagnoses would foster better services, because schools did not yet have differentiated treatments for each different subcategories of disabled pupils. See Hoffman, 48. "We have not been able to specify differentiated treatment procedures for differential diagnoses, nor have we observed thus far any relationship between diagnosis and [the] responsiveness to the school program."

63. Wheeler, 31.

64. See Milton Budoff, "Engendering Change in Special Education Practices," *Harvard Educational Review* 45:4 (November 1975). The retesting of children and the discovery of misdiagnoses was not limited to Boston; it had also occurred in Washington, D.C. See n. 69.

65. Task Force on Children Out of School, 41.

66. J. Anthony Lukas, *Common Ground: A Turbulent Decade in the Lives of Three American Families* (New York: Vintage Books, 1985), 39. See also Schrag, 43: "Recently the message of black power has been heard in the city, and been translated into a putative 'Committee of 80,000 for Roxbury Self Help.'"

67. See Carlton Maybee, "A Negro Boycott to Integrate Boston Schools," *New England Quarterly* 41 (September 1968), 258.

68. "300 City Leaders Form Boston Urban Coalition," *Boston Herald-Traveler* (March 23, 1968). See also Boston Urban Study Group, *Who Rules Boston? A Citizen's Guide to Reclaiming the City* (Boston: Institute for Democratic Socialism, 1984), 12: "The top executives of major downtown businesses and banks came together to discuss how to 'redevelop' the city, especially to improve its 'business climate.' . . . The vehicles for this transformation were several business-dominated organizations that emerged in the post-war decade. The first was the New Boston Committee, formed in 1950 (after [Mayor John Michael] Curley's defeat) to promote a new breed of business-oriented mayors and other city officials. The second was 'The Vault' (officially called the 'Coordinating Committee'), a group composed primarily of Yankee businessmen that was founded in 1959 to catalyze the city's economic recovery."

69. "300 City Leaders Form Boston Urban Coalition," *Boston Herald-Traveler* (March 23, 1968).

70. See Schrag, 172.

71. The idea of school-community cooperation was not new in 1968. Two years earlier, Boston adopted a new organizational structure with six assistant superintendents whose responsibilities were assigned by neighborhood rather than grade level. See William H. Ohrenberger, *Annual Report of the Superintendent* (1967), 11. "The administration of the Boston public schools was decentralized on September 1, 1966, with the appointment of six assistant superintendents. Each was assigned a geographic area of the city having approximately 16,000 students and 750 teachers. The broad purpose of decentralization is to provide a close relationship between the administration, the schools, and the community." This decentralization process led to the consolidation (and isolation) of particular programs in particular neighborhoods under the direction of particular assistant superintendents.

72. School Committee of the City of Boston, *An Alliance for Educational Progress: Application for a Planning and Operational Grant under Title III, Central Cities Task Force* (May 13, 1968). Though funded by federal aid under HEW, the School-Community Advisory Council emphasized "local control."

73. School Committee of the City of Boston, *An Alliance for Educational Progress* (May 13, 1968), 3–4, iii, ii.

74. See "Hub's Title I School Plans Lack Approval," *Christian Science Monitor* (August 16, 1968).

75. See "Suit Threatened On School Aid," *Boston Herald* (September 7, 1968) and "$154,000 U.S. Grant to Aid Hub Schools," *Boston Advertiser* (August 25, 1968).

76. "Hub's Title I School Plans Lack Approval," *Christian Science Monitor* (August 16, 1968).

77. Schrag, 173.

78. Quoted in Jeffrey, 156. See also Civil Rights Commission, *Racial Isolation in the Public Schools* (February 20, 1967), quoted in Jeffrey, 153.

79. The conflict between racial integration and special-compensatory programs persisted throughout the late 1960s. See Schrag, 42–43. Black leaders, Schrag noted, "have not really made themselves felt, in spite of the growing population of the Negro community, because they are not sure—and this is true within the Negro protest movement at large—whether to demand equality or special opportunity, whether to ask for compensatory or parity education. Many Negroes in Roxbury are as opposed to busing for example, as are the Dorchester whites, a sentiment that the neighborhood [school] advocates have often quoted against the civil rights people. Many Negroes are not certain whether to ask for a high quality academic program oriented to college admission or to follow the 'realists' who insist that the major thrust be devoted to relevant vocational education and to developing job opportunities for skilled Negro labor. They are divided on the proper degree of militancy, with CORE generally at a radical extreme and the middle-class members of the NAACP at the other; they are not certain what makes all-Negro schools *per se* inferior to all-white ones (assuming good faith on the part of the administration in allocating resources), are not certain what racial imbalance really means, and are emphatically confused on ways to achieve it in Boston."

80. See Mark Goldberg, "An Interview with Harold 'Doc' Howe II: 'Stirring the Pot,'" *Phi Delta Kappan,* http://www.pdkintl.org/kappan/kgol0010.htm: "When Richard Nixon spoke in the South in the fall of 1968 in his bid for the presidency, the opening line of most speeches was a promise to fire Harold Howe."

81. See Paul E. Peterson and Barry G. Rabe, "The Role of Interest Groups in the Formation of Educational Policy: Past Practice and Future Trends," *Teachers College Record* 84:3 (Spring 1983), 708–32.

Chapter Four

1. Quoted in "Sullivan Proposal: Ask U.S. Aid for Ghetto Schools," *Boston Herald Record* (June 28, 1969).

2. "Sullivan Made Integration Work," *Boston Globe* (n.d.); newspaper clipping in the files of the Beebe Communications Library, Boston University. Regarding the lack of consensus in Boston on the desirability of racial integration, Sullivan said, "I will not wait for a consensus to develop. . . . The cities will burn before a consensus develops. It is the job of leaders to mold a consensus."

3. Quoted in "Wolfeboro Publisher Still Making Difference," *New Hampshire Union Leader and Sunday News* (May 24, 2002). See also Neil V. Sullivan, *Bound for Freedom: An Educator's Adventures in Prince Edward County, Virginia* (Boston: Little, Brown, and Co., 1965).

4. For more information on Sullivan's busing program in Berkeley, see "Busing—A Symposium," *Ramparts* 13 (1975), 38–48. See also Neil V. Sullivan, "Implementing Equal Educational Opportunity," *Harvard Educational Review* (Winter 1968).

5. The most famous of the voluntary urban-suburban busing agreements was the Metropolitan Council for Educational Opportunity program, or METCO, program. For more information on METCO, see Susan E. Eaton, *The Other Boston Busing Story: What's Won and Lost Across the Boundary Line* (New Haven: Yale University Press, 2001).

6. See *U.S. News and World Report* (March 10, 1969), quoted in "Say It Isn't So, Mr. Finch," *Boston Globe* (March 12, 1969).

7. "Busing Success Story," *New York Times* (n.d.); newspaper clipping in the files of the Beebe Communications Library, Boston University. In the Pasadena desegregation case, *Spangler v. Pasadena City Board of Education*, the U.S. Supreme Court relied heavily on *Hobson v. Hansen* (and its successor, *Smuck v. Hobson*) to rule that black parents had a constitutional right to demand equal educational opportunities for their children but not a right to demand a *specific* plan of racial integration. In other words, parents could not demand cross-district busing per se as the best way to foster desegregation. See *Spangler v. United States* 415 F.2d 1242 (1969) and *Spangler v. Pasadena City Board of Education* 427 F.2d 1352 (1970).

8. See David R. Jackson, *My Long Island Memories and More*, http://www.angelfire.com/ny5/limemories/JamesEAllen/JEAtheman.html.

9. Quoted in Jerome T. Murphy, "Title I of ESEA: The Politics of Implementing Federal Education Reform," *Harvard Educational Review* 40:4 (February 1971), 46.

10. "An Interview with James Allen," *Harvard Educational Review* 40:4 (November 1970), 536–37, 539.

11. Washington Research Project, *Title I of ESEA: Is It Helping Poor Children?* (Washington, D.C., 1969). See also "Are Boston Schools Passing Title I Test?" *Christian Science Monitor* (April 22, 1970), "Amid national reports that federal money from Title I of the Elementary and Secondary Education Act is being flagrantly misused, the 18 Boston public 'Title I' schools continue the attempt to upgrade their education level with the funds."

12. Murphy, 55. See also Julie Roy Jeffrey, *Education for Children of the Poor: A Study of the Origins and Implementation of the Elementary and Secondary Education Act of 1965* (Columbus: Ohio State University Press, 1978), 120: "Although [the ESEA] required states to evaluate their programs periodically and to report [evaluation results] to the [federal] commissioner of education, no one pushed this requirement. Massachusetts, for example, never fulfilled its obligations under the law. The [federal] Office of Education . . .

was hesitant to push for evaluations, realizing that these might show the act was not working and, thus, would provide the enemies of federal aid with political ammunition."

13. In 1967, the Boston public schools created a new office of research and evaluation specifically to track the effectiveness of special-compensatory programs. See William H. Ohrenberger, *Annual Report of the Superintendent* (1967), 27.

14. Quoted in Murphy, 56. In 1969, Boston put all its Title I programs under the supervision of a single department. See William H. Ohrenberger, *Annual Report of the Superintendent* (1969), no page numbers.

15. See "New Focus in Hub School Changes," *Boston Globe* (November 11, 1969).

16. Murphy, 56.

17. See Council of Chief State School Officers, "Development of Special Conference Report" (June 22-24, 1967). See also Murphy, 43-44: "Since the beginning of the program [Title I], evaluation has been high on the list of federal rhetorical priorities, but low on the list of actual USOE priorities. . . . The matter is further complicated by the lack of agreement on what would prove whether Title I is 'working.' . . . If one views the program primarily as a vehicle to provide fiscal relief for a city school system, achievement test scores are hardly an appropriate way to measure success; the program is successful if fiscal collapse is avoided. The legislation, however, calls for objective measures, and if they show that children are not gaining in achievement, it makes it difficult for congressmen to justify their continued support of the program. At the same time, it is politically dangerous to be opposed to program evaluation. Therefore, inconclusive evaluations are politically acceptable, although they may provoke rhetorical wrath in the Congress and exasperation in the Executive agencies."

18. All quotations in Jeffrey, 131, 130. The National Advisory Council on the Education of Disadvantaged Children was created with funds from the ESEA.

19. Quoted in Murphy, 41.

20. Jeffrey, 125.

21. Stephen K. Bailey and Edith K. Mosher, *ESEA: The Office of Education Administers a Law* (Syracuse, N.Y.: Syracuse University Press, 1968).

22. Quoted in Jeffrey, 128.

23. Quoted in Jennings, "Title I: Its Legislative History and Its Promise," *Phi Delta Kappan* (March 2000), 516-22.

24. Murphy, 54.

25. See Daniel C. Jordan and Kathryn Hecht Spiess, "Compensatory Education in Massachusetts: An Evaluation with Recommendations" (March 1970), 48: "In the case of Title I and other federally funded programs, a considerable amount of financial support could be made available without even increasing the current budgets simply by using all that has been allocated rather than sending back large unused amounts to Washington."

26. See "Are Boston Schools Passing Title I Test?" *Christian Science Monitor* (April 22, 1970).

27. Jordan and Spiess, 4-5.

28. See Lee Spoull and David Wolf, *Organizing an Anarchy: Belief, Bureaucracy, and Politics in the National Institute of Education* (Chicago: University of Chicago Press, 1984).

29. "An Interview with James Allen," 535.

30. See Task Force on Children Out of School, *The Way We Go To School: The Exclusion of Children in Boston* (Boston: Beacon Press, 1970).

31. Task Force on Children Out of School, 5.

32. Ibid., *ii*.

33. Ibid., 54–55, 70. "Instead of mobilizing to meet the educational needs of various groups of children, the [Boston] School Department places the onus upon the children to fit into the existing school structure. Hence, the School Department excludes so many children because it demands that they conform to its image, while ignoring its moral and legal mandate to provide an education for them all."

34. Ibid., 70.

35. See Susan Gilbert Schneider, *Revolution, Reaction, or Reform: The 1974 Bilingual Education Act* (New York: Las Americas Publishing Company, 1976), 40.

36. J. Stanley Pottinger to School Districts with More Than Five Percent National Origin-Minority Group Children (Washington, D.C.: U.S. Office of Civil Rights, May 25, 1970).

37. See Herbert Teitlebaum and Richard J. Hiller, "Bilingual Education: The Legal Mandate," *Harvard Educational Review* 47:2 (May 1977), 141–42. The litigation in *Lau* began before Pottinger's memo of May 25, 1970; indeed, the federal district court's ruling in the case appeared the following day, May 26, 1970. See unreported district court opinion, Civil No. C-70, 627 LHB (N.D. Cal. May 26, 1970) and *Lau v. Nichols*, 483 F.2d 791, 793 (1973).

38. See Teitlebaum and Hiller, 143–44. "The lower courts had ruled that offering identical services to all children is sufficient to meet the strictures of the Equal Protection Clause and implicitly of Title VI, even though students actually received disparate benefits because of significant differences in their opportunities to take advantage of those services. Rejecting this analysis, the Supreme Court relied on the Title VI regulations and guidelines which speak to equality in the offering and receipt of benefits: 'It seems obvious that the Chinese-speaking minority receives fewer benefits than the English-speaking majority from respondents' school system which denies them a meaningful opportunity to participate in the educational program—all earmarks of discrimination banned by the regulations.' A critical underpinning of the Court's decision was a memorandum issued by HEW on May 25, 1970, regarding children of national-origin minority groups with limited English-language skills. The memorandum informed school districts that they must take affirmative steps to rectify English-language deficiencies—steps that would go beyond providing the same books and teachers to all pupils. The Court reinforced this requirement. Construing Title VI broadly, it found that the statute proscribes treating different people identically when the results will be unidentical."

39. Quoted in Schneider, 29.

40. See Charles Glenn and Ivonne LaLayre, "Integrated Bilingual Education" in Massachusetts Department of Education, *Two-Way Integrated Bilingual Education* (April 1990). "In 1970, the federal government agency responsible for civil rights issued guidelines to all school districts in the nation with five percent or more linguistic minority pupils, on the basis of language in the 1964 Civil Rights Act prohibiting discrimination or segregation on the basis of national origin as well as of race. For the first time, an *instructional* goal—remedying English-language deficiencies—was defined as a *civil rights* obligation."

41. In *Lau,* the U.S. Supreme Court did not advocate any particular form of instruction for non-English-speakers, nor did it weigh the relative merits of integrated versus isolated programs. See Teitlebaum and Hiller, 144. "Although bilingual education was the relief originally demanded in the complaint, by the time *Lau* reached the Ninth Circuit Court, this request for specific relief had been abandoned, and all that was sought was effective affirmative steps on the part of the school district. The Supreme Court opinion did not mandate a specific approach to teaching national-origin students with

English-language problems. As Justice Douglas noted at the outset of the Court's opinion: 'No specific remedy is urged upon us. Teaching English to the students of Chinese ancestry who do not speak the language is one choice. Giving instruction to this group in Chinese is another. There may be others. Petitioners ask only that the Board of Education be directed to apply its expertise to the problem and rectify the situation.'"

42. Task Force on Children Out of School, 17.

43. J. Stanley Pottinger to School Districts with More Than Five Percent National Origin-Minority Group Children (Washington, D.C.: U.S. Office of Civil Rights, May 25, 1970).

44. The issue of numbers—or "numerosity"—was central to the debate over non-English-speaking students' right to bilingual education. Civil rights usually apply to citizens on an *individual* basis, but Pottinger's memo required local school districts to provide bilingual programs only when twenty or more students from a particular language group were enrolled. The idea of a numerical threshold of twenty students went unchallenged in the Supreme Court's *Lau* ruling. See Stephen R. Applewhite, "The Legal Dialect of Bilingual Education" in Raymond V. Padilla, ed., *Bilingual Education and Public Policy in the United States* (Ypsilanti, Mich.: Easter Michigan University Press, 1979).

45. "'Showdown' Pupil Tour Tomorrow," *Boston Herald* (September 30, 1970).

46. See "Hub Children Census Set," *Boston Herald* (November 18, 1970).

47. "Third of Spanish Speakers Out of School," *Boston Globe* (November 19, 1970).

48. Task Force on Children Out of School, 72, 73, 75.

49. "Schools 'Can't Afford' Spanish Aid," *Boston Globe* (November 18, 1970).

50. See Teitlebaum and Hiller, 156-57. "Even where school districts can show that bilingual programs require additional expenditures, the budget defense may not hold. Federal rights are not to be denied or deferred because of budget constraints, whether the rights flow from the Constitution or, like the claimed rights under *Lau*, from a federal statutory guarantee of equal educational opportunity. . . . When a district claims that insufficient resources preclude instruction in a language that students understand, there may be grounds for a reordering of expenditures. Items of less educational importance may have to yield to programs necessary to meet effectively the mandate of Title VI."

51. "Schools 'Can't Afford' Spanish Aid," *Boston Globe* (November 18, 1970).

52. See Walter Rosly, "Proposal for Bilingual-Transitional Clusters Within Boston Public School Districts" (Boston: Educational Development Center, 1969). See also Task Force on Children Out of School, 19. In making a case for bilingual education as a necessary component of equal educational opportunity for non-English-speakers, the Task Force relied on Boston's own application for Title VII aid in 1968, in which the school committee acknowledged that "the Spanish-speaking child finds himself in a classroom where the total curricula, methods, and medium of language are geared toward the native English speaker," and added, "it is unrealistic for us to suppose that, if we then place a number of non-English-speakers in this urban classroom, the teachers can meet the special needs of these children."

53. "10,000 Barred From Schools, Panel Charges," *Boston Herald* (October 14, 1970).

54. See an untitled *Boston Herald* clipping dated January 24, 1971, located in the files of the Beebe Communications Library, Boston University.

55. See Massachusetts Department of Education, "The New Bilingual Law and Beyond" (Boston, 1972).

56. Quoted in "Bilingual Classes Are Law This Fall," *Boston Globe* (July 31, 1972).

57. See Cumner and Greenwood, IV-58. One Boston elementary school noted that

virtually the "whole school is bilingual because Title VII target classrooms constitute most of the school anyway."

58. See Teitlebaum and Hiller, 157. Teitlebaum and Hiller noted that "school officials should bear in mind that a failure to reallocate resources [toward bilingual education] could ultimately result in a cutoff of federal assistance for noncompliance with Title VI. Thus, to deny non-English-speaking students their *Lau* rights on the grounds of fiscal plight may only reduce further the local education budget."

59. William H. Ohrenberger, *Annual Report of the Superintendent* (1972), no page numbers.

60. See "Latin Pupils Treated Fairly, 2 Educators Say," *Boston Herald Record* (January 21, 1972).

61. Massachusetts Advisory Committee to U.S. Commission on Civil Rights, *Issues of Concern to Puerto Ricans in Boston and Springfield* (February 1972; written in May 1971), 113, 11. "Federal funds from Title VII support most of the bilingual education programs in Springfield and Boston. For 1971-72, Boston will receive $175,225 to run seven bilingual classes."

62. See Cumner and Greenwood, IV-55. Often, after spending time in an isolated and racially homogeneous bilingual cluster, students were reluctant to join racially diverse English-speaking classrooms: "One parent we interviewed noted a related problem with the half-day transitional programs. She complained that in some Bay City transitional programs (in which only persons of non-English-background participate), the kids resist leaving the comfortable fold of the transitional program to attend half-day regular classes such as art and social studies."

63. Brenda Beelar, "Schools for the City: The New Bilingual Law—and Beyond," Model Cities Bulletin 2 (Massachusetts Department of Education, Bureau of Equal Educational Opportunities, January 1972), 6, 9-10.

64. Quoted in "Latin Pupils Treated Fairly, 2 Educators Say," *Boston Herald Record* (January 21, 1972).

65. William H. Ohrenberger, *Annual Report of the Superintendent* (1972), no page numbers. See also Massachusetts Department of Education, "Two Way Integrated Bilingual Education" (Boston, April 1990), 79. The Raphael Hernandez Elementary School was built with federal assistance under the Model Cities Program. It was founded by "a group of parents, community leaders and educators . . . to provide good quality bilingual education to a growing Latin American population. Although accommodated in cramped quarters attached to the Boston Public Schools' central kitchen, the academic reputation of the school improved steadily."

66. William H. Ohrenberger, *Annual Report of the Superintendent* (1972), no page numbers.

67. In Boston, community activists supported bilingual education, but general parent opinion was hard to gauge. Many parents evidently preferred integrated English instruction to isolated bilingual instruction. See, for example, "Third of Spanish Speakers Out of School," *Boston Globe* (November 19, 1970), "The survey, conducted by the Action for Boston Community Development, . . . has produced several other tentative insights into the city's Spanish-speaking community: Most Spanish-speaking parents prefer to have their youngsters taught entirely in English rather than by bilingual instructors." Despite this preference for integrated English instruction, Chapter 71A permitted schools to place students in isolated bilingual clusters without their parents' consent. As Brenda Beelar noted, state regulations stipulated only that "the school committee shall notify the parents or legal guardians of the students enrolled in the program no later

than 10 days after the student is enrolled. The notification of enrollment must be both in English and in the native language of the parents or guardian and must include the following information: (1) a clear statement of the purpose, method, and content of the transitional bilingual education program; (2) a statement of parental rights which shall include: (a) visits to the transitional bilingual classes; (b) conferences with school personnel; and (c) [the] right to withdraw the student at any time upon written notification to the school authorities." See Beelar, 10.

68. "HEW Report Could Cost Hub $10 Million in U.S. School Aid," *Boston Globe* (November 30, 1971).

69. See Cumner and Greenwood, IV-66, 70.

70. Untitled *Boston Herald* newspaper clipping dated 24 January 1971, located in the files of the Beebe Communications Library, Boston University. See also Cumner and Greenwood, IV-61-IV-62. "During the third year [1971-72], a major change was mandated by the federal program office when they began to worry about the segregation effect [of bilingual classes]. At this time, they required the Bay City project to include at least 40 percent Anglos [in each bilingual class]. Although that ratio has not persisted, the project has remained open to native English speakers." In order to meet the federal requirement for 40 percent "Anglo" students, many schools counted black English-speakers as "Anglos." As the *Boston Herald* noted, "English-speaking students, largely black children from the area, were placed in the bilingual classes." See untitled *Boston Herald* clipping dated January 24, 1971. Yet, when it became clear that "Anglos" did not have to be white—but, rather, only English-speaking—many Hispanic parents began to put their second-generation, English-speaking children into bilingual programs. Cumner and Greenwood explained that "in the fifth year, . . . Hispanic parents were putting their non-Spanish-speaking kids into the program to learn fluency in Spanish. . . . They come into the attendance area and opt for a bilingual program . . . even though they may be native English speakers." When only minority students—both English-speaking and non-English-speaking—were placed in bilingual programs, however, it was easier to charge that their placement (and, thus, their isolation, or segregation, from predominantly white, English-speaking classes) was based *not* on language needs but, rather, on race.

71. See Teitlebaum and Hiller, 161-62. Federal regulations prohibited the use of Title VII funds to teach "foreign languages" to English speakers, so, technically, the inclusion of English-speaking students in Title VII-funded bilingual classes was illegal.

72. "HEW Report Could Cost Hub $10 Mill in U.S. School Aid," *Boston Globe* (November 30, 1971). See also Teitlebaum and Hiller, 160. According to Teitlebaum and Hiller, concentrating bilingual programs in racially imbalanced schools did not necessarily constitute racial discrimination. "Both HEW's 1968 regulations for the Bilingual Education Act and the May 25, 1970, HEW memorandum bar 'segregation and separate treatment,' but neither should be read as precluding bilingual programs in schools that are predominantly minority-attended. What they prohibit are programs that fail to rectify English-language deficiencies and instead separate and exclude students. The *Lau* remedies interdict the creation and, arguably, the perpetuation of ethnically identifiable schools in order to meet the special language needs of children of national-origin minority groups. But they do not forbid maintaining existing bilingual program in ethnically identifiable schools which have not been created or maintained through unlawful practices."

73. See Massachusetts State Advisory Committee to U.S. Commission on Civil Rights, *Issues of Concern to Puerto Ricans in Boston and Springfield* (February 1972), 12. According to this report, "in 1970-71, Boston spent $346,000 or 7.2 percent of its total Title I

budget on ESL." The average federal per-pupil allocation was $300 annually for Title I ESL programs and $750 annually for Title VII bilingual programs.

74. Murphy, 48. "One of the critical issues addressed in the original draft guidelines was the concentration of limited resources for a limited number of students. USOE officials believed that, if Title I was to have any impact, the money could not be spread thin."

75. See U.S. Office of Education, *The Effectiveness of Compensatory Education: Summary and Review of the Evidence* (Washington, D.C.: Department of Health, Education, and Welfare, 1972), 13. "We know that federal compensatory education has not been effective as a whole."

76. Murphy, 41.

77. Murphy, 41, 45, 57–58.

78. See Murphy, 58–59. "As we saw earlier with the HEW audits, USOE has been quite reluctant to take any action even when the purported violations [of federal education directives] were blatant. In fact, not only are incentives [for compliance] missing, but federal efforts to persuade the states to follow the federal directives have been almost nonexistent. The Massachusetts Department [of Education] for the most part does not hear from USOE except for occasional memoranda, and USOE is looked upon mainly as a consultant. The Massachusetts Title I director states: 'USOE provides technical and administrative assistance. They are helpful. . . . They won't come out flatly and say what you can't do. I don't feel any kind of control. It just isn't there.'"

79. Tyll van Geel, "Evaluation and Federalism" (Special Qualifying Paper, Harvard Graduate School of Education, April 1970), 34, quoted in Murphy, 60.

80. See Schrag, 142–43. "The tragedy of Boston is that the best, the most earnest, the most intelligent efforts defeat themselves. The Racial Imbalance Law is directed to the wrong targets; the independent schools [such as the bilingual-transitional clusters]— even in the talking stage—to the wrong people; the busing programs to the wrong children and the wrong places. All of them represent diligent, sincere efforts to alleviate some of the city's most vexing problems; yet all of them, in a situation of incredible complexity, are likely to exacerbate the very problems they are supposed to solve. . . . The city's schools are now 25 percent Negro; the elementary schools are 28 percent Negro, and the lower grades are over 30 percent Negro. Any insistence on arbitrary acts of balancing [in a few schools] will merely accelerate imbalance [in other schools and, ultimately, in the system in general], just as it has in other cities; and to demand balance in a community where the public schools may become predominantly Negro . . . is absurd."

81. Schneider, 40.

82. See National Advisory Council on the Education of Disadvantaged Children (NACEDC), "Educating the Disadvantaged Child: Where We Stand" (Washington, D.C., 1972), 23–24. "The NACEDC has identified a major problem in the implementation of Title I services to eligible children who are dispersed as a result of desegregation plans. The choices are clear: serve the same children with diluted programs; do not serve the same children who were being served before the desegregation plan became effective; or, resegregate the same eligible population being served for a portion of the school day. This is not a theoretical crisis, but a practical experience of the school year 1971–72. . . . Current regulations stipulate that funds be concentrated on those children determined to be 'most in need' of special assistance. If such children are diffused among a number of classrooms as the result of a desegregation plan, [T]itle I services cannot be provided to them without the school's being guilty of (1) 'general aid' violation, i.e., extending compensatory services to *all* children in the classrooms, or (2) resegregating [T]itle I children for some length of time in order that they exclusively may receive such services."

83. For more on Kevin White, see George V. Higgins, *Style versus Substance: Boston's Kevin White and the Politics of Illusion* (New York: Macmillan Co., 1985); Alan Lupo, *Liberty's Chosen Home: The Politics of Violence in Boston* (Boston: Little, Brown, and Co., 1977), 97–121; and Barbara Ferman, *Governing the Ungovernable City: Political Skill, Leadership, and the Modern Mayor* (Philadelphia: Temple University Press, 1985).

Chapter Five

1. Herbert Teitlebaum and Richard J. Hiller, "Bilingual Education: The Legal Mandate," *Harvard Educational Review* 47:2 (May 1977), 160–61. Classifying non-English-speaking students as an "ability group" did not prevent schools from putting these students into different educational tracks, thus creating "ability groups within ability groups." See Gerald C. Cumner and Peter W. Greenwood, "Bay City" in *Federal Programs Supporting Educational Change, Vol. III: The Process of Change, Appendix C. Innovations in Bilingual Education;* R-1589/3-HEW (April 1975), IV-59. "One of the problems at Newton [a pseudonym] was the diverse ability levels of the kids for various language arts subjects. For this reason, they developed seven ability levels in the bilingual program for language arts, and kids spend part of their day grouped accordingly."

2. See Burton Blatt and Frank Garfunkel, *Massachusetts Study of Educational Opportunities for Handicapped and Disadvantaged Children* (Massachusetts Advisory Council on Education, January 1971), 23. "One of the focal points [of this study] was the issue of integration, the question being, 'Is integration justifiable for its own sake?' It was decided that if the quality of the regular educational program is not as high as that in the special class, then the integration of this child into the mainstream is not only questionable but, more importantly, might even be detrimental."

3. Task Force on Children Out of School, *The Way We Go to School: The Exclusion of Children in Boston* (Boston: Beacon Press, 1970), 74–75.

4. Task Force on Children Out of School, 71. See also Harriet T. Bernstein and Daniel W. Merenda, "Categorical Programs: Past and Present," in Robert A. Miller, ed. *The Federal Role in Education: New Directions for the Eighties* (Washington: Institute for Educational Leadership, 1981), 67. "It is ironic that some poor minority children with normal intelligence are being pulled out of regular classes several times a day to partake of various supplementary services while some handicapped children with a degree of mental insufficiency are sitting in regular classrooms all day. Such a conceptual nightmare begs for some thoughtful consideration by the best thinkers in the nation."

5. The issue of biased testing came to the fore in 1970, when a federal district court in California ruled in the case of *Diana v. California State Board of Education,* Civil No. 70-37 RFP (N.D. Calif. 1970), that schools could not place students in isolated classes on the basis of (1) culturally-biased tests or (2) tests given in a language the students did not understand.

6. Task Force on Children Out of School, 70, 56. According to the Task Force, "the very machinery—'special services'—which is supposed to help children do well in the regular classroom often functions in their removal from the classroom. Special programs become the vehicle through which children who don't 'fit in' are removed from the regular classroom and often from school altogether."

7. See Task Force on Children Out of School, 5. The need to document a uniform distribution of disability in the general population led the Task Force to stress the existence of disabilities in every segment of society, including white and middle-class families from the suburbs. Disability, the Task Force asserted, "is not the problem of one partic-

ular neighborhood, or race, or social group. Rather, it transcends cultural, social, and economic boundaries. Parents and citizens in the North End, South Boston, Roxbury, and all other parts of Boston, share the same problem."

8. See *Stewart v. Phillips*, Civil No. 70-1199-F (D. Mass, February 8, 1971), reprinted in Harvard University Center for Law and Education, *Classification Materials* (Cambridge, MA, 1972), 234.

9. Shortly after the filing of *Stewart v. Phillips*, a similar case emerged in California. See *Larry P. v. Riles* 345 F. Supp. 1306 (N.D. Calif. 1972), affirmed 502 F. 2nd 963 (9th Cir. 1974). In this case, the court found IQ tests to be racially discriminatory and prohibited schools from using them to place black students in classes for the mentally retarded.

10. For more on the origins of *Stewart v. Phillips*, see Milton Budoff, "Engendering Change in Special Education Practices," *Harvard Educational Review* 45:4 (November 1975), 509-12.

11. See Budoff, 509-12; 513-14.

12. See David L. Kirp, "Student Classification, Public Policy, and the Courts," *Harvard Educational Review* 44:1 (1974), 21. "A challenge to tracking on grounds that it impairs equality of educational opportunity may well be a disguised demand that schools eliminate disparities between student outcomes. The difficulty with that demand is simply that it cannot be accomplished through any educationally sound and administratively feasible remedy presently available. Since individuals' capabilities clearly differ, it would be a cruel hoax, a 'deceit of equality,' to premise a challenge to tracking on the argument that tracking caused school failure, implicitly promising that the educational differences would vanish if tracking were done away with." In sum, Kirp concluded, "tracking should not be judicially abolished unless harm can be empirically demonstrated."

13. *Pennsylvania Association for Retarded Children (PARC) v. Pennsylvania*, 343 F. Supp. 279 (E.D. Pa. 1972). See also Leopold Lippman and Ignacy Goldberg, *Right to Education: Anatomy of the Pennsylvania Case and Its Implications for Exceptional Children* (New York: Teachers College Press, 1973).

14. *Mills v. Board of Education*, 348 F.Supp. 866 (D. D.C., 1972). It was not clear in *Mills* whether the "equitable" expenditure of resources would be measured according to flat dollar figures or the educational outcomes of specific groups of students, that is, whether disabled students would be entitled to *more* resources than their nondisabled peers in order to ensure "equitable" educational results.

15. *Association for Mentally Ill Children v. Greenblatt*, Civil Action No. 71-3074-J (D.C. Mass, filed December 30, 1971); *Barnett v. Goldman*, Civil Action 71-3074 (S.D. Mass, filed July 1974), quoted in Alan Abeson and Nancy Bolick, eds. "A Continuing Summary of Pending and Completed Litigation Regarding the Education of Handicapped Children" (Washington, D.C.: Council for Exceptional Children, December, 1974), 12-13.

16. *Mills v. Board of Education*, 348 F.Supp. 866 (D. D.C., 1972).

17. *Barnett v. Goldman* was decided in 1974. A year earlier, the U.S. Supreme Court ruled in *San Antonio Independent School District v. Rodriguez* 411 U.S. 1 (1973) that public education was not, in fact, a "fundamental right" guaranteed or enumerated in the U.S. Constitution. Attorneys for the plaintiff in *Barnett v. Goldman* probably chose to define education as a fundamental right because of a widely publicized ruling in California's state supreme court, *Serrano v. Priest*, 5 Cal. 3d 584; 487 P.2d 1241 (August 30, 1971). For more on *Rodriguez* and *Serrano*, see chapter 6.

18. For more on the question of education as a fundamental right, particularly for the disabled, see Rosemary C. Salomone, *Equal Education Under Law: Legal Rights and Federal Policy in the Post-Brown Era* (New York: St. Martin's Press, 1986), 139-40, 237. "It is

noteworthy that in both *PARC* and *Mills*, the courts sidestepped the issue of whether the handicapped constitute a suspect class or whether education is a fundamental right and thereby avoided strict scrutiny analysis. The courts upheld the plaintiffs' claims even under the less stringent rational basis test. The denial of educational services was not reasonably related to any legitimate governmental interest, not even the avoidance of undue financial burdens. . . . It is also noteworthy that neither decision required any particular substantive level of education but merely held that handicapped children must be given access to an appropriate (*PARC*) or adequate (*Mills*) publicly supported education. Ten years later, the Supreme Court picked up this standard of adequacy in an effort to define the parameters of the *appropriate education* provisions of federal legislation (*Board of Education of the Hendrick Hudson Central School District v. Rowley*)." For more on *Rowley*, see chapter 8.

19. See Kirp, "Student Classification, Public Policy, and the Courts," 19. "Challenges to within-school placements pose . . . difficult constitutional problems. They demand that the court weigh the different benefits and costs associated with varied educational approaches, a task usually—and quite properly—left to educators. The difficulty is compounded because the balancing process is riddled with ambiguity. If, for example, few students return from special to regular classes, does the explanation [for their continued isolation] lie with the structure of the educational offering or the capacities of the child?"

20. William H. Ohrenberger, *Annual Report of the Superintendent* (1972), no page numbers.

21. See Lorraine M. McDonnell, Margaret J. McLaughlin, and Patricia Morison, eds., *Educating One and All: Students With Disabilities and Standards-Based Reform* (Washington, D.C.: National Academy Press, 1997), 60. "Generally, the courts have held that the least restrictive environment mandate is secondary to provision of an appropriate program and services, and that both program and placement decisions should be individualized. Thus, the degree of integration into general education is intertwined with determinations of what the educational goals should be and whether specialized services can be effectively provided in general education environments."

22. See Budoff, 515.

23. Emphasis added. Chapter 766 was signed into law on July 18, 1972. It created Chapter 71B of the Massachusetts General Laws but was popularly known as Chapter 766.

24. See Budoff, 522, 525.

25. Many of the problems surrounding Chapter 766 stemmed from the fact that the new law failed to specify the meaning of *disability;* thus, virtually any student could qualify for special educational services. See Budoff, 516: "With the emphasis on labeling removed, [Chapter] 766 opens the way for a dramatic expansion of eligibility for special services. The law takes the radical step of dealing with all children in actual or potential educational risk. Thus if a child is in danger at midyear of not being promoted, or indeed fails, he or she can be referred for services."

26. Budoff, 523-24. See also William H. Ohrenberger, *Annual Report of the Boston Public Schools* (1972), no page numbers. "It was an unusually busy year for Boston's staff of 23 school psychologists. They were mandated to give top priority to appraisal of all special class children who were to be tested for integration into regular classes." Because the diagnosticians were poorly trained, it was unlikely that these new diagnoses would be any better than the old diagnoses. According to Budoff, "the school psychometrists had little formal clinical training in dealing with special needs children and as a result commonly administered only routine achievement and intelligence tests. . . . The

DEIM's response to the suit [*Stewart v. Phillips*] was largely cosmetic: the testers, formerly known as research assistants, were renamed 'psychologists'" (512–13).

27. See William H. Ohrenberger, *Annual Report of the Boston Public Schools* (1972). "The new John Marshall, Joseph Lee, and Dennis C. Haley schools which opened in September, 1971, already are well-established as true examples of *Tomorrow's Schools Today*. . . . They join the nationally known William Monroe Trotter Elementary School, opened in 1969, to illustrate that, while modern construction provides the superb setting, no school becomes [a] good school without superior planning. That planning placed emphasis on designing programs to fit the individual needs of children, rather than requiring them to adapt themselves to pre-structured programs. Testing, long valued as a measure of achievement, was extended to what is perhaps its most important use as a basis for designing personalized learning programs."

28. The racially imbalanced Marshall School faced a similar dilemma with respect to its federally funded remedial-reading program. See William H. Ohrenberger, *Annual Report of the Boston Public Schools* (1972), no page numbers.

29. In 1972, federal aid to Boston's public schools included $8,817,298 under Title I; $145,371 under Title II; more than $500,000 under Title III; $33,645 under Title VI; $100,914 under the NDEA; $176,046 for vocational education; roughly $100,000 for career education; and $643,976 for impact aid. See *Morgan v. Hennigan* 379 F. Supp. 410 (1974).

30. The effects of federal housing policies on residential segregation was well known. See Boston Urban Study Group, *Who Rules Boston? A Citizen's Guide to Reclaiming the City* (Boston: Institute for Democratic Socialism, 1984), 18–19. "Real estate brokers and speculators scared away white homeowners in several neighborhoods with 'block-busting' tactics—starting rumors that blacks were about to 'invade' the neighborhood—leading to a rapid racial turnover. The most notorious example was the Boston Banks Urban Renewal Group (BBURG), a consortium of 22 local banks which, for several years after 1968, dumped over $28 million worth of federally-insured mortgage loans into the pockets of speculators in Dorchester and Mattapan. The BBURG program was advertised as a way to 'cool' tensions in the black community, following two revolts in Roxbury in 1968, by promoting black homeownership through mortgages guaranteed by the Federal Housing Administration (FHA). But, instead of allowing Black families to buy homes wherever they wanted, the BBURG loans were confined to houses in certain neighborhoods, particularly white areas of Dorchester and Mattapan. As revealed in a series of exposes in the *Globe* (September 1–2, 1974), realtors frightened whites into leaving; speculators then paid less, and black families paid more, for their new homes. The banks profited by being able to make more than $20 million in guaranteed high-interest loans, insured by the federal government."

31. The events surrounding the opening of the Joseph Lee School in 1971 were complex. See "The Lee School Incident" in Center for Law and Education, *A Study of the Massachusetts Racial Imbalance Act* (Cambridge, Mass.: Harvard University, February 1972), 306–9.

32. An extraordinary number of works have addressed the case of *Morgan v. Hennigan* and its aftermath. See, for example, U.S. Commission on Civil Rights, *Desegregating the Boston Public Schools: A Crisis in Civic Responsibility* (Washington, D.C.: Government Printing Office, 1976); Jon Hillson, *The Battle of Boston: Busing and the Struggle for School Desegregation* (New York: Pathfinder Press, 1977); Robert A. Dentler and Marvin B. Scott, *Schools on Trial: An Inside Account of the Boston Case* (Cambridge, Mass.: Abt Books, 1981); Charles V .Willie and Susan L. Greenblatt, eds., *Community Politics and Educa-*

tional Change: Ten School Systems under Court Order (New York: Longman Press, 1981); Richard H. Buell Jr. with Richard A. Brisbin Jr., *School Desegregation and Defended Neighborhoods: The Boston Controversy* (Lexington, Mass.: D.C. Heath and Co., 1982); J. Brian Sheehan, *The Boston School Integration Dispute: Social Change and Legal Maneuvers* (New York: Columbia University Press, 1984); and Ronald P. Formisano, *Boston Against Busing: Race, Class, and Ethnicity in the 1960s and 1970s* (Chapel Hill: University of North Carolina Press, 1991).

33. The relevance of the Trotter School remained unclear throughout the trial. Some attributed its purported success to racial balance achieved through busing. Others attributed its success to Title I funds that paid for well-designed and well-staffed special-compensatory programs. Still others argued that the Trotter School was not a model of "success" at all. See, for example, Pamela Bullard and Judith Stoia, *The Hardest Lesson: Personal Accounts of a School Desegregation Crisis* (Boston: Little, Brown, and Co., 1980).

34. *Morgan v. Hennigan* 379 F. Supp. 410 (1974).

35. For a contemporary study of the relationship between integration and achievement, see Meyer Weinberg, "The Relationship Between School Desegregation and Academic Achievement: A Review of Research," *Law and Contemporary Problems* 39:2 (1975), 240-70.

36. J. Anthony Lukas, *Common Ground: A Turbulent Decade in the Lives of Three American Families* (New York: Random House, 1985), 230.

37. "Leaders Urge Congress to Act Now," *Boston Globe* (March 18, 1972). For media coverage of Nixon's busing moratorium, see Judith F. Buncher, ed., *The School Busing Controversy, 1970-1975* (New York: Facts on File, 1975), 99-184.

38. For more on Joseph Moakley's campaign, see James Jennings and Mel King, eds., *From Access to Power: Black Politics in Boston* (Cambridge, Mass.: Schenkman Books, 1986), 27.

39. "Elliot Richardson Talks About Busing," *Boston Globe* ([?] 1972). See also *Swann v. Charlotte-Mecklenburg Board of Education* 402 U.S. 1 (1971); Bernard Schwartz, *Swann's Way: The School Busing Case and the Supreme Court* (New York: Oxford University Press, 1986); Frye Gaillard, *The Dream Long Deferred* (Chapel Hill: University of North Carolina Press, 1988); and Frank Goodman, "De Facto School Segregation: A Constitutional and Empirical Analysis," *California Law Review* 60 (1972), 275-436.

40. *Keyes v. School District No. 1, Denver, Colorado* 413 U.S. 189 (1973). See also John C. Hogan, *The Schools, The Courts, and the Public Interest,* 2nd ed. (Lexington, Mass.: Lexington Books, 1985), 30. In 1973, arguing that local officials had "intentionally segregated" minority students was still relatively new in constitutional jurisprudence concerning northern school systems. Before *Keyes,* the prevailing precedent concerning northern schools was *Gomperts v. Chase* 404 U.S. 1237 (1971) in California. Under *Gomperts,* Hogan noted, any number of "state actions" could contribute to racial isolation without necessarily leading to a finding of intentional segregation. As Hogan observed, "a state-built and publicly financed freeway that effectively isolates blacks from whites and results in a separate and predominantly black high school; the actions of state planning groups that fashion and build the black community around the school; realtors, licensed by the state, who keep 'white property' white and 'black property' black; banks, chartered by the state, that shaped the policies that handicapped blacks in financing homes other than in black ghettos; residential segregation, fostered by state-enforced restrictive covenants, that results in segregated schools—whether [in the words of justice William O. Douglas in *Gomperts v. Chase*] 'any of these factors add up to *de jure* segregation in the sense of that state action we condemned in *Brown v. Board of Education*

is a question not yet decided.'" In *Keyes*, however, the court ruled that each of these "state actions" could lead to a finding of "intentional segregation" on the part of a northern school system.

41. In *Morgan v. Hennigan*, the plaintiffs emphasized that the school committee had "intentionally brought about and maintained racial segregation in the Boston public schools by various actions." Yet, to blame the school committee alone for the persistence of racial imbalance in the schools was to ignore the culpability of many *other* government actors at both the state and the federal level. Garrity himself admitted that "we shall never know whether Boston's segregated housing patterns would have evolved as they are today absent longstanding and thorough governmental complicity. Local, state and federal agencies historically followed discriminatory policies with respect to housing with consequences that remain clearly visible. Nor is there any present prospect of a reversal of the segregated housing patterns which were brought about by governmental action." While Garrity did not suggest that the school committee could have controlled housing patterns throughout the city, he did suggest that the school committee could have *responded* more effectively to these patterns and, in this way, could have mitigated the extent of racial imbalance in the schools. It was a lofty expectation.

42. In *Morgan v. Hennigan*, Garrity dealt at length with the issue of intent, though his attempt to clarify this key concept was not entirely successful, even in technical legal terms. In the end, he stated that he had simply inferred the existence of discriminatory intent from the *consequences* of the school committee's actions, that is, from the evidence of racial imbalance in the Boston public schools. In his words, "Intent ordinarily may not be proved directly, because there is no way of fathoming or scrutinizing the operations of the human mind; but may be inferred from the surrounding circumstances." *Morgan v. Hennigan* 379 F. Supp. 410 (1974). Justice Powell, however, doubted that such an approach to intent could withstand constitutional scrutiny. As he wrote in *Keyes*, "the decision of the court today, emphasizing as it does the elusive element of segregative intent, will invite numerous desegregation suits in which there can be little hope of uniformity of result. The issue in these cases will not be whether segregated education exists. This will be conceded in most of them. The litigation will focus as a consequence on the court's decision on whether segregation has resulted in any 'meaningful or significant' portion of a school system from a school board's 'segregative intent.' The intractable problems involved in litigating this issue are obvious to any lawyer. The results of litigation—often arrived at subjectively by a court endeavoring to ascertain the subjective intent of school authorities with respect to action taken or not taken over many years—will be fortuitous, unpredictable and even capricious."

43. In his *Keyes* dissent, Justice Powell asserted that mandatory busing was not a constitutionally required remedy to the problem of unequal educational opportunities. "The Equal Protection Clause does, indeed, command that racial discrimination not be tolerated in the decisions of public school authorities. But it does not require that school authorities undertake widespread student transportation solely for the sake of maximizing integration." *Keyes v. School District No. 1, Denver, Colorado* 413 U.S. 189 (1973).

44. Garrity was not the first federal judge in Massachusetts to look toward busing as a remedy for racial imbalance. See *Barksdale v. Springfield School Committee* 237 F. Supp. 543 (January 11, 1965). The busing remedy in this case was overturned six months later by the First Circuit Court of Appeals. See *Barksdale v. Springfield School Committee* 348 F. 2d. 261 (First Circuit, 1965).

45. *Keyes v. School District No. 1, Denver, Colorado* 413 U.S. 189 (1973). In ordering a busing remedy in Boston, Garrity wrote, quoting *Keyes* (which, in turn, quoted *Green v.*

County School Board of New Kent County, Virginia, which quoted *Brown v. Board of Education II*), "'school authorities are "clearly charged with the affirmative duty to take whatever steps might be necessary [to foster racial balance].'" . . . This means that busing, the pairing of schools, redistricting with both contiguous and non-contiguous boundary lines, involuntary student and faculty assignments, and all other means, some of which may be distasteful to both school officials and teachers and parents, must be evaluated; and, if necessary to achieve a unitary school system, they must be implemented. The Supreme Court has recognized that, [quoting *Swann,*] 'the remedy for such segregation may be administratively awkward, inconvenient, and even bizarre in some situations and may impose burdens on some; but all awkwardness and inconvenience cannot be avoided . . . when remedial adjustments are being made to eliminate the dual school systems.'"

46. See "The Birth, Death, and Legacy of the Massachusetts Racial Imbalance Law," *Boston Globe* (July 15, 1974).

47. "Anrig Sets State Priorities," *Boston Globe* (July 8, 1973).

48. See "Leadership, Not Race, Seen as Key Factor," *Boston Globe* (April 1, 1985).

49. *Keyes v. School District No. 1, Denver, Colorado* 413 U.S. 189 (1973).

50. See "Report and Recommendations of Louis L. Jaffe, Esq." (May 28, 1973).

51. *Morgan v. Hennigan* 379 F. Supp. 410 (1974).

52. In his decision, Garrity quoted an earlier ruling from the Massachusetts state supreme court suggesting that "it would be the height of irony if the racial imbalance act, enacted as it was with the laudable purpose of achieving equal educational opportunities, should, by prescribing school pupil allocations based on race, founder on unsuspected shoals in the Fourteenth Amendment [by failing to ensure equality of educational opportunities]." See *School Committee of Boston v. Board of Education,* 1967 supra, 352 Mass. At 698, 227 NE.2d at 733, quoted in *Morgan v. Hennigan* 379 F. Supp. 410 (1974).

53. *Morgan v. Kerrigan* 401 F. Supp. 216 (1975)

54. See Lukas, *Common Ground,* 241.

55. U.S. Code, Title 20, Chapter 39, subchapter II, sections 1755 and 1751. See also U.S. Commission on Civil Rights, *Equal Educational Opportunity and Nondiscrimination for Students with Limited English Proficiency: Federal Enforcement of Title VI and* Lau v. Nichols (November 1997), 83n111. "President Nixon specifically addressed his administration's goals with regard to equal educational opportunity when he first proposed the Equal Educational Opportunities Act in 1972. He stated that the statutory purpose would be to shift the emphasis on busing as a remedial scheme for civil rights violations and to focus instead on the quality of education programs as a means of remedying past civil rights violations and at the same time preventing new ones. He suggested that an emphasis on the quality of education programs would accomplish civil rights goals far more effectively than the remedy of busing. With this legislation, he sought to portray equal educational opportunity as an *alternative* to busing."

56. See "The Birth, Death, and Legacy of the Massachusetts Racial Imbalance Law," *Boston Globe* (July 26, 1974). Moderating the racial imbalance law made it possible for a public school to be considered integrated without necessarily achieving 50-percent white enrollments. As Garrity wrote in his remedy-phase decision, *Morgan v. Kerrigan* 401 F. Supp. 216 (1975), "The plan which the court adopts as a remedy in this case does not rest on any supposed constitutional right of a student to attend a school that has a particular ethnic composition or whose ethnic composition, matches that of the school system as a whole."

57. "Busing—A Symposium," *Ramparts* 13 (1975), 46.

58. See Jim Green and Allen Hunter, "Racism and Busing in Boston," *Radical America* 8:6 (November-December, 1974), 1-32; and Frank Brown and Waithira Mugai, "Court-Ordered School Desegregation: One Community's Attitude," *Journal of Black Studies* 13 (March 1983), 355-68.

59. "Busing—A Symposium," 42. Many agreed that predominantly white schools in South Boston offered no greater educational opportunities than predominantly black schools in Roxbury—that is, if opportunities were measured in terms of academic achievement. See "Report and Recommendations of Louis L. Jaffe, Esq." (May 28, 1973). See also Mwalimu Shugaa, ed., *Beyond Desegregation: The Politics of Quality in African American Schools* (Thousand Oaks, Calif.: Corwin Press, 1996).

60. "Busing—A Symposium," 43, 42.

61. See Lupo, 157-58. "Garrity had spent little time physically looking at Boston schools. He may not have really understood the sense of neighborhood most whites felt, nor the extent of their fear of black crime. Perhaps he would be surprised in the days to come to read and hear of black and Puerto Rican parents protesting busing, complaining that their children would be removed from community schools that they, the adults, had worked so hard to improve."

62. *Morgan v. Kerrigan* 401 F. Supp. 216 (1975). In some cases, racial-ethnic parent councils worked well; in other cases, they did not. See U.S. Commission on Civil Rights, *Fulfilling the Letter and Spirit of the Law: Desegregation of the Nation's Public Schools* (Washington, D.C., 1976), 21, 18.

63. "Busing—A Symposium," 38, 41. Noel Day commented that "black parents have often been the ones who were most apprehensive about busing programs like METCO or Operation Exodus. They've been worried about their children being so far from home, and in a lot of cases, they have felt insulted by 'one-way' busing plans."

64. Ibid., 39. Herb Kohl, a friend of Neil Sullivan's from his days as superintendent in Berkeley, California, commented that racial integration had not improved the academic achievement of poor black students in that city's schools. In his words, "people thought that just getting black kids to rub elbows with white kids meant that a few I.Q. points would rub off onto the blacks. Of course it didn't happen. . . . The problem that came up in Berkeley, and will probably come up everywhere else, is that desegregation doesn't solve their learning problems because the schools [themselves] are so miserable."

65. Governor's Commission to Establish a Comprehensive Plan for School District Reorganization and Collaboration, "A Plan for Advancing Quality and Excellence by the Organization and Management of Public Education" (Boston: Massachusetts Advisory Council on Education, December, 1974), 52, v. "There is a deep disillusionment in some cities about [the quality of the] public schools. As a result of this disillusionment the Commission has encountered a lack of agreement within the urban population, doubts about the racial imbalance law, a perceptible trend among some minority citizens toward the 'separate but equal' concept and a natural reluctance to participate in 'another study that will get us nowhere.'"

66. *Morgan v. Hennigan* 379 F. Supp. 410 (1974).

67. *Lau v. Nichols* 414 U.S. 563 (1974). Senator Edward Kennedy was a key advocate of bilingual education. According to the Senate Subcommittee on Education, which he chaired, the purpose of bilingual education was "to develop the proficiency in English that permits the child to learn as effectively in English as in the child's native language—a vital requirement to compete effectively in society. This requires continuation of basic-education instruction in both languages until that level of proficiency in English is

achieved." If non-English-speaking students joined English-speaking classes before they were ready, then, Kennedy argued, their placements could be considered discriminatory. See Susan Gilbert Schneider, *Revolution, Reaction, or Reform: The 1974 Bilingual Education Act* (New York: L.A. Publishing Co., 1976), 58.

68. *Morgan v. Kerrigan* 401 F. Supp. 216 (1975). In *Milliken v. Bradley* 418 U.S. 717, 740-41, 41 L. Ed. 2d 1069, 94 S. Ct. 3112 (1974), the U.S. Supreme Court held that the U.S. Constitution "does not require any particular racial balance in each school, grade, or classroom."

69. Cumner and Greenwood, IV-69.

70. See James Crawford, *Bilingual Education: History, Politics, Theory, and Practice,* 4th ed. (Los Angeles, Calif.: Bilingual Educational Services, Inc., 1999), 50-51. "There was no question that bilingual programs in the late 1970s tended to separate language-minority students from their English-speaking peers. . . . In the year the Bilingual Education Act was passed, 65 percent of Spanish-background children in elementary school and 53 percent of those in high school were attending predominantly minority institutions. . . . By 1976, the figures had increased to 74 percent and 65 percent, respectively. Most Title VII grants were going to highly segregated school districts. Bilingual education was a complicating factor in several civil rights cases, as federal courts sought to reconcile the goals of racial balance and quality programs for limited-English speakers." See also Cumner and Greenwood, IV-53. "Bay City [Boston] is now under a court order to desegregate its schools. The plan requires closing down many existing schools and moving children around by busing, mostly for short distances. The desegregation objectives are in conflict with the district's bilingual program, since it is the aim of the district to cluster together kids who need bilingual help."

71. *Morgan v. Kerrigan* 401 F. Supp. 216 (1975). For detailed statistics on student numbers by race, see Metropolitan Planning Project, "Metro Ways to Understanding: A Plan for the Voluntary Elimination of Racial and Ethnic Isolation in the Schools of the Boston Metropolitan Area" (Winchester, Mass.: MASBO Cooperative Corporation, 1974).

72. Schneider, 41, 60, 145.

73. Ultimately, the appeals court based its decision in *Serna v. Portales* on Title VI of the Civil Rights Act instead of the Fourteenth Amendment, but it affirmed the lower court's use of the Fourteenth Amendment in its own ruling. Apparently, the reason for the appeals court's shift to the Civil Rights Act was the issue of discriminatory *intent.* Proof of discriminatory intent is necessary in rulings based on the Fourteenth Amendment but not in rulings based on the Civil Right Act. See *Serna v. Portales Municipal Schools* 499 F.2d 1147 (1974). In the court's words, "The trial court noted in its memorandum opinion that appellees claimed deprivation of equal protection guaranteed by the Fourteenth Amendment and of their statutory rights under Title VI of the 1964 Civil Rights Act, specifically § 601. While the trial court reached the correct result on equal protection grounds, we choose to follow the approach adopted by the Supreme Court in *Lau;* that is, appellees were deprived of their statutory rights under Title VI of the 1964 Civil Rights Act. . . . The Portales school curriculum, which has the effect of discrimination even though probably no purposeful design is present, therefore violates the requisites of Title VI and the requirement imposed by or pursuant to HEW regulations [of May 25, 1970]."

74. *Serna v. Portales Municipal Schools* 499 F.2d 1147 (1974). "Undisputed evidence shows that Spanish surnamed students do not reach the achievement levels attained by their Anglo counterparts. For example, achievement tests, which are given totally in the English language, disclose that students at Lindsey [Elementary School in Portales] are

almost a full grade behind children attending other schools in reading, language mechanics and language expression. Intelligence quotient tests show that Lindsey students fall further behind as they move from the first to the fifth grade." For non-English-speaking minority students, it seemed that bilingual instruction was educationally "effective," but classroom integration was not. Indeed, according to Jose Cardenas, superintendent of schools in San Antonio, Texas, the pursuit of integration actually *diminished* academic achievement among non-English-speaking minority students by dispersing them throughout a school system and making parent participation as well as curricular coherence difficult to achieve. As Cardenas asserted, "desegregation efforts consistently have jeopardized special programs for minority populations" (quoted in Crawford, 51).

75. See Teitlebaum and Hiller, 167. "Whereas in *Serna* the violation was the failure of the school district to offer a curriculum to meet the educational needs of minority students, in *Keyes* the focus was segregation. Indeed, the Tenth Circuit found that the district court's plan [which allowed for the existence of four Hispanic-only pilot schools] was not sufficient to dismantle segregation in the Denver schools. The court [therefore] could not be expected to approve identifiable minority schools, particularly when it was simultaneously ruling that the remedy had not gone far enough to desegregate the system as a whole. The ethnic groupings in the four pilot schools could not even be justified on the basis of the students' language disabilities, because evidence on that issue had not been proffered. Even with such evidence, it is doubtful whether the court would have ruled differently, since desegregation was its overriding concern. Moreover, the thrust of desegregation is to offer the same education to all students regardless of race or national origin. To establish identifiable Chicano schools in the name of developing a greater sense of culture or self-concept may also permit the establishment of identifiable Black schools for the same reasons. Even if the creation of such schools might be educationally sound, it does not pass muster under the Constitution, especially when a system is found to be operating segregated schools and the mandate is to desegregate them. If bilingual programs are to be part of a desegregation remedy, they cannot jeopardize the court's paramount concern to integrate."

76. *Morgan v. Kerrigan* 509 F. 2d 580 (1974); emphasis in original.

Chapter Six

1. *Morgan v. Kerrigan* 401 F. Supp. 216 (1975).

2. Center for Law and Education, *A Study of the Massachusetts Racial Imbalance Ac*t (Cambridge, Mass.: Harvard University, February 1972), 21. "In . . . attempts by black spokesmen to end racial imbalance, a demand for equalized educational resources (e.g., buildings, teachers, equipment) became a central theme. While the arguments presented to whites often cited the social and cultural damage caused by separation, resource balancing gained greatest currency among blacks. Many blacks supported integration less for its own sake than as a way of guaranteeing that black and white alike would share in whatever resources were available."

3. "Busing—A Symposium," *Ramparts* (1975), 41.

4. "Sullivan Wants Results 'Worthy of Imitation,'" *Boston Globe* ([?] 1969).

5. Boston Municipal Research Bureau, "School Pay Raises Vary Widely" (November 1969), 1.

6. Boston Municipal Research Bureau, "A Report on Bureau Success with 1970 City Budgets" (May 1970).

7. Boston Municipal Research Bureau, "City Debt Continues to Increase" (March 15, 1971).

8. Boston Municipal Research Bureau, "School Costs Soaring" (May 1972), 1.

9. Federal budgetary policies in the 1970s had unanticipated effects in Massachusetts. See "Massachusetts in '80," *Boston Globe* (February 10, 1980). Editorialist Robert Turner argued that "the Massachusetts miasma of the seventies has national as well as local roots and may be dated from the policy decisions of August 15, 1971, when Richard M. Nixon (and then-treasury secretary John B. Connally) imposed wage and price controls. The impact was felt nationwide, of course, but in Massachusetts it was compounded by a hard squeeze on contracts for the Defense Department and the National Aeronautics and Space Administration. Before 1972 was over, nearly 100,000 Massachusetts jobs were lost in those two areas alone. . . . Unemployment rose by more than 50 percent in a single year—1974-75[—to 11.2 percent, well above the national average of 8.5 percent]."

10. Michael Barone, *The Almanac of American Politics* (New York: Dutton, 1978), 374.

11. See Center for Law and Education, *A Study of the Massachusetts Racial Imbalance Act* (Cambridge, Mass.: Harvard University, February 1972), 307.

12. William J. Leary, *Annual Report of the Superintendent* (1973), unpaginated typescript. Between 1972 and 1977, Boston closed 44 elementary schools and built several larger schools in their place.

13. See Bruce William Perlstein, "Taxes, Schools, and Inequality: The Political Economy of The Property Tax and School Finance Reform in Massachusetts" (Ph.D. dissertation, Brandeis University, 1981), 541. The Massachusetts Teachers Association (MTA) was a major political force in the state, but teachers in Boston had a separate union, the Boston Teachers Union.

14. Boston Municipal Research Bureau, "School Pay Raises Vary Widely" (November 1969), 4, 3, 5. The rise in teacher salaries in the 1970s could not be attributed to a teacher shortage. See Joseph M. Cronin, "Plan for Reorganization" (Boston: Executive Office of Educational Affairs, January 1973), 8. "As of 1972 the teacher shortage in most fields was solved [in Massachusetts]—after fifteen years of trying to catch up to the baby boom of the 1940s and 50s."

15. Concerns about the school budget (and, specifically, teacher salaries) had been mounting for at least a decade. See Boston Municipal Research Bureau, "Boston's School Budget" (March 1964) and Boston Municipal Research Bureau, "School Budget Controversy" (May 4, 1965).

16. See "Hub Teachers' Pact: How Will Cliffhanger End?" *Boston Globe* (August 28, 1980). "Boston teachers struck for the first time in the city's history in March 1970, when they staged a one-day walk-out. . . . Five weeks later in 1970 they went out again and that walk-out resulted in a thirty-day jail sentence for teachers union president John P. Reilly and heavy fines for the union for defying an injunction barring the strike."

17. Steven J. Weiss, *Existing Disparities in Public School Finance and Proposals for Reform* (Research Report to the Federal Reserve Bank of Boston, no. 46, February, 1970), 41; quoted in Charlotte Ryan, "The State Dollar and the Schools: A Discussion of State Aid Programs in Massachusetts and Promising Reforms" (Boston: Massachusetts Advisory Council on Education, 1970), 4.

18. Massachusetts Department of Education, "Report of Subcommittee A: Equal Education Opportunities Committee" (December 1971), 2-3.

19. André Danière, *Cost-Benefit Analysis of General Purpose State School-Aid Formulas in Massachusetts* (Boston: Massachusetts Advisory Council on Education, 1969), 123.

20. Boston Municipal Research Bureau, "The New State Aid System and Boston" (November 1969).

21. Perlstein, 421.

22. Governor's Commission to Establish a Comprehensive Plan for School District Reorganization and Collaboration, "A Plan for Advancing Quality and Excellence by the Organization and Management of Public Education" (Boston: Massachusetts Advisory Council on Education, 1974), 88. See also Danière, 69. "As communities adjust from year to year to the reimbursements they receive, high reimbursements one year will reduce the local tax contribution that year and generate lower reimbursements the next year. The reverse will then occur, with the result that reimbursements and expenditures will exhibit a 'yo-yo' pattern over time."

23. See Danière, 55. "The indication . . . is that (1) the state takes back a portion of the federal aid received by communities, and (2) this portion is higher the larger the federal aid received in relation to public school expenditures and the larger that community's school aid percentage. This is in direct contradiction with the principle . . . according to which the proportion of [federal aid] withdrawn by the state would be *least* the more impacted the community. . . . Furthermore, the withdrawal of a larger portion of their federal receipts from communities with high aid percentages, i.e., from the poorer communities, has no justification. As things now stand, a community with federal receipts amounting to 1/5 of its reimbursable expenditures would keep it all if its valuation per pupil is $30,000 but would lose 1/5 of it if its valuation per pupil is only $8,000." Of course, the opposite contention was also possible, namely, that Boston might at times *refrain* from applying for certain federal grants for fear that receiving them might jeopardize its state aid the next year. Either way, Boston received less-than-optimal resources.

24. See Ryan, 19–20, 10.

25. *Serrano v. Priest*, 5 Cal. 3d 584; 487 P.2d 1241; 96 Cal. Rptr. 601 (August 30, 1971). In its *Serrano* decision, California's supreme court asserted that wealth was a "suspect classification" (akin to race or national origin) requiring strict scrutiny under the equal protection clause of the state constitution. In order to make this assertion, the court had to find that different levels of funding resulted in different levels of educational opportunity for different groups of students based on family income. This finding was difficult to support. "Although we recognize that there is considerable controversy among educators over the relative impact of educational spending and environmental influences on school achievement," the court wrote, "we note that the several courts which have considered contentions [that spending does *not* affect achievement] . . . have uniformly rejected them." Citing the opinion of the federal district court in Illinois in *McInnis v. Shapiro* (293 F. Supp. 327, November 15, 1968), the court in *Serrano* held that "presumably, students receiving a $1,000 education are better educated than those acquiring a $600 schooling." The court also cited the case of *Hobson v. Hansen* (269 F. Supp. 401, 1967), in which Judge Wright noted that "comparative per pupil figures do refer to actual educational advantages in the high cost schools, especially with respect to the caliber of the teaching staff." *Serrano* acknowledged that the "extent to which high spending . . . represents actual educational advantage is, of course, a matter of proof [i.e., outcomes]" but concluded that California's system placed students in poor districts at a clear educational disadvantage and was therefore unconstitutional.

26. See "Report of Subcommittee A," 3, 2, 6. "This decision [*Serrano v. Priest*]," the subcommittee noted, "considers only the *availability* of fiscal resources to the local school district, not their *utilization* [in local classrooms]. . . . Whether or not future judicial de-

cisions in Massachusetts or elsewhere reach to this issue, it seems to the committee that equal educational opportunity for children is not really achieved if local unwillingness to use available resources is allowed to go unchallenged. Our recommendations, therefore, contemplate state intervention in local effort [that is, state supervision over resource utilization], if not through effective leadership, goal-setting, and standard-enforcing by the state, then by means of mandated floors under local spending or tax effort."

27. See John E. Heffley, "Financing Public Education in Massachusetts: A Process for Revision" (Boston: Massachusetts Advisory Council on Education, February 1975), 50. "Underestimated property values in equalizing the values for use in state aid formulas result in a penalty for those cities and towns which have revalued their property. The result of this is that the communities which have not made an effort to revalue their property appear as being poorer than they are and, therefore, those towns receive significantly more in state aid than they [should be] entitled to receive."

28. James B. Conant, "Full State Funding" in Federal Reserve Bank of Boston, *Financing Public Schools: A New England School Development Conference Held in Cooperation with the Harvard Graduate School of Education and the Federal Reserve Bank of Boston* (January 1972), 114.

29. Robert T. Capeless, "Tax Equity and Educational Equality" in Federal Reserve Bank of Boston, 85.

30. Capeless, 82. Capeless advocated "complete state financing of the cost of education and, as an absolutely necessary consequence, complete state determination of the levels of spending for education."

31. See "U.S. Urged to Help States Take Over Cost of Schools," *Boston Globe* (March 7, 1972).

32. Paul W. Cook Jr., *Modernizing School Governance for Educational Equality and Diversity* (Boston: Massachusetts Advisory Council on Education, September 1972), 63, 65.

33. *San Antonio Independent School District v. Rodriguez,* 411 U.S. 1 (March 21, 1973). The Achilles heel of the plaintiffs' argument in *Rodriguez* was the ambiguity of the "injured" class. As the court explained, "the individuals or groups of individuals who constituted the class discriminated against in [prior cases seeking equal protection for a class defined by wealth] shared two distinguishing characteristics: because of their impecunity they were completely unable to pay for some desired benefit, and as a consequence, they sustained an absolute deprivation of a meaningful opportunity to enjoy that benefit." According to Justice Powell, writing for the majority, the plaintiffs in *Rodriguez* met neither of these criteria: "The argument here is not that the children in districts having relatively low assessable property values are receiving no public education; rather, it is that they are receiving a poorer quality education than that available to children in districts having more assessable wealth." Since, as Powell noted, "where wealth is involved, the equal protection clause of the Fourteenth Amendment does not require absolute equality or precisely equal advantages," the plaintiffs had no case. See also Douglas S. Reed, *On Equal Terms: The Constitutional Politics of Educational Opportunity* (Princeton: Princeton University Press, 2001).

34. See *San Antonio v. Rodriguez* 411 U.S. 1 (1973). On the question of education as a "fundamental right," Powell's answer was curt: "Education, of course, is not among the rights afforded explicit protection under our federal Constitution. Nor do we find any basis for saying it is implicitly so protected."

35. *San Antonio v. Rodriguez* 411 U.S. 1 (1973). The measure of an "adequate" education was much debated in this case. According to the majority opinion, "Texas asserts that the Minimum Foundation Program [for school aid] provides an 'adequate' educa-

tion for all children in the state. By providing 12 years of free public-school education, and by assuring teachers, books, transportation, and operating funds, the Texas legislature has endeavored to 'guarantee, for the welfare of the state as a whole, that all people shall have at least an adequate program of education. This is what is meant by 'A Minimum Foundation Program of Education.'"

36. *San Antonio v. Rodriguez* 411 U.S. 1 (1973).

37. Ibid. In a dissenting opinion in *Rodriguez*, Justice Marshall asserted that a legal solution to the problem of funding inequities was necessary when a political solution could not be found. "The court seeks solace for its action today in the possibility of legislative reform. The court's suggestions of legislative redress and experimentation will doubtless be of great comfort to the schoolchildren of Texas' disadvantaged districts, but considering the vested interests of wealthy school districts in the preservation of the status quo, they are worth little more. The possibility of legislative action is, in all events, no answer to this court's duty under the Constitution to eliminate unjustified state discrimination."

38. Cronin, 10.

39. Governor's Commission to Establish a Comprehensive Plan for School District Reorganization and Collaboration, 70, 69, 101.

40. Cronin, 57.

41. Cronin, 29. The National Assessment of Educational Progress was established in 1969.

42. See DeLone, 25. According to DeLone, "current information about comparable, competitive school districts" could show parents in lucid terms "how their own school operation stacks up against the rest of the Commonwealth." Equipped with such information, they could decide whether their schools warranted additional resources or not.

43. Governor's Commission to Establish a Comprehensive Plan for School District Reorganization and Collaboration, 105. See also Cook, 74. "If all that public education tried to do was, for example, assure age-in-grade attainment levels in basic skills, it is relatively easy to measure effectiveness and not much more difficult to obtain statistically meaningful bases for comparison of effectiveness between school systems and over time. If [however,] public education has a broader mission, and if that mission may vary substantially from situation to situation, the problem becomes immensely more difficult. Not only that, but the effort to develop and apply universal measures of effectiveness may cause an unwanted shift of goals toward achieving good marks on those measures, even if they are regarded as inappropriate. Simplistic applications of systems analysis could set education back to the days when what schools did was prepare children to take certain tests."

44. See Governor's Commission on School District Organization and Collaboration, "Effectiveness, Efficiency, and Equal Opportunity in the Public Schools of Massachusetts" (Boston: Massachusetts Advisory Council on Education, October 1974), 84.

45. Ryan, 18.

46. *Almanac of American Politics* (1978), 374.

47. "Special Education—Plenty of Problems," *Boston Globe* (June 12, 1975).

48. "From Trouble to Tranquility: Hub Schools Chief During Busing Era Enjoys Gloucester Post," *Boston Globe* (February 27, 1990).

49. See Boston Municipal Research Bureau, "Control of Desegregation Costs Needed" (July 3, 1975).

50. Quoted in, Susan Gilbert Schneider, *Revolution, Reaction, or Reform: The 1974 Bilingual Education Act* (New York: Las Americas Publishing Company, 1976), 144.

51. W. Vance Grant and C. George Lind, *Digest of Education Statistics: 1975 Edition*

(Washington, D.C.: U.S. Department of Education, 1975), 150. See also John Brademas, *The Politics of Education: Conflict and Consensus on Capitol Hill* (Norman, Okla.: University of Oklahoma Press, 1987).

52. See "Special Education—Plenty of Problems," *Boston Globe* (June 12, 1975). "Few . . . have criticized Chapter 766 for its intent to provide the educational services for physically, mentally, and emotionally handicapped children in Massachusetts. Quite a few, however, are highly critical of its enormous financial impact on local communities at a time when their school costs are soaring and the state's fiscal crisis is worsening. The results are coming through loud and clear: less state money for general school purposes and rising expenses in scores of cities and towns that could force cuts in spending for regular school programs in favor of Chapter 766 children."

53. "Chapter 766 Compliance 'Uneven,' Groups Charge," *Boston Globe* (February 19, 1975).

54. "Special Education—Plenty of Problems," *Boston Globe* (June 12, 1975).

55. Ibid.

56. Milton Budoff, "Engendering Change in Special Education Practices," *Harvard Educational Review*, 45:4 (November 1975), 519; see also 521.

57. See Ryan, 17. As early as 1970—before the passage of Chapter 766—Ryan noted that "with more than one category of aid available, administrators tend to 'play the percentages' in developing programs [by placing students in programs most likely to maximize state aid]."

58. Chapter 70 for general state aid to schools also prioritized special education over regular education. See Boston Municipal Research Bureau "Millions for Boston at Stake" (December 1966). "The 1966 law establishing the sales tax says that 80 percent of net sales tax receipts shall be distributed *first* to reimburse communities for the state's share of the cost of special education programs for the physically handicapped and mentally retarded" (emphasis added).

59. Perlstein, 423, 426, 436. "The time lag between local expenditures and the receipt of state aid was . . . longer in the case of Chapter 70 aid for regular day programs than for special and bilingual education. State aid for special and bilingual education program costs during a given school year was paid in the following November. . . . [But] expenditures incurred during a given school year for regular day programs were not reimbursed under Chapter 70 until the second following school year. Thus, while spending on special and bilingual education (and vocational education) during school year 1974-75 was partially reimbursed in November 1975, spending on regular day programs during 1974-75 was not reimbursed until school year 1976-77. Obviously, in an inflationary period, the longer the lag the lower the real value of the final state reimbursement."

60. University of Massachusetts Institute for Governmental Services, *The Children's Puzzle: A Study of Services to Children in Massachusetts* (February 1977), 6.

61. See Massachusetts Board of Education, "School Finance Reform Legislation: Equity and Relief" (Boston, 1975), 5. In 1976, the state legislature changed Chapter 70 from an automatic appropriation set by statute (amounting to 80 percent of sales-tax revenues) to an annual appropriation set by majority vote. This change made Chapter 70 increasingly susceptible to political vicissitudes and economic fluctuations while Chapter 766 remained a guaranteed distribution. See Massachusetts Department of Education, *Taxes, Schools, and Inequality in Massachusetts: Chapter 70 School Aid and School Finance* (June 1977), 15.

62. See Paul William Cox, "The Impact of State Funding of Special Needs Programs,

Under Chapter 766, Acts of 1972, on the Funding of Other State and Local Educational Programs in Massachusetts" (Ed.D. dissertation, Boston College 1980).

63. See Gerald S. Coles, "The Learning Disabilities Test Battery: Empirical and Social Issues," *Harvard Educational Review* 48:3 (August 1978), 376. "Using a medical model and equipped with their own black bag of diagnostic instruments, the learning-disabilities specialists, sometimes together with other specialists, examine child patients. If they think there are learning disabilities, they write authoritative diagnoses stating that, based on the results of certain tests, it has been determined that the children have neurological problems that impede learning. Parents and teachers will be likely to accept these findings as true. Because the children have been given a set of seemingly scientific and valid tests, the conclusions must also be valid."

64. See Harriet T. Bernstein and Daniel W. Merenda, "Categorical Programs: Past and Present," in *The Federal Role in Education: New Directions for the Eighties*, ed. Robert A. Miller (Washington, D.C.: Institute for Educational Leadership, 1981), 53–71. As Bernstein and Merenda noted, "categorical aid and the concept of 'targeting' was in the first instance the product of a long and frustrating search for a politically acceptable way to help the schools, and [was] not the product of a search for an educationally sound method of raising the achievement levels of poor and minority children." They added that "the proliferation of [categorical] programs, each with their supporting interest group, has created an educational environment more concerned with who gets federal education money than with the education gotten."

65. James McGarry, *Final Report: Implementing Massachusetts' Special Education Law: A Statewide Assessment* (1982), 25.

66. *The Children's Puzzle*, 4. See also John C. Pittinger and Peter Kuriloff, "Educating the Handicapped: Reforming a Radical Law," *The Public Interest* (Winter 1982), 81. "Because parents who were wealthy or well-educated tended to live in the more affluent districts (districts that complied more faithfully with the law [Chapter 766]), and because such parents were better able to articulate their concerns, demand evaluations, and appeal when necessary, the effect of the law was to *increase* the disparity between the special education services available to children at opposite ends of the social ladder. (Boston children . . . were probably least well served)."

67. Massachusetts Department of Education, *Taxes, Schools and Inequality in Massachusetts: Chapter 70 School Aid and School Finance* (June 1977), 28.

68. Adding to the budget crisis in the fall of 1975 was another teachers strike. See "Hub Teachers' Pact: How Will Cliffhanger End?" *Boston Globe* (August 28, 1980).

69. Heffley, 27. In 1974–75, Boston placed 44.5 percent of public-school students in special-compensatory programs, including Title I. Comparisons found that Houston placed 27.9 percent of public-school students in such programs, and Chicago, topping the list, placed 63.4 percent of all students in these programs.

70. Ibid., 28. Heffley pointed to two states that were already moving toward a "pupil-weighting" system. The first was Utah, which, according to the National Educational Finance Project, ranked second only to Hawaii in the degree to which its school-aid formula equalized funding throughout the state. The second, New Jersey, was under a recent court order to update its state school-aid formula. See *Cahill v. Robinson* 62 N.J. 473 (April 3, 1973), decided two weeks after *Rodriguez*.

71. Heffley, 32, 51–52.

72. Massachusetts Board of Education, "School Finance Reform Legislation: Equity and Relief" (1975), 7, 8.

73. Quoted in Reed Martin, *Educating Handicapped Children: The Legal Mandate*

(Champaign, Ill.: Research Press Company), 17, 15. Both quotations in this paragraph come from the Senate Committee on Labor and Public Welfare, of which Edward Kennedy was a long-time member. See also Pittinger and Kuriloff, 88–89: "The central issue [in special education policy and law], although none of the various judges address it squarely, is the meaning of 'appropriate' in the [Education for All Handicapped Children] Act. In commanding the states to provide a 'free appropriate education' to all handicapped children, was Congress simply ordering the schools to open their doors to handicapped children and devise programs which plausibly address their needs? Or does 'appropriate' mean 'optimal'—whatever services and programs are needed to maximize a particular child's learning capacity? The Third Circuit [Court of Appeals in the case of *Armstrong v. Kline* 476 F. Supp. 583 (1979)] comes very close to endorsing the latter view—and thus opens the door to demands for a range of programs and services which cannot at this point even be described, let alone assigned a cost figure." This issue was eventually resolved by the U.S. Supreme Court in favor of the former view—merely "opening the door" to handicapped children—in the case of *Board of Education of the Hendrick Hudson Central School District, Westchester County v. Rowley* 458 U.S. 176 (1982). For more on this case, see chapter 8.

74. Quoted in Martin, 15–16.

75. Several interest groups lobbied for P.L. 94-142, most prominently the Council for Exceptional Children. See June B. Jordan, ed., *Exceptional Child Education at the Bicentennial: A Parade of Progress* (Reston, Va.: Council for Exceptional Children, 1977), 2, 6, 12.

76. Quoted in Frederick J. Weintraub, Alan R. Abeson, David L. Braddock, *State Law and the Education of Handicapped Children: Issues and Recommendations* (Reston, Va.: Council for Exceptional Children, 1972), viii.

77. Quoted in Bruce O. Boston, "Education Policy and the Education for All Handicapped Children Act (P.L. 94-142), A Report of Regional Conferences" (January-April 1977), 11. For the full text of Ford's message, see http://www.ford.utexas.edu/library/speeches/750707.htm.

78. Perlstein, 441.

79. Massachusetts Advocacy Center, "Double Jeopardy: The Plight of Minority Students in Special Education" (1978), 3.

80. U.S. Commission on Civil Rights, *Fulfilling the Letter and Spirit of the Law: Desegregation of the Nation's Public Schools* (Washington, D.C., 1976), 129.

81. David L. Kirp, "Student Classification, Public Policy, and the Courts," *Harvard Educational Review* 44:1 (1974), 17.

82. See William H. Ohrenberger, *Annual Report of the Superintendent* (1972), 33.

83. See Richard A. Weatherly and Michael Lipsky, "Street-Level Bureaucrats and Institutional Innovation: Implementing Special Education Reform," *Harvard Educational Review* 47:2 (May 1977), 101. "Data obtained from an official of the state department of education indicate that children were actually shifted from less to more restrictive programs during the first year of implementation. . . . Ironically, by providing separate rooms staffed by specialists to provide special education services, school systems *decreased* the proportion of fully integrated children by sending them out of the regular classrooms for special help." See also Burton Blatt and Frank Garfunkel, *Massachusetts Study of Educational Opportunities for Handicapped and Disadvantaged Children* (Massachusetts Advisory Council on Education, January 1971), 273–87.

84. The accretion of separate programs for disabled students resulted in a complex system of differentiated services. See Burton Blatt and Frank Garfunkel, *Massachusetts*

Study of Educational Opportunities for Handicapped and Disadvantaged Children (Massachusetts Advisory Council on Education, January 1971), 283. "There are, in fact, very substantial differences in services as one moves from one category to the next. Two of the categories (aphasic and speech handicapped) make no provision for special classes. Only two categories (physically handicapped and emotionally disturbed) provide for home instruction, although home instruction is also provided for retarded physically handicapped. Only three categories (hearing impaired, learning impaired and speech handicapped) provide for special instruction periods. Two categories (deaf and aphasic) contain no authorization for joint programs between towns. Five categories (hearing impaired, mentally retarded, speech handicapped, learning impaired and visually handicapped) contain no provisions for placement in special schools. . . . There is only a single provision (deaf) for construction grants. Two categories (deaf and mentally retarded) provide salary differentials of up to $500 for teachers. Only two categories (mentally retarded and physically handicapped) make any provision for special recreational programs. In general, the statutes provide certain services to some children but not to others, with no apparent logic or bases for the differences. The process of awarding funds to disability areas has, thus, resulted in an unequal, discriminatory and rigidly defined system of services."

85. Quoted in Jordan, 8. See also Weatherly and Lipsky, 112: "Chapter 766's aim to eliminate labels was also foiled by federal requirements demanding continued use of the traditional designations. Thus, the State Division of Special Education compelled school systems to report, as they had in the past, the numbers of and expenditures for children specifically classified as mentally retarded, physically handicapped, partially seeing, speech-hearing handicapped, emotionally disturbed, and learning disabled. Even as old labels persisted, new ones were invented. When a psychologist and counselor were contrasting programs for 'LD [learning-disabled] kids' and 'our kids,' the observer asked who 'our kids' were. The psychologist replied, 'Oh, they used to be called retarded.'"

86. See *Morgan v. Kerrigan* 401 F. Supp. 216 (1975) and *San Antonio v. Rodriguez*, 411 U.S. 1 (1973). In October 1979, Congress passed the U.S. Department of Education Organization Act (P.L. 96-88), and in May 1980, the new Department of Education became operational. See Beryl A. Radin and Willis D. Hawley, *The Politics of Federal Reorganization: Creating the U.S. Department of Education* (New York: Pergamon Press, 1988).

Chapter Seven

1. Joseph P. Viteritti, *Across the River: Politics and Education in the City* (New York: Holmes and Meier, 1983), 183. See also Bruce W. Perlstein, "Taxes, Schools, and Inequality: The Political Economy of the Property Tax and School Finance Reform in Massachusetts" (Ph.D. dissertation, Brandeis University, 1981), 441. "The widespread impression at the time among many local and state school officials, legislators, and the advocacy groups was that a large number of districts were shifting significant numbers of pupils and resources from regular-day to special education programs in response to these financial incentives."

2. See Richard A. Weatherly and Michael Lipsky, "Street-Level Bureaucrats and Institutional Innovation: Implementing Special Education Reform," *Harvard Educational Review* 47:2 (May 1977), 106-7.

3. Ibid., 107, 102. Expenditures for Chapter 766 in Massachusetts grew from $143,566,970 in 1974 to $243,262,827 in 1978.

4. See Jeffrey J. Zettel, "Implementing the Right to a Free Appropriate Public Edu-

cation" in Joseph Ballard, Bruce A. Ramirez, and Frederick J. Weintraub, *Special Education in America: Its Legal and Governmental Foundations* (Reston, Va.: Council for Exceptional Children, 1982), 25. According to Zettel, between 1976-77 and 1980-81, "the number of children labeled mentally retarded declined by over 12 percent, or by 119,656 students [nationwide]; and those identified as speech impaired decreased by 124,874, or by nearly 10 percent. Students classified as emotionally disturbed increased by over 24 percent during this period. Even with the addition of 68,388 individuals, this particular subpopulation remains the only disability area that has not reached the 2 percent prevalence level anticipated by the Congress and most experts in 1974. Finally, it can be seen that an additional 657,922 children have been identified as having a learning disability since 1976, an 83 percent increase. Whereas in school years 1976-77, 1977-78, and 1978-79, the largest subpopulation of handicapped students were those having speech impairments, beginning in 1979-80, the largest number of handicapped children now served are the learning disabled." In 1981, the federal office of special education found that Massachusetts identified 12.27 percent of all students as disabled in some way—more than any other state.

5. The increase in special education enrollments was particularly alarming in that it coincided with a *decrease* in the overall student population. See Perlstein, 424-25, 431.

6. Warren T. Brookes, "What Chapter 766 is Doing to City's Regular Education," *Boston Herald American* (May 15, 1977) quoted in Caroline Marie Cunningham, "Special Education: A Cost Analysis of the Financial Impact of Chapter 766 on Local School Systems" (Ph.D. dissertation, Boston College, 1979), 4, 6-7.

7. See John C. Pittinger and Peter Kuriloff, "Educating the Handicapped: Reforming a Radical Law," *The Public Interest* (Winter 1982), 80-81. "In many cases parents seem to have used due-process procedures for purposes which run contrary to the dominant philosophy of both Chapter 766 and P.L. 94-142. That philosophy is 'mainstreaming'— the notion that handicapped children should be educated in circumstances which are as close to normal as their condition permits. Massachusetts parents have often sought to keep or place their children in more restrictive environments."

8. State Auditor's Report on Special Education in Massachusetts (March 1991), 6.

9. In 1977-178, the actual average costs for regular and special education students in Massachusetts were $1,261 and $4,915, respectively. See Massachusetts Department of Education, "Facts on Special Education in Massachusetts" (Quincy, Mass., March 1988), 7. See also Weatherly and Lipsky, 115: "As for cost considerations, school systems continue to be concerned about expenditures, but now try to assign many regular education items to the special education budget, since Chapter 766 expenditures have first claim in the state's educational-reimbursement program."

10. Perlstein, 423-25. State commissioner of education Gregory Anrig sought ways to increase federal aid by placing more students in isolated programs likely to be covered by the Medicaid program. See records of Governor's Invitational Conference on Issues in Education (October 18, 1979).

11. Stearns, M., C. Norwood, D. Kaskowitz, and S. Mitchell, *Validation of State Counts of Handicapped Children*, 2 vols. (Menlo Park, Calif.: Stanford Research Institute International, 1977).

12. See Zettel, 28-29. One possible explanation for the fact that Hawaii did not place as many students in high-cost categories was the fact that, in Hawaii, the state covered 100 percent of school costs on a general-aid basis, so it made little (or less) difference from a budgetary perspective if schools placed low-achieving students in the category of "learning disabled," "mentally retarded," or "emotionally disturbed."

13. McGarry, *viii*.

14. See "Chapter 766 in Massachusetts Education," *Boston Globe* (October 27, 1980).

15. See David L. Kirp, "Student Classification, Public Policy, and the Courts," *Harvard Educational Review* 44:1 (1974), 19–20.

16. See Weatherly and Lipsky, 116. "Rather than encouraging concentration of resources on a limited number of children, Chapter 766 cries out for increasing the scope of coverage. . . . Indeed, the vision of many educators with whom we spoke was that the law would open the way to treating *every* child as deserving individual assessment and an individualized learning plan. This would be particularly true for the brightest students, generally thought to be a neglected group whose ordinary treatment in school provides suboptimal education and nurtures emotional problems. In short, the thrust of Chapter 766 is, if anything, to increase and expand services."

17. Perlstein, 426.

18. See Children's Defense Fund of the Washington Research Project, Inc., *Children Out of School in America* (Children's Defense Fund of the Washington Research Project, Inc., October 1974), 102, quoted in Massachusetts Advocacy Center, "Double Jeopardy: The Plight of Minority Students in Special Education" (1978), 1.

19. Quoted in Zettel, 34.

20. See U.S. Commission on Civil Rights, "Fulfilling the Letter and Spirit of the Law: Desegregation of the Nation's Public Schools" (Washington, D.C.: U.S. Commission on Civil Rights, 1976), 129.

21. "Double Jeopardy," 7, 28, 1. According to the Massachusetts Advocacy Center, due-process guarantees did not necessarily suffice to avoid discriminatory placements. As the MAC wrote, "the procedural safeguards built into Chapter 766 are extremely important in minimizing the opportunities for discrimination. Even when rigorously followed, however, they provide no absolute guarantee that racial and ethnic considerations will be avoided."

22. See Massachusetts Department of Education, "Equal Educational Opportunity in Special Education: Legal Mandates and Strategies for Planning" (Boston, 1980).

23. Perlstein, 433.

24. "Double Jeopardy," 7.

25. See Ibid., *i*.

26. Ibid., 10. See also "Hub Instruction Costs High," *Boston Globe* (December 16, 1979). "According to the data [from a survey conducted by the National School Boards Association], Boston has 5,400 students in bilingual programs with a staff of 286. It appears to be one of the cities with a heavy bilingual enrollment compared to the overall student numbers."

27. See U.S. Commission on Civil Rights, "Fulfilling the Letter and Spirit of the Law: Desegregation of the Nation's Public Schools" (Washington, D.C., 1976), 129.

28. Janice J. Weinman, *Declining Test Scores: A State Study* (Boston: Massachusetts Department of Education, 1978), 74–75. See also College Board, *On Further Examination: Report of the Advisory Panel on the Scholastic Aptitude Test Score Decline* (New York: College Board, 1977).

29. "Report of the Massachusetts Advisory Committee on High School Graduation Requirements" (June 1978), quoted in Massachusetts State Board of Education, "Policy on Basic Skills Improvement" (August 29, 1978), 4, 7, 21. "The Committee is well aware of the pressures on the State Board of Education from various publics to address vigorously the alleged lack of minimal competency in basic skills on the part of a number of high school graduates. This public concern is evidenced by several bills before the [state

legislature] which would mandate some form of statewide competency testing. The Advisory Committee is also aware that this is a national concern. The State Boards of Education in over thirty states have already adopted policies to meet this real or apparent need."

30. Joseph Tremont, "The Massachusetts Right to Read Effort: A Plan for the Seventh and Final Year" (March 1979), *i*, 4, 22.

31. See Lorrie A. Shepard, "The Contest between Large-Scale Accountability Testing and Assessment in the Service of Learning, 1970-2001" (unpublished paper, 2002).

32. "Any Technique—or None—Will Work for the Geniuses," *Washington Post* (1977).

33. Massachusetts Department of Education, "Basic Skills Improvement Policy Implementation Guide #1" (April 1979), unpaginated typescript.

34. "Wood Terms Ouster Old Politics," *Boston Globe* (August 22, 1980).

35. Robert C. Wood, "Professionals at Bay: Managing Boston's Public Schools," *Journal of Policy Analysis and Management* (1982), 457.

36. Ibid., 458.

37. See Perlstein, 445, 529-32.

38. Ibid., 531, 571.

39. Massachusetts Department of Education, "Guide to the New School Aid Law: A Section by Section Analysis" (Boston: August 1978), 4. The accuracy of pupil weights was subject to political dispute. See Perlstein, 536. "The choice of an add-on weight of 0.2 for low-income pupils was somewhat arbitrary, since no discrete data were available on per pupil costs for low-income children, although the weight was similar to that used by other school finance reform states, including Florida and Indiana. In any case, the low-income pupil weight was quite accurately assessed by all sides as another key element in the State Board and Dukakis's 'tilt' toward the large cities."

40. Ibid., 599. The use of pupil weights gave cities an advantage over suburbs, but suburbs could boost their aid vis à vis cities if they placed students in special education at a faster rate than cities. See Perlstein, 580-81.

41. See ibid., 528. Perlstein highlighted "a basic underlying conflict between the goal of equalization (targeted aid) and the need for political feasibility (spreading the aid as broadly as possible). . . . most legislators voted for that formula under which the Department of Education's simulations showed the greatest increase for their respective communities. This pattern of 'voting the printout' continued to characterize the behavior of most legislators throughout the 1978 school finance reform effort. Even a cursory examination of the legislative roll calls taken during its enactment shows a direct trade-off between the degree of *ex ante* equalization and the relative political appeal of each version of a reform proposal."

42. "Massachusetts in '80," *Boston Globe* (February 10, 1980).

43. See Michael Barone, *The Almanac of American Politics* (New York: Dutton, 1980), 390.

44. Perlstein, 547, 603-4.

45. Boston Municipal Research Bureau, "Boston Does It Again: Budget Overspent by $18.3 Million in FY 1979" (October 4, 1979).

46. Wood, 463.

47. Ibid., 463, 465, 461, 462-63.

48. "Wood Pulls Back on Move to Cut Hub 100 School Aids," *Boston Globe* (March 13, 1980).

49. Under Chapter 375, passed in 1975, state-aid reimbursements went to the city council rather than directly to the school committee. See Boston Municipal Research Bureau, "Boston's School Budget" (March 1964).

50. "Wood Asks $227 Million School Budget," *Boston Globe* (June 17, 1980).

51. "Special Education Target of Cuts," *Boston Globe* (March 31, 1980).

52. Wood, 467.

53. The idea of school personnel evaluations raised thorny legal questions. See Massachusetts Board of Education Study Committee, "Evaluation of Educational Personnel" (June 1980), 182, 2, 163.

54. Boston Municipal Research Bureau, "School Cuts: A Second Effort Needed" (February 13, 1976) and "Past Time to Reduce School Personnel" (January 30, 1976). The instructional budget of the Boston public schools was extremely difficult to cut. During Superintendent Fahey's administration, the Boston Municipal Research Bureau noted that "between 400 and 500 teaching positions could be eliminated without jeopardizing the educational process or desegregation effort. Failure of school officials to reduce teachers to reflect present enrollment is the primary factor in the School Department's projected $20 million deficit."

55. "Wood Asks $227 Million School Budget," *Boston Globe* (June 17, 1980).

56. Boston Municipal Research Bureau, "Facing Up to the Problem of Excess Schools: Why Nineteen Boston Elementary Schools Should Be Closed Now" (November 14, 1977).

57. "The New Heat on Garrity," *Boston Globe* (April 9, 1980).

58. Governor's Commission to Establish a Comprehensive Plan for School District Reorganization and Collaboration, "A Plan for Advancing Quality and Excellence by the Organization and Management of Public Education" (Boston: Massachusetts Advisory Council on Education, 1974), 52.

59. Boston Municipal Research Bureau, "The State of the Boston Public Schools: A Pessimistic Diagnosis by the Numbers" (September 17, 1981). "Blacks and other minorities represented 36 percent of total enrollment in 1970, 53 percent in 1975, and 65 percent in 1980. . . . Analysis of Boston's desegregation progress as of September, 1979, showed that only 35 percent of the 149 city schools, or 24 percent, complied with the court's desegregation standards for all races in their respective districts. Only 22 percent of all schools met the court's criteria for two of the three racial groups, 37 percent met the criteria for just one race, and 17 percent did not meet the standards for any race. Difficulties in achieving desegregation goals have mounted even as the court-approved criteria for each race have eased each year. The percentage of white pupils required to desegregate a school was reduced, and the percentage of black and other minority students permitted to attend a desegregated school was increased. For example, the Department of Management Information System's internal analysis showed that, in District IV, Hyde Park, the court-approved racial criteria for blacks was 35 percent in 1975 but was increased each year until in 1979 60 percent was acceptable."

60. "Garrity Criticizes Remarks by Wood on School Delays," *Boston Globe* (March 7, 1980).

61. "Garrity Asked to Reduce Role," *Boston Globe* (April 11, 1980) and "Garrity Criticizes Remarks by Wood on School Delays," *Boston Globe* (March 7, 1980).

62. Wood, 456, 461–62, 467.

63. See George R. Metcalf, *From Little Rock to Boston: The History of School Desegregation* (Westport, Conn.: Greenwood Press, 1983), 215–16. "Time and again, Judge Garrity emphasized the point that *Morgan* concerned itself with race, not education. Only the School Committee's unalterable opposition to change induced him to assume responsibilities that he knew properly belonged to the Committee. According to Garrity, the sine qua non was integration. If the results boosted the system's scholastic achievement, fine;

he sincerely hoped they would, but his primary interest was elsewhere. Consequently, Garrity would not monitor *Morgan* on the basis of test scores."

64. Wood, 468, 467. See also John Portz, Lana Stein, and Robin R. Jones, *City Schools and City Politics: Institutions and Leadership in Pittsburgh, Boston, and St. Louis* (Lawrence, Kans.: University Press of Kansas, 1999), 90: "Court orders can serve a useful role in bringing different parties together, but they cannot mandate the trust, consensus, and voluntary compliance that are critical to associations and networks. In Boston, the federal district court sparked considerable collaboration, but its long duration cast a lengthy shadow over the development of civic capacity."

65. "School Board's Balance of Power Uncertain," *Boston Globe* (January 7, 1980).

66. "Study Finds Imbalance in 76 Percent of Hub Schools," *Boston Globe* (June 7, 1980). "According to the study, submitted to the U.S. Office of Education last December in support of the school system's bid for more federal funds to aid in the desegregation process, 114 of the system's schools failed to meet one or more of the three (black, white and other minority) court-ordered racial-ethnic guidelines. Without substantial increases in federal funds, the study asserted, more white students will leave the system and desegregation will become even more difficult. . . . The study was sent to federal officials in support of the school system's bid for a five-year commitment of federal funds under the Emergency School Aid Act, which provides aid for school systems undergoing desegregation. School officials are still waiting for word from Washington on their request for $6 million in funds for fiscal 1981."

67. Wood, 460-61, 467. See also James T. Patterson, *Grand Expectations: The United States, 1945-1974* (New York: Oxford University Press, 1996).

68. "School Superintendent Wood Fired on Committee's 3-1 Vote," *Boston* Globe (August 22, 1980). See also "Boston Schools in Crisis," *Boston Globe* (February 8, 1981), "Warned last April that he already was running a record deficit of $14 million, Wood was optimistic that City Hall would recognize his attempts at upgrading the schools and willingly finance the changes. But Wood could not influence Kevin White. The mayor's reading of the city's political pulse suggested to him that the schools were no longer an issue and that he would lose no points by denying Wood the extra money."

69. "The Hope . . . The Anger," *Boston Globe* (August 22, 1980).

70. See "Boston Schools in Crisis," *Boston Globe* (February 13, 1981). "In the federal desegregation suit, Garrity resorted to a rare remedy in 1976 by ordering South Boston High School into receivership. That order overrode union rights so that administrators and teachers could be replaced without complying with the seniority requirements of collective bargaining agreements. While the receivership has promoted better education for Southie's students, it created a hostility that has placed the school's administration, brought in from St. Paul, Minn., in the role of suspect 'outsiders.'"

71. "Paul A. Kennedy: A Climb to the Top of Hub's Public School System," *Boston Globe* (August 23, 1980).

72. "Shakeup of School Brass Expected," *Boston Globe* (October 2, 1980).

73. "Paul A. Kennedy: A Climb to the Top of Hub's Public School System," *Boston Globe* (August 23, 1980). See also "Boston Schools in Crisis," *Boston Globe* (February 8, 1981). "Making unauthorized expenditures and personnel appointments or transfers has been simple over the years, because the school department maintains three separate accounts: one for budget, a second for payroll and a third for personnel. 'There is no communication among those departments,' said School Superintendent Kennedy. 'People are hired through various offices, without notifying personnel, and there is no meshing the openings and appointments with the budget.'"

74. "Shakeup of School Brass Expected," *Boston Globe* (October 2, 1980).

75. "Black Leaders Decry Plan for School Reorganization," *Boston Globe* (October 3, 1980).

76. See Wood, 455, 460.

77. See Boston Municipal Research Bureau, "Mayor and School Committee Must Compromise on School Budget: Research Bureau Recommends $220 Million for FY 1981" (September 3, 1980).

78. "Battle Continues on School Budget," *Boston Globe* (August 26, 1980). See also Alexander Thomas Tennant, "Proposition 2½: An Impetus for Change in the Budget Development Process of the Boston public schools for FY83" (Qualifying Paper, Harvard University, September 1982), 26: "Over the five year period prior to fiscal year 1982, the White administration spent $53 million more than it budgeted and the School Department, under several Superintendents, contributed its share to Boston's financial problems, spending over $50 million beyond its budgets since fiscal year 1977."

79. "Chapter 766: Progress and Problems," *Boston Globe* (October 6, 1980). See also "Hard-Pressed Schools Threaten 766 Trims," *Boston Globe* (March 20, 1980), "The state legislature heard warnings yesterday that some schools in Massachusetts will trim special education programs for the handicapped unless insurance companies and the federal government chip in with cash. Gregory T. Anrig, state education commissioner, . . . urged the Legislature's Education Committee to endorse a major change in the financing of the Chapter 766 special education program. They said private health insurance firms should be required to pay certain medical and diagnostic costs in the program. Anrig estimated those charges would run no more than about $17 million. Such an arrangement, he said, would qualify the state for about $6 million in federal Medicaid funds, relieving property taxes by a total of $23 million. If nothing is done, Anrig said, 'what we are jeopardizing are services to handicapped children.'"

80. Paul William Cox, "The Impact of State Funding of Special Needs Programs, Under Chapter 766, Acts of 1972, on the Funding of Other State and Local Educational Programs in Massachusetts" (Ed.D. dissertation, Boston College, 1980), 29-30, 34-36. As early as June, 1977, Cox found, the National Education Association (NEA) had speculated about the effect of underfunding P.L. 94-142 (which took effect in the fall of that year). "In order to fulfill federal mandates if the law was underfunded, local school districts would have to compensate by cutting other services, laying off teachers, and slashing other programs. These cutbacks would seriously undermine the quality of education provided for all children, and would generate hostility and outrage in the parents of normal children, parents of handicapped children, and teachers."

81. "School Board Seeks Talks on Budget Curb," *Boston Globe* (August 25, 1980). See also "Chapter 766—Progress and Problems," *Boston Globe* (October 26, 1980). As Bambi Levine of the state Department of Education noted, "a number of schools are needing to hire more people [to comply with both Chapter 766 and P.L. 94-142] at a time when regular education teachers are being laid off—and that's viewed by a number of people as not equitable. In some situations, I'm sure it's creating animosities."

82. "School Department Begins Retreat," *Boston Globe* (September 20, 1980).

83. "School Board's O'Leary Charged in Extortion Try," *Boston Globe* (October 3, 1980). FBI inquires also linked committee members John McDonough and Elvira "Pixie" Palladino to the extortion case.

84. "School Contract Probe to Continue," *Boston Globe* (October 4, 1980).

85. "School Department Warned," *Boston Globe* (October 29, 1980).

86. Governor's Invitational Conference on Issues in Education (October 18, 1979).

87. James McGarry, *Final Report: Implementing Massachusetts's Special Education Law: A Statewide Assessment* (1982), *vii*.

88. Massachusetts Advocacy Center, *Massachusetts: The State of the Child* (Boston, 1980). See also Cox, 32, 39. "The additional costs of supporting education through the local property tax became so severe that, on June 21, 1977, the Lieutenant Governor of Massachusetts, Thomas P. O'Neill III, who represented the National Governors' Conference, told the U.S. Senate Subcommittee on the Handicapped that because of [the] extreme property tax burden, support for Chapter 766 had been seriously undermined in Massachusetts." O'Neill added that "In my home state of Massachusetts we have learned a bitter lesson[:] one level of government cannot mandate programs and their costs on other jurisdictions in troubled fiscal times."

Chapter Eight

1. See Martha Wagner Weinberg, "Boston's Mayor Kevin White: A Mayor Who Survives," *Political Science Quarterly* 96:1 (Spring 1981), 87-106.

2. "An Unpredictable Start for the Boston Schools," *Boston Globe* (September 6, 1981); "Anrig: Proposition 2½ Not a Scare Story," *Boston Globe* (February 10, 1981).

3. See "Proposal Will Hurt Education, Anrig Warns School Officials," *Boston Globe* (October 16, 1980).

4. See James Catterall and Timothy Thresher, *Proposition 13: The Campaign, the Vote, and the Immediate Aftereffects for California Schools* (Stanford: Institute for Research on Education Finance and Governance, Stanford University, March, 1979).

5. See Bruce William Perlstein, "Taxes, Schools, and Inequality: The Political Economy of The Property Tax and School Finance Reform in Massachusetts" (Ph.D. dissertation, Brandeis University, 1981), 571.

6. Lawrence E. Susskind and Jane Fountain Serio, eds., *Proposition 2½: Its Impact on Massachusetts* (Cambridge, Mass. 1983). "In June 1978, just three days after California voters approved Proposition 13, four Republican legislators introduced the first version of Proposition 2½ into the Massachusetts legislature. As only one month remained in the session, they combined several small property tax reform bills that had been defeated in the past and added a 2.5 percent tax rate limit."

7. For more on the passage of Proposition 2½, see Helen Ladd and Julie Wilson, *Proposition 2½: Explaining the Vote* (Boston: Program in City and Regional Planning, 1981).

8. Susskind and Serio, 8. For information on Boston precinct voting statistics for Proposition 2½ by race and income, see James Jennings and Mel King, eds., *From Access to Power: Black Politics in Boston* (Cambridge, Mass.: Schenkman Books, 1986), 44, 49.

9. See Boston Municipal Research Bureau, "The State of the Boston Public Schools: A Pessimistic Diagnosis by the Numbers" (September 1, 1981). "The rise in school costs from 1969-70 to 1979-80 ran well ahead of the inflation in the economy. In constant 1972 dollars, total school costs over the past ten years increased by 38 percent, while net average [enrollment] fell over 34,000, or 36 percent. . . . The rise in instructional expense was due partially to retention of 1969-70 staff levels despite reduced enrollment, but also due to federal court desegregation orders and state mandated programs such as special and bilingual education."

10. See "Schools Feel the Budget Ax," *Boston Globe* (December 28, 1980).

11. See "An Unpredictable Start for the Boston Public Schools," *Boston Globe* (September 6, 1981).

12. Susskind and Serio, *vii*.

13. Untitled, *Boston Globe* (October 6, 1980).

14. See John Lawson, *Report on Federal Aid to Massachusetts School Districts* (October 19, 1983). As Lawson noted, fourteen districts that had been forced by Proposition 2½ to cut programs receiving federal matching grants were "further penalized by so-called maintenance-of-effort regulations." In his words, "any district that cuts expenditures faster than the rate of enrollment decline is liable to be penalized by losing federal aid." See Catherine Flynn and George McDowell, *Cutback Management: Coping with Proposition 2½* (Cooperative Extension Service, University of Massachusetts-Amherst 1981), 9.

15. See "O'Bryant First Black to Head School Board," *Boston Globe* (January 6, 1981).

16. Ibid.

17. "400 Layoffs Asked for Hub Schools," *Boston Globe* (February 24, 1981).

18. "Superintendent Kennedy Dies at 53," *Boston Globe* (March 27, 1981).

19. "Spillane Eager to Take Charge of Hub Schools," *Boston Globe* (July 1, 1981). See also "Class Act," *Boston Globe* (June 30, 1985).

20. "Spillane Eager to Take Charge of Hub Schools," *Boston Globe* (July 1, 1981). Many of the personnel cuts Spillane pursued had been started by his interim predecessor. See "An Unpredictable Start for the Boston Public Schools," *Boston Globe* (September 6, 1981).

21. See Massachusetts State Advisory Committee to the U.S. Commission on Civil Rights, *Minority Teachers in an Era of Retrenchment: Early Lessons in an Ongoing Dilemma* (December 1982), 21. "Judge Garrity's order was appealed by the Boston Teachers Union, an action causing severe division in the union along racial lines with effects up to the national level. The court of appeals for the First Circuit upheld the lower court in February 1982. The Teachers Union then appealed to the [U.S.] Supreme Court. In October 1982, the U.S. Supreme Court decided not to hear *Morgan v. O'Bryant*, effectively upholding the lower court's ruling." Four years later, however, the Supreme Court's ruling in *Wygant v. Jackson Board of Education* 476 U.S. 267 (1986) essentially supported the Boston Teachers Union's claims.

22. Not all the targets of Spillane's personnel cuts were tenured white teachers. See "Political Past Haunts Schools in Boston," *Boston Globe* (July 1, 1982).

23. "Spillane Goals: Accountability, Instruction," *Boston Globe* (September 15, 1981).

24. Ibid.

25. For information on the Individual Criterion Reference Test, see "Boston Schools in Crisis: What Pushed Schools to the Brink of a Shutdown," *Boston Globe* (February 8, 1981).

26. "Spillane Goals: Accountability, Instruction," *Boston Globe* (September 15, 1981).

27. See "Class Act," *Boston Globe* (June 30, 1985). As the *Globe* noted, "the Spillane administration has set up annual evaluations for teachers and administrators. 'As a result, over 50 teachers have been dismissed for incompetence, and approximately 60 principals and headmasters are newly assigned,' Spillane said in a recent interview. Among them was Thomas O'Neill, [the] new principal of the Solomon Lewenberg [Middle] School in Mattapan. 'I was not a Spillane supporter,' says O'Neill, who has been a teacher for the past 16 years. 'I did not like him. I thought he was too aloof and distant. It took me a while to come around and realize that this man is an organizer. He is interested in results.'"

28. "Massachusetts Tests Say Pupils Weakest in Writing," *Boston Globe* (October 28, 1981).

29. "Testing Competently," *Boston Globe* (December 27, 1981).

30. Ibid.

31. "Hub Schools Lack Key Guides for Teaching Basic Skills," *Boston Globe* (June 22, 1982).

32. For legal consideration of the link between state tests and local curricula, see George Madaus, *The Courts, Validity, and Competency Testing* (Boston: Kluwer-Nijhoff, 1983).

33. "Anrig to Take New Jersey Job," *Boston Globe* (May 5, 1981).

34. "Lawson Named Education Chief," *Boston Globe* (October 15, 1981).

35. "Why New State Education Commissioner Went After Job," *Boston Globe* (October 18, 1981). "A major priority for Lawson will be a re-examination of the status of public education in the state. 'I want to know how well all students are reading, writing and computing, and, if needed, I would push for developing priorities in those areas that could go beyond the state's current basic skills policy,' he said. If academic standards are generally low, he said, 'then I would not be averse to having the state communicate to school districts that there are minimum expectations—whether you can mandate them, I'm not sure.' Lawson, who is an acquaintance of new Boston school superintendent Robert Spillane, says he has 'a high regard for Dr. Spillane, and I'll do everything I can to see that he is supported in his goal of turning the Boston school system around.'"

36. "Massachusetts Tests Say Pupils Weakest in Writing," *Boston Globe* (October 28, 1981).

37. See "Lawson Named Education Chief," *Boston Globe* (October 15, 1981). "Lawson said the most serious issues facing public education are the financing of public schools, restoring public confidence in public education, and reviewing academic standards."

38. "Impact of Budget Chaos Lingers," *Boston Globe* (June 28, 1982). In the past, the *Boston Globe* noted, schools had no "means of limiting the number of employees. If there was a need for another staff member—either [for] legitimate or for political reasons— he or she could be added to the payroll by any number of school officials without any regard to the budgetary impact and often with no notice to the personnel department."

39. Quoted in Eleanor Farrar and Anthony Cipollone, "After the Signing: The Boston Compact, 1982 to 1985," *American Business and the Public School: Case Studies of Corporate Involvement in Public Education,* ed. Marsha Levine and Roberta Trachtman (New York: Teachers College Press, 1988), 96.

40. "The Solution(s) to School Crisis?" *Boston Globe* (May 31, 1981). As John O'Bryant argued, "as long as we have a city government which refuses to respond to that constituency which is, for the most part, made up of the working poor, black and minority citizens, we are going to continue to be a city in crisis."

41. "Boston's Schools: Signs of Change After Decade of Confusion, Fear," *Boston Globe* (December 9, 1982).

42. See "Class Act," *Boston Globe* (June 30, 1985). "Certainly, one of Spillane's greatest triumphs is his success in recruiting private money for school purposes. At the end of his fourth year he could point to $5 million in endowments and gifts from the Bank of New England, John Hancock, New England Life, and Bank of Boston, contributions that have been unprecedented in this city."

43. Farrar and Cippolone, 89–90, 98. The organizers of the Boston Compact deliberately avoided a grass-roots strategy. "The Compact document was written by a small core group of people who decided to forgo broad-based participation, with its inevitable political maneuvering and haggling, in favor of speed and decisiveness. 'It's always a tough choice whether to begin with something at the grassroots level and get a lot of participation or, particularly with something of this complexity, to negotiate behind closed

doors with a limited number of people and then deal with the flack you get from those who weren't included,' Bob Schwartz [assistant to Mayor White on educational issues] admitted. The Compact staff felt they had to operate the latter way because the business community had little understanding of, or tolerance for, the processes required in working with the public sector. 'If we had said to the business leadership that in addition to having to negotiate with the superintendent, we would have to go out and consult with 25 different community-based organizations and interest groups, they would have said, "Hey, sorry."'"

44. Quoted in Farrar and Cippolone, 93. See also "Business, Schools Join Forces on Jobs," *Boston Globe* (February 20, 1983), which was reprinted from *Rolling Stone.*

45. Farrar and Cippolone, 93–94. As Farrar and Cippolone pointed out, business-school partnerships already "existed as a result of the [federal] Youth Entitlement Program, which Boston had participated in from 1978 to 1980. As one part of the Youth Employment Demonstration Project Act under the 1977 amendments to the Comprehensive Employment Training Act, the Entitlement poured over $40 million into the city over a two-year period." Farrar and Cippolone noted that many leaders of the Boston Compact, including William Spring, Paul Grogan, Al McMahill, and Robert Schwartz, had worked together in the Carter administration. "They knew and trusted each other and hand many years of experience working together on youth employment issues. 'The original people—the plotters and conspirators—we all knew each other. We had similar views, similar ends, a very long track record in public life, and accessibility to all the powers in town,' Paul Grogan said. McMahill and others agreed. 'This was an example of what can happen when you get a group of people together who have known each other for awhile. You've known one another in various disguises so you don't necessarily haul around your turf baggage with you.' Bill Spring agreed but thought that their years of working on youth education and employment issues, some of them in Washington during the Carter Administration, were more important. They had just about crafted a new federal youth education and training bill when Carter lost the Presidency; in some sense, they were doing the same kind of thing all over again in Boston."

46. Quoted in Farrar and Cipollone, 96.

47. "Boston Schools: Signs of Change After Decade of Confusion, Fear," *Boston Globe* (December 9, 1982).

48. "Garrity Ruling Praised and Panned," *Boston Globe* (December 24, 1982).

49. "The Boston Experience: A Decade of Busing," *Boston Globe* (March 21, 1982).

50. "After 8 Years, Garrity Prepares to Curtail His Role in the Schools," *Boston Globe* (December 8, 1982).

51. Ibid. Garrity had begun his withdrawal from the case as early as 1979. "By October,1979, Garrity was sufficiently satisfied with the operation of the Department of Implementation to end reviews of student assignments by his court experts, Marvin B. Scott and Robert A. Dentler. . . . In November 1981, Garrity ruled that all but two of the system's 123 schools were either desegregated or so close to compliance that discrepancies were insignificant under law."

52. See "Boston Blacks Split on Plan to Replace Busing With Choice," *Boston Globe* (February 28, 1982) and "Board Cordial to Blacks' School Plan," *Boston Globe* (March 9, 1982).

53. "Garrity Provides Fuel to Critics Who Say He Meddles in the Schools," *Boston Globe* (May 8, 1982).

54. "Spillane Cites Split Over Garrity Decree," *Boston Globe* (May 12, 1982); "Spillane Criticizes Garrity Intrusions," *Boston Globe* (May 19, 1982).

55. "Spillane Hits Hard at Garrity Over School Ruling," *Boston Globe* (January 23, 1985).

56. See "Garrity Shifts Court Roles in Boston Schools to State," *Boston Globe* (December 24, 1982). "The judge indicated that the time was finally ripe for the court's partial withdrawal because of a cooperative school committee, a strong state Board of Education and the involvement of concerned parent and business organizations."

57. "100 Blacks Meet, Endorse Dukakis," *Boston Globe* (June 20, 1982).

58. See "King, Dukakis, and Minority Vote," *Boston Globe* (August 30, 1982).

59. "Dukakis' Acceptance Speech," *Boston Globe* (May 23, 1982).

60. "Dukakis Says No to Tests for Teacher Competency," *Boston Globe* (October 22, 1982).

61. Ibid.

62. "Governor's Speech Was Educational Because of What He Didn't Say," *Boston Globe* (May 14, 1983).

63. Thomas P. "Tip" O'Neill was Speaker of the House and a member of the Rules Committee when the Omnibus Budget Reconciliation Act of 1981 passed. See Michael Barone, *The Almanac of American Politics* (New York: Dutton, 1984), 557-58. According to Barone, O'Neill "steadfastly refuses to use procedure and rules to obstruct the legislative process. Some Republicans would quarrel with that [assessment], and cite the procedures the Rules Committee (now solidly controlled by O'Neill) supported on the major votes on the Reagan tax cuts in 1981. But the very fact that the vote took place at all that year is a tribute to O'Neill's sense of fairness: he kept the legislative process on schedule—not an easy task—and kept his word to the president that the House would vote on his program. It did, beating O'Neill on the rule and then on the substantive vote as well. . . . His long-term strategy in 1981 and 1982 was to put the Republicans on record in favor of the Reagan program and against a Democratic alternative, not only on budget and taxes, but particularly on Social Security, and then to jam those votes down their throats in the 1982 elections."

64. See Richard N. Holwill, ed., *The First Year: A Mandate for Leadership Report* (Washington, D.C.: The Heritage Foundation, 1982), 73-75. For more on the ECIA, see Brenda J. Turnbull, Marshall S. Smith, and Alan L. Ginsburg, "Issues for a New Administration: The Federal Role in Education," *American Journal of Education* 89 (1981), 396-427; Bette Everett Hamilton and Daniel Yohalem, "The Effects of Federal Deregulation: The Case of Handicapped Children," *Education and Urban Society* 14:4 (August 1982), 399-423; Richard F. Elmore and Milbrey Wallin McLaughlin, "The Federal Role in Education: Learning from Experience," *Education and Urban Society*, 15:3 (May 1983), 309-30; and Allan W. Odden and Dean L. Webb, *School Finance and School Improvement: Linkages for the 1980s* (Cambridge, Mass.: Ballinger Publishing Company, 1983). For preludes to the Reagan educational policies, see Chester E. Finn, Jr., *Education and the Presidency* (Lexington, Mass.: Lexington Books, 1977); Sar A. Levitan and Robert Taggart, *The Promise of Greatness* (Cambridge, Mass.: Harvard University Press, 1976); and Stephen S. Kaagan, "Executive Initiative Yields to Congressional Dictate: A Study of Educational Renewal, 1971-1972" (Ed.D. dissertation, Harvard University, 1973).

65. See "Bell Backs U.S. Role Shift on Education," *Boston Globe* (March 15, 1981). See also Terrel H. Bell, *The Thirteenth Man: A Reagan Cabinet Memoir* (New York: Free Press, 1988).

66. See U.S. Department of Education, *Toward More Local Control: Financial Reform for Public Education* (Washington, D.C., February, 1982). See also Terrel H. Bell, "Educa-

tion Policy Development in the Reagan Administration," *Phi Delta Kappan* (March 1986), 487-88, 490, 493.

67. Chapter 1 was similarly flexible when it came to eligibility guidelines. See Milbrey Wallin McLaughlin, "States and the New Federalism," *Harvard Educational Review* 52:4 (November 1982), 570. "In addition to the former Title I provisions, which permit[ted] funds to be allocated to attendance areas with the highest concentration of low-income families or to all attendance areas of a district that have uniformly high concentration of such children, Chapter 1 allows use of 'part of the available funds' for services 'which promise to provide significant help for all such children served by such agency.' It does not, however, provide a definition of either 'part' or 'all such children' (Sec. 556[b]). It is possible to interpret this language to permit the dispersion of Chapter 1 funds throughout the district, thereby undoing the past decade's efforts to concentrate federal funds for compensatory education. Moreover, if 'all such children' is interpreted to mean children from low-income families, but not educationally disadvantaged [i.e., low-achieving] youngsters, there is no apparent mandate to spend Chapter 1 funds on compensatory education. A district could choose, for example, to use these funds to support gifted and talented programs for low-income students."

68. See John H. Lawson, *Report on Federal Aid to Massachusetts School Districts* (October 19, 1983).

69. Richard Jung and Michael Tashjian, "Big Districts and the Block Grant: First-Year Fiscal Impacts," *Phi Delta Kappan* (November 1983), 203.

70. Quoted in Anne T. Hastings, "Snipping the Strings: Local and State Administrators Discuss Chapter 2," *Phi Delta Kappan* (November 1983), 197. See also Anne Henderson, "Chapter 2: For Better or Worse?" *Phi Delta Kappan* (April 1986), 600. According to Henderson, block grants did not necessarily foster deregulation at the state level. "In cases where money is passed through the states to the localities, the states have often added requirements that cause additional administrative burdens on localities. Moreover, as the block grants have come up for reauthorization, Congress frequently has added new controls to restrict the actual or alleged misuse of federal funds."

71. Quoted in Milbray W. McLaughlin, "States and the New Federalism," *Harvard Educational Review* (November 1982), 575.

72. Holwill, 78. In December 1979, the Heritage Foundation launched a project to outline priorities for a conservative administration. See *Mandate for Leadership: Policy Management in a Conservative Administration* (Washington, D.C. Heritage Foundation, 1981).

73. See David R. Mandel, "ECIA Chapter 2: Education's First Taste of the New Federalism," *Education and Urban Society,* 16:1 (1983), 29-43.

74. National Commission on Excellence in Education, *A Nation at Risk: The Imperative for Educational Reform* (April 1983).

75. David L. Clark, Terry A. Astuto, and Paula M. Rooney, "The Changing Structure of Federal Education Policy in the 1980s," *Phi Delta Kappan* (November 1983), 189.

76. Terrel Bell, "Education Policy Development in the Reagan Administration," *Phi Delta Kappan* (March 1986), 492-93.

77. *Board of Education of the Hendrick Hudson Central School District, Westchester County v. Rowley* 458 U.S. 176 (1982). "Noticeably absent from the language of the statute [P.L. 94-142] is any substantive standard prescribing the level of education to be accorded handicapped children. Certainly, the language of the statute contains no requirement like the one imposed by the lower courts—that states maximize the potential of handicapped children 'commensurate with the opportunity provided to other children.'"

78. *Board of Education of the Hendrick Hudson Central School District, Westchester County v. Rowley* 458 U.S. 176 (1982).

79. A comparison of handicapped students and non-English-speaking students arose in the case of *New Mexico Association for Retarded Citizens (NMARC) v. State of New Mexico* 495 F.Supp.391 (D.N.M., 1982), *rec'd in part* 678 F.2d 847 (Tenth Circuit, 1982). See Rosemary C. Salomone, *Equal Education Under Law: Legal Rights and Federal Policy in the Post-Brown Era* (New York: St. Martin's Press, 1986), 239-40.

80. See "Boston Schools in Crisis: A School System Caught in the Chapter 766 Crossfire," *Boston Globe* (February 12, 1981). "Right now, almost one out of every five of Boston's more than 63,000 students is in some kind of Chapter 766 program. . . . The bill this year for these 12,000 students comes to $46 million."

81. For the U.S. Supreme Court decision upholding the standard of "maximum feasible potential" in Massachusetts, see *Massachusetts Department of Education v. David D.* 475 U.S. 1140 (1986). See also Massachusetts Board of Education, "Report No. 3 to the United States District Court, District of Massachusetts, on Boston School Desegregation" 1 (July 15, 1984), 492-93. According to this report, "the student desegregation plan of May 10, 1975, which mandates multiple sites for K-12 bilingual programs in all districts where bilingual students reside (except districts 3 and 4) makes compliance with the Lau Guidelines regarding minimum cluster size extremely difficult or altogether impossible."

82. See "Now and Then a Different System; Schools Changed, But For Better or Worse?" *Boston Globe* (September 4, 1985). Massachusetts State Board of Education, "Policy on Basic Skills Improvement" (August 29, 1978), 5-6. See also Massachusetts Department of Education, "Evaluating Basic Skills Achievement" (April 1979), 4. "Each public school district shall exempt, from all provisions of these regulations, students who have limited English ability as defined by General Laws, Chapter 71A. Notwithstanding the previous sentence, students who have completed an appropriate transitional bilingual education program in accordance with General Laws, Chapter 71A . . . shall be considered as any other students for the purpose of these regulations." The state did not specify whether "limited English ability" was a label that could apply to students who, despite the completion of a transitional bilingual program or the completion of a regular education program, *still* performed below average (or below minimum standards) on tests of English language ability.

83. See Massachusetts Department of Education, "Schools for the City: Educating Linguistic Minority Students" (1988), 16. "The Board of Education has a responsibility to hold every school accountable for educational outcomes, and this can only be done through statewide, standardized measures that inevitably fall short of reflecting the complex achievements of each student. For linguistic minority students such tests are especially inadequate, but at the same time it is they (and other high-risk categories of students) for whom the Board's accountability must be exercised most vigorously. There is no way out of this dilemma. We must insist upon standardized testing of [linguistic minority] students while continually stressing that the test results do not adequately reflect their overall ability and potential."

84. U.S. Department of Health, Education, and Welfare, "Memorandum for Chief State School Officers and Local School District Superintendents" (August 1975), quoted in Massachusetts Department of Education, "Equal Educational Opportunity in Special Education: Legal Mandates and Strategies for Planning" (Boston, 1980), 6.

85. Massachusetts Department of Education, "Equal Educational Opportunity in

Special Education: Legal Mandates and Strategies for Planning" (Boston, 1980), 6. "The statutory and judicial mandates seek to guarantee equal treatment for all children. However, the law has never stated that equal treatment means identical treatment for different types of persons."

86. "Class Act," *Boston Globe* (June 30, 1985). See also "Test Scores Jump For Hub Students," *Boston Globe* (June 20, 1984) and College Board, *Equality and Excellence: The Educational Status of Black Americans* (New York: College Entrance Examination Board, 1985).

87. "Too Many Education Tests, Says ETS Chief," *Boston Globe* (June 30, 1985). "'There are too many tests,' Gregory Anrig, president of the service, last week told the joint College Board-Harvard University Summer Institute on College Admissions. 'It's gotten to the point where if it moves, we test it,' he said, while defending his company's college entrance examinations against recent criticisms."

88. "A Man with a King-Sized Job Ahead," *Boston Globe* (August 4, 1985).

89. Bell, "Education Policy Development in the Reagan Administration," 492–93. In 1984, in response to Reagan's appeals for new categorical programs in mathematics, science, and technology, Congress passed the Education for Economic Security Act (P.L. 98-377).

90. "Kennedy Blasts Cuts in Education Funds," *Boston Globe* (March 14, 1982).

91. Harriet T. Bernstein and Daniel W. Merenda, "Categorical Programs: Past and Present," in *The Federal Role in Education: New Directions for the Eighties,* ed. Robert A. Miller (Washington, D.C.: Institute for Educational Leadership, 1981), 64.

92. "Dukakis Proposes $100 Million in School Aid," *Boston Globe* (September 20, 1984). See also "'85 School Reform Law Is Credited with Improving Education in State," *Boston Globe* (March 4, 1987), "The state has allocated more than $25 million in equal educational opportunity grants to 129 school districts. The grants are slated for communities that are spending less than 85 percent of the state average per-pupil expenditure, which is currently $3,400. . . . [The] grants have allowed dozens of school districts to resume many of the programs that fell victim to Proposition 2½."

93. Massachusetts Department of Education, "Chapter 188, Massachusetts Public School Improvement Act of 1985: A Snapshot of Implementation as of March 1987" (Boston, 1987), 1.

94. "Children of the Cities Fare Worst in Statewide Test of Basic Skills," *Boston Globe* (August 18, 1987). It was important for legislators to tie rewards to increases in the *absolute* number of students with improved scores rather than the *proportion* of students with improved scores so schools would not have an incentive to encourage low-scoring students to drop out (if low-scoring students dropped out, then the proportion of students with improved scores might rise even as the absolute number of students with improved scores fell). The danger of this approach, however, was that *overall* increases or decreases in enrollment would distort the data on the absolute number of students with improved scores.

95. In the period from the mid-1970s to the mid-1980s, enrollments in special and bilingual education grew rapidly. Moreover, the number of students placed in substantially separate programs increased from 11 percent in 1977-78 to 20 percent in 1986-87. See Massachusetts Department of Education, "Facts on Special Education in Massachusetts" (Quincy, Massachusetts, March 1988), 3. See also Boston Municipal Research Bureau, "The State of the Boston Public Schools: A Pessimistic Diagnosis by the Numbers" (May 14, 1982). Between fiscal year 1976 and fiscal year 1981, the BMRB ex-

plained, "special education enrollment increased by 4,917 or 90 percent. . . . In bilingual classes, which may not exceed eighteen students without an aide, enrollment increased by 2,498 or 68 percent after fiscal year 1976."

96. Boston Urban Study Group, *Who Rules Boston? A Citizen's Guide to Reclaiming the City* (Boston: Institute for Democratic Socialism, 1984), 61–63.

97. "Dukakis Proposes $100 Million in School Aid," *Boston Globe* (September 20, 1984).

98. Massachusetts Department of Education, "Chapter 188: Massachusetts Public School Improvement Act of 1985: A Snapshot of Program Implementation" (March 1987), 27–28.

99. "Garrity May Stay On, Sources Say," *Boston Globe* (September 6, 1984).

100. "After 8 Years, Garrity Hopeful," *Boston Globe* (December 25, 1982). See also "Garrity Proposes School Enrollment Quotas," *Boston Globe* (April 4, 1985). "The proposed 80 percent ceiling is intended to deal with the increasing concentration of black students in Hyde Park, Mattapan and Dorchester schools. The hope, Dentler said, is that 'white students would be encouraged not to withdraw or find a way to transfer elsewhere . . . and that this device would prevent the racial isolation of black students.' Garrity noted that the assigned black enrollments at a 'half dozen to a dozen' schools in those neighborhoods are presently 'at or near the 80 percent mark.' In many cases they could go as high as 90 percent and still comply with his orders."

101. "Class Act," *Boston Globe* (June 30, 1985).

102. "Boston's New Schools Head," *Boston Globe* (August 2, 1985).

103. "Laval S. Wilson Changed Rochester Schools' Image," *Boston Globe* (July 14, 1985).

104. "Forum on Hub's Busing Crisis: Familiar Faces, New Questions," *Boston Globe* (September 29, 1985). See also "School Desegregation Cases Take On a New Look in United States; Local Boards Become Plaintiffs Suing for More Aid," *Boston Globe* (October 6, 1985): "Wilson . . . emphatically rejected the idea of seeking a metropolitan plan for Boston's schools. 'Most urban systems are headed toward large numbers of minority children,' he said. 'It is a false expectation that things will improve if you have enough money to bring kids together.'"

105. "In Search of Common Ground," *Boston Globe* (October 1, 1985).

Conclusion

1. "Standard Tests Under Fire," *Boston Globe* (November 20, 1989). "Complaints about the abuse of student testing procedures and scores are prompting educators and test publishers to take steps to reduce cheating and to stop the use of test results as measures of school quality." See also "Testing the Testers?" *Boston Globe* (May 20, 1990). The *Globe* described the activities of "teachers who circumvent the intent of testing by giving their classes the answers; in the most extreme instances, teachers have altered the children's answers. The fear of having their salaries, pay increases or promotions tied to the results of standardized tests has frightened some teachers."

2. "Wilson Blames Politics for His Ouster; Calls School Vote 'Miscarriage of Trust," *Boston Globe* (February 15, 1990).

3. See Lorrie A. Shepard, "The Contest between Large-Scale Accountability Testing and Assessment in the Service of Learning, 1970–2001" (unpublished paper, 2002).

4. See "School Chief Picks Panel on Tracking, Retention," *Boston Globe* (October 12, 1990).

5. See Thomas Timar, "Federal Education Policy and Practice: Building Organizational Capacity Through Chapter 1," *Educational Evaluation and Policy Analysis* 16:1 (Spring 1994), 51–66.

6. Quoted in Nick Penning, "An Administrator Goes to Congress," *School Administrator* (January 1989), 30.

7. See William H. Clune, "The Shift from Equity to Adequacy in School Finance," *World and I* 8:9 (September 1993), 397–98. "With new high educational standards being adopted, everyone is wondering who will be held accountable. . . . If high expectations are created without adequate resources, the whole system can easily turn into one for shifting blame."

8. See Harvey Kantor, "Equal Opportunity and the Federal Role in Education," *Rethinking Schools* 11:2 (November 2002). "There is not much the federal government can do directly to make [urban] schools better and reduce the disparities in achievement between low-income children and their more advantaged peers. The federal programs begun in the 1960s and 1970s, together with the civil rights movement, have gone a long way toward expanding educational services for economically disadvantaged students. But the experience of the last three decades has also taught us to temper our expectations about the potential effects of large-scale federal interventions on classroom learning."

9. See Arthur E. Wise, "On the Limits of Reforming the Schools Through Educational Measurement," *Cross References* 1:4 (August 1978).

10. Robert D. Gaudet, "The Status of Education Reform in Massachusetts" at www.edbenchmarks.org/schoolimprovement/status2.htm.

11. See Steven F. Wilson, *Reinventing the Schools: A Radical Plan for Boston* (Boston: Pioneer Institute, 1992), *xiv.* "The average combined Scholastic Aptitude Test (SAT) scores of Boston public school students continue to decline. In 1988, Boston's average score was 764; in 1989, 759; in 1990, 750; and, in 1991, 745—fully 151 points below the 1991 state and national average of 896."

12. Boston Public Schools, "Reducing the Racial/Ethnic Gap: Analysis of Performance on the MCAS by Racial/Ethnic Group, May 1998 to May 1999" (Boston, April 2000), unpaginated typescript.

13. See Marsha L. Brauen, "Issues and Options in Outcomes-Based Accountability for Students with Disabilities" (Reston, Va.: Council for Exceptional Children, 1994).

14. See Mary F. Ehrlander, *Equal Educational Opportunity: Brown's Elusive Mandate* (New York: LFB Scholarly Publishing, 2002), 300. "Many educators and activists who had followed the course of school desegregation closely now prioritized raising achievement levels over continued efforts at integration. Blacks who had chafed at the notion that black children needed the presence of white children in order to learn looked forward to rebuilding a sense of community in their neighborhood schools."

15. Public Agenda, *Time to Move On: African American and White Parents Set an Agenda for Schools* (1998). This report is available online at http://www.publicagenda.org/specials/moveon/moveon.htm. The school committee's decision to end the use of race as a factor in making student assignments evolved over the course of several years. In 1995, the parents of a white student denied admission to the Boston Latin School won a federal suit charging that the use of race unconstitutionally discriminated against white students. See *Wessman v. Gittens* 160 F.3d 790 (First Circuit, 1998). According to Harvard professor Gary Orfield, the reversal of court-ordered integration in northern schools resulted from a shift in the federal judiciary. See Harvard Graduate School of Education, "Busing in Boston: Looking Back at the History and Legacy" (September 1, 2000) at http://www.gse.harvard.edu/news/features/busing09012000_page1.html.

"'Desegregation is being lost in Boston not because the people of Boston decided to stop it or because the Boston school committee wanted to stop it, but because Ronald Reagan changed the federal courts by appointing conservative, anti-desegregation judges,' Orfield says."

16. See "W. Arthur Garrity, Jr.," *Boston Globe* (September 18, 1999) and "Many Refuse to Mourn Man Viewed As Foe," *Boston Globe* (September 18, 1999).

17. See Carl F. Kaestle and Marshall S. Smith, "The Federal Role in Elementary and Secondary Education, 1940–1980," *Harvard Educational Review* 52:4 (November 1982), 403. "The late 1960s had seen a variety of school-based policies, such as community control, compensatory education, and affirmative action, that competed with the goals of desegregation."

18. See Ehrlander, 288. "Ironically, while the purpose of high stakes competency or exit exams was to increase student performance and school system and student accountability, such exams were encountering legal challenges because of the disproportionate failure of minority students." See also Barry M. Franklin, *From 'Backwardness' to 'At-Risk': Childhood Learning Difficulties and the Contradictions of School Reform* (Albany: State University of New York Press, 1994).

19. See Jackie Kimbrough and Paul T. Hill, *Problems of Implementing Multiple Categorical Education Programs* (Santa Monica, Calif.: Rand Corporation, 1983); and Molly McCusic, "The Use of Education Clauses in School Finance Reform Litigation," *Harvard Journal on Legislation* 28 (1991), 307, 308.

20. "City Students Show Improved Test Scores," *Yale Daily News* (March 26, 2003). The emphasis on standardized tests put many schools in a difficult situation. On the one hand, if they erred on the side of high scores, then program auditors might conclude they were receiving money for special-compensatory services their students did not really need. On the other hand, if they erred on the side of low scores, then auditors might conclude they were squandering money on programs that did not work. Either way, standardized test scores were used to justify the *withdrawal* of supplemental aid.

21. See Kaestle and Smith, 405. "Supplemental activities for low-scoring students in poverty areas, special classes for bilingual youngsters, new procedures for handling handicapped children, and equal levels of sports activities for boys and girls are all important issues, and they take much time and energy to work out. Yet, they are not central to the workings of the regular school program. Taken together these activities assumed great weight because of their symbolic value; taken separately they were often seen as interfering with the real business of the schools. . . . To be sure, in inner-city schools where multiple problems abound, the federal programs and mandates create bureaucratic and pedagogical confusion. Students are pulled out of regular classes for Title I, integrated into regular classes under ESAA and the Handicapped Act, and segregated again for bilingual education."

22. See Wilson, 212. "Boston's regular and special education programs function in a vicious cycle. As the regular classroom declines, students are shunted to special education. Since special education's small class sizes and generous staffing levels are guaranteed by state regulations, costs skyrocket as enrollment burgeons. As a larger portion of the district's budget flows to the mandated program, the resources for regular education diminish further. Remedial programs are eliminated, instructional supply budgets slashed, and regular education programs debilitated, leading to still more special education referrals." In 1991, the Massachusetts board of education found that, between 1974 (the year before P.L. 94-142) and 1990, the proportion of disabled students in *isolated* classes had increased from 9.4 percent to 20.7 percent (an increase of 120 per-

cent). See Massachusetts Board of Education, "A Comprehensive Report of the Issue of Mainstreaming Children With Special Needs" (September 1991), 5-6.

23. Paul T. Hill, "Getting It Right the Eighth Time: Reinventing the Federal Role" (unpublished paper, March 1999). See also Hamilton Lankford and James Wyckoff, "Where Has the Money Gone? An Analysis of School District Spending in New York," *Educational Evaluation and Policy Analysis* 17:2 (Summer 1995), 195-218.

24. *State Auditor's Report on Special Education in Massachusetts* (March 1991). In 1980, total state spending for special education was $266.9 million; in 1985, it was $389.2 million; in 1990, it was $739.5 million—a jump of 177 percent in ten years. P.L. 94-142 had promised to cover 40 percent of special education expenditures by 1981, but, in 1989, federal aid reimbursed only 6 percent of actual costs. Similarly, Chapter 766 had promised to cover *all* excess costs associated with special education, but, in 1989, state reimbursements covered only 5.8 percent, or $43 million, of the $739.5 million total. Localities, therefore, covered an average of 88.2 percent of the costs of special education in Massachusetts. See also Julie Berry Cullen, "The Impact of Fiscal Incentives on Student Disability Rates," *National Bureau of Economic Research Working Paper* 7173 (1999).

25. See David K. Cohen, "Policy and Organization: The Impact of State and Federal Educational Policy on School Governance," *Harvard Educational Review* 52:4 (November 1982), 477-99.

26. See, for example, the language used in the remedy phase of *Keyes v. Denver School District No. 1* 576 F. Supp. 503 (D. Colorado, 1983). "The defendant [the Denver public schools] considers *Lau* C children to be bilingual, presumably with equal proficiency in English and another language. That view disregards the other element of the applicable definition in the Colorado Language Proficiency Act that the English language development and comprehension of such bilingual students is at or below the district mean or below an acceptable proficiency level on a national standardized test or a test developed by the Colorado Department of Education." In other words, education for non-English-speaking children was considered to be sufficient only when it helped them score at or above "the district mean" or "an acceptable proficiency level" on a national standardized test or on a test developed by the state department of education.

27. *Lau v. Nichols* 414 U.S. 563 (1974).

28. *San Antonio Independent School District v. Rodriguez* 411 U.S. 1 (1973) and *Lau v. Nichols* 414 U.S. 563 (1974). See also William H. Clune, "New Answers to Hard Questions Posed by *Rodriguez:* Ending the Separation of School Finance and Educational Policy by Bridging the Gap Between Wrong and Remedy" 24 *Connecticut Law Review* 721, 735 (1992).

29. See U.S. Commission on Civil Rights, *Equal Educational Opportunity and Nondiscrimination for Students with Limited English Proficiency: Federal Enforcement of Title VI and Lau v. Nichols* (November, 1997), 187-93, 134. "Federal civil rights laws require schools to comply with the *Brown* decision's requirements for equal treatment and integration; the nondiscrimination provisions under Title VI; the effective participation requirements of *Lau;* and, if necessary, the remedies for discrimination described in the Equal Educational Opportunities Act [of 1974]. These obligations require schools to strive towards two somewhat conflicting goals: integration and effective participation." See also *Castaneda v. Pickard* 648 F. 2d. 989 (Fifth Circuit, 1981). Incidentally, the Supreme Court in *Board of Education of the Hendrick Hudson Central School District, Westchester County v. Rowley* 450 U.S. 176 (1982) used the Fourteenth Amendment, not the Civil Rights Act, to uphold Rowley's right to a "meaningful" education.

30. Explicit mention of academic achievement or standardized test scores in Supreme Court decisions is a relatively recent phenomenon. For one example, see *Missouri v. Jenkins* 515 U.S. 70 (1995). Justice David Souter, in his dissenting opinion in this case, insisted that, when considering the effectiveness of schools marked by past segregation and racial discrimination, courts would have to consider academic achievement as measured by standardized tests: "In the development of a proper unitary status record, test scores will undoubtedly play a role. It is true, as the court recognizes, that all parties to this case agree that it would be [an] error to require that the students in a school district attain the national average test score as a prerequisite to a finding of partial unitary status, if only because all sorts of causes independent of the vestiges of past school segregation might stand in the way of the goal. That said, test scores will clearly be relevant in determining whether the improvement programs have cured a deficiency in student achievement to the practicable extent."

31. See Herbert Teitlebaum and Richard J. Hiller, "Bilingual Education: The Legal Mandate," *Harvard Educational Review* 47:2 (May 1977), 169. "At a minimum, the courts and the school districts as well need reliable indexes for gauging programs by the standard of equal benefits, the touchstone of Title VI. . . . Grades, scores on standardized achievements tests, and dropout and absentee rates are certainly probative as to whether a remedy is effective in securing equality of benefits."

32. See Massachusetts Department of Education, "Students with Special Needs in Massachusetts by Federal Disability Category for the Year 1991-1992" (Boston, March 1992), 20. From 1980 to 1991, the proportion of all handicapped students in Massachusetts defined as "learning disabled" increased from 36.7 percent to 61.0 percent. This percentage (the highest in the country) was 21 percent higher than the national average. According to the state department of education, "the large percentage of students with learning disabilities may not reflect actual disabilities, but the decreased capacity of regular education to appropriately meet the needs of diverse learners."

33. See William C. Lannon, "Responses," *Harvard Educational Review* 52:4 (November 1982), 532-33. Lannon, a school official in Cambridge, Massachusetts, noted that federal aid for the disabled under P.L. 94-142 had drawn resources away from regular classrooms.

34. *McDuffy v. Robertson* 415 Mass. 545 (1993). This litigation began in 1978 as *Webby v. Dukakis*.

35. See Bradley W. Joondeph, "The Good, the Bad, and the Ugly: An Empirical Analysis of Litigation-Prompted School Finance Reform," *Santa Clara Law Review* 35 (1995), 763.

36. See Wilson, 303. "Boston's problem is not a lack of funds. In the spirit of 'reform,' Boston has dramatically increased its total school spending and teacher salaries over the last decade. Yet neither quality nor equity of educational opportunity improved for Boston's children—if anything, they declined. As in other states, including California, where similar financing reforms have been implemented, equalizing financial 'inputs' will not equalize educational 'outputs.'"

37. See Hill, "Getting It Right the Eighth Time: Reinventing the Federal Role" (unpublished paper, March, 1999). "Of the new net money spent on education, about 38 percent went to special education for severely handicapped and learning-disabled children. Increasing numbers of parents sought individually tailored accommodations for their children, and the definitions of 'handicapping conditions' proliferated. Virtually any child who had trouble learning to read or adjusting to the behavioral demands of schools could be considered handicapped and was therefore entitled to a special accommodation."

38. See Wilson, 201–3. In the Boston public schools, special education classes enrolled 8.4 percent of all students in 1970–71, 18.0 percent of all students in 1980–81, and 22.0 percent of all students in 1990–91. By 1991–92, 22.9 percent of all students in the Boston public schools were enrolled in special education. As Wilson pointed out, only part of this growth was attributable to state and federal policies, because, even within the same state, different school districts enrolled different proportions of students in special education. "While Boston had 21.2 percent of its students in special education in 1988," Wilson noted, "Lawrence had 12.1 percent, Worcester 17.5 percent, and Springfield only 13.3 percent, though all are subject to the same provisions of state law. . . . Just as Chapter 766 enrollment varies sharply from community to community, so do costs per FTE (full-time equivalent) student. In 1989, Boston spent $17,411 per FTE, substantially more than Lowell, New Bedford, Springfield, and Worcester. Lawrence spent only $8,367."

39. See "Special Education Law Change Approved: Massachusetts Legislators End 'Maximum' Benefit Rule," *Boston Globe* (July 18, 2000).

40. Massachusetts Department of Education, "Follow-Up on Students with Extended Stays in the Boston Transitional Bilingual Education Program" (April 29, 1986), *ii, iv.* "In Spanish middle school programs, 325 of a total of 762 (43 percent) have participated in [the transitional bilingual education program] for 6 years or longer. In Spanish high school programs, 194 of 609 (32 percent) have participated in [the transitional bilingual education program] for 6 years or longer." The study added that "approximately 30 percent (167 of 519 students) of Spanish students in the program 6 years or more also receive bilingual special education services. Data from the past three years indicate that nearly half of this group (73 students) has not been moved to a higher level of English proficiency during that time."

41. "Boston Schools Steer Hispanics Down a Path to Failure; Curriculum, Attitudes Form Core of Problem," *Boston Globe* (June 10, 1990). "Some educators contend that bilingual education, once viewed as a panacea for Hispanic students, has become another part of the problem. Hispanics in bilingual programs—nearly half of those in the [Boston Public School] system—drop out an annual rate of 17 percent compared to 16 percent for Hispanics in regular programs." For a different view, see Catherine E. Walsh, "Transitional Bilingual Education in Massachusetts: A Preliminary Study of Its Effectiveness" (Boston: Massachusetts Department of Education, April, 1986), 73–75.

42. See "English Immersion Plan Wins Over Bilingual Education," *Boston Globe* (November 6, 2002).

43. See Bradley Scott, "The Fourth Generation of Desegregation and Civil Rights" in Civil Rights in Education: Revisiting the *Lau* Decision" (San Antonio: Intercultural Development Research Association, January, 1995).

44. See James Q. Wilson, "Responses," *Harvard Educational Review* 52:4 (November 1982), 415–18.

INDEX

Abraham Lincoln Elementary School, 63–64, 260n60

accountability, 164–66, 179, 195, 196–97, 207–9, 228, 243–45, 316n83, 320n18; budgeting and, 198–99; Chapter 188 and, 236; court orders and, 201–3; personnel management and, 217; racial balance and, 205; Robert C. Wood and, 193–94, 203–5; testing and, 218–20, 225–26, 233–34, 242–44

Action for Boston Community Development (ABCD), 38, 43, 87, 108, 266n25, 267n44, 268n56, 283n67

Allen, James E., Jr., 93–94, 99, 119, 176, 192

American Institutes for Research (AIR), 69, 192–93

Anrig, Gregory T., 141, 194–95, 199, 201, 208, 211–12, 214, 218–19, 234, 304n10, 309n79, 317n87

Association for Mentally Ill Children v. Greenblatt. See *Barnett v. Goldman*

Association Promoting the Constitutional Rights of the Spanish-Speaking (APCROSS), 78, 198

Barnett v. Goldman, 129-30, 131, 133, 159, 175, 287n17

Batson, Ruth, 222-23, 265n17

Bell, Terrell H., 176, 229-30, 235

bilingual education, 103-4, 253, 275n43; bilingual teachers and, 75-76; enrollment and, 197-98, 233, 252, 282n44, 284n70; funding, 108-10, 178, 282n50; pullout programs, 77-78, 105-7, 121, 126, 232, 282n52, 283n67; racial imbalance and, 76-79, 111-19, 137, 142; special education and, 189-90. *See also* Bilingual Education Act; Chapter 71A; *Lau v. Nichols; Serna v. Portales Municipal Schools*

Bilingual Education Act, xiv-xv, 89, 103, 142, 169, 204, 282n52, 283n61, 284nn71-73, 294n70; effect on enrollments in bilingual programs, 78-79, 283n57; passage of, 76

black migration, 20, 260n60

Black Panthers, 73, 83

Black Parents' Committee, 223

Black United Front, 83, 85

Board of Education of the Hendrick Hudson Central School District, Westchester County v. Rowley, 231-33, 252, 288n19, 310n73, 315n77

Boston Association for Retarded Children, 2, 3, 256n1

Boston Banks Urban Renewal Group (BBURG), 289n30

Boston Child Betterment Association, 2

Boston Compact, 221, 312n43, 313n45

Boston Latin School, 109, 319n15

Boston Municipal Research Bureau (BMRB), 56, 78, 153, 155, 157, 199, 206, 269n85, 270n93, 300n58, 307n54, 307n59, 310n9, 317n95

Boston Private Industry Council, 221

Boston Redevelopment Authority (BRA), 23-24, 78

Boston Teachers Union, 197-99, 201, 217, 225, 311n21. *See also* unions, teachers'

Boston Urban Coalition, 84-85, 221

Brennan, William J., Jr., 142

Briggs v. Elliot, 48, 268n59

Brooke, Edward III, 139

Brown v. Board of Education of Topeka, Kansas, xv, 6, 140, 146

Brown v. Board of Education II, 6, 14

Budoff, Milton, 133, 170, 277n68, 288nn25-26

busing, ix, 52, 54, 149, 151-53, 161-62, 166-67, 193, 200, 202-3, 207-8, 224, 239-40, 279nn4-5, 279n7, 293n59, 293nn61-63, 318n104; court-ordered, 140-43, 147-48, 168-69, 179-80, 196, 255n1, 289-90nn32-33, 291nn43-45, 292n55, 294n70; opposition to, 92-93, 118, 138-39, 144-46, 222-23, 278n79, 285n80; voluntary, 219, 268n68

Capeless, Robert T., 161, 269n88, 298nn30-31

Cardenas, Jose, 294n74

Cardinal Cushing Center, 78

Carmichael, Stokely, 73, 83

Carter, Jimmy, 179, 213, 313n45

Casey, Alice, 101, 170, 174, 176

Castaneda v. Pickard, 321n29

Celebreeze, Anthony J., 45, 62

Chapter 1. *See* Educational Consolidation and Improvement Act

Chapter 70, 142, 155-56, 171-72, 173, 269nn88-89, 300nn58-59, 300n61

Chapter 71, 4-5, 126, 260n52

Chapter 71A (Transitional Bilingual Education Act), 110-13, 123, 132, 135, 142, 147, 152, 233, 283n67; demise of, 253

Chapter 188, 236-37

Chapter 514, 4-5, 68, 256n11

Chapter 650, 39-40, 58

Chapter 660, 28

Chapter 750, 18-19, 81-83, 260n52, 276n57, 277nn58-59

Chapter 766, 142, 208-9, 233, 252, 300n52, 300n61, 303n3, 304n7, 304n9, 305n16, 305n21, 309nn79-81, 310n88, 321n24; effect on special education enrollments, 177-78, 316n80, 323n38; implementation of, 152, 154-55, 169-75, 182-90, 300n57, 301n66, 303n85; passage of, 132-35, 288n23, 288n25

Chinatown, 63-64, 66

Chinese students, 64–66
choice plans, 223, 230, 238, 246
Christopher Gibson Elementary School, 53
Citizens Education Advisory Council (CEAC), 87
Citywide Coordinating Council, 193
Citywide Education Coalition, 236
Civil Rights Act, 51, 104–6, 113–14, 146–48, 249–50, 266n31, 268n60, 269n79, 271n2, 272n14, 281n38, 281n40, 282n50, 283n58, 289n29, 292n55, 294n73, 321n29, 322n31; de facto segregation and, 44–48, 58, 267n54; passage of, 40–42
Clavell, Mario, 101, 109
Clinchy, Evans, 44, 49–50
Cohen, Raquel, 101, 107
Cohen, Wilbur J., 41
Coleman, James S., 65–66, 272n14
Committee for the Full Funding of Education, 176
compensatory education, xiv, 152; de facto segregation and, 35–36, 37; for disabled students, 131, 134, 177; for disadvantaged students, 26–27, 32–35; effectiveness of, 98–99, 190–91, 280n13, 280n25, 285n75; federal aid and, 38, 40, 78–79, 89, 167–69, 271n4, 315n67; racial balance and, 46–47, 50–54, 56, 58–59, 63, 65, 72–73, 88, 116, 118, 135–36, 142–43, 146, 266n28, 267n48, 269n86, 271n5, 272n6, 276n56, 278n79, 285n82; testing and, 68, 320n20. See also bilingual education; Chapter 650; Lau v. Nichols; Operation Counterpoise; School-Community Advisory Council; special education; Task Force on Children Out of School; Title I
Comprehensive Employment Training Act (CETA), 221, 313n45
Conant, James B., 40, 160, 258n31
Congress of Racial Equality (CORE), 45, 265n19, 278n79
Cook, Paul W., Jr., 162, 299n43
Council for Exceptional Children (CEC), 176, 302n75
Council of Chief State School Officers (CCSSO), 72, 176, 280n17

Council of Great City Schools (CGCS), 24–25, 176
Cronin, Joseph M., 164–65, 296n14

Daly, Michael J., 101, 110, 132, 194, 199
Daly-Bartley-Sargent Special Education Act. See Chapter 766
Danière, André, 156, 158, 297nn22–23
Day, Noel, 145, 153, 261n62, 265n19, 293n63
desegregation, 14, 42, 61, 72, 93–94, 138–40, 179, 197–98, 202–3, 227–28, 230, 239–40, 246–47, 290n35, 293n64, 294n70, 307n59, 308n66, 308n70; court ordered, xiii, 162, 200, 224, 291n42, 295nn74–75; legislation and, 167, 285n82. See also busing; Keyes v. Denver School District No. 1; Lau v. Nichols
diagnosis of disabilities, 100, 170–74, 181–87, 191, 257n18, 257nn20–21, 286n5, 288n26, 301n63, 304n12, 322n32, 322n37; minorities and, 5–7, 38–39, 68–71, 80–82, 121–26, 286n7. See also Chapter 766; Education for All Handicapped Children Act
Dorchester, 3, 10, 73, 75, 84, 85, 134, 222, 238
Dorchester High School, 222
Dukakis, Michael S., 166, 183, 194–96, 224–26, 236–37, 306n39, 322n34

East Boston, 50, 263n3
ECIA. See Educational Consolidation and Improvement Act
Economic Opportunity Act, 40, 41, 46
Educational Consolidation and Improvement Act, xv, 226–29, 242–43, 314n66
Education for All Handicapped Children Act (P.L. 94-142), xv, 175–78, 181, 183–86, 187, 208–9, 302n73, 304n7, 309nn80–81, 315n77, 320n22, 321n24, 322n33; Board of Education of the Hendrick Hudson Central School District v. Rowley and, 231–33; as unfunded mandate, 198, 207
Education for Economic Security Act, 317n89
Eisenhower, Dwight D., 7, 8, 11–14, 22, 106, 226, 258n27

El Comite de Padres Pro Defensa de la
Educacion Bilingue, 147, 201

Elementary and Secondary Education
Act, xiv-xv, 57, 89, 111, 167, 205,
267n40, 268n56, 270n97, 271n4,
279-80nn11-12, 280n14, 280n25,
284n73, 285n74, 289n29; amendments to, 72, 76; civil rights and, 44-
46; de facto segregation and, 62, 63,
272n6, 285n82; effectiveness of, 85,
94-99, 280n17, 290n33; implementation of, 49-51, 54, 55, 58, 81, 116,
141-42, 168, 226-28, 236, 315n67,
320n21; passage of, 42-43, 103-104,
245. *See also* Bilingual Education Act;
Civil Rights Act

Elliott, Carl, 13, 259n39

Emergency School Assistance Act (ESAA),
167, 203, 227-28, 308n66, 320n21

English as a Second Language (ESL), 21,
65, 75-79, 112, 284n73

English High School, 154, 222

Equal Educational Opportunity Act, 144

equalization formula for state aid to
schools, 57-58, 156, 270n91, 270n94

Fahey, Marion J., 166-70, 173, 193, 205,
307n54

Federal Housing Act, 22, 24

Federal Housing Administration,
289n30

Federal Reserve Bank of Boston, 156,
161, 222, 269n88

Finch, Robert H., 93, 95-96, 106

Flannery, Richard, 136-38, 140

Folsom, Marion B., 13, 14

Ford, Gerald R., 168, 176, 177

foundation formula for state aid to
schools, 27, 57

Furcolo, J. Foster, 8-9, 51, 161

Gardner, John W., 62, 84, 85, 88

Garrity, Wendell Arthur, Jr., xiii, 136, 138,
140-49, 151-53, 162, 166, 167, 176,
180, 199-203, 219, 223, 224, 238,
239, 246, 291nn41-42, 291nn44-45,
292n52, 292n56, 293n61, 307n63,
308n70, 311n21, 313n51, 314n56,
318n100

Gartner, Alan, 45

George A. Lewis Middle School, 39, 137

George Bancroft Elementary School, 21,
76, 261n64

Georgia, Sister Frances, 75, 77, 107,
276n50

Gertrude Godvin School for Boys, 2

gifted education, xiv, 11, 16, 167, 227,
258n31, 315n67

Gillis, Frederick J., 16-29, 31-32, 36, 62,
68-69, 256n7, 257n20, 259n45,
260n52, 260nn55-56, 260n58,
260n60, 261n62, 261n64, 261n69,
262n75-76, 262n79, 263n88,
263nn2-4, 264nn8-9, 268n62,
273n19

Glenn, Charles, Jr., 115, 281n40

Goals 2000: Educate America Act, 245

Goldwater, Barry, 14

Great Cities Program for School Improvement. *See* Council of Great City
Schools

Griffith, Rollins, 101, 265n14

Guscott, Kenneth, 84

Haley, Dennis C., 2-4, 5, 7, 9-10, 15-17,
29, 31, 127, 256n2, 256n6, 256n13,
257n18, 257n21, 258n23, 258n26,
259nn42-44, 260n57, 268n56,
275n38, 289n27

Harrington, Michael, 26, 28

Harvard Center for Law and Education,
223

Harvard Graduate School of Education,
9, 23, 40, 92, 93, 95, 141, 161, 218,
319n15

Hawkins-Stafford School Improvement
Amendments, 242-43

Heffley, John E., 173-74, 194, 298n27,
301nn69-70

Henry L. Higginson Elementary School,
34, 264n10

Hicks, Louise Day, 37, 45, 47-51, 52, 56,
59, 63-67, 74, 93, 118-19, 139, 196,
266nn23-24

Hill, Lister, 13

Hobson v. Hanson, 70-72, 88, 98, 124,
273nn25-27, 274n28, 274nn30-31,
274n33, 279n7, 297n25

Horace Mann School for the Deaf, 2

Howe, Harold II, 62, 72-73, 88, 93, 96,
271n2, 278n80

Humphrey, Hubert H., 89, 91, 175, 205

Hyde Park, 10, 50, 238, 307n59, 318n100
Hyde Park High School, xiii–xiv, 39, 222

Immigration and Naturalization Act, 275n38

Jaffe, Louis L., 142, 143, 293n60
James P. Timilty Junior High School, 85–86, 225
John Greenleaf Whittier Elementary School, 3, 17, 19
Johnson, Larry, 223
Johnson, Lyndon B., 37, 40, 41–42, 47, 62, 76, 78, 84–85, 89, 138, 193, 204
John W. McCormack Middle School, 222
Jones, Hubert E., 101, 187–88
Joseph Lee Elementary School, 134–37, 154, 289n28, 289n32. See also *Morgan v. Hennigan*
Josiah Quincy Elementary School, 222
juvenile delinquency, 24, 32, 77
Juvenile Delinquency and Youth Offenses Control Act, 19, 32, 260n56, 266n25

Kennedy, Edward M., 43, 51, 52, 76, 103, 175–76, 177, 196, 213, 235, 269n70, 293n67, 302n73
Kennedy, John F., 17–18, 19, 22, 24, 26, 27, 31, 32, 34, 37, 40, 41, 138, 175, 259n49, 260n50, 266n25
Kennedy, Paul, 205, 206, 211, 215–16, 308n73
Kennedy, Robert F., 51, 86, 92, 95, 138
Kennedy, Rosemary, 18, 175
Keppel, Francis, 40–43, 45, 47, 55, 62, 88, 93
Kerner Commission (National Advisory Commission on Civil Disorders), 85
Keyes v. Denver School District No. 1, 139–42, 146, 147–49, 162, 290n40, 291nn42–43, 291n45, 295n75, 321n26
Kiernan, Owen, 8–10, 45, 50, 51, 55, 72, 87–88, 92, 266n27, 267n48, 270n95, 271n2
King, Edward J., 195–96, 225
King, Martin Luther, Jr., 36, 45, 83, 85, 86, 92
Kozol, Jonathan, 52–53, 66–67, 269n77, 269n86

Lau v. Nichols, 104, 146–49, 249–50, 281n37, 281n41, 282n44, 282n50, 283n58, 284n72, 292n55, 293n67, 294n73, 316n81, 321n26, 321n29
Lawson, John H., 219–20, 224, 225, 311n14, 312n35, 312n37
Leary, William J., 141, 154, 166–67
Lee, Joseph, 108–9
Lincoln Filene Center for Citizenship and Public Affairs, 53–54
Lukas, J. Anthony, 239

Manpower Development Act, 19, 22
Marland, Sidney, 176
Marshall, Thurgood, 299n37
Martin Luther King, Jr., Middle School, 85, 236
Massachusetts Advisory Council on Education (MACE), 28, 162, 173
Massachusetts Advocacy Center (MAC), 169–70, 178, 187–90, 305n21
Massachusetts Commission Against Discrimination (MCAD), 104–6, 113–14, 118, 222, 225
Massachusetts Comprehensive Assessment System (MCAS), 245, 247, 251
Massachusetts Education Reform Act, 245, 251
Massachusetts High Technology Council, 237
Massachusetts Institute of Technology (MIT), 78, 84
Massachusetts Mental Retardation Planning Project, 38, 39, 43, 50, 67, 256n1
Massachusetts Psychological Association, 133
Massachusetts School for Idiotic and Feebleminded Youth, 1, 2
Massachusetts Teachers Association (MTA). *See* unions, teachers'
Mattapan, 10, 238, 289n30, 311n27, 318n100
Maurice J. Tobin Elementary School, 223–24
McCormack, John W., 18, 43, 118
McDonough, John, 203–4, 309n84
McDuffy v. Robertson, 251, 322n34
McGovern, George S., 139
McGuire, Jean, 224
Medicaid, 183, 304n10, 309n79

Metropolitan Council for Educational
Opportunity (METCO), 219, 224,
222, 279n5, 293n63
Milliken v. Bradley, 200, 294n68
Mills v. Board of Education, 128-29, 130,
131-32, 149, 287n14, 288n18
Missouri v. Jenkins, 322n30
Moakley, J. Joseph, 139, 290n38
Mode, Walter H., 45, 46, 59, 107
Morgan v. Hennigan, 136-38, 140-41,
142, 144-45, 146, 147, 148, 149, 151,
153, 159, 162, 202-3, 289n29,
289n32, 291nn41-42, 292n52
Morgan v. Kerrigan, 151, 180, 292n56,
293n62, 294n68, 294n71, 303n86
Morse, Wayne L., 41
Moynihan, Daniel P., 275n37
Murphy, Jerome T., 95, 116-17, 280n17,
285n74, 285n78

National Advisory Council on the Educa-
tion of Disadvantaged Children, 96,
280n18, 285n82
National Association for Retarded Chil-
dren (NARC), 3, 7, 176
National Association of School Boards,
176
National Catholic Welfare Conference
(NCWC), 41
National Commission on Excellence in
Education, 229
National Defense Education Act (NDEA),
xiv, 11-14, 167, 259n39
National Education Association (NEA),
41-42, 176, 309n80
National Plan to Combat Mental Retar-
dation, 18, 31
Nation at Risk, A, 229-30
Nixon, Richard M., 13, 17, 89, 91, 93,
106, 116, 138-39, 153-54, 161-62,
168, 229, 278n80, 290n37, 292n55,
296n9
No Child Left Behind Act, 252

O'Bryant, John D., 204, 206, 214-15,
239, 311n21, 312n40
Office of Economic Opportunity (OEO),
46-47
Ohrenberger, William H., 28-29, 31-39,
43-46, 54, 59, 69, 71-72, 75, 76, 79,
108, 111, 112-13, 131, 134, 141-42,
166-67, 168, 263n2, 263n4, 266n25,

266n27, 268n58, 271n4, 276n50,
278n71, 280nn13-14, 288nn26-28
O'Leary, Gerald, 203, 204, 208, 214
O'Neill, Thomas P., 17, 18, 43, 166, 196,
314n63
O'Neill, Thomas P., III, 166, 310n88,
311n27
Operation Counterpoise, 34-38, 39-40,
44-45, 46, 50, 52-53, 63, 65, 66, 77,
87, 264n8, 265n14, 266n24,
269n78
Operation Second Chance, 32, 39,
263n3
Oram, Phyllis, 101
Orient Heights, 10

Palladino, Elvira "Pixie," 203, 204,
309n84
Parents Association for South End
Schools, 67-68, 69-70, 82
*Pennsylvania Association for Retarded
Children (PARC) v. Pennsylvania*, 127-
28, 149, 172, 288n18
Perkins Institute for the Blind, 1, 3
Perlstein, Bruce W., 186, 194, 195,
300n59, 303n1, 304n5, 304n10,
306nn39-41
Pettigrew, Thomas F., 61, 88, 271n1
P.L. 81-815, 10
P.L. 81-874, 10
P.L. 94-142. *See* Education for All Handi-
capped Children Act
Pottinger, J. Stanley, 103-7, 113-15, 116-
19, 146, 281n37, 282n44
Powell, Adam Clayton, 258n35
Powell, Lewis F., Jr., 163-64, 291nn42-
43, 298nn33-34
property tax, xv, 10, 26-28, 50, 58, 154-
61, 164, 196-97, 212, 213, 270n93,
303n1, 309n79, 310n6, 310n8. *See
also* Proposition 2½; Proposition 13
Proposition 2½, xv, 212-15, 216, 219,
220, 225, 309n78, 310nn6-8,
311n14, 317n92
Proposition 13, 212, 213, 310n6
Public Housing Act, 22

Quinn, Robert H., 92, 166

racial imbalance law, 50-51, 56-58, 63-
64, 81, 92, 110, 111, 118, 135, 141,
271n2, 285n80, 292n56, 293n65

racial violence, xiii–xiv, 47, 73–74, 84–86, 92–93, 143–44, 167

Raphael Hernandez Elementary School, 112–13, 236, 283n65

Reagan, Ronald, xv, 213, 225, 226, 228–29, 230, 235, 314nn63–64, 317n89, 320n15

Rehnquist, William H., 231–32

Richardson, Elliot L., 12–14, 17, 40, 41, 51, 55, 91, 92, 106, 138, 139, 140

Right to Read, 99, 192

Roslindale, 10, 238

Roxbury, xiii, 10, 34, 37, 50, 53, 73–74, 75, 83–85, 101, 112, 205, 216, 225, 238, 260n60, 262n73, 265n19, 277n66, 278n79, 287n7, 289n31, 293n59. *See also* Joseph Lee Elementary School; Maurice J. Tobin Elementary School

Ruddy, Charles, 67, 80

Rules Committee, 18, 259n49, 314n63

Ryan, Charlotte, 158–59, 160, 166, 269n90, 296n17, 300n57

Saltonstall, Leverett, 12–13, 43

San Antonio Independent School District v. Rodriguez, 162–63, 164, 228, 249–50, 278n37, 287n17, 298nn33–35, 321n28

Sargent, Francis W., 91–92, 110, 132, 140–41, 144, 164, 166

Sargent Report, 23–24, 262n73, 262n75

Scholastic Aptitude Test, 190–91, 229, 305n28, 319n11

school boycotts, 36, 143, 145, 222, 265n19

School-Community Advisory Council, 85–87, 278n72

school construction, 9–11, 12, 17, 20, 23–24, 28, 32, 38, 42, 113, 154–55, 160, 258n26, 289n27, 303n84

schoolwide reform, 243

Science Institute for Able Learners, 15, 259n43

Seelye, David, 47–48

Serna v. Portales Municipal Schools, 148, 149, 294nn73–75

Serrano v. Priest, 159–61, 163, 194, 287n17, 297nn25–26

Smith-Hughes Act, 8

Solomon, Harry, 38

Solomon Lewenberg Junior High School, 73, 311n27

Souter, David, 322n30

South Boston, 37, 50, 145, 287n7, 293n59. *See also* South Boston High School

South Boston High School, xiii, 144, 145, 222, 236, 308n70

South End, 10, 66–67, 71, 74, 75, 78, 82, 84, 85, 100, 107, 111, 126, 172, 225, 273n24, 276n50

Spangler v. Pasadena City Board of Education, 279n7

special education, 1–3, 208, 256nn3–4, 256nn8–9, 264n6; budget cuts and, 198, 207; enrollment levels, 80, 175, 181–82, 184, 187–90, 256n6, 263n4, 301n69, 304nn4–5, 323n38; federal funding for, 7, 32–33, 175, 177–78, 207, 251, 322n33; integrated with regular education, 5–7, 18–19, 179, 252, 260n55, 286n2, 286n4, 288n21, 302n83, 304n7; legislation, 4–5, 8, 127, 184, 256n11, 257n19; state funding for, 132–34, 171–74, 176, 183, 260n52, 300n58, 302n73, 303n84. See also *Barnett v. Goldman;* bilingual education; *Board of Education of the Hendrick Hudson Central School District, Westchester County v. Rowley;* Chapter 750; Chapter 766; compensatory education; diagnosis of disabilities; Education for All Handicapped Children Act; Elementary and Secondary Education Act; *Mills v. Board of Education; Pennsylvania Association for Retarded Children (PARC) v. Pennsylvania; Stewart v. Phillips;* Task Force on Children Out of School

Spillane, Robert R., 216–17, 220–22, 224, 225, 237–39, 246, 311n20, 311n22, 311n27, 312n35, 312n42

Sputnik, 11, 13, 14, 16, 229, 258nn30–31

standardized tests, 68–70, 98, 100, 124–25, 190–91, 217, 218, 225–26, 229, 230, 233–36, 241–45, 253, 274n31, 274n33, 318n1, 320n20, 322n30. See also *Hobson v. Hansen*

Stewart v. Phillips, 126–28, 131, 149, 172, 273n24, 287nn8–10, 289n26

Sullivan, Marguerite, 46, 52–53

Sullivan, Neil V., 92–93, 118, 141, 279nn2–4, 293n64, 295n4

Swann v. Charlotte-Mecklenburg Board of Education, 139, 290n39, 292n45

Task Force on Children Out of School, 100–103, 106–9, 111–12, 118, 119, 122–26, 282n52, 286n4, 286nn6–7
Thurmond, Strom, 14
Tierney, Paul, 108–9, 115
Title I. *See* Elementary and Secondary Education Act
Title VI. *See* Civil Rights Act
Title VII. *See* Bilingual Education Act
Transitional Bilingual Education Act. *See* Chapter 71A
Tri-Lateral Council, 201, 222

unions, teachers', 155, 197–99, 212, 217, 225, 296n13, 296n16, 311n21. *See also* Boston Teachers Union
United South End Settlements, 67–70, 225
urban renewal, 22, 26, 32, 41, 141, 153, 261n69, 262n75, 289n30

Vocational Rehabilitation Act, 8
Volpe, John A., 51, 55, 91–92

Wallace, George C., 139
Walter E. Fernald School for the Retarded, 2, 4, 256n9
West Roxbury, 50, 262n73
White, Kevin, 74–75, 84, 110, 118, 144, 166, 196, 206, 215, 220, 286n83, 308n68
William Lloyd Garrison Elementary School, 39
William Monroe Trotter Elementary School, 137, 289n27, 290n33
Willis-Harrington Commission, 28, 50
Wilson, Laval S., 238–40, 241–42, 318n104
Wood, Robert C., 193–94, 196–99, 201–8, 268n64, 307n68
Wright, J. Skelly, 70–72, 88, 124, 273n23, 273nn26–27, 274nn30–31, 274n33, 297n25